# Energising Rural Development through 'Panchayats'

*The Editors :*

**BIBEK DEBROY** is Director, Rajiv Gandhi Institute for Contemporary Studies (RGICS), Rajiv Gandhi Foundation, New Delhi. He is a professional economist and was educated in Presidency College (Calcutta), Delhi School of Economics and Trinity College (Cambridge). He has worked at Presidency College (Calcutta), Gokhale Institute of Politics and Economics (Pune), Indian Institute of Foreign Trade (Delhi), National Council of Applied Economic Research (Delhi) and as Consultant, Department of Economic Affairs, Ministry of Finance, Government of India. He was also the Director for a project known as LARGE, set up by the Ministry of Finance and UNDP to examine legal reforms. He is the author and editor of several books, papers and popular articles and is also Consulting Editor with Financial Express. Bibek Debroy's special interests are international trade (in particular the WTO), law reform and the political economy of liberalisation in India. He has been listed in many bibliographies and has been a member of several government committees.

**P. D. KAUSHIK** is a Fellow at the RGICS. He is an engineer, MBA and Ph.D. During his Ph.D., he was awarded Jawahar Lal Nehru Fellowship. He has wide experience of industry and academics. He was also associated with consultancy work for the FAO, Commonwealth Secretariat and World Bank. He is a visiting faculty at leading business schools in Delhi. He has publications on policy issues emerging from electronic commerce and WTO. He has co-authored two books on the WTO.

*About RGICS :*

The **Rajiv Gandhi Institute for Contemporary Studies (RGICS)**, New Delhi is part of the Rajiv Gandhi Foundation and functions as a think tank. The target audience of the RGICS includes parliamentarians, legislators and representatives of political parties, public policy-makers and their advisers, the intelligentsia, the media and various interest groups. To interface with these groups, RGICS uses different modes of communication like books, monographs, working papers, symposia, discussions, talks and lectures. The RGICS research work is focused on international economic relations, law reforms, IT and economic reforms in India.

# Energising Rural Development through 'Panchayats'

Editors

Bibek Debroy

P.D. Kaushik

Published by
ACADEMIC FOUNDATION
in collaboration with
RAJIV GANDHI INSTITUTE FOR
CONTEMPORARY STUDIES
NEW DELHI

Academic Foundation
NEW DELHI

First published in 2005 by

**Academic Foundation**
4772-73 / 23 Bharat Ram Road, (23 Ansari Road), Darya Ganj, New Delhi - 110 002 (India).
Phones : 23245001 / 02 / 03 / 04. Fax : +91-11-23245005. E-mail : academic@vsnl.com
www : academicfoundation.com

Published in collaboration with :
**Rajiv Gandhi Institute for Contemporary Studies (RGICS)**
New Delhi



*Energising Rural Development through 'Panchayats'*
Editors : Bibek Debroy and P.D. Kaushik

**ISBN 81-7188-417-2**

Designed and typeset by Italics India, New Delhi.
Printed and bound in India.

# Contents

...CONTD. ..

...CONTD. ..

# List of Boxes and Figures

## BOXES

...CONTD. ..

## FIGURES

# List of Tables and Annexure Tables

## TABLES

...CONTD. ..

## ANNEXURE

### *Suggested Activity Mapping for Panchayati Raj Institutions (As Approved by the Cabinet Sub-Committee)*

...Contd. ..

# Contributors to this Volume


**Bibek Debroy** ............. Director, Rajiv Gandhi Institute for Contemporary Studies, New Delhi.

**Y.K. Alagh** ................ Chancellor, Nagaland University and Vice Chairman, Sardar Patel Institute of Economic and Social Research, Ahmedabad.

**Debashis Chakraborty** ...... Research Associate, Rajiv Gandhi Institute for Contemporary Studies, New Delhi.

**Arup Guha** ................ Research Student, Indian Statistical Institute, New Delhi.

**Laveesh Bhandari** ........... Chief Economist, Indicus Analytics, New Delhi.

**P.D. Kaushik** .............. Fellow, Rajiv Gandhi Institute for Contemporary Studies, New Delhi.

**Mohammed Saqib** .......... Fellow, Rajiv Gandhi Institute for Contemporary Studies, New Delhi.

**Rajiv Lall** .................. Founder and Chairman, Lok Capital, Mumbai.

# 1

# Rural Development and *Panchayats*

## *An Introduction*

BIBEK DEBROY

"Do we have a holistic view of rural development in which all the activities currently being undertaken are integrated? Do we share a vision for a prosperous rural India, a vision which sees agriculture and allied activities as the growth engine for rural development complemented by promotion of non-farm activities for value addition and sustainable in a healthy competitive environment? Are our strategies effective in increasing the productive potential of our agriculture, developing viable non-farm occupations and provision of basic human needs in a holistic manner?" This quote is from a speech delivered by Dr. Manmohan Singh, the Indian Prime Minister.[1] And that same speech said, "We need to learn from the Chinese model of rural business hubs that add value to agricultural produce within the rural areas." And finally, "Together we have an opportunity to make a radical departure from current ways of doing things. Incrementalism will not take us very far as sometimes the fault may be in the very design of the programmes imposed from above."

According to Census 2001, out of India's total population of 1.027 billion, 285 million lived in urban areas. That's an urbanisation ratio of 27.78 per cent, up from 23.34 per cent in 1981. 72.22 per cent of the population continues to live in rural areas. Textbooks often list the characteristics of developing countries. While the foremost characteristic is that of per capita income, invariably such textbooks also state that significant percentages of populations in developing countries live in rural areas. *Ipso facto*, there is a normative element

1. PM's inaugural address at the Chief Ministers' Conference on Poverty Alleviation and Rural Prosperity through *Panchayati Raj*, 29 June 2004, New Delhi.

to this suggestion, implying that somehow, living in rural areas is undesirable. Such normative statements don't characterise developed countries, even though some percentage of the population in those countries also lives in rural areas. For instance, 23 per cent of the US population lives in rural areas. Cross-country, the definitions of rural *vis-à-vis* urban often vary, although there is usually a cutoff in terms of the number of people residing in a habitation. Such cutoffs are not the point. The point is that in rural areas there is usually a complete absence of physical and social infrastructure and that is the reason one tends to be normative about life in rural areas. The pastoral paradise of Arcadia simply doesn't exist.

Consider a variable like the percentage of households with *pucca* houses. Urban India has a figure of 70.70 per cent, but rural India has a figure of 29.20 per cent.[2] 63.85 per cent of urban households have access to toilet facilities, but the figure is 9.48 per cent for rural India. 81.38 per cent of urban households have access to safe drinking water, but the figure is 55.54 per cent for rural households. 75.78 per cent of urban households have electricity connections, the figure is 30.54 per cent for rural India. The urban literacy rate is 80.06 per cent, but the rural literacy rate is 59.21 per cent. The life expectancy at birth is 66.3 years for urban India and 59.4 years for rural India. The infant mortality rate is 51 per thousand for urban India and 84 per thousand for rural India. 73.3 per cent of urban births were attended by health professionals, with a figure of 33.5 per cent for rural India. Barring the sex ratio, there is not a single socio-economic indicator that is better for rural India than for urban India. And it is hardly surprising that we should finally recognise this and talk about providing urban amenities in rural areas (PURA). Lack of rural infrastructure, spliced with explicit and implicit subsidies that pour into urban India, provide the trigger for rural to urban migration.

Add to that the lack of employment opportunities in rural India. Between 1993-94 and 1999-2000, the two data points for the NSS (National Sample Survey) large samples, the annual average increase in employment was 1.6 per cent.[3] But this had a breakup of 2.4 per

2. The figures in this paragraph are from *National Human Development Report 2001*, Planning Commission, Government of India, 2002. Consequently, they are dated, since subsequent figures have become available. However, even with these later figures, the fundamental contention will not change.

3. *National Human Development Report, op.cit.*

cent for urban India and 1.3 per cent for rural India. As is fairly obvious, unemployment rates mean very little in rural India. However, in the 1990s, there has been slackening growth in agriculture and non-agricultural rural sector employment growth has failed to compensate. Inevitably, this creates a push towards migration into urban areas. One element of the Chinese model is agro-cum-rural sector reforms required to reduce this push factor. Rural growth is also critical to handling the political economy of reforms, with a general impression that liberalisation has thus far had a pro-urban focus and little of the benefits have percolated through to rural India. The National Common Minimum Programme (NCMP) of the UPA government takes explicit cognisance of the rural sector.

The Tenth Five-Year Plan (2002-07) has an annual average real GDP growth target of 8 per cent, although that looks increasingly unlikely. The NCMP has an annual average real GDP growth target of between 7 and 8 per cent. Whether it is 7 per cent or 8 per cent, such growth rates are impossible without the primary sector growing at close to 4 per cent a year, even if the primary sector's contribution to GDP progressively declines from the present figure of around 25 per cent. That this is a primary or agriculture and allied sector growth rate, rather than an agricultural sector growth rate, needs to be emphasised. There doesn't seem to be an official annual employment generation target any more. But at one point, there used to be a target of creating 10 million jobs a year. Such jobs cannot be created only in agriculture and certainly not in crop production, or its sub-set, food-grain production. The Chinese model, so to speak, is one of encouraging diversification of agriculture and creating non-farm employment in rural areas, in rural industries and services.

Obviously, this requires implementation of the reform agenda, more often than not, the purview of State governments. In this agenda of pending agro-cum-rural sector reforms one would include rural infrastructure, public investments, decentralisation, credit, insurance, removal of restrictions on production, storage, trading and marketing, creation of land markets, extension services and the like.

In the agriculture context, here is the NCMP's version of the reform agenda. "The UPA government will ensure that public investment in agricultural research and extension, rural infrastructure and irrigation is stepped up in a significant manner at the very earliest. Irrigation will receive the highest investment priority and all ongoing projects will be completed according to a strict time schedule. The rural cooperative credit system will be nursed back to health. The UPA government will ensure that the flow of rural credit is doubled in the next three years and that the coverage of small and marginal farmers by institutional lending is expanded substantially. The delivery system for rural credit will be reviewed. Immediate steps will be taken to ease the burden of debt and high interest rates on farm loans. Crop and livestock insurance schemes will be made more effective. The UPA government will introduce a special programme for dryland farming in the arid and semi-arid regions of the country. Watershed and wasteland development programmes will be taken up on a massive scale. Water management in all its aspects, both for irrigation and drinking purposes, will receive urgent attention. The UPA administration will ensure the fullest implementation of minimum wage laws for farm labour. Comprehensive protective legislation will be enacted for all agricultural workers. Revenue administration will be thoroughly modernised and clear land titles will be established. The UPA government will bring forward a Constitutional Amendment to ensure the democratic, autonomous and professional functioning of cooperatives. Controls that depress the incomes of farmers will be systematically removed. Farmers will be given greater say in the organisations that supply inputs to them. The UPA government will ensure that adequate protection is provided to all farmers from imports, particularly when international prices fall sharply. The UPA government will ensure that government agencies entrusted with the responsibility for procurement and marketing will pay special attention to farmers in poor and backward states and districts. Farmers all over the country will receive fair and remunerative prices. The terms of trade will be maintained in favour of agriculture. The UPA government will take steps to ensure that dues to all farmers including sugarcane farmers will be cleared at the earliest." This is specifically on agriculture and needs to be considered in conjunction with the NCMP's agenda on employment, education and health, women and children, food and nutrition security, *panchayati raj*, infrastructure, water resources and regional development. For instance, under the infrastructure head, "The UPA will pay special attention to augmenting and modernising rural infrastructure consisting of roads, irrigation, electrification, cold-chain and marketing outlets. All existing irrigation projects will be completed within three to four years. Household electrification will be completed in five years."

The first paper in this volume is by Y.K. Alagh, on the problems confronting agriculture and rural development and the reform issues. The road map proposed envisages diversification away from low productivity foodgrains, with land and water development schemes, transparency in land rights of the tiller, market reforms and support to commercial infrastructure in rural areas. The point is made that producer cooperatives, in partnership with non-profit organisations and the private sector can establish strategic alliances, even for contract farming.[4] There is also the suggestion that there can be focused programmes for processing, market and transport development and information and communication strategies, designed to foster non-farm employment growth in existing *mandi* towns and artisan-based growth clusters. A more detailed fleshing out of this reform agenda is available in the "Overview" volume of the Millennium Study on the State of the Indian Farmer.[5]

Census 2001 tells us that India has 638,000 villages and 5,161 towns. Should there be so many villages? Are so many villages viable? The existence of habitations requires delivery of services, usually public in nature. Schools have to be set up, there have to be health centres, roads are required, electricity must be provided. Because there are economies of scale, such delivery requires a minimum economic size. Understandably, the minimum economic size varies from category to category. However, it is plausible that such service delivery becomes impossible if the number of inhabitants is fewer than 1500. The average population of an Indian village in 2001 was 1161. Tracking across States for the average population per village, the figure was more than 1500 in Chandigarh, Haryana, Delhi, Bihar, Tripura, Gujarat, Daman & Diu, Dadra & Nagar Haveli and Andhra Pradesh. Everywhere else, it was below 1500 and these are just averages. This is not to suggest that there should be a quantitative restriction on the number of villages India should have. But if rural transport

4. To state the obvious, because it needs to be stated, contract farming need not be the same as corporate farming.

5. Y.K. Alagh, Volume 1, *An Overview, State of the Indian Farmer: A Millennium Study*, Ministry of Agriculture and Academic Foundation, 2004.

connectivity improves, many of these villages will perforce disappear and that wouldn't necessarily be undesirable.

The second paper, by Debashis Chakraborty and Arup Guha, is on India's villages, about which, not much has been written. The 58$^{th}$ round (July-December 2002) of NSS (National Sample Survey) has village-level data. Using five broad categories (proximity to administrative centres, access to the rest of the economy, physical and social infrastructure, coverage of government support programmes and presence of private initiatives), the authors attempt an inter-State ranking of village-level development. This is done separately for large States and small States. Perhaps inevitably, in the overall ranking of large States, the BIMARU (undivided Bihar, undivided Madhya Pradesh, Rajasthan and undivided Uttar Pradesh) perform poorly. But so do Jammu & Kashmir, Assam and Orissa. There is variation within the small States and also within the North-East. For instance, in the overall rankings, Arunachal Pradesh performs poorly in the North-East.

Tangentially, this paper also raises the issue of convergence *vis-à-vis* divergence among States, especially in the decade of the 1990s. Increasing inter-State disparities across India has received some attention and the question of convergence versus divergence across States is often debated. Did the reform decade of the 1990s accentuate inter-State disparities? And what can be done to ensure that trickle down benefits of growth percolate to all regions and some backward areas are not bypassed? India is not *sui generis* in raising such questions. The divergence between North-West China and the Southern Coastal Provinces has probably received much more attention. Divergence or convergence is of course a function of the variable used to measure it. The two most commonly used indicators are growth in per capita State domestic product (SDP) or the poverty ratio (head count ratio). On the former, the growth records of Gujarat or Maharashtra in the 1990s are hardly comparable to the growth records of Orissa or undivided Bihar and Uttar Pradesh (UP). If growth in per capita SDP is the yardstick, then inter-State disparities existed in the 1980s as well. But the conclusion that these disparities increased in the 1990s also seems fairly robust. Similarly, on poverty ratios, Goa, Punjab or Haryana are hardly comparable to Orissa or undivided Bihar. Arguably, the post-1991 reforms shifted the focus of policy change from the Centre to the States. In a federal country, most factor markets are either on the State or Concurrent Lists. Hence, the agenda of second-generation reforms includes items that require changes at State level. Agriculture, social infrastructure and most areas of physical infrastructure are cases in point. If reform inclinations vary across States, it logically follows that so must growth rates. And this is compounded by the phenomenon that many faster growing States tend to have lower rates of population growth. Sick public sector units (PSUs) also tended to be concentrated in certain geographical regions and these are not the regions that have exhibited high (private sector driven) employment growth in the 1990s.

In discussing inter-State disparities, the East versus the West or the North versus the South dichotomy is often emphasised. This East versus the West dichotomy, with a vertical line drawn through Kanpur, has some validity, subject to the caveat that undivided UP is an extremely heterogeneous State, with the Eastern parts somewhat different from the Western, NOIDA being an obvious example. The North versus the South dichotomy, with a horizontal line drawn through the Vindhyas, also has some validity, with growth rates in Tamil Nadu, Karnataka and Andhra Pradesh picking up in the 1990s. But like all generalisations, these hide as much as they reveal. Conventionally, the backward States have been identified as the BIMARU ones.[6] However, undivided Madhya Pradesh and Rajasthan no longer belong to the conventional BIMARU fold, which should perhaps be redefined as BIMAROU, to include Orissa. This is a debated issue, but is also a function of the variable used to measure convergence or divergence. For example, per capita State domestic product or poverty ratios may not be the only indicators used. Arguably, there is increasing convergence across States on many education-related indicators, but not on health-related ones. But beginning in central India and extending eastwards, all the way up to the North-East, there are vast regions of poverty, deprivation and backwardness.

More importantly, why is one interested in identifying pockets of deprivation? While not negating the possibility of differential relative growth rates across the country or attempting to neutralise it, the answer must be that one is interested in policy interventions that

---

6. As every Indian knows, there is a pun on the word *bimar*.

ensure uniform access to market opportunities across the country, quite apart from the socio-economic tensions that marginalisation leads to. Liberalisation does not mean an abdication of the State's responsibility. Instead, it should be interpreted as a refocusing of State intervention, with an emphasis on social (education, health) and physical (power, water) infrastructure, or even governance. The tension over better performing States effectively cross-subsidising States that have relatively inferior track records needs to be viewed in this light. However, development or deprivation does not necessarily follow State boundaries, which are at best, administratively determined. Unfortunately, policy intervention in India is too centralised. This doesn't only mean overwhelming emphasis on the Centre in Centre-State relations, as all States invariably argue, it also means negligible emphasis on decentralisation and devolution within States, a point that States rarely make. Hence, while policy intervention is indeed needed to tackle problems of poverty and deprivation, identification of backward regions needs to go beyond State boundaries.

This takes one to the issue of backward districts, because poverty or deprivation doesn't always follow neat administrative boundaries. As such, outside BIMAROU, backward districts also feature in Gujarat, Maharashtra, Karnataka, Tamil Nadu, Andhra Pradesh, West Bengal and the North-East. Using objective criteria, it is not very difficult to figure out which are India's worst districts. For instance, in Assam one would pick Dhubri. In Bihar, one would pick Araria, Deoghar, Kishangunj, Palamu, Purnia, Sahibganj and Sitamarhi. In MP, one would pick Bastar, Betul, Chhattarpur, Damoh, Datia, East Nimar, Guna, Jhabua, Mandla, Panna, Raisen, Rajgarh, Rajandgaor, Ratlam, Rewa, Sagar, Satna, Sehore, Shahdol, Shajapur, Shivpuri, Sidhi, Surguja, Tikamgarh and West Nimar. In Orissa, one would pick Ganjam, Kalahandi, Koraput and Phulbani. In Rajasthan, one would pick Banswara, Barmer, Bhilwara, Dholpur, Dungarpur, Jaisalmer, Jalor, Jhalawar, Nagaur, Pali, Sirohi and Tonk. In UP, one would pick Bahraich, Banda, Basti, Budaun, Gonda, Hardoi, Lalitpur, Shahjahanpur, Siddrathnagar and Sitapur.[7]

---

7. See, Bibek Debroy and Laveesh Bhandari edited, *District-Level Deprivation in the New Millennium*, Konark Publishers, 2003 and Aasha Kapur Mehta, "Multidimensional Poverty in India: District Level Estimates", *Working Paper No. 9*, Chronic Poverty Research Centre, Indian Institute of Public Administration, 2004.

The objective of such a identification is the following. India doesn't become developed until these backward districts are also mainstreamed into the development process. Can one direct specific attention to these backward districts? Such as in health, primary education, drinking water, electricity, sanitation and rural road connectivity. Can centrally sponsored schemes only be directed towards these districts? Can local area development funds granted to Members of Parliament be restricted to these districts in areas like physical and social infrastructure? It is by no means obvious that such targeting violates the Constitutional provisions of equality before the law, especially if one remembers that many of these backward districts have significant ST populations. What it does violate is the perennial problem of populism, whereby one fails to target State intervention because one fears a backlash from existing beneficiaries of unwarranted subsidies. Therefore, the resistance to such targeted intervention will be from State governments. The NCMP does incorporate the idea of specifically targeting backward districts. For instance, "A special programme for social and physical infrastructure development in the poorest and most backward districts of the country will be taken up on a priority basis."

The third paper, by Laveesh Bhandari, is provocatively titled - more rural roads are equivalent to fewer villages. That is, if village infrastructure, especially road infrastructure is improved, the number of villages will decline.[8] As things stand, States that have a higher share of villages connected with *pucca* roads tend to have fewer smaller villages. The statistical testing suggests that the greater the degree of un-connectivity, the greater has been the growth in villages. Stated differently, the number of villages is also a function of economic growth and population growth. But if road connectivity improves, the rate of growth in villages declines, which is a weaker proposition than suggesting that the actual number of villages declines. Extrapolating to the future, one expects an increase in the size of villages (many of which will become towns), a fall in the number of villages (because of rural-rural migration) and a takeover of rural areas by fast-expanding urban areas. The paper ends on the note that these transformations have a clear policy angle, not just in

8. There is of course a distinction between a village and a habitation.

fiscal terms, but also in improving governance and greater decentralisation.

P.D. Kaushik's fourth and fifth papers form a continuum. Both are on *panchayati raj* institutions (PRIs). While the first of these two papers has a sketch of how PRIs evolved and undertakes a stock taking exercise, the second is specifically on women's empowerment. In principle, PRIs can transform governance, empowerment and even delivery of public services. But many of the continuing problems stem from the fact that despite the 73rd Constitutional amendment, the authority to *panchayats* is a delegated one and is therefore contingent on State-level commitment and action, including provisions on *gram sabhas*, elections, dissolution, reservations, devolution, District Planning Committees (DPCs), relationships among the three layers of PRI institutions and *the Panchayats (Extension to the Scheduled Areas) Act, 1996*. While there are legitimate reasons for optimism about the evolution of PRIs, the euphoria needs to be muted because of these constraints. The stock taking paper also has a sketch of *panchayat* role in rural development and the functioning of centrally sponsored schemes (CSSs), which can, in principle, be delivered through PRIs, thereby improving accountability and efficiency, but continue to be delivered through the bureaucratic system or parallel institutions. There is also a section on *panchayats* and rural markets and the possibility of developing rural business hubs using PRIs. This is part of the Eleventh Schedule mandate and is also the thrust of this volume. The paper on women's empowerment is also a stock taking exercise, but is more specific. And in addition to the general constraints, there is also a listing of specific constraints and problems that women face.

The quote from the PM's speech, reproduced at the beginning of this introduction, has a reference to the Chinese model of rural business hubs. The sixth paper, by Mohammed Saqib and Debashis Chakraborty, is on the Chinese experience of township and village enterprises (TVEs) and the working of agricultural cooperatives in India. In the mid-1990s, rural enterprises (*xiangzhen qiye*) in China were estimated to account for 36 per cent of national industrial output, compared to 9 per cent in 1978. Three-fourths of that came from community-owned TVEs (*xiangcun qiye*). In the mid-1990s again, there were estimated to be 23.4 million TVEs with 135 million workers, a figure that seems to have declined subsequently, either because the original figures were over-estimates or because some TVEs have now been transformed. These TVEs were not State-owned, nor were they private or cooperatives. Their origins can be traced to the communes and the brigades of the Great Leap Forward period, but they rapidly evolved in the 1980s, transiting to export-linked industrial production, ancillary functions and agro and rural industries. Despite the Chinese reforms, the private sector wasn't initially quite acceptable. Given that mindset, community-owned TVEs were more acceptable and they were also used to deliver local public goods like sanitation, roads and family planning. It was also thought that community-owned enterprises would be able to surmount the individual credit problem, with community governments borrowing from banks to lend to TVEs. Expectations about credit delivery may have been somewhat belied, since there continue to be question markets about credit access by TVEs, compared to credit access by SOEs (State-owned enterprises). There also question marks about the geographical spread of TVEs, since most are located in the coastal provinces of Guangdong, Fujian, Zhejiang and Jiangsu and sub-contracting functions (to SOEs) primarily restricted to Beijing, Shanghai and Tianjin. Often, TVEs flourished because of less rigid and relatively lax procedures, labour and environmental standards being obvious examples. They are also small and cannot exploit economies of scale, the typical size of a township enterprise being 73 employees per firm and that of a village enterprise being 26 employees per firm. Conflicts between community ownership and professional management are also not unknown. Nevertheless, a review of the Chinese experience is useful, especially in decentralisation and devolution, and this is what the authors set out to do. There is an obvious analogy with Indian cooperatives and the paper also lists problems that Indian cooperatives faced, often due to unnecessary government interference, and suggests solutions.

P.D. Kaushik's seventh paper is on civil society and ICT initiatives. Civil society has various definitions, but a subset of civil society is certainly the NGO movement. Sometimes, though not always, this voluntary sector supplements and reinforces the role of PRIs. With case studies, the first half of the paper documents some successful instances of civil society intervention and some of these are in areas of market dis-intermediation. In agriculture, India has one of the longest distribution chains in the world. Successful dis-intermediation, with or without the use of information technology, can allow producers to obtain better prices, without the final consumer having to pay higher prices. Dis-intermediation also spills over into better extension services and even credit and insurance. The second half of the paper is on ICT initiatives. Some of these are purely public (especially of the e-governance type), others are purely private and the remainder is best described as public-private partnerships. While the paper mentions ITC's *e-choupal* initiative, it doesn't mention the *Choupal Sagar* experiment in Rafiqganj, near Sehore in Madhya Pradesh. This is a natural extension of the *e-choupal* idea and is an outlet for selling FMCG products, as well as consumer durables. Perhaps one should mention the explosion in rural consumption demand that has come about in the 1990s, documented for example by NCAER, an explosion that is expected to continue in the next decades, especially if spliced with rural sector reforms. If *Choupal Sagar* succeeds, the existing 1700 *e-choupal*s will also be transformed. However, there remains a question. Most of these successful experiments are restricted to certain parts of the country and not others. Any bypassed parts of the country continue to be bypassed also in these interventions. What can be done to mainstream these relatively deprived regions also and is there a role for PRIs in this? The first two maps on identified industry clusters show that these too tend to be located in certain parts of the country. The next map on India's identified agro export processing zones (AEPZs) also has a regional concentration, in so far as foodgrains are concerned. But the fourth map is on AEPZs for fruits and the fifth on AEPZs for vegetables. Given India's agro-climatic zones, it is understandable that these should be spread throughout the country. There is no part of India that doesn't possess a static comparative advantage in some agro product or the other. The sixth map indeed shows a concentration of artisan clusters in relatively disadvantaged regions. And the seventh and final map depicts existing *mandi*s. The *mandi*s do have a geographical concentration and are extremely clustered in the North. However, they exist everywhere. It is a separate matter that *mandi* infrastructure may often be unsatisfactory and this is also true of the many more *haat*s. If PRIs can work through a public-private partnership mode in building infrastructure in these *mandi*s and *haat*s, many rural development problems may in fact be addressed.

Credit and micro-credit is a subset of the rural development problem and the eighth paper by Rajiv Lall is on micro-credit. Rural credit figures prominently in the UPA government's reform agenda. The NCMP states, "The rural cooperative credit system will be nursed back to health. The UPA government will ensure that the flow of rural credit is doubled in the next three years and that the coverage of small and marginal farmers by institutional lending is expanded substantially. The delivery system for rural credit will be reviewed. Immediate steps will be taken to ease the burden of debt and high interest rates on farm loans. Crop and livestock insurance schemes will be made more effective." Quite rightly, this recognises the link between credit and insurance. For the poor, the credit problem is often an insurance problem, with an inability to face exogenous shocks. However, do dictates that rural lending be at a few percentage points below PLR (prime lending rate) serve any purpose, especially because the poor are often denied access to organised capital markets? Micro-credit is only a subset of the overall credit issue and Rajiv Lall sketches the concept of social investing, that is, investing for objectives that are not purely financial. This displays many public good characteristics, with an explicit or implicit subsidy. Having reviewed micro-finance, and its viability, in Asia, the paper sketches the micro-finance scenario in India, ending with a case study of Lok Capital.

The ninth paper by P.D. Kaushik is on the role of PRIs in fostering and creating rural markets. Having reviewed poverty and inequality in rural India, the paper turns to rural infrastructure represented by the *mandis* and the *haats*. The model proposed is of an *apna bazaar*, involving PRIs and a strategic private party through a public-private partnership. There is an obvious analogy with what has happened in China. The hub can also be used to deliver public sector services, including a rationalised and harmonised CSS menu. Instead of beginning a fresh exercise, the idea obviously would be to start where the beginnings of such clusters already exist. Even in backward areas, it is not very difficult to figure out where any initial infrastructure development attempt should be focused. Consider for instance the backward districts mentioned earlier. In Assam, Dhubri is one of these and in Dhubri one would focus on infrastructure development in Dhubri, Bilasipara, Mankachar, Chapar, Bagribari and Golokganj. If one picks Ganjam district in Orissa, one would focus on Brahmapur, Kabisuryanagar, Chhatrapur, Bhanjanagar, Asika, Hinjili and Surada. Araria in Bihar leads to the identification of Forbesganj and Araria. Bahraich in UP leads to the identification of Bahraich, Nanpara and Kaiserganj. In Betul district of Madhya Pradesh, one identifies Betul, Amla, Multai, Bhainsdehi and Shahpur. And in Banswara district of Rajasthan, one identifies Banswara, Garhi and Kushalgarh. This is merely illustrative, but is indicative of the kind of identification that can be done.

The tenth and final paper in this book is by Debashis Chakraborty and is on food security, one element of what may be called public intervention of the anti-poverty type. The 2004-05 budget promised, "In the Tenth Plan document, the Planning Commission had suggested that a system of distributing food stamps should be tested on a pilot basis. Every eligible family will be entitled to collect its monthly quota of food stamps from a designated distribution centre, and such stamps could then be used to buy foodgrains from any food shop. I propose to introduce a pilot scheme for distributing food stamps, instead of distributing food through fair price shops, in two or three contiguous districts in a selected State." Any subsidy, food stamps or otherwise, involves targeting and identification of beneficiaries, and in the rural sector, the involvement of PRIs in such an exercise is certainly possible. Having sketched the food security issue and the unsatisfactory performance of the PDS, including the targeting experience, the paper reviews the cross-country experience with food stamps, food coupons, food vouchers, food cash and in-kind food transfers. The conclusion that emerges is a somewhat negative one. Food stamps are not without their problems. And other options need to be explored first.

The ten papers in this volume don't pretend to have all the answers. But collectively, one forms a very good idea of what the rural development issues are and what the PRIs can do to address rural development concerns. In the process, a menu of options also emerges. If some of these ideas get transformed into pilot projects, that can thereafter be successfully replicated, the objectives of the volume will have been met.

# 2

# Agriculture and Rural Development: Towards A Policy Framework

YOGINDER K. ALAGH[1]

## Introduction

This paper:

- Discusses the trends towards agricultural diversification from the eighties and the reversals since the mid-nineties: also the falling profitability of agriculture in the nineties;
- Examines the external context for Indian agriculture in the current policy phase;
- Suggests a targeted programme of land and water development in different agro-climatic regimes in the next phase and the organisational and resource strategies for it;
- Suggests that there should be a road map for policies for major crops;
- Suggests focused programmes for first stage processing, market and transport development, information and communication strategies for the agricultural sector embedded in larger policies of non-farm employment growth in *mandi* towns and artisan based growth clusters;
- Suggests that the State plays a facilitating role for such development and recommends some operational rules for this, including incentives for start-up costs, support to farmers, artisans, cooperatives and other strategic alliances and disincentives for non-sustainable growth so that the farmer and

1. This paper was prepared as a presentation to the first meeting of the Task Force on Agriculture and Rural Development of the RGCIS. It was subsequently presented at a Seminar on Agriculture organised by the RGICS and then at the Conference of Congress Chief Ministers at Abu. The paper carries the flavour of a power point presentation.

worker is clearly shown a practical way out of his current economic dilemmas. Policies should be fiscally neutral, if not resource conserving;

- Recommends that such strategies would be a part of a programme of food security for poor households, but that there should also be a targeted programme for hungry households, generally women headed or with handicapped earners; and
- Finally suggests a dual strategy of arguing for reform at the national level as also pushing reform at the State level.

## Diversification and Structural Change

Expansion and diversification of the consumption basket is basically driven by a higher growth performance since the Eighties. Agro-based items of consumption are important in the demand baskets of different income groups. These consumer items are not for elite consumption alone. As people are better off, they eat more eggs, drink more milk and eat vegetables, fruit and cheese. This has happened in the nineties and by now this diversification of the food basket is well known.[2]

**Table 2.1**

*In Some States More Change (Shift in Employment Share)*

| *Sl. No.* | *State* | *Share of Total 1991* | *Agriculture Workers % 2001* |
|---|---|---|---|
| 1. | Gujarat | 56.3 | 51.0 |
| 2. | Haryana | 57.8 | 51.6 |
| 3. | Karnataka | 63.1 | 55.9 |
| 4. | Punjab | 55.3 | 39.4 |
| 5. | Tamil Nadu | 59.5 | 49.5 |
| **6.** | **India** | **64.8** | **58.4** |

It is no longer true that 74 per cent of the work force depends on agriculture. In fact even in 1961, while 75.9 per cent of the work force was dependent on agriculture, only 73.5 per cent was depending on crop production. This has now gone down to 54.3 per cent, according

2. See Y.K. Alagh, 1994, ICAR.

to the National Sample Survey's 55th Round. However, even the Planning Commission's Steering Group on Agriculture says that 69 per cent and other experts say two thirds, sometimes three fourths, of our people depend on agriculture. There may be some change in the Census numbers when they come, but that will not change the big picture. While 54 per cent workers are engaged in crops, those in livestock, dairying, poultry and so on has doubled, from 2 per cent to 4 per cent of the work force.

The Ninth Plan period, however sees a slowing down of this process of diversification and this needs a quick turn around. The following statistics show this:

### Table 2.2

*Slowing Down in Diversification*

*(mn. tonnes/bales for cotton)*

| *S.No* | *Crop/Sector* | *1996/97* | *Highest 1997/99* | *Target Ninth Plan* |
|---|---|---|---|---|
| 1. | Foodgrains | 199.44 | 205.91 | 234.00 |
| 2. | Oilseeds | 24.38 | 25.21 | 30.00 |
| 3. | Sugarcane | 277.56 | 309.31 | 338.00 |
| 4. | Cotton | 14.23 | 12.18 | 15.70 |
| 5. | Fruits and Vegetables | 141.00 | 122.00 | 179.00 |
| 6. | Milk | 69.00 | 78.10 | 96.50 |
| 7. | Eggs (bn. Nos.) | 27.50 | 30.32 | 35.00 |
| 8. | Fish | 5.35 | 5.80 | 7.00 |
| 9. | Tea | 0.78 | 0.85 | 1.00 |

*Source:* Planning Commission, *Annual Plan, 2000/01*, p. 301

The diversification of the agricultural demand basket became a significant feature of the Tiger economies from the mid-eighties onwards. FAO projected that up to 2010, GDP growth would be 7 per cent annual in East Asia and 4.4 per cent in the Near East and North Africa, with the West Asian (Near East) component growing faster.[3] Per capita income growth was 5.7 per cent annual for East Asia. With this kind of income growth there was a shift of demand to non-cereal food items and commercial crops. Countries projected to have high volumes and growth of agricultural imports were Japan, Hong Kong,

3. See Nikos Alexandratos, 1995.

the Republic of Korea, Saudi Arabia, Singapore, Malaysia, Indonesia, the Islamic Republic of Iran, Thailand, Kuwait and Oman. These countries were estimated to be large and growing markets for fruit and vegetables, and meat and countries like Japan and Korea, of fish. In fact, up to the mid-Nineties the agricultural import of each of these countries was growing between 4 to 8 per cent annual. They account for 40 per cent of India's agricultural exports.[4]

More recently the East Asian slowdown seems to have led to a slowdown in the diversification of the agrarian economies of the NIE's. We developed a simple indicator of 'diversification', namely the change in the index of livestock production in a country divided by the index of agricultural production. According to the World Development Indicators, the long-term annual GDP growth rate through 1997 was 7 to 8 per cent for Indonesia, Malaysia, Thailand and the Republic of Korea. In the period 1984 to 1994, the incremental livestock to agricultural production ratio was 2.12, 2.18, 2.59 and 2.56 respectively for these countries. The GDP growth of these countries went down to 4.7, 2.9, 0.3 and 4.4 per cent and the incremental livestock to agricultural production ratio went down to minus 1.79, 1.01, minus 1.61 and minus 0.72 respectively in these countries, from 1994 to 1999. On the other hand, countries like China which grew at around 8 per cent since 1980, and where the growth did not decelerate, had the incremental livestock to agricultural production ratio of 1.82 in the earlier period and 1.59 in the later period, suggesting that the momentum of diversification and widespread agricultural growth was kept up. Data on vegetable and fruit production is available only for the nineties (FAOSTAT), and the incremental vegetable to cereal production ratio is minus 1.14 in Indonesia, minus 2.58 in Malaysia, minus 0.3 in Thailand and 1.43 in South Korea from 1994 to 1999.[5]

## The Road Map

The road map is clear. Diversification away from low productivity foodgrains, diverse land and water development schemes, transparency in land rights of the tiller, market reforms and support to commercial

4. See Y.K. Alagh, *First Dantwala Lecture*, 1999 and ESCAP, 1995.

5. I am grateful to Munish Alagh for these ideas.

infrastructure in rural areas with an emphasis on delivery systems covering the last mile, all complement each other. Market reform, tax and monetary and credit policy reform can be integrated with crop level revival policies. For specific crops details have been worked out elsewhere.

There is at the present stage considerable synergy in different policies in pushing the different agro climatic regimes of India to pursuing the objective of a more competitive agriculture oriented to national and global markets. The Indian farmer has demonstrated the ability to grow more grains. Diversification, in areas with low yields and widespread agricultural growth, together with a targeted distribution policy will create the incomes to achieve the objectives of food security.

The existing policies are in the reverse direction. Rajiv Gandhi's agro climatic policymaking packages have been given up in operational terms in the Tenth Plan. There is a lack of harmonisation in tariff, credit, price and trade policies, *e.g.*, large unintended imports of sugar, cotton, forestry products and now vegetables and fruits. Again, macro objectives are not operationalised at the regional level by giving appropriate positive and negative signals in terms of incentives and disincentives. The earlier policies of lending through weather and project cycles have been given up. Organisational reform is slow as the experience with the Farmer's Producer's groups legislation shows. There is lack of convergence in land, water and technology policies.

Approaches such as that contained in Robert Wade's well-known *World Politics* paper on East Asia's economic success and his famous 'strategic trade theory' is, I believe, still relevant. Later, for example John Stopford, was to place this experience in a larger strategic global political economy perspective and draw management implications for the global firm from it in a contemporary perspective.[6] As Stopford argues, a strategic approach to policy in a globalised economy is not easy, since mindless intervention can breed sloth and vested interests, but there is no question that, as Stiglitz has recently shown, there is no unique way to reform and the agricultural and poverty agenda should be a part of the agenda. For me personally, Wade's paper shows

6. J. Stopford, Carnegie Mellon, 1994, p. 5.

that it is a small world, since he begins and ends his paper with a reference to an Indian description of South Korea's policy perspectives in the early phases of industrialisation.[7] The reference by Wade to a South Korean perspective from Y. K. Alagh's view from South Asia in the Asian Development Bank's journal the *Asian Development Review*[8] became a widely cited part of the strategic trade theory literature. The Nineties reversed all this and I believe that is a mistake.[9]

## Perverse Economics

Since output prices are not rising fast enough, agricultural profitability rates are going down. Profitability rates in Indian agriculture have fallen by 15 per cent in the Nineties. In a market-driven agriculture this would have serious consequences and drive away investment to other sectors. In the Nineties, when the role of the private sector expands very considerably in supply of seeds, agrochemical and credit inputs, prices go up in a significant manner and in a relative sense. Of course, with this structure, growth would go down. Agricultural growth has also gone down, because of a collapse of public investment. So we have both diminishing returns and cost-push declines in profitability, in a period of substantial privatisation of agriculture. The rise in input prices and falling profitability can only be explained by inefficiency and the trend to low value added crops (Table 2.3). The case for reform in the state sponsored pricing system to encourage diversification of Indian agriculture is very clear. So is the need to remove bureaucratic controls on commodity movements in India and for exports. But the effectiveness of existing systems in supplying cheaper inputs in village markets of small size needs study. The existing private channels of distribution are not enough.[10]

The real policy options then are to build markets, develop information systems of the economic opportunities available, provide financial institutions which work and provide finances for communication, processing, standardisation, quality upgradation and

7. See R. Wade, 1992, p. 270 and p. 320.

8. Y.K.Alagh, 1989.

9. See my "Globalisation Without Theory: India in the Nineties", forthcoming, *Economic and Political Weekly*.

10. See Lele, Alagh, *et al.*, 2001.

trade. Simultaneously, the harmonised tariff, monetary, fiscal and trade policy package at individual crop levels will have to be prepared as the road map presentation argues. Improving cereal productivity and diversification is not possible if the farmer does not have access to improved energy and water supplies and becomes much easier if the land development technologies are accessible. It is well known that he pays for such facilities when the service is good. A great initiative is required to release the Indian farmer's energies by improving his access to inputs and services. This requires market-driven input supplies. A number of organisations which cannot cover the last mile have to close down and this becomes difficult when they live on government subsidies and many others who succeed need organisational support and have access to bank finance. Newer organisational forms like Producer Associations need support.[11]

**Table 2.3**

*Profitability is Falling in Agriculture*

*Price Index (CACP Estimates)*

| *Year* | *Input Items* | *Output Sold* |
|---|---|---|
| 1989/90 | 401.4 | 393.5 |
| 1997/98 | 920.1 | 785.4 |
| Per cent Increase 97/98 over 89/90 | 229 | 199 |

## Land and Water Development Strategies

The Agro Climatic Project has identified the major components. Farmer-led distribution systems in existing commands; watershed development - rehabilitation of tanks, *beels*, ponds, *talaavs*; aquifer management, particularly in coastal areas, have high returns; a massive programme for land and water development has to be the centre piece. Growth of private investment in groundwater has been spectacular and needs further support, particularly in the Eastern region. It must be led by a public initiative, with a very large financing component. Newer institutional forms like cooperatives, NGOs, non-profit companies and others must be designed.[12]

11. Alagh, 2001.
12. Alagh, FAO, 2002.

Ideally we need a national land and water development plan, with responsibilities fixed for implementation. It is recommended that the Chief Ministers personally supervise the preparation and implementation of such a programme at the agro-climatic regional level of 3 to 5 districts. A study sponsored at the Mumbai University Department of Civics by the Rajiv Gandhi Institute for Contemperary Studies has shown that in Madhya Pradesh there is high congruence between State-level and District-level perceptions in the water sector, which drives the system hard.

## Road Map: Some Details

It will be a mistake to ignore the strengths built up in the food-grains area. In my *Interim Report* to WTO adjustment in the Punjab, I have argued for a Commodity Board to ride through the global grain price cycle and technological support to the sector. In the final report I will document this with more facts and analysis. The new technologies in cereals like the *bajra,* which can store paddy, including the hybrids, must get off the research success stage. States like Punjab, Harayana, and Western UP will show the way, but if price policy gives appropriate incentives for quality and transport differentials are introduced, the rice economy in MP, Chhattisgarh and speciality cereals like the Durhams will revive. Shorter duration cereals will pave the way for diversification to oilseeds, pulses, fruits and vegetables. Markets and their development and processing are the key. Strategic alliances must be encouraged.

A bifocal policy initiative is required. Subsidies with adverse consequences on productivity of land must be phased out. Simultaneously profitability of alternate crops and activities must improve through market, economic and financial reform. This is again the road map for each crop. If this approach fails, the State must intervene in markets. The role of sponsoring policies for alternative distribution channels so that there is genuine competition in input supplies is very necessary. Cooperatives, non-profit organisations and partnerships between the private sector, Cooperatives, NGOs or local governments are required. A Committee presented a draft law for cooperatives to set up producer companies with corporate alliances. It saved the cooperative principle by providing the one share one vote basis and the legislation has now been passed. Producer cooperatives, working on a cooperative principle, can be a very powerful instrument of growth and the required level of diversification. Producers groups should be encouraged to enter into strategic alliances, say with the corporate sector for Contract Farming.

## Financial Reform and Issues

The Rural Infrastructure Fund was meant to give loan finance for infrastructure. But it became a vehicle to finance the official irrigation plan. It has to revive or develop a new vehicle to power the Indian farmer and his organisations to diversify, trade and improve his income. All of that will now be WTO compatible. After Doha, the main challenge is at home. The road map abroad is no longer hazy.

There have to be well-identified shelves of a large number of small projects on land, water and other infrastructure projects available for financing. Financial institutions have to design structures such that community collateral is possible for viable projects. Self-help financing groups are only one such group. Land and water development groups, local infrastructure projects, in road or communication sectors, productionising products developed in R&D institutions, training for production with improved techniques, market development schemes developed by local and community groups would be other examples. These could be drainage, soil shaping, contour management, improvement and management of lower level canals, de-silting of tanks, raising embankments, fish culture, market development, controlled grazing and so on. Studies show high economic rates of return, making them very productive investments. They involve household labour, but also need outside finance.[13]

Some of the policy reform required for the replication on a required scale of such projects includes: lending through a weather or project cycle, NABARD had started a scheme of this kind as a part of the agro-economic regionalisation strategy of Rajiv Gandhi, gave it up in 1993 and is again starting it now.[14] Financial institutions have to design structures such that community collateral is possible for viable projects.

Policy "champions" are necessary for sorting out administrative, financial and procedural issues at local, regional and national levels,

---

13. For details, see Alagh, 2003.

14. See *Kapur Committee*, Reserve Bank of India, 2000 for details.

when problems arise with these kind of development strategies. It is reasonably certain that problems are going to arise in development experiments that are off the beaten track. The question then is, is there somebody in the policy decision-making structure who will sort out the problem? ADB reports in a detailed study of farmer managed irrigation systems, that the failure cases were those where such support did not exist. Failure here is defined as performance levels in water delivery lower than by government agencies.

The policy champions should be personally selected by the CMs and should be held accountable to them with defined time bound targets.

## Hunger and Poverty

Endemic poverty can be different from both hunger and vulnerability. Poverty in India is now estimated at 28 per cent of the population, but we know from the NSS that people who claimed that they did not have two square meal a day, went down to less than a twelfth of the population in 1993 from around a fifth in 1983.

**Table 2.4**

*Incidence of Hunger in Rural India - 1983/1993*

| *S.No.* | *Year* | *Incidence of Hunger (%)* |
|---|---|---|
| 1. | 1983 | 19.0 |
| 2. | 1993 | 7.0 |

*Source:* National Sample Survey Organisation

This 7 per cent of the population consists largely of women-headed households and handicapped-earner households. With large grain stocks, they can be given free grain in a targeted programme. Recent work with participative rural appraisal analysis suggests that the earning power of hungry households is related in a significant manner with the demographic status of the household (hungry households more often tend to be women headed or consist of disabled workers) and health status of the members of the household (morbidity significantly reduces economic status). On the positive side, hungry households in rural areas showed considerable dignity and desire to improve their status The democratic polity was seen as a factor empowering them and in fact there was considerable resistance in classifying themselves as destitute or hungry. Food security policies have to be embedded in more general human security approaches.

An Employment Guarantee scheme, with a food for work programme with linkages with health and education programmes with a self-selection bias for the hungry is necessary. There has in this decade been new understanding in the area of food that the agenda is not just grain production and targeted employment and food security distribution programmes for poor populations. Such programmes have a role, but only as a part of a strategy and a policy framework of widespread growth and income generation and this may also in fact, under fairly plausible circumstances, require diversification away from grains. Land and water development programmes are a central part of this approach. Widespread agricultural growth based on sustainable land and water development and management programmes, has a dual effect: "food commodities" become available at cheaper prices and sufficient and sustainable employment and income is generated. Targeted employment and food distribution programmes for poor populations have a role, but only as a part of a strategy and a policy. A large part of the poor and hungry segments of the work force are low productivity food producers. Demarcation of "hunger zones" and targeted programmes, have to take a larger context into account. A hunger removal programme, embedded in a food security strategy, will have to be a part of the wider process of diversification and growth of agriculture.

It is mainly the poor that suffer from famine, hunger and malnutrition. But not all poor people are equally vulnerable to hunger, and it is not always the poorest who are exposed to the greatest risks. There are many other factors that determine the vulnerability to hunger. These include the risk of exposure to crises, stress and shocks. There is also the population that is subjected to risk by civil breakdowns and violence on a community scale. Economic development without corresponding development in civil society organisations can lead to greater vulnerability. Earthquakes are natural, but damage depends on land use, the nature of development and social and governance institutions to cope up. Disaster management is at a rudimentary scale in India. The possibility of setting up a National Fund for immediate assistance in such cases may be considered.

## Forests

The ban on logging is absolutely necessary, but the forests should be nurtured to produce everything else. This is not happening and India is becoming one of the largest importers of forest products, while many other countries are large exporters, say of medicinal plants, organic chemicals of forest origin and so on. These are all on OGL. Import duties in many cases are 10 to 15 per cent. The first thing to do is to reform the tax system, so that forest produce, particularly what is called minor forest produce, is not discriminated against. Apple trees get protection at 60 per cent, some trees at 40 per cent, but most at 10 per cent. The second element is to do a market reform and let producer and joint forestry management committees enter into contracts with those who can sell. The role of cooperatives is clear. The third is to clean up the financing and technology support systems. Today a tribal who grows a tree on his own land, can't get financial accommodation for the sixth year, if he has seen the tree through five years with his own savings. Trees are not collateral. If policy supports nurturing our forests, the sector will lead the next agricultural revolution. Poultry and dairying grew at 5 to 7 per cent annual. Forest produce demand is growing at that rate. But production growth is zero. This must be reversed.

## Fish

In the fish sector, major projects like the FFDA were completed, but now new strategies need to be worked out. East Asia was our dynamic market and when they stagnated, one part of the fast growing market crashed out. 40 per cent of the market growing between 8 to 10 per cent stopped growing, but that should be only half the story. A revival should now be possible. The experience of export of fish and seafood suggests that quick responses to foreign demand changes are also required.

## Land Reform

Updating of land records and creating secure title for small landholders and tenant farmers, is essential; for creating access to inputs and finance. An improved land market will also trigger large farm investments and enable alliances and contracts between farmers, cooperatives and companies. A large programme of land development based on fallow and marginal lands can follow.

## Small Towns and Rural Linkages

Decentralised urbanisation will supplement broad-based agricultural and rural development. Recent work shows that artisan based responses to national and global markets can be powerful sources of growth and in any case are not an insignificant part of exports. As much as a third of India's engineering exports are attributed to them. 112 towns account for 80 per cent of India's small industry. The success studies here involve training and improvement of inherited community-based artisan skills. The organisational pattern is generally based on fierce competition between small firms, with considerable mobility between self-employment and wage labour. However, the communities (in Indian castes) are also engaged in training and skill enhancement, access to larger markets through traditional networks, and technology enhancement, both of production and markets/communication. Support to such clusters can provide widespread employment opportunities.

There are a number of such success stories, such as in Tiruchengodu in Salem district of Tamil Nadu[15] or for diamond-cutters in Surat.[16] We must support artisan based industrialisation and services with a nation-wide technology, market access and training programme supporting communities which are integrating with regional, national and global markets. We must develop a national programme to train the poor and disadvantaged youth for the jobs of tomorrow.[17]

---

15. Hullier, V. Bener, L. Kennedy, 1994.

16. S.P. Kashyap and R.S. Tiwari found in a study an organisational structure of distribution, processing and markets, strongly based on trust, with the roughs (*passas*, as they are called), and polished diamonds changing hands without any written documentation; constant upgradation of technology on the production side, with hand polishing giving way to semi-automatic tools; intense competition and mobility in the lowest polishing formations; and community (caste) based training efforts of a decentralised nature, going on in each *taluka*. Replication would require support to artisan-based networks for technology upgradation, standardisation, training, market tracking and modern communication; solutions should not be from above or imposed.

17. Alagh, OECD, 2003.

## Conclusion

The reform process should always show the farmer and artisan the way out from unsustainable activities in concrete terms in the local context. Within the budget constraint at the local level, the challenge is to design ways of withdrawing unproductive programmes and subsidies and creating support mechanisms for newer more profitable paths of growth.

# 3

# How Well are the Villages Equipped

*Creating a Future Growth Potential Index at the State Level*

DEBASHIS CHAKRABORTY
ARUP GUHA

## Introduction

In India we have more than six lakh villages spread over the States and the Union Territories. The quality of life across these villages, as well as the available facilities, differs significantly from one State to the other. The qualitative difference in life of the villagers could be seen from the village level consumption data across States as seen from NSSO (1999-2000). While the per capita monthly consumption expenditure of the rural population for food items in Punjab and Kerala is Rs. 467.86 and Rs. 458.37 respectively, the same for Madhya Pradesh and Orissa stands at a meager figure of Rs. 286.28 and Rs. 289.14 in that order. The difference originates from a number of factors, structure of the rural workforce, the existing level of endowments, access to government support programmes, spread of human capital and many others.

The success of the economic reform programme, although it had a much greater effect on the urban centres,[1] has slowly transmitted to the villages as well. The overall poverty ratio, as obtained from various NSS rounds, has been reported in Table 3.1. It is clearly seen that although the poverty rate declined steadily in consecutive rounds, the reduction has been quite sharp during the 55$^{th}$ round, from 36.0 per cent in 1993-94 to 26.1 per cent in 1999-2000. In particular, the reduction has been more prominent in the rural sector, where the

1. Bhandari and Khare (2002), p. 326.

majority of the population resides. The trend appears to be satisfactory, but it deserves a closer analysis.

### Table 3.1

*Poverty Scenario in NSSO Rounds*

| *Year* | *Poverty Ratio (%)* | | | *Number of Poor (Million)* | | |
|---|---|---|---|---|---|---|
| | *Rural* | *Urban* | *Combined* | *Rural* | *Urban* | *Combined* |
| 1973-74 | 56.4 | 49.0 | 54.9 | 261.3 | 60.0 | 321.3 |
| 1977-78 | 53.1 | 45.2 | 51.3 | 264.3 | 64.6 | 328.9 |
| 1983 | 45.7 | 40.8 | 44.5 | 252.0 | 70.9 | 322.9 |
| 1987-88 | 39.1 | 38.2 | 38.9 | 231.9 | 75.2 | 307.1 |
| 1993-94 | 37.3 | 32.4 | 36.0 | 244.0 | 76.3 | 320.3 |
| 1999-2000 | 27.1 | 23.6 | 26.1 | 193.2 | 67.1 | 260.3 |

*Source:* Economic Survey, 2002-03.

Saxena (2000) says, "During the period 1989-90 to 1998-99, the growth rate of production for both foodgrains and non-foodgrain crops taken together has declined to 2.35 per cent per annum from 3.72 per cent per annum achieved during 1979-80 to 1989-90. The decline in the rate of growth for foodgrains was sharper from 3.54 to 1.80 per cent per annum. This has also resulted in slower increase of real agricultural wages from 4.68 per cent during 1981-91 to 2.04 per cent between 1991-99."

In Table 3.2 the percentage of population below the poverty line across the States in 1999-2000 is shown and also compared with that of 1993-94. Chakraborty and Babu (2004) have pointed that while in all other States rural poverty has recorded a massive decrease, the margin is not too high in Orissa and Madhya Pradesh. Another interesting point is that, urban poverty is generally higher than the rural poverty, barring the exceptions of Bihar, Orissa, Punjab, Uttar Pradesh and West Bengal, where the reverse scenario exists. The exception is classic in the sense that there is no similarity among these States in terms of the rural scenario. While agriculture in Bihar and Orissa is in a very shabby state, it is moderately manageable in Uttar Pradesh and West Bengal. However, Punjab is the sole developed State in this group. In addition, the poverty ratios in Bihar, Uttar Pradesh, West Bengal and Madhya Pradesh are still above the national average. In addition, the rural infrastructure level also varies widely across these States. However, it has often been argued by economists that the extent of poverty reduction is less dramatic, and the choice of methodology is a source of biasedness.[2] In particular, the sharp decline in rural poverty is less convincing in the light of the falling productivity in agriculture[3] and absence of any special emphasis on non-farm activities before the month of July. On the other hand, rural employment has exhibited a declining trend throughout the 1990s and a similar situation has been noticed in case of agricultural wages.[4] Besides, given the growth rate of population, a sizable chunk of the population is still living below the poverty line.

## Table 3.2

*Percentage of Population Below the Poverty Line*

*(Percentage)*

| *States* | *1993-94* | | | *1999-2000* | | |
|---|---|---|---|---|---|---|
| | *Rural* | *Urban* | *Total* | *Rural* | *Urban* | *Total* |
| Andhra Pradesh | 15.92 | 38.33 | 22.19 | 11.05 | 26.63 | 15.77 |
| Bihar | 58.21 | 34.50 | 54.96 | 44.30 | 32.91 | 42.60 |
| Gujarat | 22.18 | 27.89 | 24.21 | 13.17 | 15.59 | 14.07 |
| Haryana | 28.02 | 16.38 | 25.05 | 8.27 | 9.99 | 8.74 |
| Karnataka | 29.88 | 40.14 | 33.16 | 17.38 | 25.25 | 20.04 |
| Kerala | 25.76 | 24.55 | 25.43 | 9.38 | 20.27 | 12.72 |
| Madhya Pradesh | 40.64 | 48.38 | 42.52 | 37.06 | 38.44 | 37.43 |
| Maharashtra | 37.93 | 38.15 | 36.86 | 23.72 | 26.81 | 25.02 |
| Orissa | 49.72 | 41.64 | 48.56 | 48.01 | 42.83 | 47.15 |
| Punjab | 11.95 | 11.35 | 11.77 | 6.35 | 5.75 | 6.16 |
| Rajasthan | 26.46 | 30.49 | 27.41 | 13.74 | 19.85 | 15.28 |
| Tamil Nadu | 32.48 | 39.77 | 35.03 | 20.55 | 22.11 | 21.12 |
| Uttar Pradesh | 42.28 | 35.39 | 40.85 | 31.22 | 30.89 | 31.15 |
| West Bengal | 40.80 | 22.41 | 35.66 | 31.85 | 14.86 | 27.02 |
| **India** | **32.77** | **32.36** | **35.97** | **27.09** | **23.62** | **26.10** |

*Source:* NHDR (2001)

2. For a detailed discussion, see Abhijit Sen (2000).
3. For a detailed discussion, see Sidhu (2002), who has shown that even Punjab, the key agricultural producer State, is displaying near stagnation in agricultural production and crop yields. Chakraborty (2003b) through a plan-wise comparison, arrived at a similar conclusion.
4. For a detailed analysis on rural employment in the nineties, see Chadha and Sahu (2002).

Although opinions vary about the extent, there is no doubt that the economic reforms have resulted in a fall in poverty. The route through which the reforms are likely to have caused the reduction is by causing increased decentralisation at the level of policymaking and funds disbursement, increased dissemination of information, and obviously through increased private participation. So that the growth through reforms continues to reduce poverty, the above areas play a crucial role and the regions, which have achieved the most, will be able to take the maximum advantage of the reform process. In this paper, we have selected the variables that reflect the above broad areas. Our exercise in this work has been to rank the States using these variables. The ranking tells us which State is comparatively better equipped to take advantage of the reforms, and which is not, and consequently reflects their future growth potential. Consequently, it will not be wrong to call the index on the basis of which the ranking is made, a growth potential index.

## Choice of Variables

We obtain the data required for the State level ranking analysis from the NSS 58$^{th}$ Round (July – December 2002) on facilities available to the villages. The distribution of various facilities across the States is provided per thousand villages. Thirty variables are selected under five broad categories. The major categories, as well as their components, are discussed below:

1. Proximity to administrative centres

    1a Location of *panchayat* head quarter (within 2 km)

    1b Location of *tehsil* head quarter (within 2 km)

2. Access to rest of the economy

    2a Location of railway station (within 2 km)

    2b Location of bus stop (within 2 km)

    2c Location of metalled road (within 2 km)

    2d Location of post office (within 2 km)

    2e Location of telegraph office/PCO/e-mail facility (within 2 km)

    2f Location of market/weekly market (within 2 km)

    2g Number of cable TV connections

2h Location of bank (within 2 km)

3. Physical and social infrastructure

3a Location of veterinary hospital (within 5 km)

3b Location of fertiliser/pesticide shop (within 5 km)

3c Location of primary health centres (within 2 km)

3d Location of community health centres (within 2 km)

3e Location of primary schools (within 2 km)

3f Location of higher secondary schools (within 2 km)

3g Location of vocational training centres (within 5 km)

3h Intensity of electricity use (for more than two purposes)

3i Intensity of non-conventional energy use (for more than two sources)

3j Coverage of drainage system (underground and covered *pucca*)

3k Distribution of drinking water source (tap and tubewell)

3l Distribution of irrigation system (canal and tubewell)

3m Location of metalled road (within 2 km)

3n Location of bank (within 2 km)

4. Coverage of government support programmes

4a Government programme coverage (drinking water)

4b Government programme coverage (sanitation)

4c Government programme coverage (approach roads)

4d Government programme coverage (employment)

4e Government programme coverage (electricity)

4f Government programme coverage (irrigation)

5. Presence of private initiatives

5a Presence of self-help groups

5b Presence of cooperatives

## Proximity to Administrative Centres

The proximity of administrative centres enhances the growth potential of the villages since the inconveniences, if any, are readily reported and consequently the probability of introducing corrective measures is usually higher. We select two variables under this group, namely – the proportionate presence of *panchayat* headquarters and *tehsil* headquarters within two kilometers of the village. However, we do not calculate a separate ranking for this category because the extent of decentralisation depends on both the distribution of formal administrative bodies (like the two above) and informal ones. The placement of formal bodies is purely an administrative decision and data on the distribution of informal administrative bodies are associated with lots of problems. In that case, we may rank a region lower just because it is distant from formal administrative centres, while actually it is quite near to informal ones. Until we can eliminate this error, unfortunately we have to forego this ranking.

## Access to Rest of the Economy

The access to the rest of the economy determines the productive capacity of a region. While absence of access signifies prevalence of a self-reliant village economy, with little development opportunities and low growth potential, increasing access augments the possibility of diversification and higher growth. We have included eight variables in this category - location of railway station, bus stop, metalled road, post office, telegraph office/PCO/e-mail facility and market/weekly market and bank within two kilometers. The number of cable TV connections is also included in the list of variables. For instance, the importance of the fifth and the sixth variables for the rural community could be explained as follows. The government of India provides price data for various crops over the Internet, which cannot be accessed by the farmers in the absence of the facility. In other words, the farmers are forced to accept the price paid by the purchaser. On the other hand, absence of agricultural markets near the village implies that the average small farmer is not taking part in it, since it is not economic for him to go to a distant market with a tiny marketable surplus. Instead, he sells the product to an intermediary, accepting a lower remuneration, which in turn results in lower investment on land, and further lower yield in future years. The presence of a bank network enhances financial transactions on the one hand, and lowers the dependence on moneylenders on the other. A similar argument could be placed in favour of including other variables. In short, increasing access to the rest of the economy plays an instrumental role in breaking the traditional mode of operation in villages.

## Physical and Social Infrastructure

The infrastructure level of the villages, both social and physical, is extremely important in the realisation of development potential. We select fourteen variables for this ranking. The location of veterinary hospital (within 5 km), primary health centres and community health centres (within 2 km) are included to judge the health scenario. The location of primary schools and higher secondary schools (within 2 km), and of vocational training centres (within 5 km) shows the access to education. Location of fertiliser/pesticide shop (within 5 km) is also included. Electricity and non-conventional energy use has increased in villages quantitatively, but qualitative improvement is still lacking. For instance, electrification has been done in a large number of villages for lighting the lamp-posts, which does not help much to increasing productivity. Similarly, a number of villages have been confined to the use of biogas as a source of energy, and not any other form. We consider only those villages, which are utilising electricity for at least two purposes and non-conventional energies from more than two sources. Similarly, in the case of sanitation and drinking water, we adopt a relatively high standard. We do not consider open *pucca* drainage system in the analysis and include the number of underground and covered *pucca* system only. For drinking water, we consider tap and tubewell as the sources. The distribution of irrigation system includes canals and tubewells. Finally, we include the location of metalled road and banks (within 2 km) in this analysis from the earlier category, as we think it should also be included under infrastructure.

## Coverage of Government Support Programmes

While the current growth rate of a region is dictated by the current level of access to the rest of the economy and the infrastructure level, the government support programmes in the current period is a determinant of the future growth potential. We consider six key areas of government operation, instrumental for enhancing the future growth potential of the villages. Most of the selected activities in practice strengthen the earlier two categories. That is government support, quite naturally, either improves the access of the villages to the rest of the economy or enhances the level of the physical or social infrastructure. The variables are – government support programmes to drinking water, sanitation, approach roads, electricity and irrigation. The support programmes on the creation of employment are also noted, because of their usage as a corrective measure in poorer States.

## Presence of Private Initiatives

The importance of various government policies is obvious for improving the economic condition of the village population, but private initiatives are also capable of complementing the same. Here, for the purpose of the ranking analysis, we select two variables – presence of self-help groups (SHGs) and presence of cooperatives. Over the last couple of years, the operation of SHGs has increased manifold in the area of microfinance, and they have significantly contributed in restricting rural poverty. Similarly, the cooperatives are also capable of improving the lot of the rural population owing to the potentially lower transaction costs and pooling of member resources.

## Methodology

We first divide the sample into two sets, the first consists of twenty large States, and the other one of ten small States. The following exercise is first performed with both sets, and then for each category within them. For each collection of variables we choose, the assumption is that the set determines a particular capability of the States. For instance, all the variables for physical and social infrastructure, when combined for a certain State, should reflect the general atmosphere for infrastructure available to the villages in that State. This general atmosphere however is a latent variable, in the sense that it cannot be observed. This is true for all the different sets of variables we select. For analytical convenience, we assume that this latent variable is a linear function of the chosen variables. Under this assumption, had the latent variable not been such, we would have automatically known about the relative position of the States and could also have applied econometric methods to obtain ordinary least square estimators of the coefficients of each of the variables. This would have enabled us to know the sensitivity of the general atmosphere to each of the relevant variables and more importantly, how much improvement is required in each to cause a targeted magnitude of improvement in the dependent variable. The variable though, continues to remain latent and we must device other methods to attain the stated objectives. In this paper, however, our objective is only to rank the States according to the various criteria and so we must leave the second point of analysis for some future work. One such method is principal component analysis (PCA). Before we explain the methodology for that, we must make the important point that the total variance in the index for general atmosphere is equal to the total variance in all the selected variables. Here we are obviously assuming that the variance in the index accounted for by the variance in the omitted variables is small enough to be negligible. Now, we must explain the specific advantages of PCA relevant for our analysis. Firstly, we must note that the number of principal components extracted is equal to the number of variables. Moreover, like the variables, the total variance in the principal components also accounts for the variance in the index (given our earlier assumption). So the variables can be replaced with the principal components in any analysis. However, the principal components must promise us some specific advantage in order to justify the replacement of the variables with the former. This advantage is that the principal components can not only be ranked in the order of the proportion of the total variance they explain, but also that the first principal component accounts for a very significant proportion of the total variance, usually more than fifty per cent. Consequently, the ordering of the first principal component can reflect the ordering of the States in terms of the relevant latent variable, had it been actually known, very accurately.

We compute the PCs as follows:

*Step 1*

Transform the indicators into their standardised form, *i.e.*,

$$X_k = \frac{X_k - \text{Min } X_k}{\text{Max } X_k - \text{Min } X_k} \qquad k = 1 \ldots\ldots 30$$

*Step 2*

Then, we solve the following determinantal equation

$| R - \lambda . I | = 0$ for $\lambda$

where R is the 30 X 30 correlation matrix; this provides a $30^{th}$ degree polynomial equation in $\lambda$ and hence 30 roots. These roots are the eigen values of R. Now let us arrange $\lambda$ in descending order of magnitude,

$$\lambda_1 > \lambda_2 > .........> \lambda_{30}$$

*Step 3*

Corresponding to each value of $\lambda$, we solve the matrix equation $(R - \lambda. I). c = 0$, for the 30 X 1 eigenvector c, subject to the condition that $c'c = 1$. We write the eigenvectors as below:

$c_1 = [\ ]$, ..................., $c_k = [\ ]$

which correspond to $\lambda 1_1 > \lambda_2 > .........> \lambda_{30}$

$c_{11}$ $c_{1k}$

... .....

*Step 4*

$c_{k1}$ $c_{kk}$

The principal components are obtained as,

$P_1 = c_{11}. X_1 + ................... + c_{k1}. X_k$

$P_k = c_{1k}. X_1 + ................... + c_{kk}. X_k$

Thus we can compute all these PCs using elements of successive eigenvectors corresponding to eigen values, $\lambda 1_1$, $\lambda_2$, ........., $\lambda_{30}$ respectively, where $\lambda_1 = var(P_1)$, $\lambda_2 = var(P_2)$, ..., $\lambda_k = var(P_k)$. The principal components are linear combinations of the actual variables weighed by their respective eigenvectors. So, $\lambda_1 + \lambda_2 + ... \lambda_k$ is equal to the total variation in the index. Therefore, $\lambda_i / \Sigma\lambda_i$ is equal to the proportion of total variance accounted for by $P_{I.}$

Since,

$$\lambda 1_1 > \lambda_2 > .........> \lambda_{30},$$

thus,

$$\lambda_1 / \Sigma\lambda_i > \lambda_{i2} / \Sigma\lambda_i > ....... > \lambda_{30.} / \Sigma\lambda_i$$

then $P_I$ accounts for the largest proportion of the total variance and following the argument made above can be expected to reflect the ranking of the States by the latent variable, if actually observed, very closely.

## Table 3.3

*Ranking for the Large States*

| Rank | Overall Ranking | | Access to the Economy | | Physical and Social Infrastructure | | Reach of Government Support Programmes | | Presence of Private Initiatives | |
|---|---|---|---|---|---|---|---|---|---|---|
| | State | Score | State | Score | State | Score | State | Score | State | Score |
| 1 | Kerala | 10.00 | Kerala | 10.00 | Kerala | 10.00 | Kerala | 10.00 | Kerala | 10.00 |
| 2 | Haryana | 6.24 | Tamil Nadu | 7.06 | Haryana | 7.06 | Haryana | 6.95 | Tamil Nadu | 7.36 |
| 3 | Tamil Nadu | 6.20 | Punjab | 5.79 | Punjab | 6.08 | Chhattisgarh | 6.87 | Andhra Pradesh | 6.94 |
| 4 | Andhra Pradesh | 5.04 | Haryana | 5.28 | Tamil Nadu | 5.06 | Andhra Pradesh | 6.52 | Maharashtra | 5.86 |
| 5 | Maharashtra | 4.55 | Andhra Pradesh | 4.52 | Karnataka | 4.27 | Tamil Nadu | 6.36 | Haryana | 4.92 |
| 6 | Punjab | 4.53 | Uttar Pradesh | 4.04 | Uttar Pradesh | 4.21 | Maharashtra | 6.06 | Karnataka | 4.47 |
| 7 | Karnataka | 4.31 | West Bengal | 3.82 | Maharashtra | 4.16 | West Bengal | 5.63 | Chhattisgarh | 3.79 |
| 8 | West Bengal | 4.14 | Karnataka | 3.77 | Himachal Pradesh | 4.10 | Karnataka | 4.89 | Madhya Pradesh | 3.43 |
| 9 | Uttar Pradesh | 3.95 | Gujarat | 3.50 | Jammu & Kashmir | 3.91 | Uttar Pradesh | 4.78 | West Bengal | 3.42 |
| 10 | Himachal Pradesh | 3.74 | Rajasthan | 3.49 | West Bengal | 3.86 | Madhya Pradesh | 4.49 | Gujarat | 3.38 |
| 11 | Gujarat | 3.35 | Jammu & Kashmir | 3.45 | Andhra Pradesh | 3.73 | Gujarat | 4.40 | Himachal Pradesh | 3.30 |
| 12 | Rajasthan | 3.19 | Maharashtra | 3.34 | Rajasthan | 3.61 | Orissa | 3.92 | Punjab | 3.18 |
| 13 | Chhattisgarh | 2.89 | Himachal Pradesh | 3.23 | Uttaranchal | 2.81 | Himachal Pradesh | 3.81 | Rajasthan | 2.21 |
| 14 | Madhya Pradesh | 2.72 | Uttaranchal | 2.81 | Gujarat | 2.59 | Rajasthan | 3.12 | Uttar Pradesh | 2.18 |
| 15 | Jammu & Kashmir | 2.65 | Bihar | 2.35 | Madhya Pradesh | 2.30 | Assam | 2.82 | Assam | 1.91 |
| 16 | Uttaranchal | 2.23 | Jharkhand | 2.09 | Assam | 2.00 | Bihar | 2.20 | Jammu & Kashmir | 1.35 |
| 17 | Assam | 1.94 | Assam | 1.45 | Chhattisgarh | 1.86 | Punjab | 1.55 | Orissa | 0.73 |
| 18 | Bihar | 1.80 | Orissa | 1.18 | Jharkhand | 1.84 | Uttaranchal | 1.29 | Bihar | 0.69 |
| 19 | Orissa | 1.74 | Madhya Pradesh | 1.15 | Bihar | 1.75 | Jharkhand | 1.14 | Uttaranchal | 0.55 |
| 20 | Jharkhand | 1.51 | Chhattisgarh | 0.65 | Orissa | 1.48 | Jammu & Kashmir | 0.68 | Jharkhand | 0.15 |

## Table 3.4

*Ranking for the Small States*

| Rank | Overall Ranking | | Access to the Economy | | Physical and Social Infrastructure | | Reach of Government Support Programmes | | Presence of Private Initiatives | |
|---|---|---|---|---|---|---|---|---|---|---|
| | State | Score | State | Score | State | Score | State | Score | State | Score |
| 1 | Delhi | 10.00 | Delhi | 10.00 | Delhi | 10.00 | Tripura | 10.00 | Pondicherry | 10.00 |
| 2 | Goa | 7.91 | Goa | 6.79 | Pondicherry | 8.29 | Nagaland | 9.36 | Delhi | 8.30 |
| 3 | Nagaland | 7.38 | Pondicherry | 5.59 | Goa | 7.82 | Goa | 8.85 | Arunachal Pradesh | 7.62 |
| 4 | Tripura | 7.30 | Tripura | 4.96 | Tripura | 7.30 | Delhi | 6.15 | Meghalaya | 7.49 |
| 5 | Pondicherry | 6.06 | Sikkim | 4.35 | Nagaland | 7.23 | Sikkim | 5.03 | Tripura | 7.15 |
| 6 | Sikkim | 5.17 | Nagaland | 4.25 | Sikkim | 5.02 | Meghalaya | 4.65 | Manipur | 4.82 |
| 7 | Manipur | 2.92 | Manipur | 2.33 | Manipur | 3.15 | Mizoram | 3.79 | Mizoram | 4.53 |
| 8 | Meghalaya | 2.28 | Meghalaya | 1.30 | Meghalaya | 1.91 | Manipur | 3.75 | Goa | 3.63 |
| 9 | Mizoram | 1.79 | Mizoram | 0.61 | Arunachal Pradesh | 1.54 | Arunachal Pradesh | 2.68 | Nagaland | 3.51 |
| 10 | Arunachal Pradesh | 1.20 | Arunachal Pradesh | 0.13 | Mizoram | 1.20 | Pondicherry | 0.15 | Sikkim | 3.14 |

## Interpretation of the Results

### *Overall Ranking*

In case of the large States, we see that Kerala, Haryana, Tamil Nadu, Andhra Pradesh and Maharashtra are in the top spot. The difference in the normalised scores between Kerala and other States is noteworthy. On the other hand, States like Assam, Bihar, Orissa and Jharkhand with relatively lower rates of growth are at the other end of the spectrum. A slightly astonishing result is that Punjab is in the sixth spot and Uttar Pradesh (ranked nine) is above Gujarat (ranked eleven). However, the seemingly startling result could be explained by looking at the data. In spite of achieving a very commendable rural growth, and having high values for most of the indicators, certain variables are quite low in Punjab. The coverage of government support programmes is understandably low and drainage system as well as access to CHCs is relatively lower, as compared to various other States. The relative positions of the other two States, Uttar Pradesh and Gujarat could also be successfully explained from the data, and the same is done in the following analysis of individual categories.

In case of small States, Delhi, Goa, Nagaland and Tripura are at the top positions, while five North-Eastern States are at the bottom. The position of Nagaland (ranked third) before Tripura and Pondicherry is slightly surprising. However, it is seen from the data that the proximity to administrative centres (both *panchayat* headquarters and *tehsil* headquarters) is highest in the case of Nagaland. Besides, surface connectivity, access to health (location of CHC, PHC), education (location of primary schools), certain government expenditures and presence of cooperatives are also quite high there. All these factors jointly contribute in obtaining a high rank for Nagaland.

### *Access to the Economy*

The villages located in Kerala, Tamil Nadu, Punjab, Haryana and Andhra Pradesh are most efficiently connected with rest of the economy. This result is hardly surprising, as these five States are the most developed ones. However, there is a need to explain the positions of Uttar Pradesh (ranked sixth), West Bengal (ranked seventh), Gujarat (ranked ninth) and Maharashtra (ranked twelfth). While in the case of Uttar Pradesh, surface as well as postal connectivity has played a key role, West Bengal has earned its position from better railway and postal connectivity. The relatively lower rank of Gujarat could be explained by a relatively lower village level penetration of telegraph office/PCO/internet facility and the banking network, although surface connectivity is quite high there. Finally in the case of Maharashtra, the coverage of railway, telegraph office/PCO/internet facility and the banking network is not very high, and presumably accounts for its position. The importance of access to the economy is reinforced by the presence of relatively less developed States like Bihar, Jharkhand, Assam, Orissa, Madhya Pradesh and Chhattisgarh at the lower extreme.

Similarly, the ranking of the smaller States is hardly surprising, as Delhi, Goa, Pondicherry and Tripura are placed in the top positions. The other North-Eastern States are placed at the bottom. Sikkim and Nagaland are better placed among other North-Eastern States owing to better surface connectivity (*e.g.* – metalled roads).

*Physical and Social Infrastructure*

It is seen from the Table 3.3 that Kerala, Haryana, Punjab, Tamil Nadu and Karnataka are among the best performing large States. On the other hand, Chhattisgarh, Jharkhand, Bihar and Orissa are at the bottom. The positions of Andhra Pradesh (ranked eleven) and Gujarat (ranked fourteen) are slightly surprising. It is seen from the data that while in Andhra the usage of electricity (for more than two purposes) and availability of drinking water is very high across villages, the health infrastructure (*e.g.* – PHC, CHC) is not very appreciable. Besides, the practical education centres, *i.e.*, the presence of VTCs are also very low there. In addition, the drainage system, as defined in our analysis, is not very extensive in Andhra. In case of Gujarat, although the variables primary schools, electricity use and drinking water sources are quite high as compared to other States, the access to health is quite moderate. The relatively high position of Uttar Pradesh (ranked six) could be explained by its relatively good performance of the variables – availability of fertiliser shops, primary schools, electricity use (for more than two purposes), drinking water and irrigation.

In case of small States, Delhi, Pondicherry, Goa and Tripura take the top four places respectively. As seen from the Table 3.4, the other

North-Eastern States are at the bottom. The result becomes obvious by comparing the data points of these with the top three States.

*Coverage of Government Support Programmes*

It is seen from Table 3.3 that Kerala, Haryana, Chhattisgarh, Andhra Pradesh, Tamil Nadu and Maharashtra are receiving the maximum amount of government support among the large States. This ranking is justified, looking at the data sources. For instance, West Bengal is ranked seventh in the analysis. Although it receives a decent coverage of government support in infrastructure building (e.g. – approach roads and electricity), the extent of coverage in case of irrigation is very low. On the other hand, Orissa is ranked twelfth since the coverage of government support is quite low in all areas, barring drinking water and approach roads. Assam, Bihar, Punjab, Uttaranchal, Jharkhand and Jammu and Kashmir are at the other extreme. The position of Punjab (ranked seventeenth) stems from the fact that because of its developed status, the coverage of government support programmes is quite limited. The result suggests that there is ample scope to enhance the penetration of government support programmes in States like Uttaranchal, Jharkhand and Jammu and Kashmir.

A somewhat similar scenario is noticed in the case of small States (Table 3.4). It was expected that the relatively less developed States of the North-East region would have topped the list. Although Tripura and Nagaland are in the first two positions, Goa and Delhi hold the following two places. A look at the data reveals that government support in sanitation, approach roads, and electricity is very high in these two States, and hence the result. As in the case of large States, it seems that the ongoing government programmes are yet to effectively cover a major section of the villages located in backward regions.

*Presence of Private Initiatives*

In case of large States, Kerala, Tamil Nadu, Andhra Pradesh, Maharashtra and Haryana are at the top spot, signifying that the presence of private initiatives is quite high in these States (Table 3.3). In light of their high ranking in the overall index, this implies that the private initiatives are proportionately present in a greater frequency in the relatively well off States as compared to the worse-off ones. The hypothesis is further supported by the fact that Assam, Jammu and Kashmir, Orissa, Bihar, Uttaranchal and Jharkhand are at the bottom in this case as well. In other words, the private initiatives failed to bridge the gap left by the inadequate coverage of government support programmes in these relatively backward States.

For small States, Pondicherry and Delhi top the list (Table 3.4). It is worth noting that the variability of the normalised score across States is relatively low in this case, signifying lower inequality. The underlying reason is that SHGs and Cooperatives are present in the North-Eastern States in large numbers.

*Policy Implications*

A complete and unbiased list of policy prescriptions would involve studying the factor loadings, as we have noted in our methodology section. However, that is a vast area and can form the content of some future work on its own. But we can still make some comments about policy implications from the rankings of this paper itself. The first thing to be noted from the rankings is that in almost all States, the pre-reform better performers are at the top of the list even after liberalisation. This, we feel has an important message for the government. Better information, decentralisation, better quality physical and social infrastructure, are still concentrated in a few States. Since the main tool of growth through reforms, private participation, is guided by the availability of the above, future growth can happen in the backward States only if the facilities listed above are improved. Consequently, we see that the government still has a very significant role to play even in the post-liberalisation scenario. It must concentrate on the States lagging behind and make them attractive for private initiative. This is easier now, that is after liberalisation, than before, since currently, with increased private participation in the forward States the government can free more of its funds than before and concentrate them on the backward States. On a different dimension, the government must also concentrate more on villages than on urban centres, since the latter are better equipped to attract private initiatives on their own than the former. Until this policy shift takes place, the rankings reported are unlikely to change.

# 4

## More Rural Roads = Fewer Villages

LAVEESH BHANDARI[1]

### Background

This paper takes the view that by improving infrastructure, especially road infrastructure, the government would inadvertently create conditions where the number of villages would fall. This in the view of the authors is a **desirable** outcome, as fewer villages would lead to lower costs of supplying essential services. In other words, not only would the government's fisc be affected positively, but it would also lead to better lifestyles for the masses.

As is true of urban residents, rural residents also chose their residential location based on a host of factors. Broadly however, we can categorise these factors as lifetime income related and lifetime consumption related. First consider income. Most rural economies are based on an agriculture base. Location of the residence close to the work-place (read farms) is desirable as it reduces the time, effort, and monetary costs of frequent travel to and forth from the workplace. A well-distributed road network combined with mechanised (not necessarily motorised) transport means reductions in these costs, and therefore the costs of being farther from the farm are reduced. Next, consider those in non-agri based services. For such occupation groups (whether in services or manufacturing), it is extremely important to be close to markets. Non-agro occupations involve many more market interactions. A better spread road system would enable them to relocate close to the larger markets (larger villages) as well.

Next consider consumption. We can roughly categorise that into two parts: private and public. Private or exclusive consumption

---

1. I am grateful to Bibek Debroy for suggesting this topic and line of argument. All errors are mine. All data are from Census of India and Ministry of Rural Development, unless otherwise mentioned.

involves private consumption such as food and manufactured items, *etc.* With a better road infrastructure a large part of these services would be better supplied at a lower cost, **but only as long as relatively larger scales exist.** In other words, exclusive consumption commodities are cheaper to supply to larger villages. Provided that larger villages with larger number of consumers would ensure lower monopolistic power of suppliers of such commodities, they would be available at lower cost in larger villages.

Public consumption elements include those that require physical and/or social infrastructure. These include education, health, electricity, communications, post offices, banks, and other social infrastructure such as religious locations, places of entertainment, *etc.* Each of these has high levels of fixed costs and consequently enjoys scale economies to the last mile.

In other words, fewer villages imply lower costs for all – private providers and government. Moreover, larger concentration of people also supports better functioning of markets, as forces that create small localised monopolies are weakened. As a result, these lower costs can be passed on to the consumers (residents). Finally, larger concentrations also bring with them a better choice of commodities and services.

The net result is that, not only would a better road system lead to better and cheaper lifestyles and easier supply of public utilities and services, but would create conditions where it would be in the interest of those living in very small villages to relocate to larger villages. The above arguments can all be tested, however, the available data do not allow us that liberty. For that we would need to undertake specific village level surveys that would include among other things, details on costs and prices across a representative cross-section of villages.

It is however possible to test the final outcome of the above arguments – that is, does better road connectivity lead to a reduction in the number of villages? The rest of the paper shows that indeed that has been the case in the past. This will have significant ramifications on the cost of supply of basic services and utilities, and as a consequence, on future policy.

The size and numbers of villages change over time for many reasons. These range from economic factors to geographic to policy related. But one of the most important factors affecting this is population growth. Greater population in rural areas might either result in growth of number of villages and increase in size of the villages. We argue that the rate of this increase in the number of villages would be lower in those areas that have better road connectivity. On the other hand, in areas that are not as well connected, the need to be closer to the place of work will tend to push people to the peripheries and form new villages.

## The Facts

But first the facts. The Tables that follow show four important aspects about villages.

- Inhabited village numbers have been increasing only marginally since Independence – about 0.1 per cent per annum from 1951 to 2001.
- Villages are typically getting larger in terms of population residing in them.
- Smaller villages are becoming less and less important in terms of the percentage population contained.
- Smaller villages are reducing in absolute numbers as well.
- The most important – fewer people live in smaller villages now than they ever did.

### Table 4.1

*Percentage of Total Population in Rural Areas by Size of Villages in India*

| *Population Range* | *1961* | *1971* | *1981* | *1991** |
|---|---|---|---|---|
| Less than 200 | 3.83 | 2.68 | 1.78 | 1.18 |
| 200-499 | 12.55 | 9.91 | 7.49 | 5.48 |
| 500-999 | 18.33 | 16.45 | 14.21 | 11.78 |
| 1000-1999 | 19.80 | 19.90 | 19.25 | 18.13 |
| 2000-4999 | 17.22 | 18.71 | 20.09 | 21.34 |
| 5000-9999 | 5.05 | 5.44 | 6.90 | 8.17 |
| 10000 and above | 2.80 | 4.07 | 4.56 | 5.16 |
| Total Population (Million) | 439.24 | 548.16 | 683.33 | 846.30 |
| Population in villages of size less than 1000 | 152.46 | 159.19 | 160.45 | 156.06 |
| Population in villages of size less than 500 | 71.95 | 69.01 | 63.34 | 56.36 |

*Source: India Yearbook 2002,* Manpower Profile.

* Excludes Jammu and Kashmir (which accounted for less than 1 per cent of total rural population)

## Table 4.2

*Population Size-wise Distribution of Villages in India*

| *Population Range* | *Number of Villages* | | | *% of Total Number of Villages* | | | *% of Population* | | |
|---|---|---|---|---|---|---|---|---|---|
| | *1971* | *1981** | *1991$* | *1971* | *1981** | *1991$* | *1971* | *1981** | *1991$* |
| Less than 500 | 318633 | 270795 | 245095 | 55.3 | 48.6 | 42.2 | 16.4 | 12.5 | 9.5 |
| 500-999 | 132990 | 135928 | 144998 | 23.1 | 24.4 | 25.0 | 21.5 | 19.1 | 16.8 |
| 1000-1999 | 81973 | 94486 | 114395 | 14.2 | 17.0 | 19.7 | 25.8 | 25.9 | 25.7 |
| 2000-4999 | 36005 | 46892 | 62915 | 6.3 | 8.4 | 10.8 | 23.8 | 27.1 | 29.8 |
| 5000-9999 | 4974 | 7202 | 10597 | 0.9 | 1.3 | 1.8 | 7.4 | 9.3 | 11.2 |
| > 10000 | 1358 | 1834 | 2779 | 0.2 | 0.3 | 0.5 | 5.1 | 6.1 | 7.0 |
| **Total** | **575936** | **557137** | **580779** | **100.0** | **100.0** | **100.0** | **100.0** | **100.0** | **100.0** |

*Note:* * : Excludes Assam. $: Excludes the population of J & K where 1991 census was not conducted.

*Source: Rural Development Statistics,* National Institute of Rural Development, Govt. of India.

On the whole, therefore, we find that the size of Indian villages has been increasing across the country, and across time. More importantly, States that have a higher share of villages connected with *pucca* roads tend to have **fewer smaller villages.** The Figure 4.1 below shows the correlations of percentage of villages connected by roads with village sizes.

## Figure 4.1

*State-level Correlation, bw % Villages of Different Sizes and Village Connectivity: 24 States, 1991*

## Table 4.3

*Number of Inhabited Villages*

| *States/UTs* | *1901* | *1911* | *1921* | *1931* | *1941* | *1951* | *1961* | *1971* | *1981* | *1991* |
|---|---|---|---|---|---|---|---|---|---|---|
| Andhra Pradesh | 29950 | 27748 | 28362 | 28432 | 26355 | 26306 | 27084 | 27221 | 27379 | 26586 |
| Arunachal Pradesh | | | | | | | 2451 | 2973 | 3257 | 3649 |
| Assam** | 10133 | 12,239 | 14,304 | 17703 | 18601 | 18965 | 20565 | 21995 | — | 24685 |
| Bihar | 73616 | 68826 | 66761 | 65297 | 66526 | 68148 | 67665 | 67566 | 67546 | 67513 |
| Goa | 102 | 102 | 165 | 166 | 166 | 251 | 251 | 383 | 386 | 360 |
| Gujarat | 17919 | 17598 | 18161 | 18301 | 17821 | 18724 | 18584 | 1827 | 18114 | 18028 |
| Haryana | 6783 | 6811 | 6739 | 6743 | 6725 | 6580 | 6669 | 6731 | 6745 | 6759 |
| Himachal Pradesh | N.A. | 6326 | 6539 | 10211 | 11016 | 11133 | 13060 | 16916 | 16807 | 16997 |
| Jammu & Kashmir | 6836 | 7052 | 7086 | 7085 | 7049 | — | 6559 | 6503 | 6477 | — |
| Karnataka | 29288 | 28548 | 29349 | 28365 | 28290 | 27629 | 26377 | 26826 | 27028 | 27066 |
| Kerala | 5725 | 5383 | 5362 | 4910 | 4358 | 4618 | 1573 | 1268 | 1219 | 1384 |
| Madhya Pradesh | | | | | | 70037 | 70414 | 70883 | 71352 | 71526 |
| Maharashtra | | | | | | 35526 | 35851 | 35778 | 39354 | 40412 |
| Manipur | | | | 1372 | 1521 | 1601 | 1866 | 1949 | 2035 | 2182 |
| Meghalaya | 2865 | 4077 | 4262 | 4589 | 4658 | 4059 | 407 | 4583 | 4902 | 5484 |
| Mizoram | | | | | | | 730 | 229 | 721 | 698 |

*Contd...*

*...Contd....*

| *States/UTs* | *1901* | *1911* | *1921* | *1931* | *1941* | *1951* | *1961* | *1971* | *1981* | *1991* |
|---|---|---|---|---|---|---|---|---|---|---|
| Nagaland | 292 | 407 | 449 | 481 | 497 | 512 | 814 | 960 | 1112 | 1216 |
| Orissa | N.A. | N.A. | N.A. | 48092 | 45387 | 48393 | 46466 | 46992 | 46553 | 46989 |
| Punjab | 12309 | 12235 | 12318 | 12223 | 12186 | 11526 | 11947 | 12188 | 12342 | 12428 |
| Rajasthan | 30986 | 32594 | 32739 | 34080 | 32081 | 31693 | 32241 | 33305 | 34968 | 37889 |
| Sikkim | 125 | 315 | 407 | 367 | 99 | 99 | 462 | 215 | 440 | 447 |
| Tamil Nadu | 24677 | 21530 | 20784 | 20139 | 18712 | 18470 | 14124 | 15735 | 15831 | 15822 |
| Tripura | 1463 | 2316 | 3373 | 3382 | 4387 | 3453 | 4932 | 4727 | 856 | 855 |
| Uttar Pradesh | 108646 | 108210 | 109726 | 111003 | 105775 | 111724 | 112626 | 112561 | 112566 | 112803 |
| West Bengal | | | | | | 38474 | 38465 | 38074 | 38024 | 37910 |
| **India** | **351582** | **350078** | **352582** | **357146** | **393609** | **557409** | **562183** | **556561** | **556014** | **579688** |

*Source:* Census of India, 1991; Rajya Sabha, Unstarred Question No. 383, dated 14.07.2004.

The figure 4.1 graphs the various correlation coefficients between villages of different sizes and percentage villages connected across the major 24 States of India. The data are from 1991 and are from the Census of India as well as Ministry of Rural Development. These show a very unambiguous relationship. Across the States of India, the larger the percentage of villages connected, the fewer are the proportion of small villages. And conversely, the larger the percentages of villages connected, the higher are the percentage of villages that are larger.

## Figure 4.2

*Un-connectivity of Habitations and Growth in Villages in 1990s*

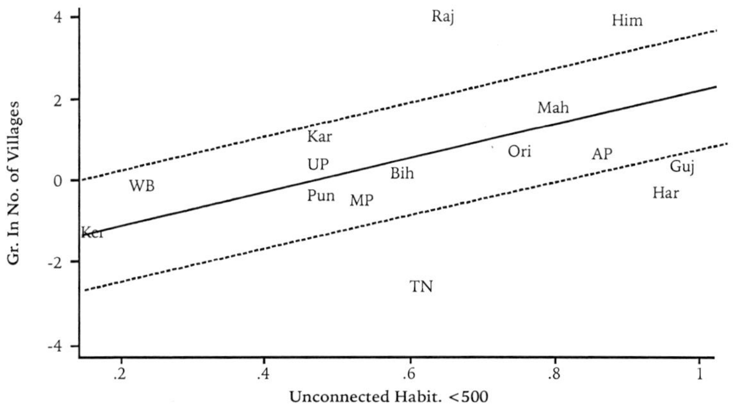


Figure 4.2 (above) graphs the percentage growth in the number of villages through the nineties against the proportion of small unconnected habitations in total unconnected habitations for the year 2001. The term small here refers to population less than 500. Villages are of course not homogenous entities, a village may consist of more than one habitations. Circumstantial evidence suggests that a habitation tends to be more homogenous with fewer households living together in a more concentrated manner than in the village it is a part of. Here as well we find a positive relationship. In other words, the greater the degree of un-connectivity, the greater has been the growth in villages. More important, note the outliers. Rajasthan

and Himachal, both have large areas that are difficult to reach in a manner that is difficult for simplistic data such as this to capture. And poor accessibility as discussed before is the primary force behind increase in villages. Next consider the States that have had a fall in the number of villages not commensurate with the pattern. These States are also those that have had a large increase in urbanisation levels. This in turn tends to reduce the number of villages for many reasons – expanding towns take over outlying villages, rural to urban migration, *etc.*

**Figure 4.3**

*Habitation Connectivity and Village Growth in Large States*

| | *States where <40% of habitations remain unconnected in 2001* | *States where >40% of habitations remain unconnected in 2001* |
|---|---|---|
| States where number of villages has increased in the nineties | [3] Maharashtra, AP, Gujarat, Karnataka | [2] Bihar, UP, Orissa, Rajasthan, Himachal, West Bengal |
| States where number of villages has fallen in the nineties | [1] Haryana, Punjab, Tamil Nadu | [4] Kerala, MP |

Consider Figure 4.3 above. Cell 1 shows that States such as Haryana, Punjab, and Tamil Nadu that have high levels of road connectivity have had a fall in the number of villages. Whereas States such as Bihar, Uttar Pradesh, Orissa, Rajasthan (Cell 2) have had an increase in the number of villages and these are precisely the States that have had a large number of villages that remain unconnected. But there are outliers. Kerala (Cell 4) for instance, can be explained in terms of connectivity through waterways due to its terrain.

However, States such as Maharasthra and Gujarat (Cell 3) have seen a rise in the number of villages despite generally having better connectivity. On the other hand, these States also have large parts that have low levels of connectivity. Kuchh in Gujarat, Telangana and Rayalseema in AP, Marathwada in Maharasthtra, the Gulbarga area in Northern Karnataka, all have low levels of infrastructure. (This however cannot be tested as sub-State data on these aspects are as yet unavailable.)

## The Future

Whichever way we see it, it is fairly clear that the number of smaller villages is going to fall in India. This will be due to many factors – the three key ones being road connectivity, economic growth and population growth. This is leading to a fall in the proportion of population in such small villages by about 3.5 percentage points every decade. By 2010 therefore, we should expect about 6 per cent of the population living in the smaller villages and about 3 per cent by 2020.

However, note the important factors – GDP growth is likely to be higher in the coming years, and with the greater emphasis on rural roads, the connectivity would also be significantly higher. In all likelihood, therefore, we should expect that the number of people in such small habitations to be insignificant. This is not a pattern that is peculiar to India. It is well known that rural populations fall with economic growth. What is normally not well known, is that this fall in rural population is not merely due to migration. It is also the result of (i) increase in the size of villages - many of which eventually become towns; (ii) fall in the number of villages – due to rural-rural migration; and (iii) take-over of rural areas by fast expanding urban areas.

**Figure 4.4**

*Villages with less than 500 People*

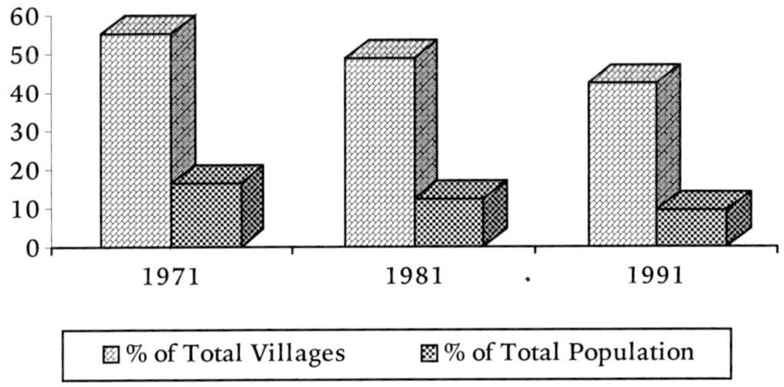

**Figure 4.5**

*Projected Fall in Small Villages*

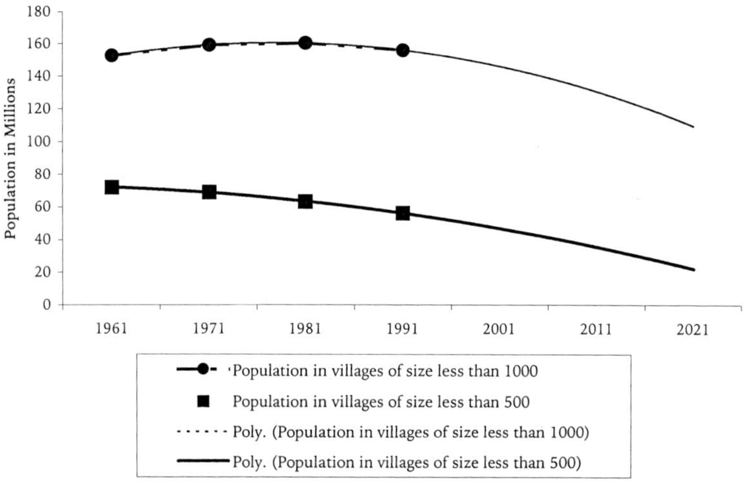


Of course, these relationships with village size/numbers are not exogenous. Two crucial elements are economic growth and road connectivity. Since economic growth itself is a function of infrastructure, communications, markets and lowering of costs of transactions, road connectivity is the critical element that completes the picture. As has already been argued, greater connectivity would lead to lower need for peripheral villages. In other words, both number of villages connected, as well as the increase in rural roads should be negatively related to the change in the number of villages.

## Road Connectivity

Rural roads are the most important element of rural development. Whether it is the usage of new technologies, the availability of inputs, the presence of a good economic climate, the presence of a large number of buyers and suppliers, the reach of mass media, delivery of services, all are intimately connected with rural roads. Not surprisingly, we find that all advanced countries tend to have high road penetration in the hinterlands. What causes this is for others to deliberate, the point being made here is that rural development and road penetration go together. And as road penetration increases, the number of villages fall.

An important aspect of road connectivity is in the reduction of costs of transactions. What are these costs of transactions? These are the costs of transportation, search costs, costs of finding the relevant buyers and sellers for products and services that can be produced by village dwellers, *etc.* These costs might be seen purely as monetary, but time and effort costs (that could be quantified in money terms) are not insignificant and can strongly affect production and resource allocation decisions of both public and private entities.

What then would make a good road transport network? Others have written significantly about this – many factors have been identified as important. Should the connectivity be to other villages? Should it be to nearby towns, or should it be to large markets or frequently held *haats*? Or should a hub and spoke system be the standard norm?

Rural road and transportation networks affect both production and consumption. And for different areas the answers will be different. For instance, for villages that tend to cater to predominantly producers and exporters of a single commodity, the kind of road connectivity required would be different than one for regions that produce heterogeneous commodities.

It is well known that since village connectivity has been under the policy radar, administrations in different parts of India have generally been aiming at improving the number of villages connected. However, what is not so well known is what has been the process of determining which village should be connected to which location. The current practice in India considers connectivity based on the population of the villages and the small-sized villages tend to be neglected. By improving the spread of rural roads to the hinterlands, these small habitations and villages will become redundant. For this to occur, the planning of the rural road network has to be done in a systematic manner in a comprehensive and coordinated manner.

## Conclusion: The Windfalls and Concerns

According to the 1961 Census, there were 5,67,169 inhabited villages and 54,891 uninhabited villages in the country. The numbers for 1991 were not very different at 5,87,226 inhabited and 47,095 uninhabited and all indications are that the totals have stabilised and will start to fall, especially for the smaller villages. Given that we are going to see a fall in the villages, what should be the policy reform to gain from this eventuality? There are many and some are discussed below.

First, flexibility at the lower levels of governance in deciding on provision of public services and public utilities need to be enhanced. The 73rd and 74th amendments do on paper provide that flexibility, but in reality that is hardly the case. Take for instance, the norms of a primary school within 1 km walking distance. In the coming years, many if not most of the schools servicing small habitations will become redundant. Similar issues apply for police stations, health centres, post offices, drinking water, *etc.* Many such utilities/services would be 'freed' up in the coming years due to the fall in small villages. The re-allocation of these facilities – infrastructure, as well as manpower, would be an important issue.

Second, the per head costs of supply of many such facilities/ infrastructure would fall. As a consequence, if managed well, there would not be a negative impact on the State governments' budget. Provided migration improves lifestyles, it may even be easier to impose user charges for some services.

Third, as villages expand, the need for better systems of village administration will become more and more important. The *Gram Panchayat* would need to function more like *Nagar Panchayat*s and perhaps even municipalities. One very important aspect of this would be issue of revenues for such larger habitations. In all likelihood, some form of property tax would have to be imposed by many such local governments.

Fourth, village connectivity and rural road building efforts should not be top down. A democratic process should be followed. That is, the largest numbers of the rural population should benefit, not necessarily those that produce or consume high values. This mechanism will have the highest impact for opening up the possibilities and opportunities for everyone. And the number of villages will fall further.

# 5

# *Panchayati Raj* Movement in India: Retrospective and Present Status

P.D. KAUSHIK

This paper is in two Sections. Section 1 is a retrospective description of the *panchayati raj* movement in India. Section 2 is a status report on devolution of functions and powers.

## SECTION 1: RETROSPECTIVE

The most significant experiment in reforming governance in India from a participatory democratic decentralisation point of view has been the introduction of the constitutionally mandated *Panchayat* system through the 73rd Constitutional Amendment in the early 1990s. It was expected that the newly created *Panchayat* system, drawing strength from the Constitutional provisions, would emerge as effective tools of local self-governance and would strongly further the primary objectives of economic growth and social justice.

### 1.1 Introduction

Self-governing village communities characterised by agrarian economies existed in India during the *Rig-Vedic* period. Not only it is evidenced in the *Rig Veda,* which dates from approximately 1200 BC, but there is also definite evidence available of the existence of village *sabhas* and *gramins* until 600 BC. These local bodies were the points of contact with higher authorities on matters affecting the villages and residents. Later, such village bodies metamorphosed into *panchayats*[1], which looked after the affairs of the village. Prevalent customs and religion elevated the *panchayats* to a sacred position of authority, which bestowed on them executive and judicial powers.

1. A local body consisting of five village elders.

The rural society also witnessed emergence of other *panchayats*, like the *jati panchayats* and *nyaya panchayats*, for ensuring that the people belonging to a particular caste adhered to its code of social conduct and ethics. These *panchayats* still exist in rural India today. In all fairness, such local bodies were the pivot of administration, the centre of social life, and a focus of social solidarity.[2] However, changing times and influence of foreign rule curtailed the scope and role of *panchayats*. With the advent of British rule, the *panchayats* were replaced by formally constituted institutions of village administration. Although British rule usurped the administrative and judicial powers of the *panchayats*, it willingly refrained from interfering in the functioning of the *jati/nyaya panchayats* for reasons well known.

## 1.2 *Panchayati Raj*: Road to the 73rd Constitutional Amendment

Decentralisation remained a major issue during the British Raj period, however India's national commitment to democratic decentralisation took a back seat while drafting the Constitution in the post-independence period. On the insistence of Mahatma Gandhi and others, the subject of decentralisation was included in Part IV of the Constitution[3] (*Directive Principles of State Policy*).

At another place in the Indian Constitution, local government is mentioned in Schedule VII, List 2.[4] This inclusion ambiguously defined local government without giving due recognition to *panchayats*. India's development in the early fifties was planned without taking cognisance of the idea of '*gram swaraj*'. The *panchayati raj* movement in India picked up momentum in 1957 with the constitution of the Balwant Rai Mehta Committee to suggest an institutional set up to secure participation of Community Development and National Extension Service programmes.

---

2. Charles Metcalfe, Provisional Governor General (1835-36) had called such village communities 'little republics'.
3. "The state should take steps to organise village *panchayats* and endow them with such power and authority as may be necessary to enable them to function as units of self-government."
4. "Local government, that is to say, the constitution and powers of municipal corporations, improvement trusts, district boards, mining settlement authorities and other local authorities for the purpose of local self-government or village administration."

**Box 5.1**

*Decentralisation: Key Facts under British Raj*

| | |
|---|---|
| 1687 | British formed the first Municipal Corporation in Madras |
| 1870 | Mayo Resolution to bring about administrative efficiency |
| 1870 | Revival of *gram panchayats* through Bengal Chowkidari Act |
| 1880 | Famine Commission highlighted inefficient disbursement of relief measures due to absence of local bodies |
| 1882 | Ripon Resolution elevated the role of local administration |
| 1906 | Indian National Congress adopted self-government as the political goal for the country under the Presidentship of Dadabhai Naoroji |
| 1909 | Government constituted the Royal Commission on Decentralisation |
| 1909 | Lahore Resolution of INC – "to make all local bodies from village *panchayats* upwards elective with elected non-official Chairmen". |
| 1919 | Montague & Chelmsford Reforms – bringing the local bodies under the domain of Indian ministers in the provinces |
| 1925 | Eight provinces in British India adopted the reforms – Madras, Bombay, Bengal, Central Provinces & Berar, UP, Punjab and Assam |
| 1926 | Six native States – Cochin, Travancore, Indore, Baroda, Kolhapur, Mysore adopted village *panchayat* laws |
| 1935 | Government of India Act allowed provincial autonomy, facilitating the evolution of *gram panchayats* |

The Balwant Rai Mehta Committee recommended setting up of a three-tier structure of the PRIs for effective decentralisation. According to the committee, it was imperative to give power and responsibility to the community for the successful continuation of the process of development. Consequently, statutory elective local bodies with adequate resources, power and authority were recommended. On the basis of these recommendations the *Panchayati Raj* institutions were established for people's participation and the effective implementation of Community Development Projects. The structure envisaged directly elected *Panchayats* for a village or a group of villages, an executive body called *Panchayat Samiti* for a block with directly elected and co-opted members and an advisory body, *Zilla Parishad*, with an ex-officio member from the lower tier and the District Collector as the Chairman.

Rajasthan became the first State to implement the recommendations of the Balwant Rai Mehta Committee at Nagaur in 1959. Pandit Jawahar Lal Nehru hailed the system as "the most revolutionary and historical step in the context of new India". S.K. Dey, Minister for Community Development in Nehru's Cabinet, became the chief architect of *panchayati raj* in the post-Independence period.

By 1959, all the States had passed the *panchayat* acts and by the mid-1960s, *panchayats* were established throughout India. More than 217,300 village *panchayats*, covering over 96 per cent of the 579,000 inhabited villages and 92 per cent of the rural population, were established. On an average, a *panchayat* covered a population of about 2400, covering 2-3 villages. As a result of conferring power on people's representatives, there was improvement in the attendance of teachers in primary schools, block administration became more responsive, *panchayats* emerged as an effective grievance redressal system for the rural masses, *etc*. Besides, they were successful in curbing petty corruption among the subordinate staff and newly elected leaders.[5]

**Box 5.2**

*The Balwant Rai Mehta Committee's Recommendations*

- Constitution of statutory elected local bodies with the necessary resources, power and authority.
- Decentralised administrative system working under the control of statutory bodies.
- Basic unit of democratic decentralisation should be located at the block/*samiti* level.
- Envisaged elected bodies '*panchayats*' for a village or group of villages
- An executive body called *Panchayat Samiti* for a block, with directly elected and co-opted members
- An advisory body called *Zila Parishad* at the district level
- Chairman as the district chief, elected through ex-officio members from the lower tier and others.

With the passage of time, a variety of weaknesses in the *panchayati raj* system surfaced. Indubitably, the resources were meagre for the *gram sabha*, but the major drawback of the system was hijack of the *gram panchayats* by economically and social elites. Further, local

5. Report of Association of Voluntary Agencies for Rural Development (AVARD) - 1962.

administration resisted devolution of functions and powers to *panchayats*. As a consequence, regular elections were not held, and traditional rivalries emerged in rural society. In fact, Mathews (2001) reports that there was a deliberate attempt by the bureaucracy, vested interest groups and elected representatives to thwart regular elections to *panchayats*, because their ascendancy was feared. Even the Government of India bypassed the *panchayats* and *zila parishads* and launched programmes like the Intensive Agricultural District Programme, Small Farmers Development Agency, Drought Prone Areas Programme, Intensive Tribal Development Programme, *etc*. This ultimately resulted in the downgrading of the Ministry of Community Development into a Department under the Ministry of Food and Agriculture, marking an end of both the 'community' and '*panchayats*' as agents of change and agencies of rural development.

The *panchayat* movement in India reached a turning point in 1977 with the constitution of the Ashok Mehta Committee. This Committee was set up to inquire into the working of the *panchayati raj* institutions, and to suggest measures to strengthen them so as to enable a decentralised system of planning and development to be effective. The Ashok Mehta Committee Report (1978) paved way to make *panchayats* an integral part of Indian democracy and formed the foundations for second-generation *panchayats*.

### Box 5.3

*The Ashok Mehta Committee's Recommendations*

- Favoured two-tier model for *panchayati raj - zila parishad* & *mandal panchayat*.
- Direct elections to these bodies, reservation of constituencies for SC/STs and women.
- State governments should not supercede the PRIs, all development functions should be put under the *zila parishad*.
- Preparation of exhaustive list of functions based on location-specific programmes.
- PRIs should be allowed to mobilise resources by granting them powers of taxation.
- Improved interface between PRIs, voluntary agencies, cooperatives and local government institutions for capacity building and human resource development.

The Ashok Mehta Committee's recommendations on the two-tier model at district and *mandal* level covering a population of 15,000 to 20,000 and abolition of the block as an administrative unit were subsequently rejected at the Chief Ministers' Conference in 1979, which favoured the continuation of three-tier system. Later, the G.V.K. Rao Committee was constituted in 1985 for reviewing the administrative arrangements for rural development programmes and poverty alleviation schemes. It agreed that the district should be the basic unit of policy planning and programme implementation, but it emphasised the need for regular elections to the *panchayat*s.

The 7$^{th}$ Five-year Plan recommended strengthening of PRIs through devolution of resources and greater autonomy of local bodies. It suggested radical changes in the planning process for village and block level activities. Subsequently, the Singhvi Committee was formed in 1987 for reviewing the functioning of PRIs. It recommended reorganisation of villages for creating viable *Gram Panchayat*s. The Singhvi Committee strongly recommended availability of greater financial resources to PRIs. However, the Sarkaria Commission on Centre-State relationships did not favour the PRIs, because local self-governing bodies were not working efficiently due to irregular elections and the suspension and supercession of local bodies on flimsy grounds.

The Thungon Committee (1988) made recommendations for strengthening the *panchayati raj* system by way of Constitutional recognition. As a result of which, the Ministry of Rural Development drafted the Constitution (64$^{th}$ Amendment) Bill, modeled on the bill appended to the Ashok Mehta Committee Report (drafted by L.M. Singhvi). The 64$^{th}$ Amendment was placed before Parliament on 15$^{th}$ May 1989. The Bill suggested setting up of *panchayat*s in every State at the village level, intermediate level and district level. The intermediate level was not obligatory in States with a population of less than 20 lakh. This bill was passed in the Lok Sabha in 1989, but could not be passed by the Rajya Sabha. The main reason for opposition was serious political overtones, namely the bill overlooked the States and was seen as an instrument of the Centre to deal directly with the PRIs and imposing a uniform pattern throughout, instead of permitting individual States to legislate.

## 1.3 73rd Amendment - Establishment of *Panchayati Raj* in India

Institutionalising the *panchayati raj* system in India is essentially the result of recommendations and proposals of various committees and sub-committees. Thus, all such efforts culminated in the form of the 73rd Constitutional Amendment, thereby providing Constitutional status to the *panchayati raj* institutions.

The explanation for the easy passage of the 73rd Amendment Bill and the acceptance of radical restructuring of the administrative structure with far reaching political consequences goes way beyond the committee reports and proposals. In this regard, Jain (1994), Mathews (1995), Bandopadhaya (2001), Behar and Kumar (2002), among others, have highlighted the dynamics of social and political change in the context of the Amendments. They view that several decades of centralised planning and a top-down model of development had paid dividends in terms of economic growth and industrialisation, but failed to result in the trickle-down effect that would have involved the poor and the marginalised in the process of development. As a result of which, a distorted and lopsided development process emerged, where the resources and authority became further concentrated in a few hands. The fruits of development were neither shared, nor did the poor and marginalised have access to it.

It became evident by the 1980s that for more egalitarian and balanced development to be achieved, a more participative, democratic and decentralised bottom-up model of development was needed. The collapse of the Soviet State in the late 1980s had led to a crisis and consequently various development paradigms were being discredited or put under strict scrutiny. Simultaneously, in the liberal democratic countries, new frameworks of development and governance were emerging. Many of these discourses propounded that for achieving the objectives of democratic States, the governance systems needed substantial changes, making the structure more participative and decentralised. The paradigmatic shift was evident in the attempts to transform governance to enhance accountability and projects to reinvent government and the bureaucracy, *etc*. The dictum that 'lesser governance is better governance' was used to restructure governments and enhance their efficacy through moves towards decentralisation.

**Box 5.4**

*73rd Constitutional Amendment: Basic Features*

- Constitutional status to the *panchayats* and gives it uniformity by making the three-tier system a permanent feature.
- *Panchayats* to be constituted in every State at the village, intermediate and district level, except States with a population not exceeding 20 lakh.
- Establishing a *Gram Sabha* in each village, exercising powers and performing functions at the village level, as the State may provide by law.
- Members of *panchayats* at all levels will be elected through direct elections. The election of the chairperson at the intermediate and district level will be through indirect elections.
- Seats are reserved for SCs and STs at all levels according to their population. Not less than one-third of seats are reserved for women.
- The office of Chairperson will also be subject to this provision.
- A uniform five-year term has been granted to the *panchayats*. In case of dissolution, elections should be held within six months of the date of dissolution.
- *Panchayats* are entrusted with (i) preparing plans and implementing schemes for social justice and economic development; (ii) in regard to matters listed in the 11th Schedule.
- State legislature authorises the *panchayats* to levy, collect and appropriate suitable local taxes. The Government can make grant-in-aid to the *panchayats* from the Consolidated Fund of the concerned State.
- Review of the financial position of the *panchayats* will be undertaken by a finance commission, which shall be constituted every five years.
- State Election Commission shall be constituted to ensure free and fair elections to the *panchayats*.

During the late 1970s and 1980s, all over the world, and especially in India, various social movements and civil society initiatives were trying to reclaim their legitimate space from the State. These new social movements and civil society actors were spreading a democratic consciousness in the people and suggesting that a democratic development process had to be participative and bottom-up. According to them, development had to be based on local needs and priorities, and micro initiatives. Development should be a flexible process emanating from the grassroots level and not a blueprint given from above. For these ends, the social movements and civil society actors were demanding radical changes in the government structure, to make it more participative, decentralised, democratic, accountable and transparent. The underlying theme was to replace the State-centric development process with a people-centric development process. At this juncture the political will and support at the highest level also played a crucial role in preparing the ground for a *panchayati raj* system.

**Table 5.1**

*State-wise Conformity Acts with the 73rd Amendment Act*

| S.No. | State/UT | Year | Name of the Act |
|---|---|---|---|
| 1. | Andhra Pradesh | 1993 | *The Andhra Pradesh Panchayati Raj Act 1993* |
| 2. | Bihar | 1993 | *The Bihar Panchayati Raj Act, 1993* |
| 3. | Gujarat | 1993 | *The Gujarat Panchayati Raj Act, 1993* |
| 4. | Himachal Pradesh | 1994 | *The Himachal Pradesh Panchayati Raj Act, 1994* |
| 5. | Karnataka | 1993 | *The Karnataka Panchayati Raj Act, 1993* |
| 6. | Kerala | 1994 | *The Kerala Panchayati Raj Act, 1994* |
| 7. | Madhya Pradesh | 1994 | *The Madhya Pradesh Panchayat Act, 1994* |
| 8. | Maharashtra | 1994 | *The Bombay Village Panchayats and the Maharashtra Zilla Parishad & Panchayat Samitis (Amendment) Act, 1994* |
| 9. | North-East | | |
| | a) Assam | 1994 | *The Assam Panchayat Act, 1994* |
| | b) Tripura | 1993 | *The Tripura Panchayat Act, 1993* |
| | c) Manipur | 1994 | *The Manipur Panchayati Raj Act, 1994* |
| | d) Arunachal Pradesh | 1994 | *The Arunachal Pradesh Panchayati Raj Ordinance, 1994* |
| 10. | Orissa | 1993 | *The Orissa Gram Panchayat, Taluk Panchayats, Zilla Parishads (Amendment) Act, 1993* |
| 11. | Punjab | 1994 | *The Punjab Panchayati Raj Act, 1994* |
| 12. | Rajasthan | 1994 | *The Rajasthan Panchayati Raj Act, 1994* |
| 13. | Tamil Nadu | 1994 | *The Tamil Nadu Panchayati Raj Act, 1994* |
| 14. | Uttar Pradesh | 1994 | *The Uttar Pradesh Panchayat (Amendment) Act, 1994* |
| 15. | West Bengal | 1994 | *The West Bengal Panchayat (Amendment) Act, 1994* |

*Source: Task Force Status Report*, 2000

The 73rd Amendment was inserted in Part IX of the Constitution. The local government is an exclusive domain of the State, therefore the Union just provides the outline of the *panchayat* system. The

States must implement by making laws or amending their existing laws to bring them in conformity with the provisions of the 73rd Amendment. But it was made binding on the States that the implementing legislation should be undertaken within a year of the commencement of the 73rd Amendment Act.

All the State governments have passed their *State panchayat Acts* to establish *panchayats* at village, intermediate and district levels. Some States like Tamil Nadu, Andhra Pradesh, Karnataka, Orissa and Madhya Pradesh, even after passing respective Conformity Acts, have adopted amendments to further strengthen their *panchayat Acts*. There are also some instances of amendments for tightening the hold of the state government on PRIs. Many State governments have retained both regulatory, supervisory and more importantly, powers of dissolution. Such disparities raise the fundamental question - how autonomous are the *panchayats* in our federal structure of governance?

## 1.4 *Panchayati Raj* - Constitutional and Legal Framework

In the post-73rd Amendment phase, different States have responded with varying degrees of enthusiasm. A few States have responded with innovativeness and remarkable commitment to make the system sustainable and successful. Others are still exercising significant controls. The efforts to institutionalise the *panchayati raj* system are evident in the number of amendments that have been made to the respective *State Panchayat Acts* as a dynamic response to the problems at the ground level. However, for the PRIs to function as institutions of self-government, the essential pre-requisites are-

a) Clearly demarcated areas of jurisdiction;

b) Adequate power and authority commensurate with responsibilities;

c) Necessary human and financial resources to manage their affairs; and

d) Functional autonomy within the federal structure.

*Continuity*

The 1992 amendment essentially aimed at fulfilling these pre-requisites. By providing fixed tenure of five years for an elected *panchayat*, it is aimed at providing continuity to the process of decentralisation and local self-government. In the event of premature dissolution of the *panchayat*, there is a provision for holding elections within six months. Besides, the 73rd Amendment has made a provision for non-interference of courts in electoral matters. Thus, continuity in *panchayats* has been ensured.

### *Accountability*

The provision on *gram sabhas* attempts to build in accountability within the functioning of *panchayats*. All States have provided that the Chairperson of the *gram panchayat* must convene a *gram sabha*, consisting of persons registered in the electoral rolls relating to the village, at least twice a year. The following matters shall be placed before the *gram sabha*, namely, the annual Statement of accounts and audit report, report on the administration of the previous year, proposals for fresh taxation or for enhancement of existing taxes, and selection of schemes and beneficiaries.

### *Power and Authority*

It is a noteworthy development that the 73rd Amendment provides for States to endow the *panchayats* with powers and authority "to enable them to function as institutions of self-government". It allowed the setting up of mechanisms for consolidating and coordinating planning and development initiatives and actions of the *panchayats*. Functions that by tradition are uniquely assigned to *panchayats* consist of the provisions and maintenance of local public goods, like street lighting, sanitation, village commons and water supply, as opposed to 'national' public goods like justice and national defence. The amendment provides for the constitution of district planning committees (DPCs). Such committees are a significant step in the direction of initiating a process of planning from below. The DPCs are to be responsible for the consolidation of plans prepared by the *panchayats*, and preparation of draft development plans.

### *Composition*

The provisions also lay down that every State shall constitute *panchayats* at the village, intermediate and district levels with the proviso that a State having a population not exceeding two million may not constitute a *panchayat* at the intermediate-level. The Constitution makes a specific provision for the representation of women and other disadvantaged groups on the local bodies in order to ensure participation of those sections of local communities, which had been outside of the mainstream of development. Under the Constitutional amendments, not less than one-third of the total number of seats on local bodies is to be reserved for women. Other disadvantaged groups are to be represented on a proportionate basis. Thus, the amendment not only provides for a constitutionally safeguarded third stratum of government, but it also confers uniformity in the structure.

*Fiscal Responsibility*

Appropriate expenditure and tax assignment and other revenue sharing powers for each tier of government are a crucial component in any decentralisation policy. Both theory and experience suggest that it is important to specify expenditure responsibilities as clearly as possible in order to enhance accountability, and reduce unproductive overlap, duplication of authority and legal challenge. In theory, decision-making should occur at the lowest level of government consistent with the principle of subsidiarity. The Constitutional amendment has maintained the erstwhile division of subjects between the Union (Central government) and State governments, under which, the subject of local government stands assigned to State governments. The amendments maintain that the legislature of a State will continue to have powers to endow the *panchayat*s and municipalities with such powers and authority as it may consider necessary to enable them to function as institutions of self-government.

In tandem, the Constitutional amendment has maintained the prerogative of the State legislature to decide which taxes, duties, tolls and fees should be assigned to local bodies and which of them should be shared between the State and local bodies. The Amendment has provided for the setting up of a Finance Commission in every State for the purpose of reviewing the financial position of the *panchayat*s and making recommendations on the principles that would govern:

- Distribution between the State and *panchayat*s of the net proceeds of the taxes, duties, tolls and fees that may be leviable by the State;

- Determination of the taxes, duties, tolls and fees which may be assigned to, or appropriated by, the *panchayats*;
- Grants-in-aid to the *panchayats* from the Consolidated Fund of the State; and
- Any other measure that would improve the finances of the *panchayats*.

These provisions in the Constitution envision a major vertical and horizontal restructuring in the State-local and Centre-local fiscal relations. It has also provided to States an opportunity to redesign the existing fiscal system so that it is coherent and flexible enough to meet the rapidly changing local needs and responsibilities.

The 73rd Amendment has ushered in an era of democratic decentralisation, incorporating specific provisions for the empowerment of local governments. This development coincides with what is happening in the other parts of the world. It has provided Constitutional recognition of local bodies, which was non-existent in the pre-amendment period. It has also simultaneously laid out a platform for initiating a wide spectrum of reforms in areas, such as local electoral systems, mechanisms for local planning and development, and State-local relations in matters concerning functional and fiscal powers and responsibility.

## 1.5 Institutions – Changing Indian Polity

It has been almost a decade since the 73rd Amendment. Since then, two fundamental changes have come about in the Indian democratic polity – namely,

a) the democratic base of the Indian polity has widened;

b) this has brought about significant changes in India's federalism.

Before the amendment, India's democratic structure through elected representatives was restricted to the *Lok Sabha* and the *Rajya Sabha* in the Parliament, 25 State Assemblies and two Assemblies of the Union Territories. The strength of total elected representatives at the first and second strata was about 4,963. Presently, the democratic base of the Indian polity has widened considerably. Beside the erstwhile elected representatives, there are about 600 district *panchayats*, more than 6000 block/*tehsil*/*mandal panchayats* at the intermediate level and more than 2,50,000 *gram panchayats* in rural India. In fact, the third stratum has fully dominated the Indian polity. No country in the world can boast of such a number of elected representatives, which truly forms the foundation of Indian democracy.

**Figure 5.1**

*Widening Democratic Base: Post-1993*

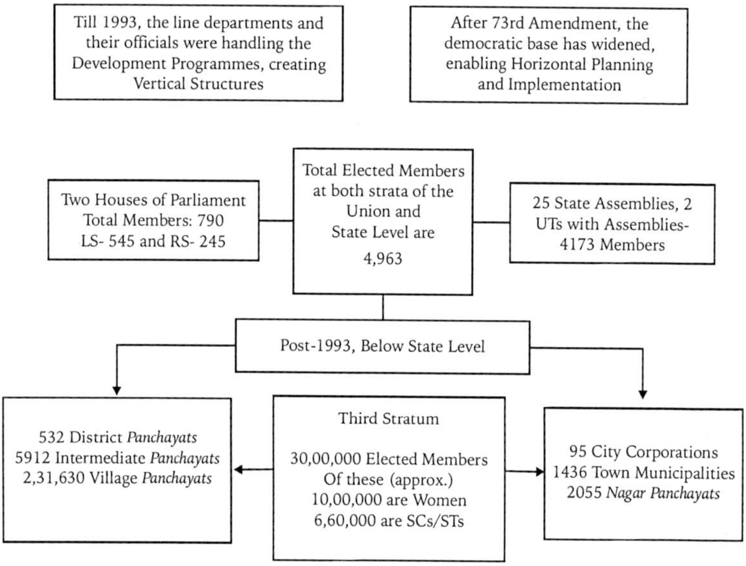


*Source:* ISS (2000)

Another significant change that has come about is in our federal structure. Our federal structure is pregnant with revolutionary possibilities following the widening democratic base as well as the structural change brought about by the *panchayats* and local bodies. India is on the move to become a multi-level federation with elected local bodies at district, *taluka/mandal/tehsil*, and village levels. Indubitably, this may be realised only when the subjects mentioned in the 11$^{th}$ Schedule of the 73$^{rd}$ Amendment (*Panchayat*) and 12$^{th}$ Schedule of the 74$^{th}$ Amendment (Municipalities) are brought under Schedule VII. Only then will this assume the status equal to that of the Union and State Lists. Although the elected bodies under the

## Table 5.2

*Number of Elected Representatives in the Panchayati Raj System*

| States/UT | Gram Panchayats (As on 31.3.1999) | | Intermediate Tiers (As on 31.3.2000) | | Zilla Parishads (As on 31.3.1999) | |
|---|---|---|---|---|---|---|
| | Number | Elected Represen-tatives | Number | Elected Represen-tatives | Number | Elected Represen-tatives |
| Andhra Pradesh | 21943 | 230529 | 1098 | 14644 | 22 | 1093 |
| Arunachal Pradesh | 2012 | a | 79 | a | 12 | a |
| Assam | 2489 | 30360 | 202 | 2564 | 21 | 845 |
| Bihar | 12181 | b | 725 | b | 55 | b |
| Goa | 183 | 1281 | — | — | 2 | 35 |
| Gujarat | 13316 | 123470 | 184 | 3814 | 19 | 761 |
| Haryana | 5958 | 54346 | 110 | 2430 | 16 | 226 |
| Himachal Pradesh | 2922 | 18264 | 72 | 1661 | 12 | 252 |
| Jammu & Kashmir | 2683 | c | — | c | 14 | c |
| Karnataka | 5675 | 80627 | 175 | 3340 | 20 | 919 |
| Kerala | 991 | 10270 | 152 | 1547 | 14 | 300 |
| Madhya Pradesh | 30922 | 47351 | 459 | 9097 | 45 | 1036 |
| Maharashtra | 27619 | 30545 | 319 | 3524 | 29 | 1762 |
| Manipur | 166 | 1566 | — | — | 3 | 61 |
| Meghalaya Mizoram, Nagaland | Traditional Councils perform duties of local government. 73rd Amendment not applicable in these states. | | | | | |
| Orissa | 5261 | 81077 | 314 | 5260 | 30 | 854 |
| Punjab | 11591 | 75473 | 138 | — | 17 | — |
| Rajasthan | 9185 | 112897 | 237 | 5494 | 31 | 1028 |
| Sikkim | 148 | 873 | — | — | 4 | 92 |
| Tamil Nadu | 12593 | 125852 | 385 | 6499 | 28 | 648 |
| Tripura | 525 | 5421 | 16 | 196 | 3 | 70 |
| Uttar Pradesh | 58605 | 799780 | 901 | 59991 | 68 | 2687 |
| West Bengal | 3314 | 49225 | 341 | 8520 | 17 | 716 |
| *Union Territories* | | | | | | |
| A&N Islands | 67 | 667 | — | — | 1 | 30 |
| Chandigarh | — | — | — | — | — | — |
| D&N Haveli | 11 | 135 | — | — | 1 | 16 |
| Daman & Diu | 10 | 63 | — | — | 2 | 15 |
| NCT Delhi | — | — | — | — | — | — |
| Lakshadweep | 10 | 79 | — | — | 1 | 22 |
| Pondicherry | 10 | 120 | c | c | 1 | 16 |
| **All India** | **227698** | **2580261** | **5906** | **128581** | **474** | **13484** |

a *Arunachal Pradesh Panchayati Raj Act* not yet passed.

b Post-73rd Amendment elections not held in the State. Elections issue *sub judice*. Figures not available.

c 73rd Amendment not applicable in the State. State proposes adopting 73rd Amendment.

*Source:* CSO, *Statistical Abstract India 2000*

amendment have no legislative powers and *de jure* the Union and States constitute federal India, the qualitative change that has come about in the Indian federal structure has far reaching consequences.

With changing political equations and coalition governments at the Centre, the second and third strata of governance are getting stronger. The Centre depends on the States, which are controlled by a number of regional parties. The regional parties derive their strength from the PRIs. Hence, PRIs have emerged as a pivot of governance at both State and Central levels. Thus, the *panchayati raj* movement is likely to result in significant changes in India's federalism.

Beside these changes in the Indian polity, *panchayati raj* has also resulted in some interesting developments, especially in terms of emergence of women's leadership and providing political space to the marginalised.

## 1.6 Emergence of Women's Leadership

One of the most interesting developments of the *panchayati raj* movement is women's participation in the democratic institutions at all the three levels - district, block and village levels. Although there are scores of instances where women representatives face culture of exclusion and violence, it is also true that lakhs of rural women have shed their inhibitions and taken up the responsibilities of governance. Panda (1996) observed that women entered into politics due to mandatory provisions of reservation. Most of the women are from non-political backgrounds and entered into politics due to persuasion by their family members or pressure from the village community. The important aspect of her study is that the women who reluctantly entered into politics showed great maturity in outlook, enthusiasm, increasing political consciousness and increasing perception of their role and responsibility. Jain (1996) found that usually women representatives are young, between 25-45 years of age. About 20 per cent of the women had previous political experience. Most of the women elected were illiterate and above all, the majority of women declared themselves as homemakers. She observed that women's experience of PRIs has transformed many of them. The elements of this transformation include empowerment, self-confidence, political awareness and affirmation of information access.

**Box 5.5**

*Malgudi Zila Panchayat*

Ms Gangamma Jayker completed her 20-month term as President of the Malgudi *Zilla Panchayat*. She now plans to contest the election to the Legislative Assembly of Karnataka. Gangamma is a product of reservations in the PRI system. She comes from a small village called Haleuru in Malgudi *taluk*, and belongs to the SC category. Her childhood story is typical of women born into the lower strata of rural society. She was married at the age of 10, had a son at 13, and struggled to get a primary education, walking 7 Km to go to school. She completed her primary education. Being educated, she felt she should do something for the women in her village, and started a *mahila mandal*. Growing to a strength of 100 members, this *mandal* was successful in accessing government loans meant for poor women under TRYSEM. This was the beginning of her political career. When the PRI institutions were set up, the *mandal* became her base, and she was elected to the *mandal panchayat*. She successfully completed her five-year term, and learned a great deal about the functioning of local government in the process. Gangamma Jayker is an example of the new politician emerging from the PRI system in Karnataka. Women like her would have found it impossible to make a mark in the system without the reservations.

## 1.7 Political Space to Marginalised Sections

Likewise, the reservation of SCs/STs in local bodies enabled the marginalised sections of the society to share political space with others. But an important development of the *panchayati raj* movement is providing political space to tribals. As the provisions of 73rd Amendment did not apply to Scheduled Areas located in eight States, namely Andhra Pradesh, Madhya Pradesh, Rajasthan, Gujarat, Maharashtra, Himachal Pradesh, Orissa and Bihar—vide clause (1) of Article 244, the Parliament extended the 73rd Amendment Act to these areas by legislating the *Panchayats (Extension to the Scheduled Areas) Act, 1996*. The Extension Act is notable for the vast powers given to tribal local bodies.

PESA gives radical self-governance powers to the tribal community and recognises its traditional community rights over natural resources. Prior to the passage of this Act, laws passed by Central and State governments were applied mechanically to tribal areas, even when these contravened traditional tribal practices and institutions. For instance, the *gram sabha*, which is the locus of political power under the PESA, may be in other States no more than a convenient administrative label for the relevant assembly. However, under PESA the law focuses on settlements, which the tribal people themselves perceive to be traditional and organic entities. In fact this is the first law that empowers people to redefine their own administrative boundaries. PESA provides that the tribal *gram sabha,* so defined, would be empowered to approve all development plans, control all functionaries and institutions of all social sectors, as well as control all minor water bodies, minor minerals and non-timber forest resources. It would also have the authority to control land alienation, impose prohibition, manage village markets and resolve internal conflicts by traditional modes. At one stroke, the Act creates a space for people's empowerment, genuine popular political participation, convergent community action, sustainable people oriented development and auto-generated emancipation.

**Box 5.6**

*PESA: Basic Features*

- Every village will have a *gram sabha* that will be competent to safeguard and preserve tradition and customs of the locals and their cultural identity.
- Prior approval from the *gram sabha/gram panchayat* is mandatory before granting permission by the government.
- *Gram sabha/panchayats* were given ownership of minor forest produce.
- *Gram sabha/panchayats* were endowed with powers to manage village markets.
- *Gram sabha/panchayats* were endowed with powers to lend money to the tribals.

A one-year time limit was given to the eight States to amend the *State Panchayat Acts* to bring them in conformity with the provisions of PESA. However, Bihar and Rajasthan did not amend their Acts within the stipulated period. Even those States which amended their respective *State Panchayat Acts*, have exhibited stiff resistance to endow so much power to the *gram panchayats*. Bureaucratic subversion of the letter and spirit of the law has been most visible in the interpretation of that provision of PESA by which *panchayats* at appropriate levels and the *gram sabha* have been vested with the ownership of minor forest produce (MFP). For tribal forest dwellers, the forest department has been the most visible oppression. Enforcement of PESA is perceived as weakening the stranglehold of the forest bureaucracy, and it is instructive to study the interpretation of PESA favoured by the State governments for its attempts to minimise the bureaucratic loss of control.

*Accountability at the Grassroots*

*Panchayati raj* has also strengthened the concept of *gram sabha*. *Gram sabha* is the only forum that can ensure direct democracy. It offers equal opportunity to all citizens of a village to discuss, criticise, approve or reject the proposals of the *panchayat* executive and assess its past performance. Besides, *gram sabha* acts as a watchdog of democracy and builds in accountability at the grassroots level. The *gram sabha* has been endowed with powers to identify beneficiaries for various poverty alleviation programmes, propose an annual plan, *etc*.

The Constitution of India envisages the creation of the *gram sabha* to ensure that the decisions made by the *panchayats* are transparent and its elected representatives are accountable to the electorate. As regards the composition, powers and functions of the *gram sabha*, the Department of Rural Development has explained that according to Article 243(b) of the Constitution of India, *gram sabha* "means a body consisting of persons registered in the electoral rolls relating to a village comprised within the area of the *panchayat* at the village level". The basic concept is that all the adult persons of the village as a collective body discuss issues and problems, needs and aspirations of the whole village and also special groups. Under Article 243-A, the *gram sabha* may exercise such powers and perform such functions at the village level as the Legislature of a State may, by law, provide.

In fact, the *panchayati raj* movement has emerged as a great influence on the Indian polity, a change agent for the rural society and building block for participative democracy. But in the implementation of *panchayati raj*, States have faced several opportunities and difficulties. The experience is extremely rich and provides vital insights into the process of institutionalising *panchayati raj*. On the one hand is the story of bureaucratic resistance, functional problems, political and institutional challenges, financial inadequacy and mismatch of capacities and roles. On the other hand, it involves the grassroots level in a democratic and participative governance system, and therefore potentially unleashes its considerable energy. It is extremely pertinent to study and document this process of transition. The process of implementation of the PRIs has raised several vital questions linked to the institutional and structural mechanism of governance. It also raises fundamental questions regarding the nature of the Indian polity. The PRIs also have far reaching implications for the political and social processes.

## 1.8 Impediments for *Panchayati Raj*: Conformity and Operational Issues

Although expectations are high with the provision made for Constitutional status to the PRIs, in actual practice, they appear to have been burdened with a variety of problems. There are many impediments affecting the functioning of the PRIs in several States with regard to structural pattern, composition of *panchayats*, linkages between PRIs, electoral process, concept of rotation in the case of reserved seats, devolution of powers and functions, bureaucratic control over local bodies, *etc*. It is useful to comment on some of the legal issues surrounding the implementation of the Act and examine the need to have further changes to revitalise PRIs, so as to make them vibrant.

Bandopadhyay (2004, 2003, 2000), Mukherjee (2004, 2002, 2001), Sharma (2004), Buch (2004, 2003, 2001, 2000), Saxena (2002, 2001), *Task Force on Panchayati Raj* (2004, 2003, 2002, 2001, 2000), UNDP (2000) among others have analysed the conformity and operational problems and issues at lengths. Some of the common issues confronting the PRIs in terms of conformity and operations are as follows:

*Distance from the Gram Sabha*

The *gram sabha*, which was a pivot of *panchayati raj* in the new dispensation, has been sidelined in most cases. It is through the *gram sabha* that the elected representative is made accountable to the electorate. This pre-supposes two things. Firstly, if the participation in *gram sabha* has to be meaningful, the gathering cannot be large. Secondly, the *gram sabha* should meet periodically and the subjects placed before it should be such that they attract public attention. Only then, will the electorate have any interest to attend the *gram sabha*, foregoing their day's income. Unfortunately, the Act does not appear to provide for both these requirements explicitly. Often, one *gram panchayat* constitutes more than one village. Therefore, the composite *gram sabha* meetings are held at one village for all the constituent villages, which constitute the *gram panchayat*. Since this composite *gram sabha* is usually held in the headquarters village of the *panchayat*, citizens from the other villages either do not attend the *gram sabha* or are reluctant to articulate their needs. Unless each village has a *gram sabha* of its own, the purpose of accountability may not be served effectively, especially when the village *panchayat* serves a population of a few thousand.

### *Rigid Structure*

The structure of the PRIs envisaged under the Act is too rigid. While the district has been defined as a normal district in a State, the jurisdiction of village and intermediate levels have not been specifically defined in the Act. While many States have more or less accepted the Constitutional dictum of three-tier structure, some prefer to have the freedom to choose the pattern of decentralisation, which in their opinion is most suited to them.

The institutional design for decentralisation should take into account not only the developmental thrusts built upon the capabilities at the local levels, but also the need to ensure local participation in decision-making. The problem of striking a balance between technical requirements and possibilities for meaningful participation by the people in development management occurs at levels below the district. What is the adequate area for a unit of administration is a quite complicated issue in any State. Such inadequacies are the results of unevenness in terms of economic resources, communication facilities, population density, level of social integration, civic commitments, *etc*. Thus, a uniform criterion cannot be applied throughout the country. On the contrary, it would be more appropriate to leave the exact pattern of local government below the district to the State governments. The Central Act at best can lay down general criteria for guidance purposes, making it compulsory to have one tier closer to the people to implement the development programmes and another at a higher level to supervise and monitor implementation.

### *Election to Panchayats*

The constitution of *panchayats* as mandated under the Act has also posed problems in some States. Under Article 243C(2), all the seats in a *panchayat* shall be filled by persons chosen by direct election from territorial constituencies in the *panchayat* area. Prior to the Act, some State governments, like Karnataka, had intermediate level *panchayats* consisting only of the elected representatives representing that area in the village as well as district *panchayats*. While the Chairman of this *panchayat* was directly elected in some States, in some other States the Chairperson of this intermediate *panchayat* was either elected from among the members or nominated by the government.

Whether direct elections should be held to constitute the *panchayats* at all the three levels or whether the intermediate *panchayats* at least can be constituted by nomination of the concerned elected members belonging to the other two tiers, is an issue explored widely. A related issue, raised in a recent Constitutional Amendment proposal, is whether the direct elections can be restricted to the village level only and have the village *panchayat* members elect their representatives for the intermediate and district level *panchayats*. While this may provide an organic linkage between the three tiers of the system, it may not perhaps satisfy the democratic norms for decentralisation, by diluting the element of direct democracy at the district level.

*Reservations*

There is a mandatory provision for reservation of seats for SCs and STs and one-third reservation for women (including women from SCs and STs). There is also an enabling provision for reservation for Other Backward Classes (OBCs). There is no reservation for OBCs in the State Assemblies and the Parliament, even though reservation is provided in these for SCs and STs. Reservation for OBCs in the *panchayats* has led to controversies and litigation in several States. Even the holding of elections were stalled on account of this anomaly in Bihar and Pondicherry, as the identification of OBCs in these places has itself run into difficulties.

There has been a debate on the desirability of prescribing reservations to the offices of Chairperson in the *panchayats*. These reservations have resulted in administrative problems in some States. There have been instances of the ruling party not having even a single elected representative from the category of SCs/STs or women, when the Chairperson's post was reserved in their favour, and under Article 243C(5), the Chairperson has to be elected from among the elected members only. Besides these practical problems, there can also be a question as to why the post of the Chairperson of a *panchayat* should only be reserved for a particular community/sex, when a similar reservation has not been made for any other public office anywhere in the country. On the other hand, it must also be borne in mind that without such a reservation, the country could produce only a handful of Chief Ministers in the States who belong to the category of SC/ST or women.

The concept of rotation prescribed under the Act in respect of the reserved seats has also posed certain practical difficulties. Article 243D clearly directs that the reserved seats, both for SCs and STs as well as women, shall be allotted by rotation to different constituencies in a *panchayat*. This has been interpreted to mean that such rotation should take place at the end of every five years. If this interpretation is given effect to, no SC, ST, or woman member will ever get the opportunity of occupying the same seat for a second term, as it is highly unlikely that these persons would be allowed to contest from the same constituencies, when the reservation is removed.

Often the elected representatives on the reserved seats are first-timers, thus most of the SC/ST and women members do not have any prior experience of governance. This shortcoming places them in great difficulty to occupy positions of power in the initial period. It will be difficult to support the idea that such leadership should not continue in their positions, beyond one term. Since the provision of rotation applies to Chairpersons also, the bureaucracy usurps the functions of novice Chairpersons and exercises indirect control over the *panchayat*'s decisions. This form of usurpation of authority becomes easier if the bureaucracy and the Chairperson are aware of the bleak chance of getting re-elected. While the concept of rotation is commendable, it is desirable to specifically prescribe the period for such rotation. This period should be long enough for the incumbent to get acclimatised to such positions and deliver the goods before completing that period and short enough to give all sections of the community a chance to get into positions of power at the local level.

*Dissolution*

Article 243E specifies the duration of tenure of *panchayats* and makes it mandatory to constitute the next *panchayat* before the expiry of the duration of the previous *panchayat* or before the expiry of a period of six months from the date of dissolution, if any. While the Constitution acknowledges the possibilities of dissolution, it however, does not deal with the running of the *panchayat* during the hiatus, which is between the dissolution and the constitution of the new *panchayat*. It may perhaps be necessary to provide for the continuance of the existing office-bearers of the *panchayat* to manage the day-to-day affairs of the *panchayat* during this inter-regnum, if necessary under the supervision of the *panchayat* at the next higher level.

*Devolution*

The Constitution expects the State Legislature, by law, to endow the *panchayat* with such powers and authority as may be necessary to enable them to function as institutions of self-government and such law may contain provisions for the devolution of powers and responsibilities upon the *panchayats* at the appropriate levels. However, the devolution of powers and functional strengthening of the different tiers of the *panchayati raj* system have not taken place in most States. Detailed executive instructions devolving powers and responsibilities on the different tiers of the PRIs have not been issued and a feeling is gaining ground that the initial momentum is somehow lost.

In addition, a review of the provisions in the Conformity Acts reveals that bureaucratic control over the *panchayats* continues to be very strong. Even where direct bureaucratic control is not visible, the *panchayats* have been placed in such a position that the Chairpersons have to make repeated trips to government offices located far away, for getting approvals and sanctions. This dismal picture obtaining in most of the States leads to the question of whether the Act should have gone to the extent of drawing up a fourth list in the Seventh Schedule of the Constitution for district subjects, instead of simply outlining 29 matters in the Eleventh Schedule.

Functions go where there is money, regardless of any list. Consequently, it is perhaps more important to install a new financial regime than to devise new lists. This further draws attention to the constitution of the Finance Commission as prescribed in the Act. Articles 280(bb) and 280(cc) require the Central Finance Commission to take into account the recommendations of the State Finance Commissions (SFCs).

The SFCs who have already submitted the reports have given their recommendations for the period 1996-2001, the Twelfth Finance Commission was constituted for the five years beginning 2001 and is currently operational. Merely projecting the requirements based on the available SFC reports by the Central Finance Commission will be a very static way of dealing with the issue. Some innovative method will, therefore, have to be devised to bring a meaningful interface between the Twelfth Finance Commission and the SFCs. One solution could be to expedite the setting up of the second SFCs. This will require an amendment to Article 243I and 243Y, as the second SFCs cannot be set up before the expiry of five years from the date when these were first set up. Unless the financial devolution from Centre to the States and the PRIs is put on a realistic and sound footing, no functional devolution can become meaningful.

*Relationships between PRI Levels*

The relationship among the different tiers of the *panchayati raj* structure is one of the most ignored aspects of decentralisation. A major area of friction and discontentment between the tiers has been the allocation of functions among them, as the Constitution has left this entirely to the discretion of the State governments. The State government is free to devise the pattern of devolution not only between the State government and the PRIs, but also between the three tiers of PRIs. It is imperative to mention that a wide variety of interests and variations coexists at the governmental and three tiered structured local self-government levels. Each institution is a stakeholder and interest group, vying for superseding others in terms of power and financial allocation.

The silence of the 73$^{rd}$ Amendment Act on the manner in which the three tiers should be linked has resulted in a variety of practices and some confusion in this regard. This frequently results in a lack of co-ordination between the three levels, which weakens the PRI structure as a whole. The lack of specification of functions and powers between the three levels results in a feeling - at each level - that the other two have greater powers and resources. The devolution of powers in the respective conformity legislation is not merely seen to be inadequate, but the Acts are also generally vague about which functions are meant to be performed by which tier. There are also no mechanisms for co-ordinating the functioning of the three tiers. The criteria of functional efficiency and economy, as also of administrative resources, could have been used to define more clearly the role of each tier in the planning and implementation of programmes.

### *Ambiguities in the Panchayat-Administrative Relationship*

The relationship between the *panchayat*s and the local administration has been interpreted differently across States. The Government of Rajasthan amended, by ordinance, some of the provisions of the *Conformity Act* to decrease the control of government over the two higher tiers. However, this is by no means definitive evidence of the superiority of elective over appointed authority. On the contrary, evidence is in abundance of the dominance of the bureaucracy over the people's representatives in all the States. In Haryana, the bureaucracy is seen to exercise inordinate control, as it substantially guides and directs the developmental activities of the *panchayat*s, instead of merely facilitating these. This relationship becomes stifling in relation to *panchayat*s headed by women, and even more so those headed by *dalit* women.

Further, lower-level government functionaries, attached to the *panchayat*s, are also in a state of confusion as they are simultaneously accountable to their superior in the government as well as to the elected leaders of the *panchayat*s. A notable exception in this regard is the *Conformity Act* of Gujarat, which provides for sectoral development staff of gazetted officers' rank to be transferred to the *panchayat* institutions to carry out developmental work. Despite this provision, Gujarat has not been able to decentralise planning, which Karnataka and Maharashtra have been able to do somewhat better, arguably due to a more long-standing engagement with *panchayat* institutions.

### *Devolution of Powers, Functions and Resources in the Conformity Acts*

While structures undoubtedly predispose institutions to evolve in particular ways, the most stringent test of any exercise in democratic decentralisation is the actual powers and functions that are devolved to democratic institutions at the local level, which must enjoy autonomy in the exercise of these.

The relevant article of the Constitution describes *panchayats* as institutions of self-government, but if the scope of self-government is externally defined and circumscribed, the institutions will be limited in this role. Article 243(G) itself provides for such circumscription, as it permits the States to endow the *panchayats* with powers, without actually making it imperative for them to do so. An examination of the powers and functions actually devolved makes evident the fact that the implications of the Constitutional Amendment were perhaps more radical in reservation provisions than in the powers and functions which were left to the States to determine and finance.

In fact, only three *Conformity Acts*, those of West Bengal, Bihar and Tripura, state that they aim to endow *panchayats* with powers and functions that can enable them to work as institutions of self-government. The Haryana Act specifically states that the objective of the *panchayat* institutions is to administer rural areas better. Indeed, Article 20, Chapter IV of *the Haryana Panchayati Raj Act of 1994*, specifies the "functions and duties" of the *gram panchayat* as follows:

"....It shall be the duty of the *Gram Panchayat* within the limits of the funds at its disposal, to make arrangements for carrying out the requirements of *sabha* area in respect of the following matters...."

It is evident that many of these problems relating to the structure of the *Panchayati Raj* system have implications for the functioning of *panchayats*, but that these become especially difficult in the context of *panchayats* headed by women is not often realised. The obstacles faced by women as members or heads of *panchayats* tend to be evaluated in terms of their own subjective perceptions, and are rarely related to the structural inadequacies of the *Panchayati Raj* framework.

## 1.9 Panchayati Raj and Rural Development

The fundamental question confronting the PRIs is - are they mandated for development functions only or for the wider purpose of self-governance. In his dissenting note to *the Ashok Mehta Committee Report*, E.M.S. Namboodiripad said, "Democracy at the central and state levels, but bureaucracy at all lower levels – this is the essence of Indian polity as spelt out in the Constitution. I cannot think of the PRIs as anything other than the integral parts of the country's administration with no difference between what are called the 'development' and 'regulatory' functions. I am afraid that the ghost of the earlier idea that PRIs should be completely divorced from all regulatory functions and made to confine themselves only to developmental functions is haunting my colleagues. What is required is that, while certain definite fields of administration like defence, foreign affairs, currency, communication *etc.*, should rest with the Centre, all the rest should be transferred to the States and from there to the district and lower levels of elected administrative bodies".

Article 243G of the Constitution, which now governs the entrustment of functions to the PRIs makes it clear that the primary role of the *panchayats* will be in the area of development. Planning and implementation of programmes of economic development and social justice ought to be the focal points of their activities. If the role envisaged for the PRIs is primarily in the field of development, it is difficult to envisage their effectiveness alongside several other governmental and non-governmental actors already in the development field. Admittedly, PRIs have entered the scene recently. All the other actors have been in the field for several years by now. The rules governing them have either been defined or evolved over a long period of time. Thus, is it a pre-requisite to bring about changes in these rules to establish PRIs in their assigned place in governance? Besides, all the three tiers of *Panchayati Raj* share a common goal of development, how to delineate their functions and powers in such a manner that there is space for each one of them without any significant overlapping?

The passage of the 73rd Constitutional Amendment has created a space and opportunity for decentralised participatory local development effort with in-built pressures for accountability. Implementation of these provisions is far from complete. Several states have not held local body elections as required by the Constitution. The PRIs have legislative powers to control rural development programmes. However, rural development programmes in India are often conceived and implemented as part of a national development strategy. Thus, serious problems remain in enabling local bodies to genuinely articulate and implement the aspirations of the poor and to remain insulated from bureaucratic interference and elite manipulation and capture. Within India there is a wide variation in the degree of success of local governments among different States. To some extent, the success has been correlated with the level of literacy and political consciousness of the electorate and the activism of civil society in the State. The major weakness observed in the devolution of powers and functions for rural development are-

a) Lack of support, both political and bureaucratic, for developing an effective framework for and management of the decentralisation process; and

b) Absence of knowledge and appropriate skills of *panchayats* to meet the requirements of their new roles as planning and implementing bodies.

The Union Rural Development Ministry is perceived to be a major impediment for *Panchayati Raj*. The Ministry is persistently fortifying bodies such as the District Rural Development Agencies. The DRDAs are empowered to bypass *panchayats* and directly handle rural development funds. What causes greater concern is the suggestion in the Ministry's *Annual Report* that the measure is not a temporary one. The move by the Rural Development Ministry to constitute District Vigilance and Monitoring Committees (DV&MCs), with Members of Parliament as chairpersons, to oversee rural development works is another case in point. This would serve to undermine the Constitutional status of *zilla parishads*. The usual argument in favour of setting up of such bodies is that these bodies will improve the efficiency of PRIs. Ironically, excessive political and bureaucratic interference are the cause of inefficiency in the *panchayati raj* system.

The democratic decentralisation using *panchayati raj* institutions seems to have been derailed. There is a lack of political will and bureaucratic support; the understanding of the constitutional perception of *panchayati raj* is also inadequate. There is an urgent need for another round of structural changes coupled with sustained pressure from the electorate. *Gram sabhas* need to be educated on decentralisation mechanisms and their rights under this process. However, it is Utopian to expect different interest groups to work in this direction. Civil society needs to be commended for their role in raising the awareness of the people so far, but the massive task of strengthening PRIs requires a new brand of politics that is genuinely committed to democratic decentralisation.

There is considerable debate on a number of major issues of development strategy that affect rural development. Neither the Statist nor the NGO programmes of rural development address the issue of poverty and regeneration of rural areas in a macroeconomic framework. While most programmes are formulated in a sector-centric framework, the NGO programmes are project-oriented and address the issues only at the micro level. This often accounts for the gap in micro level successes and failures at the overall level of the economy or the rural population. Thus, there are a few examples of successes at the level of individual projects of rural development, but the overall rural development picture remains bleak. A major weakness of the architecture of rural development programmes in general, and anti-poverty programmes in particular, is that they are conceived as having a minimal existence in "a self-contained universe of micro-oriented programmes and projects to specific groups of the poor." Such micro-programmes, from their conception, remain incapable of generating the synergy needed to eliminate poverty and tend to degenerate into welfarism. As a result, they become unsustainable without continuing access to financial assistance.

Nayak *et al* (2002) looked into the implementation of select centrally sponsored anti-poverty schemes. The study highlighted influence of political manipulation and administrative use at the time of implementing income transfers, infrastructure strengthening, employment creation and self-employment schemes.

**Table 5.3**

*Summary of Performance of Schemes*

| *Type and Name of the Scheme* | *Degree of Political Manipulation* | *Degree of Administrative Abuse* | *Impact on Productive Assets* |
|---|---|---|---|
| **Income Transfer types** | | | |
| National Old Age Pension Scheme | Low | Low | N/A* |
| Indira Awaas Yojana | High | High | N/A |
| **Infrastructure Strengthening types** | | | |
| Accelerated Rural Water Supply Project | Moderate | High | Low |
| Drought Prone Areas Programme | Moderate | Moderate | Moderate |
| **Employment Creation types** | | | |
| Sampoorna Grameen Rozgar Yojana | Low | Moderate | Low |
| Employment Assurance Scheme | Moderate | High | Low |
| **Self-employment types** | | | |
| Integrated Rural Development Programme | Low | High | Low |
| National Credit Fund for Women | Low | Low | High |

* Not applicable since these two schemes do not aim to impact on productive assets—they are concerned with income transfers only.

The evidence reviewed here suggests the following:

i) Schemes having a large component of individual subsidy, or large individual transfers, attract the attention of politicians and officials bent on diverting funds away from their intended purposes and on allocating benefits to those (usually wealthier) outside the intended beneficiary group.

ii) By contrast, small, regular payments are generally seen as not worth the trouble of embezzling or diverting, and schemes offering these are generally robust in implementation.

iii) The schemes that were implemented by NGOs appeared to be less corrupt than those administered by government, but this is a very small sample and may not be treated as a finding.

iv) Corruption in schemes involving payment in kind (such as foodgrains) appears to be concentrated at fewer points than in those involving financial payments (such as the siphoning off of grain by fair price shops).

v) Involvement of the private commercial sector in any aspect of implementation requires very close monitoring, the evidence suggests widespread collusion between middlemen and local officials in falsifying invoices and a range of other malpractices.

vi) The creation of sufficient local ownership of capital assets to ensure adequate maintenance and sustainability is exceptionally difficult for technical departments in the public sector to achieve (as in the case of water pumps under the ARWSP). Whilst recent public sector approaches (*e.g.* in DPAP) have attempted to break old top-down moulds, much remains to be done to break embedded patterns of corrupt behaviour.

vii) Equally difficult for government is the identification of the types of productive asset and opportunity that has the potential to enhance the livelihoods of the poor in sustainable ways. The negative experience of the IRDP is particularly instructive in this regard, though much the same applies to assets created under the EAS or SGRY.

Most allocations to centrally sponsored schemes can be tracked only to the district level, where they arrive either directly from the

Centre or *via* the State governments. Beyond the district level there are no mechanisms to verify whether or not, and the extent to which, expenditures materialise in the field. Nevertheless, there are definite indications that at least some funds from schemes are diverted from their given purpose. These can be for other schemes that the State government prefers, for instance, Andhra Pradesh and Madhya Pradesh. There are also examples of utilised rural development funds for general budgetary support, such as Bihar. The 'diversions' described may very well be beneficial as they could address States' priorities within the sector, for instance, watershed development being preferred over wage employment. However, there is also the potentially more serious question of whether funds allocated to centrally sponsored schemes are diverted into general support for State budgets. There are two ways this can happen within a particular financial year. It can be either with money being released to implementing agencies at the end of the instalment period with interest being earned on it in the interim (the end of year accounts will not reflect this juggling in any way), or on a more permanent basis.

**Box 5.7**

*Diversion of Funds: The Case of Andhra Pradesh*

The Employment Assurance Scheme (EAS) makes an interesting case study. In Andhra Pradesh, CAG (2000) observed that the implementing authorities of the EAS diverted funds aggregating Rs 111.3 million towards the state sponsored *Janmabhoomi* scheme and other activities not connected with the EAS, leading to a loss of potential generation of employment of 1.908 million man-days during 1994-99. Rajakutty *et al.* note that discussions with the officials who implemented the EAS scheme at the divisional level showed that most of these funds were utilised for works identified as part of the *Janmabhoomi* programme. The same study notes that in Adoni and Karnool subdivisions of Andhra Pradesh, apart from watershed development works, mostly other rural development works have been carried out under the banner of *Janmabhoomi*.

The selection of beneficiaries under the IRDP in AP followed patterns reported all over India. In an evaluation of IRDP in Anantpur district, Galab (1990) found wastage of 59 per cent of the total investment, due to the inclusion of the non-poor and the non-retention of assets. The beneficiaries were found to have spent an additional 5 per cent in pay-offs to middlemen. In another study, in East Godavari district, the socio-economic profiles of the village *panchayat* leadership and the beneficiaries were found to be closely associated. The wrong identification of beneficiaries and leakages of benefits are not accidental, they are the result of local power configurations. Various studies have found evidence of active patron-client relationships in the distribution of benefits under the anti-poverty CSS.

### *Panchayats and Rural Markets*

Rural markets are an integral aspect of the 'Eleventh Schedule'. However, multiplicity of functions, especially in creating rural marketplaces at all the three tiers of *Panchayati Raj*, has primarily acted as a major impediment. Small urban centres amidst rural areas are of great importance, especially in the context of decentralisation policies. *Panchayats* vary greatly in size and present different challenges. Lending to small business centres offers a particular challenge, though lending even to very small business hubs (below 500 inhabitants) can be efficient through the application of institutional innovation.

*Panchayats* at all levels have come up with innovative ideas to create business hubs in rural India. Although most of the examples are in pilot stages, there are quite a number of success stories. On the other side, governmental institutions like the Khadi and Village Industries Corporation (KVIC), Indian Handicrafts Guild (IHG), Small Industries Development Bank of India (SIDBI), National Bank for Agriculture and Rural Development (NABARD), *etc.*, have already made inroads into rural India and placed concerted efforts in creating rural business hubs at select locations. The common principle is to exploit the comparative advantage of a particular location.

The KVIC alone has at least one retail outlet in each district headquarter. In fact, it has a nationwide distribution network in place. Likewise, SIDBI has identified almost 400 industry clusters like readymade garments in Tirupur and scientific instruments in Roorkee. It has also identified 1600 artisan clusters at different locations, primarily engaged in capacity building and providing financial assistance for rural entrepreneurship. Indubitably, such programmes are running in parallel to the *panchayats*. However, *panchayats* have also taken the lead in setting up 2.40 lakh weekly *haats* and rural market places across India. Thus, a vibrant rural economy is gaining momentum from isolated successes. But strategic linkages between all the existing stakeholders are the key for creating rural business hubs in India.

Civil society is also not far behind. Civil society, in league with *panchayats*, is creating business networks in rural areas. Organisations like SEWA, Dastkar, Agri-Cooperatives, *etc.* are contributing more than just creating rural markets. In fact, there are many instances where the civil society is involved in safeguarding traditional culture and craftsmanship. The civil society is also one of the front-runners in creating ICT-enabled business networks in rural areas. The private sector is also not far behind the government in exploiting the advantages of ICTs for marketing of rural produce. There are ICT-enabled experiments like the Drishtee, TARAhaat, *etc.*, which are responsible for connecting rural populations to markets. Industry giants like ITC and EID-Parrys have initiated experiments like *e-choupal* and Parrys Corner in rural India for marketing agricultural inputs and outputs directly from the farmers.

State governments are also concentrating on connecting themselves with rural population for delivering ICT-enabled government services like the *Gyandoot* experiment in Madhya Pradesh, *Bhoomi* Project in Karnataka, *e-seva* in Hyderabad, *Janmitra* and *Lok Mitra* in Rajasthan. Besides, Andhra Pradesh has taken the lead in creating farm produce local markets like *Rythu Bazar* with the help of *gram panchayats*. Likewise, other States like Tamil Nadu and Kerala are trying to replicate some of the successful business experiments in their territories to benefit the local farmers.

In all, rural India is slowly emerging as a market place with small business hubs scattered all across the country with innovative linkages between the government, *panchayats*, industry and civil society. However, it is imperative to mention that major business activity hubs are those that have been already in existence in the past decade. But now they are innovating and broadening their field of activities. Most regions continue to remain in a state of neglect in the absence of any initiative from the State government, *panchayats*, industry or civil society. Thus, there is lot of scope for the *panchayats* in creating rural business hubs in these areas.

Some of the areas that surely require attention for creating vibrant rural business hubs are as follows-

- Providing services to the poor in and around small urban centres can be achieved if the constellation and responsibilities of institutions that work across the rural-municipality are understood.

- Working across the rural-urban boundary remains a challenge, requiring creative solutions.
- There are backward and forward linkages and synergies that exist between small towns and rural areas, which are important in the development process.
- The type and level of investment required to encourage economic growth is influenced by the size of the town and the population dynamics between the rural and urban areas.
- The poor status and high costs of infrastructure, social and public service delivery to rural areas is well known, especially in smaller towns, and the question arises of whether a certain "critical" size of town is needed before justifiably providing certain services. Alternatively, infrastructure and services can be provided to encourage growth, though experiences of this approach have been mixed.
- Low cost service delivery mechanisms need to be developed for smaller towns, for example, creating mobile services, ICT enabled business services, *etc.* (*e.g.* mobile banks, info-kiosks, *etc.*).

It has been a long journey from Montague Reforms to the 73rd Amendment. To conclude, the *panchayat*s have now come to stay as a Constitutionally recognised tier of governance. It is time to strengthen them so that they can discharge the duties cast on them in the best manner possible. At the same time, it must also be borne in mind that even without a further amendment to the Constitution, it is still possible to implement the spirit of decentralisation in India. In areas, which have been left to the discretion of the State governments under the Act, it is possible for the respective governments to bring in improvements either through administrative orders or by amending the conformity statutes appropriately. Only in cases where the Act comes in the way of meeting a particular field situation specific to a State, is there a need for seeking a Constitutional Amendment. Experience and research studies reveal that such cases do exist, but are not very many.

A paradox is that the 73rd Constitutional Amendment was necessitated to bring about decentralisation in India, whereas Article 40 of the Constitution could not be effectively used to establish meaningful local bodies in most of the States in India. Legal statutes may not be the best form of central intervention for bringing in decentralisation. Firm political commitment is a must for enhancing decentralised governance. Anomalies that have crept in have to be rectified and the challenge of the time has to be met. These will need a public debate to crystallise ideas, and political will to translate these ideas into workable legislation.

At present there is no strong evidence that the *panchayat*s are exercising their powers to raise revenues. The expectation that benefit taxes, where there is a direct quid-pro-quo between the taxpayer and the tax authority, can be levied more easily has not been realised. The terms of reference of the Twelfth Finance Commission require the Commission to suggest measures needed to augment the Consolidated Fund of the States to supplement the resources of the *panchayat*s and municipalities. "Measures" could be interpreted to include not only financial, but also legislative and administrative. Decentralisation has administrative, political and fiscal dimensions. The three dimensions are interdependent and the effectiveness of PRIs requires calibration of the three dimensions together.

The quest for equity cannot come about without wider representation of all groups, especially those currently denied access to power, SCs, STs and above all women. Their participation in the process of decision-making has come about through reservations. Revision of the current administrative and political structures, and their rules, is necessary in order to facilitate this broader representation and its translation into political power for those who are currently marginalised. Enshrining political change within the law has forced both the pace and direction of such change. The lesson of PRIs is clear, that if the wisdom of grassroots organisations, especially the courage and clarity of women, is to become policy, it will not be through the art of intellectual persuasion, but by the arrangements made within a political system for their voice to have power.

Bringing women into power is not only a matter of equity, but also correction of an unjust and unrepresentative system.

Rural developmental efforts are seriously constrained due to multiplicity of agencies and local actors. Parallel institutions are further transgressing the domain of PRIs, resulting in wastage of resources and duplicity of efforts. Lastly, rural development is more than ever before, linked to entrepreneurship under the new regime of local self-government. PRIs and individuals promoting rural development now see entrepreneurship as a strategic developmental intervention that could accelerate the rural development process. Furthermore, the various stakeholders of the rural economy, like government, PRIs, civil society, private sector and individuals seem to agree on the urgent need to promote rural enterprises.

## SECTION 2

## STATUS OF *PANCHAYATI RAJ*: DEVOLUTION OF FUNCTIONS AND POWERS

The 73$^{rd}$ Amendment Act (1992) of the Constitution created a uniform three-tier system of rural governments at the district, block and village levels, marking a new era of local self-government in rural India. It is more than a decade since the Act came into force. Most *Panchayati Raj* Institutions (PRIs) constituted under the new Act have by now established their credentials in the rural society and gained experience in participative governance. Therefore, it is an appropriate time for appraising the functioning of PRIs so as to reflect on emerging trends and to identify the impediments that have emerged in the process of democratic decentralisation.

The status of PRIs can be reviewed in terms of the following parameters:

(i) Conduct of *Panchayat* elections;

(ii) Devolution of Financial Powers;

(iii) Devolution of Functions and Functionaries;

(iv) Constitution of District Planning Committees (DPCs);

(v) Status of *Gram Sabha*;

(vi) *Panchayats (Extension to the Scheduled Areas) Act, 1996*; and

(vii) Checks and Balances over PRIs and Accountability.

Further, there are other issues that are central to the effectiveness of PRIs as conduits for delivery of economic and social services. These include participation, transparency and sustainability and the interface of PRIs with other parallel organisations operating at the local level.

### 2.1 Conduct of Panchayat Elections

On *panchayat* elections, the 73$^{rd}$ Amendment states "...shall be filled by persons chosen by direct election from territorial constituencies in the *panchayat* area and, ...area shall be divided into ... constituencies...that the ratio between the population of each constituency and the number of seats allotted to it shall, so far practicable, be the same throughout the *panchayat* area"[6]. The amendment required every State to pass or amend its own *panchayat* Act by April 1994, and to hold elections by April 1995. This provision resulted in a significant change in the Indian polity by creating political representation in the *panchayats*, covering almost 73 per cent of India's population.

Every five years in rural India, about three million representatives are elected by the people through the democratic process, of which, one million are women representatives. Rough estimates suggest, women head about 175 district *panchayats*, more than 2000 intermediate level *panchayats*, and more than 85,000 *gram panchayats*.

As a result of election to PRIs in States/Union Territories, 2,27,698 *Panchayats* at village level, 5906 *Panchayats* at intermediate level and 474 *Panchayats* at the district level have been constituted in the country. These *Panchayats* are being manned by about 34 lakh elected representatives at all levels; of them, one-third are women. This is the broadest representative base that exists in any country in the world. Elections to PRIs on expiry of their first term have also been held in Haryana, Karnataka, West Bengal, Uttar Pradesh and Madhya Pradesh.

Conducting *panchayat* elections confronted stiff resistance at various levels, especially in Assam, Arunachal Pradesh, Bihar and Pondicherry. On many counts, respective State Election Commissions (SECs) have been unsuccessful in holding the *panchayat* elections within the stipulated time. For Arunachal Pradesh, the Ministry of Rural Development introduced a bill for amending Article 243D of the Constitution to exempt it from the requirement of providing for reservation of seats for Scheduled Castes, in order to suit the socio-demographic ethos of the State. In Bihar and Pondicherry, the elections to PRIs could not be held because the matter was taken to Courts[7]. Assam cited law and order problems for delaying *panchayat* elections.

---

6. See Article 243(C)2 of *the Constitution 73rd Amendment Act, 1992* brought into effect on April 24, 1993.
7. In Bihar.

Table 5.4

*Number of PRIs in India**

| States/UTs | Gram Panchayats (Nos.) | Panchayat Samitis (Nos.) | Zila Parishads (Nos.) | Rural Pop. Covered (Lakh) | Villages Covered (Nos.) |
|---|---|---|---|---|---|
| Andhra Pradesh | 21943 | 1098 | 22 | 411.35 | 29293 |
| Arunachal Pradesh | 2012 | 79 | 12 | 5.72 | 3737 |
| Assam | 2489 | 202 | 21 | 171.83 | 20799 |
| Bihar | 12181 | 725 | 55 | 611.96 | 76488 |
| Goa | 183 | — | 2 | 9.69 | 406 |
| Gujarat | 13316 | 184 | 19 | 234.84 | 18550 |
| Haryana | 5958 | 110 | 16 | 100.96 | 7064 |
| Himachal Pradesh | 2922 | 72 | 12 | 42.57 | 18850 |
| Jammu & Kashmir | — | — | — | 47.27 | 6900 |
| Karnataka | 5675 | 175 | 20 | 255.67 | 27024 |
| Kerala | 991 | 152 | 14 | 201.63 | 1451 |
| Madhya Pradesh | 30922 | 459 | 45 | 415.92 | 76603 |
| Maharashtra | 27619 | 319 | 29 | 407.91 | 39354 |
| Manipur | 166 | — | 3 | 6.06 | 672 |
| Meghalaya, Mizoram & Nagaland | Traditional Council of Village Elders Exist | | | | |
| Orissa | 5261 | 314 | 30 | 234.85 | 50744 |
| Punjab | 11591 | 138 | 17 | 121.41 | 12795 |
| Rajasthan | 9185 | 237 | 31 | 270.51 | 37124 |
| Sikkim | 148 | — | 4 | 2.65 | 440 |
| Tamil Nadu | 12584 | 384 | 28 | 324.56 | 16602 |
| Tripura | 525 | 16 | 3 | 23.87 | 863 |
| Uttar Pradesh | 58605 | 901 | 68 | 909.13 | 112566 |
| West Bengal | 3314 | 341 | 17 | 394.78 | 38047 |
| Andaman & Nicobar Islands | 67 | — | 1 | 1.02 | 185 |
| Dadra & Nagar Haveli | 11 | — | 1 | 1.03 | 72 |
| Daman & Diu | 10 | — | 2 | 7.30 | 462 |
| Lakshwadweep | 10 | — | 1 | — | — |
| Pondicherry | 10 | — | 1 | — | 334 |
| **TOTAL** | **227698** | **5906** | **474** | **5214.49** | **592495** |

* As on October 1997.

Note: After 1997, some changes like creation of new States, formation of new districts, and other restructuring took place, which are not reflected in the above Table. However, the total number of PRIs is unlikely to change.

*Source: NIRD Rural Development Statistics (2001).*

## 2.2 Devolution of Financial Powers to PRIs

"Subject to the provisions..., the legislature of a State may, by law, endow the *panchayats* with such powers and authority as may be necessary to enable them to function as institutions of self government ...."[8] This provision essentially is targeted at devolution of powers, authority and responsibilities of *panchayats*. Article 243 H-J of the Act deals with the financial powers to impose taxes and collecting funds by *panchayats*, constitution of State Finance Commissions (SFCs), audit of accounts, and review of financial position after every five years.

**Box 5.8**

*Tax Assignment of Gram Panchayats*

**Major Tax Powers**

- Land tax (agricultural and non-agricultural)
- House building tax
- Vehicle tax
- Water, drainage and sanitation taxes
- Pilgrim tax
- Tax on profession, trade, and callings
- Tax on fairs and other entertainments
- Tax on advertisement
- Octroi on animals or goods or both brought for sale
- Lump sum levy of factories in lieu of taxes
- Special tax for construction and public works

**Fees and Charges Levied for Provision of Public Facilities**

- Water rate
- Lighting fee
- Street cleaning fee
- Conservancy fee
- Drainage fee
- Sanitary fee for public latrines; and pilgrimage fee (sanitation tax/fee)

**Fees for Use of Common Resources**

- Fee for the use of *panchayat* shelter
- User charges for hospitals and schools
- Fee for use of common resources like grazing land etc.
- Fee on markets and weekly *bazaars*
- Fee on animals sold *etc.*

8. See Article 243G of the Act.

**New Powers Recommended by SFCs**

- House tax
- Tax on pumps and tractors
- Tax on highway services
- Tax on village produce sold in regulated markets
- Tax on telephones and cable T.V.
- (Non-agricultural) profession tax

*Source:* Bohra (1998, 2002), Rajaraman (2001)

Keeping in view the spirit of the 11th Schedule, almost all State Acts have devolved some powers and functions to the *panchayats*. Kerala has followed the "principle of subsidarity" in allocating functions. As a result, village *panchayats* have been given more powers, functions and functionaries (schemes with necessary assets and staff), whereas intermediate level *panchayats* have fewer functions. The district *panchayats* are given second priority. The functions of *panchayats* have been grouped under obligatory, discretionary and functions entrusted by the State governments. While the mandatory and entrusted ones are binding, subject to the availability of funds, the discretionary functions can be undertaken by the *panchayats* as their own option. Table 5.5 highlights the current status of devolution at a national level.

## Table 5.5

*Status of Devolution to PRIs - Selected Indicators*

| *States/UTs* | *Status of Recommendations of the SFCs* | *Devolution of Funds, Functions & Functionaries* |
|---|---|---|
| Andhra Pradesh | Accepted 54 recommendations fully, 11 with some modifications, and 19 not accepted at all. Constituted 2-SFC. | Funds- 05, Functions- 17 & Functionaries- 02 |
| Arunachal Pradesh | Not Constituted | Not applicable |
| Assam | Recommendations accepted in parts. | No action taken yet |
| Bihar | Report awaited | Funds- 0, Functions- 20 & Functionaries- 0 |
| Chhattisgarh | Not Constituted | Funds- 10, Functions- 23 & Functionaries- 09 |
| Goa | Report under consideration | Information not available |
| Gujarat | Received but not placed before the legislature yet. | Information not available |
| Haryana | Accepted all the major recommendations. | Funds- 0, Functions- 16 & Functionaries- 0 |
| Himachal Pradesh | Accepted all the major recommendations. Constituted 2-SFC. | Funds- 02, Functions- 23 & Functionaries- 07 |

*Contd...*

*...Contd....*

| *States/UTs* | *Status of Recommendations of the SFCs* | *Devolution of Funds, Functions & Functionaries* |
|---|---|---|
| Jharkhand | Not Constituted | No action taken yet |
| Jammu & Kashmir | $73^{rd}$ Amendment Act has yet to be extended to the State. Central govt. has asked the State govt. to seek views of the legislature on extending the provisions of Act. Panchayat elections were held at some places in 2001. | |
| Karnataka | Accepted all the major recommendations. | Funds- 29, Functions- 29 & Functionaries- 29 |
| Kerala | Accepted all the major recommendations. Constituted 2-SFC. | Funds- 10, Functions- 23 & Functionaries- 15 |
| Madhya Pradesh | Accepted all the major recommendations. Constituted 2-SFC. | Funds- 10, Functions- 23 & Functionaries- 09 |
| Maharashtra | Accepted all the major recommendations. | Funds- 18, Functions- 18 & Functionaries- 18 |
| Manipur | Accepted all the major recommendations. | Funds- 0, Functions- 22 & Functionaries- 04 |
| Meghalaya, Mizoram & Nagaland | $73^{rd}$ Amendment Act is not applicable as the traditional system of local self-government exists in these states. | |
| Orissa | Accepted all the major recommendations. | Funds- 05, Functions- 25 & Functionaries- 03 |
| Punjab | Accepted all the major recommendations. | Funds- 0, Functions- 07 & Functionaries- 0 |
| Rajasthan | Accepted all the major recommendations. Constituted 2-SFC. | Funds- 0, Functions- 29 & Functionaries- 0 |
| Sikkim | Accepted all the major recommendations. Constituted 2-SFC. | Funds- 24, Functions- 24 & Functionaries- 24 |
| Tamil Nadu | Accepted all the major recommendations. Constituted 2-SFC. | Funds- 0, Functions- 29 & Functionaries- 0 |
| Tripura | Accepted all the major recommendations. Constituted 2-SFC. | Funds- 0, Functions- 12 & Functionaries- 0 |
| Uttar Pradesh | Accepted the recommendations. Constituted 2-SFC. | Funds- 12, Functions- 13 & Functionaries- 09 |
| Uttaranchal | Report awaited | Funds- 12, Functions- 13 & Functionaries- 09 |
| West Bengal | Accepted all the major recommendations. | Funds- 12, Functions- 29 & Functionaries- 12 |
| Andaman & Nicobar Islands | Report under consideration | Funds- 06 Functions- 06 & Functionaries- 06 |
| Chandigarh | Report awaited | Information not available |
| Daman & Diu | Under consideration | Funds- 05 Functions- 09 & Functionaries- 03 |
| Dadra & Nagar Haveli | Under consideration | Funds- 0 Functions- 03 & Functionaries- 03 |
| Delhi | NCT has repealed the Panchayati Raj Act, sought abolition of PRIs. Revival of PRIs is under consideration. | |
| Lakshwadweep | Under consideration | Funds- 0 Functions- 06 & Functionaries- 0 |
| Pondicherry | Elections have not been held. The matter is *sub-judice* in the Chennai High Court. | |

*Source:* GoI (2001)

States where *panchayats* exist have constituted their respective State Finance Commissions (SFCs), except for Arunachal Pradesh and newly created States, namely Chattisgarh and Jharkhand. Most SFCs have submitted their reports to respective State Governments, with the exception of Bihar, Chandigarh and Uttaranchal. Recommendations of the SFCs have been accepted in toto by ten States, *viz*; Karnataka, Kerala, Madhya Pradesh, Manipur, Punjab, Rajasthan, Tamil Nadu, Tripura, Uttar Pradesh and West Bengal. In case of Andhra Pradesh, Himachal Pradesh, Haryana and Maharashtra, the State Governments are still considering the Reports. In Gujarat, the Report is yet to be placed before the State Legislature. The Government of Assam has accepted the SFC's recommendations in part, while the Orissa Government has accepted the Report with some modifications.

It is also evident that the Reports of SFCs have not attracted serious attention from many State Governments. The recommendations of the State Finance Commissions can be divided into three categories:

(a) assignment of taxes, duties, levies and tolls to local bodies;

(b) sharing of revenue proceeds; and

(c) transfers on account of grants-in-aid and other financial assistance.

As per the SFC's recommendations, most State Governments have agreed to give PRIs a specific percentage of share in some of the State taxes like land revenue and cess on it, additional stamp duty, entertainment tax, royalties on minerals and mines, forest revenue and market fees. These taxes are less buoyant in nature and have no relation to the powers and functions to be devolved upon *panchayats*. More buoyant taxes like sales tax and excise are kept out of the purview of PRIs. All SFCs have put great emphasis on internal revenue mobilisation, but none has suggested any effective mechanism for PRIs to generate their own revenue. The SFCs also failed to recommend or foresee any noticeable change in the tax (including the non-tax) jurisdiction of local bodies. However, the SFCs suggest better use of the existing tax jurisdiction by referring the system of property taxation and giving greater autonomy to local bodies in matters relating to tax rate setting. SFCs place greater reliance on transfers for bridging the gap between the revenue and expenditure of local bodies.

## Table 5.6

*State-wise Revenue and Expenditure of Panchayats at Village Level*

*(Rs. Crore)*

| *S.No.* | *State* | *Item* | *1990-91* | *1995-96* | *1996-97* | *1997-98* |
|---|---|---|---|---|---|---|
| 1. | Andhra Pradesh | Total Reve. | 229.82 | 234.09 | 370.54 | 301.01 |
| | | Total Exp. | 196.05 | 222.83 | 345.85 | 288.03 |
| 2. | Arunachal Pradesh | Rev/Exp. | PRIs do not exist | | | |
| 3. | Assam | Total Reve. | 2.04 | 2.25 | 2.30 | 13.91 |
| | | Total Exp. | — | 30.68 | 33.38 | 29.19 |
| 4. | Bihar | Total Reve. | 0 | 358.26 | 308.57 | 295.29 |
| | | Total Exp. | 27.95 | 402.03 | 356.97 | 348.23 |
| 5. | Goa | Total Reve. | 3.67 | 7.68 | 6.81 | 10.57 |
| | | Total Exp. | 2.07 | 4.73 | 5.24 | 7.63 |
| 6. | Gujarat | Total Reve. | 90.63 | 73.53 | 141.59 | 93.38 |
| | | Total Exp. | 31.68 | 40.70 | 53.51 | 59.08 |
| 7. | Haryana | Total Reve. | 41.38 | 54.49 | 61.44 | 77.44 |
| | | Total Exp. | 62.01 | 114.84 | 87.11 | 136.52 |
| 8. | Himachal Pradesh | Total Reve. | 3.92 | 6.04 | 13.81 | 20.81 |
| | | Total Exp. | 3.92 | 6.04 | 13.81 | 20.81 |
| 9. | Jammu & Kashmir* | Rev./Exp. | * Information not furnished | | | |
| 10. | Karnataka | Total Reve. | 122.42 | 221.81 | 228.88 | 233.65 |
| | | Total Exp. | 114.59 | 198.42 | 233.82 | 243.65 |
| 11. | Kerala | Total Reve. | 96.61 | 205.00 | 400.45 | 744.27 |
| | | Total Exp. | 98.73 | 209.23 | 402.06 | 440.57 |
| 12. | Madhya Pradesh | Total Reve. | 221.41 | 401.11 | 444.83 | 682.42 |
| | | Total Exp. | 219.49 | 414.15 | 466.03 | 707.67 |
| 13. | Maharashtra | Total Reve. | 172.05 | 346.03 | 407.15 | 511.45 |
| | | Total Exp. | 200.43 | 220.35 | 444.21 | 537.55 |
| 14. | Manipur | Total Reve. | 0.33 | 0.62 | 0.36 | 0.34 |
| | | Total Exp. | 0.92 | 1.57 | 1.33 | 1.86 |
| 15. | Meghalaya | Total Reve. | 9.13 | 11.74 | 14.52 | 17.52 |
| | | Total Exp. | 11.79 | 19.64 | 21.09 | 23.56 |
| 16. | Mizoram | Total Reve. | — | 0 | 0.74 | 0.75 |
| | | Total Exp. | 0.66 | 0.81 | 1.55 | 1.49 |
| 17. | Nagaland | Total Reve. | 22.73 | 81.60 | 94.61 | 92.83 |
| | | Total Exp. | 22.73 | 81.60 | 94.61 | 92.83 |
| 18. | Orissa | Total Reve. | 85.17 | 139.07 | 132.09 | 145.73 |
| | | Total Exp. | 85.17 | 139.07 | 132.09 | 145.73 |
| 19. | Punjab | Total Reve. | 81.15 | 145.69 | 105.23 | 101.17 |
| | | Total Exp. | 81.31 | 155.94 | 127.31 | 123.82 |

*Contd...*

...Contd....

| S.No. State | Item | 1990-91 | 1995-96 | 1996-97 | 1997-98 |
|---|---|---|---|---|---|
| 20. Rajasthan | Total Reve. | 214.76 | 667.14 | 756.72 | 801.09 |
| | Total Exp. | 210.03 | 681.46 | 773.88 | 821.23 |
| 21. Sikkim | Total Reve. | 0 | 0.83 | 1.01 | 0.98 |
| | Total Exp. | 0 | 0.83 | 1.01 | 0.98 |
| 22. Tamil Nadu | Total Reve. | 92.03 | 255.49 | 242.13 | 279.29 |
| | Total Exp. | 118.46 | 174.30 | 197.15 | 237.53 |
| 23. Tripura | Total Reve. | 1.24 | 3.51 | 8.76 | 40.37 |
| | Total Exp. | 1.23 | 3.46 | 8.71 | 40.31 |
| 24. Uttar Pradesh | Total Reve. | 400.19 | 640.60 | 541.06 | 732.81 |
| | Total Exp. | 402.55 | 647.53 | 548.76 | 743.61 |
| 25. West Bengal | Total Reve. | 50.32 | 338.19 | 279.15 | 255.07 |
| | Total Exp. | 89.94 | 377.96 | 294.64 | 315.15 |
| **26. Total** | **Total Reve.** | **1941.09** | **4194.88** | **4562.84** | **5452.25** |
| **(All States)** | **Total Exp.** | **1981.81** | **4148.25** | **4644.24** | **5367.15** |

*Source:* GoI, *Report of the Eleventh Finance Commission for 2000-2005.*

In real terms, no improvement in the local resource base is visible. Moreover, the SFC reports have paid far less attention to issues of autonomy, financial management and auditing procedures. The main deficiency of the reports lies in the fact that the recommendations are not based on a clear statement of the spending responsibilities of local bodies. Indeed the absence of attention to the elementary principle, that expenditure assignment must precede any tax or revenue assignment, has made most of the SFC recommendations suspect.

All PRIs have a poor fiscal base. While resource mobilisation by the PRIs is generally limited, it is imperative to provide PRIs with revenue raising powers of their own in order to reduce their excessive dependence on the State and Central Government. But till such time that they are financially dependent on funds from the State Governments, the State Budgets should specify the amount earmarked for district sector plans under *Panchayati Raj*, as also their distribution among the three tiers. It was also suggested that 30-40 per cent of a State's Plan be devolved on local bodies as already done in the State of Kerala. In addition, a part of the finances should be in the form of untied funds so that the funds can be utilised as per the felt needs of the *panchayats*. Training and capacity building of PRI functionaries is essential and devolution of financial resources must be accompanied by suitable strengthening of PRIs through transfer of departmental functionaries.

## 2.3 Devolution of Functions and Functionaries

In respect of the 29 subjects identified in the Eleventh Schedule, it is necessary for the State Governments to be coherent on the issues of devolution at all the three tiers of PRIs. This should be based on the rule that what can be done at the lower level should be done only at that level, no higher. Furthermore, departmental functionaries who are required to implement the programmes at the *panchayat* level must be placed under their overall supervision and control.

One of the common anomalies found in the devolution of powers and functions is that there is always a gap between the powers given and powers exercised, between functions as enlisted in the Schedule and as they are carried out. In fact, such discrepancies are more noticeable at the *gram panchayat* level. It is quite evident from Table 5.5 that most States have preferred to transfer only a small fraction of functions and functionaries to *gram panchayat*s. Only Karnataka, Rajasthan, Tamil Nadu and West Bengal are States that have transferred all the 29 functions to the respective PRIs.

In States like Gujarat, Madhya Pradesh, Maharashtra, Karnataka, Kerala, Orissa, Rajasthan, Tripura, Uttar Pradesh and West Bengal, detailed instructions have already been issued and in several cases of departmental functionaries have been placed with the *panchayat*s. The Government of Madhya Pradesh has transferred 18 Departments to the PRIs, with administrative control over class III and IV employees deputed to the *panchayat*s. PRIs are actively involved in the implementation of the programmes of these Departments. The Government of Kerala has transferred Agriculture, Health, Veterinary and Primary Education Departments to the *panchayat*s. About 40,590 staff, moveable and immovable property has also been transferred to the *panchayat*s. The State Government however continues to pay the staff salaries.

The Government of Uttar Pradesh has transferred selective activities/functions and functionaries of 11 departments along with their salary to village *panchayat*s. During 1999-2000 nearly ten per cent of the Annual State Plan outlay, *i.e.*, Rs. 1,100 crore was to be directly transferred to the village *panchayat*s. The State Government has further taken a decision to declare cadres of all its employees whose services have been placed under administrative control of village *panchayat*s as "dying cadre". The Government has also posted at least one functionary

## Box 5.9

*"Eleventh Schedule" (Article 243G)*

1. Agriculture, including agricultural extension.
2. Land improvement, implementation of land reforms, land consolidation and soil conservation.
3. Minor irrigation, water management and watershed development.
4. Animal husbandry, dairying and poultry.
5. Fisheries.
6. Social forestry and farm forestry.
7. Minor forest produce.
8. Small scale industries, including food processing industries.
9. Khadi, village and cottage industries.
10. Rural housing.
11. Drinking water.
12. Fuel and fodder.
13. Roads, culverts, bridges, ferries, waterways and other means of communication.
14. Rural electrification, including distribution of electricity.
15. Non-conventional energy sources.
16. Poverty alleviation programmes.
17. Education, including primary and secondary schools.
18. Technical training and vocational education.
19. Adult and non-formal education.
20. Libraries.
21. Cultural activities.
22. Markets and fairs.
23. Health and sanitation, including hospitals, primary health centres and dispensaries.
24. Family welfare.
25. Women and child development.
26. Social welfare, including welfare of the handicapped and mentally retarded.
27. Welfare of the weaker sections, and in particular, of the Scheduled Castes and the Scheduled Tribes.
28. Public distribution system.
29. Maintenance of community assets.

as *Panchayat* Secretary in each *village panchayat*. The assets of departments whose selective functions have been transferred to village *panchayats* within the territory of those *panchayats* will be handed over to concerned village *panchayat* for maintenance in a time-bound manner.

**Box 5.10**

*Panchayati Raj in Madhya Pradesh*

- Activities of governance and development have been clearly demarcated between *Panchayat* Sector and the State Sector.
- All district and sub-district level officers and employees in respect of programmes transferred to PRIs are placed under control of PRIs at the appropriate level.
- Greater coordination among the three tiers through representation of 1/5 *sarpanchs* to *Janpad Panchayat, Janpad Panchayat Adhyakshas* to *Zilla Parishad.*
- *Gram Panchayats* are empowered to sanction development works up to Rs. 3 lakh, *Janpad Panchayats* up to Rs. 7 lakh and *Zilla Panchayat* up to Rs. 10 lakh.
- Merger of District Rural Development Agencies (DRDAs) with *Zilla Panchayats*.
- *Gram Panchayats* recruit the *Panchayat Karmi* designated as Secretaries.
- *Shiksha Karmis* are appointed by *Janpad Panchayats* and *Zilla Parishad.*
- No recruitment by State Government to 'dying cadres'.

Budgetary allocations for transferred programmes/subjects are made available to PRIs. From 2000-01, tier-wise and district wise provision would be made in the Budget to ensure efficient flow of resources to PRIs. Greater transparency in selection of beneficiaries and implementation of programmes through social audit by strengthening the *Gram Sabha/Panchayat* in the State. For instance, no technical evaluation required for *Jawahar Gram Samaridhi Yojana* (JGSY) works; instead quality and utility of works subjected to social audit through *Gram Sabhas*. First and only State to introduce the concept of "Right to Recall" of elected representatives at the *Gram Panchayat* level, once in their tenure, for greater accountability to the *Gram Sabha*.

The Government of Rajasthan has transferred nine schemes that were earlier being implemented by DRDAs to the *Zilla Parishad*. It has also set up a Village Level Standing Committee for each village under the Chairmanship of the *Sarpanch* of the *Gram Panchayat* to act as "watch dog". It will keep watch on the absenteeism of grassroots functionaries of the Departments, namely *Patwari*, Teachers, ANMS, MPW, VLW, *Anganwadi* workers and Compounder posted in rural areas. Primary and Upper Primary Education, Literacy and Continuing Education, Rajiv Gandhi Scheme for Restoration of Traditional Drinking Water Sources, Rajiv Gandhi *Swarna Jayanti Pathshalas* will all be implemented by the PRIs. Further, innovative projects like *Lok Jumbish, Shiksha Karmi* and District Primary Education Programme (DPEP) have also been brought under the umbrella of the *Panchayati Raj* Department.

In Orissa, 16 subjects listed in the Eleventh Schedule of the Constitution have been transferred to the *Zilla Parishads* and concerned District Level Officers of the line department have been declared ex-officio Additional Executive Officers of the *Zilla Parishads*.

In some States, functions and functionaries have not been transferred to PRIs. For instance, in the field of decentralisation, the State Government of Andhra Pradesh is implementing *Janmabhoomi* mainly through the State bureaucracy, which is against the spirit of the Act. However, after strong protests from Chairpersons (*Sarpanch*), the State Government has agreed to transfer 16 out of the 29 subjects of rural administration to the local bodies. Also, Haryana circulated a list of 16 subjects to be transferred to PRIs. The exercise appears to be vague, as it does not provide for any transfer of funds, personnel and powers to the elected bodies. The responsibilities relate mostly to supervision and monitoring.

In view of the above, it is evident that the initiatives such as taken by Madhya Pradesh and Kerala need to be replicated in all the States and Union Territories, if *panchayati raj* is to be established as an institution of local self-government.

## 2.4 Constitution of District Planning Committees (DPCs)

The 73rd Amendment conceptualises *panchayati raj* institutions (PRIs) as instruments of planning for economic development and social justice. The States are required to set up District Planning Committees (DPCs) to facilitate decentralised planning under Article 243(ZD). The DPCs are entrusted with the job of preparing composite plans. Large States such as Andhra Pradesh, Bihar and Gujarat have not yet set up DPCs, thus evading Constitutional responsibility without being punished. States such as Haryana and Tamil Nadu have made government officials the chairpersons of these bodies, against the very spirit of the 73rd Amendment. Madhya Pradesh has undermined the authority of local government bodies by setting up district governments around the DPCs. The DPCs in Madhya Pradesh are chaired by government Ministers. The concept of *panchayati raj* loses its significance when a Minister heads a DPC. The failure to set up DPCs and government policies that undermine the authority of these institutions speaks not only of a lack of political will, but also of a lack of conceptual clarity about the institutions of self-government as envisioned by the 73rd Amendment.

Despite long years of delay, many States are yet to constitute the DPCs. Only nine States, namely, Haryana (just in three Districts), Karnataka (10 out of 27 districts), Kerala, Madhya Pradesh, Rajasthan, Sikkim, Tamil Nadu, Tripura and West Bengal and two Union Territories, namely, Andaman and Nicobar Islands and Daman and Diu have taken action to constitute DPCs. In Tamil Nadu, operational orders for DPCs are yet to be issued. The formation of DPCs must receive top priority by the State Governments; it is only then that planning would genuinely begin from the grassroots. In Kerala, a Voluntary Technical Corps (VTC) has been created, consisting of about 10,000 technical experienced people to vet and re-work projects prepared by the *panchayats*. These include retired persons with technical expertise, bank personnel and officials of government departments.

Similarly, in other States, voluntary groups and institutions need to be identified for providing services, training and support for effective implementation of programmes at the local level. The planning model followed in the State of Kerala is worth replication in other States also.

Experiences from the field reveal that planning is yet to be taken up seriously by the *panchayats*. Usual observation is that the bureaucracy continues to predominantly play a major role in preparing *panchayat* plans. The planning process under the amendment was envisaged to start from the level of *gram sabha* and integrate with the plans mooted out at different tiers of *panchayati raj*, till it is finally integrated at the District Planning Committee level. The officials, who have been all along preparing the plans, continue to hold the final word in planning. State governments need to adopt a firm stance, especially in providing a conducive environment to make planning from below a reality.

## Table 5.7

*Status of DPCs in Various States/UTs*

| *S.No.* | *States/UTs* | *Status of Constitution of DPCs* |
|---|---|---|
| 1. | Andhra Pradesh | Not constituted |
| 2. | Arunachal Pradesh | Not constituted |
| 3. | Assam | Not constituted |
| 4. | Bihar | Not constituted |
| 5. | Goa | — |
| 6. | Gujarat | Not constituted |
| 7. | Haryana | Only in four Districts. Rest under consideration |
| 8. | Himachal Pradesh | Not yet but it is under consideration |
| 9. | J&K | Not applicable |
| 10. | Karnataka | Yes. |
| 11. | Kerala | Yes, DP Chairperson is chairman of DPC |
| 12. | Madhya Pradesh | Yes. District incharge Ministers are Chairpersons. Responsibilities of District Government given to the DPCs |
| 13. | Maharashtra | Not constituted |
| 14. | Manipur | Yes in two Distts. Out of four. *Adhyaksha*, DP is Chairperson |
| 15. | Meghalaya | Not applicable |
| 16. | Mizoram | Not applicable |
| 17. | Nagaland | Not applicable |
| 18. | Orissa | Yes, DP Chairman is Chairman of DPC |
| 19. | Punjab | Not yet but its constitution is under active consideration |
| 20. | Rajasthan | Yes, ZP President is chairperson, of DPC |
| 21. | Sikkim | Yes. |
| 22. | Tamil Nadu | Yes. Chairperson, DP is Chairperson |
| 23. | Tripura | Yes cabinet rank ministers are chairpersons. |
| 24. | Uttar Pradesh | Yes. Ministers are Chairperson of DPC |
| 25. | West Bangal | Yes. DP Chairman is Chairman of DPC. |
| 26. | A&N Islands | Yes, Chairman, DP is Chairperson of DPC |
| 27. | Chandigarh | Not in favour as 90 per cent of population covered by Municipality |
| 28. | D & N Haveli | Yes. |
| 29. | Daman & Diu | — |
| 30. | NCT Delhi | State Panchayati Raj Act is under suspension |
| 31. | Lakshadweep | Yes. Chief Development Commissioner is Chairperson |
| 32. | Pondicherry | Elections not held. Not constituted. |

**Box 5.11**

*People's Planning Campaign: Kerala*

People's Campaign for Planning was launched in 1996, with the aim of empowering local bodies to function as institutions of local self-government as well as the agents of local development. Devolution (35 per cent-40 per cent) of the State's Plan outlay for projects and programmes drawn up and implemented by local bodies. The People's Campaign has been organised in six phases, with clearly defined objectives for each phase.

**Phase I - *Gram Sabha*:** Identification of the needs of the people has been accomplished by convening *Gram Sabha*. Priorities listed and awareness created.

**Phase II - Development Seminars:** Make an objective assessment of the natural and human resources in the locality. Development Seminars also discuss the Development Reports being prepared for each *panchayat*.

**Phase III - Task Forces:** Sector-wise Task Forces have been constituted in local bodies to project the recommendations and suggestions from the development seminars.

**Phase IV - Annual Plan Finalisation:** The major task was finalisation of Annual Plan of *Gram Panchayat* by including projects approved by the local bodies.

**Phase V - Integration of Plans of Higher Tiers:** Every Block *Panchayat* has to prepare its development plan by integrating village development reports as also the Centrally Sponsored poverty alleviation programmes. Similarly, each District *Panchayat* has to prepare a development report integrating the suggestions and programmes of the lower tiers.

**Phase VI - Plan Appraisal:** This phase is organised to ensure technical soundness and viability of projects prepared by the local bodies before they are approved for implementation. For this, a new concept of Voluntary Technical Corps (VTC) has been adopted. Retired technical experts and professionals were encouraged to enroll themselves as volunteers to appraise the projects and Plan of local bodies. Further, Expert Committees were formed at Block (BLEC), Municipality (MLEC), Corporation (CLEC) and District (DLEC) levels drawing personnel from the VTC and including certain categories of mandatory officers. The Committees have Subject Committees and their tasks are technical and financial appraisal of the projects and issue of technical sanctions.

## 2.5 Status of *Gram Sabha*

*Gram Sabha* is regarded as the 'soul' of *panchayati raj*. It is political forum for the people to ensure transparency and accountability in the system. The Act defines the *gram sabha* as "... a body consisting of persons registered in the electoral rolls relating to a village comprised within the area of *panchayat* at the village level." All *State Panchayat Acts* have included a provision for the constitution of *gram sabhas* and for them to meet at least once in six months. This is primarily drawn from Article 243 A of the 73rd Amendment, which states "A *gram sabha* may exercise such powers and perform such functions at the village level as the legislature of a State may by law, provide". However, their functioning at the grassroots level is usually questionable, especially in terms of *gram sabha* meetings, attendance, *etc*. Table 5.8 highlights the stipulation laid out by the respective *Conformity Acts* for minimum attendance required for holding a *gram sabha* meeting.

### Table 5.8

*Quorum - Gram Sabha in Different States*

| *S.No.* | *Name of the State* | *Quorum for Gram Sabha* |
|---|---|---|
| 1. | Andhra Pradesh | 1/3rd of total Electorate |
| 2. | Arunachal Pradesh | 1/10th of total Electorate |
| 3. | Assam | 1/10th of total Electorate |
| 4. | Bihar | 1/10th of total Electorate |
| 5. | Chhattisgarh | 1/10th of total Electorate (out of total present in GS meeting 1/3rd should be women) |
| 6. | Goa | 1/10th of total Electorate |
| 7. | Gujarat | 1/10th of total Electorate |
| 8. | Haryana | 1/10th of total Electorate |
| 9. | Himachal Pradesh | 1/5th of total Electorate |
| 10. | Jharkhand | 1/5th of total Electorate |
| 11. | Karnataka | 1/10th of total Electorate |
| 12. | Kerala | 1/10th of total Electorate |
| 13. | Madhya Pradesh | 1/3rd of total Electorate |
| 14. | Maharastra | 15 per cent of total Electorate |
| 15 | Manipur | 1/10th of total Electorate |
| 16. | Orissa | 1/10th of total Electorate |
| 17. | Punjab | 1/5th of total Electorate |
| 18. | Rajasthan | 1/10th of total Electorate |
| 19. | Sikkim | 1/10th of total Electorate |
| 20. | Tamil Nadu | 1/10th of total Electorate |
| 21. | Tripura | 1/8th of total Electorate |
| 22. | Uttar Pradesh | 1/5th of total Electorate |
| 23. | Uttaranchal | 1/5th of total Electorate |
| 24. | West Bengal | 1/20th of total Electorate |

*Source: 37th Report of Standing Committee on Urban and Rural Development 2002*, Lok Sabha Secretariat, New Delhi, August 2002.

Nearly a decade down the line, it has been observed that most of the State Acts have not spelt the powers of *gram sabhas*, nor have any procedures been laid down for the functioning of these bodies. For instance, (i) the law in most States prescribed at least two meetings of the *gram sabha* in a year. Unfortunately, the minimum has been interpreted as a maximum. (ii) Provision doing away with the need for quorum for adjourned meetings of the *gram sabha* has reinforced the tendency to view *gram sabha* meetings as a mere formality; (iii) State laws set out highly ritualistic functions for the *gram sabhas*. *Gram sabhas* are to recommend and suggest, consider annual accounts, administrative reports, audit notes, *etc*. The *gram panchayat* cannot ignore the suggestions and recommendations put forth by the *gram sabhas*.

**Box 5.12**

*Gram Sabha: Hathras District*

The *Gram Sabha* meeting was not held since the *Panchayat* elections. Some of the village elders from the poor section of *Balmiki* caste approached the Chairperson (*Jatav* caste) to provide a tap for drinking water under the centrally sponsored scheme in their area, as they were not allowed to use the village well at times. Their request was turned down due to shortage of funds. A local retired school teacher raised this issue in the presence of the District Magistrate and made a request to arrange a *Gram Sabha* meeting. On the orders from the District Magistrate, the Chairperson convened a meeting and also mobilised support from his community. It led to wide scale violence in the village assembly, deterring other groups from supporting the cause of the *Balmiki* community. Besides, some from the *Balmiki* community were implicated in false police cases. The *Balmiki* community still awaits their tap connection.

*Source:* Author's field survey as part of a collaborative study.

There are, at the same time, large expectations from this weak and powerless *gram sabha*. It was expected that the *gram sabha* would strive to promote harmony and unity in the village, mobilise voluntary labour and contribution in kind and promote programmes for adult education and family welfare. It must be acknowledged that some State Acts do provide for powers to the *gram sabhas* to identify beneficiaries, who are to be covered under different development schemes. For instance, the *panchayati raj* legislation of Punjab, Rajasthan, Uttar Pradesh, Karnataka and Bihar did vest powers in the *gram sabhas* to select beneficiaries, but in some cases, strange qualifications were added to the state legislation.

In Rajasthan, the state legislation provides for identification of beneficiaries by the *gram sabha*. But with a rider, which states that in case the *gram sabha* is unable to select the beneficiaries in a reasonable time, the *gram panchayat* would do the needful and identify the beneficiaries. Such provisions expressed faith in the *gram sabha*, while at the same time also permitted undermining.

In contrast, Madhya Pradesh and Kerala have made legal provisions to make the advice of *gram sabha* binding on the *gram panchayat*. Finally, the membership of a *gram sabha* varies widely from State to State, usually from 250 to 8,000. It may be confined to a single village or may span 2-3 villages. Where the *gram sabha*s cover more than one village, their meetings qualitatively are seen to be very poor. The 73rd Amendment failed to anticipate that the very size of a *panchayat* may work to disempower a *gram sabha*.

Principally, the 73rd Amendment has not set down in black and white an imperative for the empowerment of *gram sabhas*. In order to accelerate the emergence of *gram sabha*s as bodies to whom the PRIs are accountable, it might be essential to spell out the powers and functions of the *gram sabha* coherently, articulating their role as planners, decision makers and auditors. The size of a *gram sabha* also needs to be carefully set out. However, despite all these shortcomings, there are several examples of how dedicated/committed, enlightened *sarpanch*es have transformed their villages into self-reliant units.

### Box 5.13

*Rajasamadhiala Village, Gujarat*

Shri Hardevsingh Jadeja, *sarpanch*, has transformed the village Rajasamadhiala into a model village, totally crime-free and characterised by self-reliance, inter-caste amity and active community participation. Nobody in the village ever locks his house; the shopkeeper does not lock the shop for his afternoon siesta. People can buy/help themselves, unattended by the shopkeeper and leave the money in a matchbox, which is also unattended/unguarded. Shri Jadeja has been using the *gram sabha* meetings to convince and motivate the village community to join hands together, rather than demanding or begging from the Government. About Rs. 100 million has been earned in 15 villages due to better irrigation through the small dams built by the village people themselves with very little government help. This charismatic *sarpanch* is now spreading his message in the neighbouring villages.

Despite reluctance of the state governments to give more powers to the *gram sabhas*, it is evident that the Central Government favours strengthening of *gram sabhas* as the bedrock of grassroots democracy. The year 1999-2000 was declared "Year of the *Gram Sabha*". To energise *gram sabhas*, all the State governments were directed to initiate measures such as vesting full powers in the *gram sabhas* for identifying beneficiaries and determining the priorities for various programmes in the village and approval of budgets. Even after four years, the Ministry has not carried out any evaluation in this regard, nor about the long-term impact of this declaration on participation and empowerment of the disadvantaged.

## 2.6 'Panchayats' (Extension to the Scheduled Areas) Act, 1996

The provisions of *the Panchayats (Extension to the Scheduled Areas) Act, 1996 (PESA)* or Act 40 of 1996 extend to tribal areas of eight States namely, Andhra Pradesh, Bihar, Gujarat, Himachal Pradesh, Maharashtra, Madhya Pradesh, Orissa and Rajasthan. It aims to enable tribal society to assume control of its own destiny to preserve and conserve the traditional rights over natural resources. All States barring Bihar have enacted requisite legislation.

PESA is a unique piece of legislation, it gives radical self-governance powers to the tribal community and recognises its traditional community rights over natural resources. In fact, this is the first law of its kind that empowers people to redefine their own administrative boundaries. It creates space for people's empowerment, genuine popular political participation, convergent community action, sustainable people-oriented development and auto-generated emancipation. PESA empowers the tribal *gram sabha* to approve all development plans, control all functionaries and institutions of all social sectors, as well as control all minor water bodies, minor minerals and non-timber forest resources. It also has the authority to control land alienation, impose prohibition, manage village markets and resolve internal conflicts by traditional modes.

## Table 5.9

### *PESA - Functional Devolution on Panchayats*

| *Components* | *Mandatory Provisions* | *Status* |
|---|---|---|
| Definition of village | A village consists of a habitation or a group of habitations or a hamlet or a group of hamlets comprising a community and managing its affairs in accordance with traditions and customs | All States adopted this definition except Maharashtra, which is silent on this subject. |
| Status and Functions of *Gram Sabha* | Every village will have a *Gram Sabha* which will be competent to safeguard and preserve the traditions and customs of the people, their cultural identity. | All State Acts follow the Central Act. However, regarding customary mode of dispute resolution, the Andhra Pradesh Act puts a condition that this will be subject to 'without detriment to any law for the time being in force'. The Orissa Act adds that it should be consistent with the relevant laws in force and in harmony with the tenets of the Constitution and Human Rights. |
| Constitution of *Panchayat* | *Panchayats* will be constituted at village level with reservations for Scheduled Tribes in the manner prescribed in Part IX of the Constitution. | The Andhra Pradesh and Himachal Pradesh Acts have extended the reservation of elective seats and Chairpersons to both *Gram Panchayats* and *Mandal*/intermediate *Panchayats*. The Maharashtra Act does not mention it. |
| Acquisition of land for development projects and resettlement of displaced persons | Prior consultation with *Gram Sabha* or *Panchayats* at the appropriate level shall be made mandatory. | In Andhra Pradesh, *Gram Sabhas* have no role. Gujarat assigned this power to *Taluka Panchayat*, however, no provision relating to coordination of such projects at State level. Orissa assigned the power to *Zilla Panchayat* with no role for the *Gram Sabha/Gram Panchayat*. |
| Planning and Management of Minor Water Bodies | Entrusted to *Panchayats* at the appropriate level. | Maharashtra Act does not make any mention of it. Orissa assigned power to *Zilla Parishad* instead of *Gram Sabha/Gram Panchayat*. |
| Components Grant of Prospecting licence or mining lease for minor minerals | Prior recommendations of *Gram Sabha* or the *Panchayats* at the appropriate level shall be made mandatory. | Andhra Pradesh gives primacy to *Gram Panchayat* in place of *Gram Sabha*. Gujarat-does not make mention of it. Himachal Pradesh retained primacy of *Gram Sabha*, but term 'shall be made mandatory' has been replaced by 'shall be taken into consideration'. No mention in the *Madhya Pradesh Panchayat Act*, but the relevant Subject Act, *Mines and Minerals (Regulation and Development Act) 1987*, amended to assign powers to *Gram Sabha* and *Panchayats* at appropriate level. Maharashtra assigns powers to *Gram Panchayat*. *Gram Sabha* has no role in the matter. Orissa gives powers to *Zilla Parishad*. |
| Grant of concession for exploitation of minor minerals by auction | Prior recommendation of *Gram Sabha* or *Panchayats* at appropriate level shall be made mandatory. | Andhra Pradesh and Maharashtra assigned the function to *Gram Panchayat* in place of *Gram Sabha*. Gujarat - No mention of it. Madhya Pradesh - *Madhya Pradesh Panchayat Act* does not make mention of it but the |

contd...

| *Components* | *Mandatory Provisions* | *Status* |
|---|---|---|
| | | Subject Act, *Mines and Minerals (Regulation and Development) Act, 1987,* amended to assign the power to *Panchayat* at appropriate level. Orissa assigned the power to *Zilla Parishad.* |
| Enforce prohibition / regulate or restrict sale & consumption of any intoxicant | *Panchayats* at the appropriate level and the *Gram Sabha* to be endowed with the powers | All State Acts followed the Central Act except Madhya Pradesh, which does not make provision for it in its PR Amendment Act. However, the Subject Act, *Madhya Pradesh Excise Act 1915,* has been amended to give powers to *Gram Sabha.* |
| Ownership of Minor Forest Produce (MFP) | *Panchayats* at the appropriate level and the *Gram Sabha* endowed with the powers of ownership | All State Acts follow central Act by assigning this power either to *Gram Sabha* or to the *Gram Panchayats* |
| Prevention & Restoration of Tribal Alienated Land | *Panchayats* at appropriate level and the *Gram Sabha* to be endowed with this power. | Gujarat, Himachal Pradesh, Madhya Pradesh *Panchayati Raj Amendment Act* do not make provision for this. However, in the case of Madhya Pradesh, *the Madhya Pradesh Land Revenue Code, 1959,* has been amended to give power to *Gram Sabha.* |
| Manage Village Markets | *Panchayats* at appropriate level and the *Gram Sabha* to be endowed with this power. | Gujarat and Maharashtra Amendment Acts are silent on this matter. |
| Money lending to the Scheduled Tribes | *Panchayats* at appropriate level and the *Gram Sabha* to be endowed with this power. | Madhya Pradesh Amendment Act does not make a mention of this subject. |
| Exercise control over institutions and functionaries in all social sectors | *Panchayats* at appropriate level and the *Gram Sabha* to be endowed with this power. | All States Acts except Madhya Pradesh assign this power either to *Gram Panchayat* or *Panchayat Samiti/Mandal Parishad.* The Madhya Pradesh Amendment Act has given this power to the *Gram Sabha* and the *Janpad Panchayat* or the *Zilla Parishad.* |
| Control over Local Plans and Resources including Tribal Sub Plans | *Panchayats* at appropriate level and the *Gram Sabha* to be endowed with this power. | State Acts of Andhra Pradesh, Gujarat, Himachal Pradesh, Orissa have assigned the power to *Panchayat Samiti/Taluka Panchayat/ Mandal Parishad,* while the Madhya Pradesh and Maharashtra Acts assign this power to *Gram Sabha.* In order to make the Central Act effective, it is necessary for the State Governments to make appropriate amendments in their State Laws/Acts which impinge on specific provisions contained in the Central Act namely, (i) *Land Acquisition Act; (ii) Excise Act; (iii) State Irrigation Act; (iv) Minor Forest Produce Act; (v) Mines and Minerals Acts; (vi) Land Revenue Code/ Act; (vii) SC/ST Land Alienation Act; (viii) Money Lenders Act;* and (ix) *Regulated Market Act.* No doubt, some State Governments (MP) have already amended some of the relevant Acts, others are yet to follow suit. |

*Source:* Saxena (2001)

Implementation of the law has been severely hampered by the reluctance of most State governments to make laws and rules that conform to the spirit of the law. What is perceived as weak-kneed political will has led to bureaucratic creativity in minimalistic interpretations of the law. Bureaucratic subversion of the letter and spirit of the law has been most visible in interpretation of that provision of PESA by which *panchayats* at appropriate levels and the *gram sabha* have been vested with the ownership of minor forest produce (MFP). For tribal forest dwellers, the forest department has been the most visible oppression.[9]

Firstly, the State governments have argued that the power of *gram sabhas* can extend only to forest located within the revenue boundaries of a village. This one provision, if accepted, would nullify the law, because reserved forest in most States is not located within a revenue boundary of a village. The spirit of the law is clearly to extend ownership to the *gram sabha* of MFP from forests located in vicinity of the village of traditional access. In fact, in the case of Joint Forest Management (JFM), the Madhya Pradesh government vested the village forest committees with authority to manage forest falling within a radius of five kilometres of the village boundaries. A similar dispensation would eminently suit the PESA case as well.

Secondly, MFP has been defined to exclude cane and bamboo. This is contrary to the common sense definition of MFP, which is that part of a tree that can be sustainably harvested without damage to the survival of the tree. More significantly, it denies access to poor tribal artisans to two types of MFP on which their livelihood is most critically dependent. On the other hand, many State policies have subsidised bamboo for private industry.

Another controversy is in the interpretation of the concept of "ownership" of MFP by the *gram sabha*. The common view is that ownership does not provide *gram sabha* the right to take any decisions related to stewardship, management or sustainable harvesting of MFPs. Contrary to a whole body of empirical evidence from the national and international experience of JFM and community control of forests, it is claimed that the exercise of "ownership" of MFPs by

9. Verrier Elwin recounts, when queried about his idea of paradise, a tribal described it as miles and miles of forest, but without a forest guard.

*gram sabhas* in this sense would inevitably lead to a destruction of forests. Therefore, "ownership" as provided for in PESA, is reinterpreted to mean the right to net revenues from MFP, after retaining administrative expenses of the forest department.

These interpretations have almost killed the concept of ownership and control of local resources by the *gram sabha*. The real danger thus is that the far-reaching changes introduced in the law will remain a pipe dream unless they are translated into action and sustained by a process of awareness and capacity building among the tribal communities. There are a number of grave problems that must be overcome if the law is to genuinely transform tribal reality, but it is important to stress that none of these barriers to tribal self-government is insurmountable.

## 2.7 Checks and Balances over PRIs and Accountability

The effective functioning of *panchayats* depends on facilitative functional relationship in terms of coordination and cooperation between the elected and official functionaries. Further, it is a prerequisite of democracy that the administrative wing should function under the deliberative wing, *i.e*, bureaucracy should be answerable and accountable to the elected political leadership. But the information provided in various expert group reports, research studies, *etc.*, indicates a disturbing trend. Under the State laws, wide powers of suspension and dismissal have been vested in the State bureaucracy. In fact, the respective legislation provides ample scope for the governments, through bureaucracy, to exercise control. Such provisions straightaway places *Panchayati Raj* Institutions in a position of disadvantage *vis-à-vis* even middle and lower rung functionaries of State Governments. It also takes away the essential characteristic of PRIs as elected representative bodies. In many States, more often the *gram panchayats* have been placed in a position of subordination *vis-à-vis* intermediate *panchayats* and so on.

A scrutiny of State laws reveals that almost all the State Governments have kept enough powers with themselves to deal with PRIs as far as ensuring checks and balances is concerned. These provisions had existed even before the introduction of 73rd Constitution Amendment Act and had been widely used in different

States. However, these provisions have in-built limitations because they directly affect the concept of democratic decentralisation on the one hand and the autonomy of the PRIs on the other.

Another important aspect of the administrative restructuring process is the merger of District Rural Development Agencies (DRDAs) with *Zilla Parishads*. In the light of the 73rd Constitution Amendment Act, DRDAs need to be restructured to suit the changed scenario. They should work under the overall control and supervision of the *Zilla Parishads*. In the States of Karnataka, Kerala and Madhya Pradesh, DRDAs have already been merged with the *Zilla Parishads*. In Himachal Pradesh, Orissa, Rajasthan, Uttar Pradesh and West Bengal, the Chairman of the *Zilla Parishad* is also the Chairman of the DRDAs. However, Maharashtra has expressed its reservation to the merger of DRDAs with the *Zilla Parishads*. Andhra Pradesh also is not in favour of a DRDA merger with the *District Panchayat*. In Andhra Pradesh, the District Collector is the Chairperson of DRDA, whereas Chairperson of the District *Panchayat* is its Vice-President.

Quite a number of instances have been reported where the Chairperson (*sarpanch*) of *gram panchayats* have to spend a good lot of time visiting Block Offices and experience harassment by Block level officials. Systems put in place by the government requires *Gram Panchayat Pradhan/Sarpanch* to approach Block office for funds and/or technical approval. Such operational systems reflect problems recurring, confrontation figuring between district *panchayat* leadership and bureaucracy. This is mainly due to the absence of coherent policy on demarcation of powers, functions and responsibilities between *panchayat* functionaries, particularly between the presidents and CEOs of the *panchayats*. This needs to be changed completely to ensure the sanctity of elected bodies before official agencies. Village bodies should be able to spend funds on their own without having to take technical approval from government officials. These interactions with Block staff distort the role of *pradhans* as elected representatives of the *Gram Sabha* and induct them into bad old ways of officialdom and also encourage corruption.

*Transparency*

Accountability and transparency are possible only if *gram sabhas* are taken seriously. Empowerment of *Gram Sabhas* would require efforts at mobilisation of the village community for mass participation in meetings of the *Gram Sabha*. Further, a massive awareness generation programme needs to be taken up to inform *Gram Sabhas* about their rights in planning, implementation and audit of development programmes and in control over natural resources, land records and conflict resolution.

In Madhya Pradesh development works of PRIs are subjected to social audit. For instance, works under *Jawahar Gram Samridhi Yojana* (JGSY) are exempted from evaluation by technical personnel. Now, instead of Junior/Sub Engineer of PWD, the *sarpanch* moves the *gram sabha* to get an expression of its satisfaction with the quality and utility of the Project. The *gram sabha* certifies the utilisation of expenditure. In the event of dissent by the *gram sabha*, the official designated by the competent authority under the Act (*i.e.* Sub-Divisional Officer) gets the evaluation done by a Committee consisting of a *panch*, a sub-engineer and social worker from the area. Social audit is not only limited to development works. An expression of dissatisfaction of the *gram sabha* about the PRI performance in individual beneficiary programmes leads to an inquiry by the competent authority through a committee. Further "Right to Recall" of elected representatives at the *gram panchayat* level has enhanced the accountability and transparency at the village level.

A key to the success of the *Panchayati Raj* system is transparency in the way these bodies function. Being closer to the people, the *Panchayats*' right to information and accessibility to the elected representatives must be ensured. A Central Government circular in 1997 proposed that each State may consider passing orders highlighting three different aspects of transparency.

First, the *Panchayati Raj* Institutions, especially *gram panchayats*, should display all vital information about development projects (especially receipt of funds and how they are being spent) in the *panchayat* offices or on a prominent board outside the village school for the information of the public.

Second, all relevant records should be open to inspection.

Third, members of public should also be able to obtain photocopies of documents related to development projects as also matters of general public interest by paying a nominal charge. Such documents would extend in particular to all bills, muster rolls, vouchers, estimates and measurement books as well as information about the criterion and procedure for selection of beneficiaries. A list of beneficiaries should not only be available for inspection, but photocopies should be given on demand from a convenient place such as Block or Tehsil Office.

Thus, it is imperative for bringing transparency in the PRIs by coherently defining the role of *gram sabhas*. The *gram sabha's* role should not be limited to preparation of proposals, but it should have the right to take a final decision in this regard. In the employment-oriented schemes, the task of selecting the beneficiaries should be the sole prerogative of the *gram sabha*. The public works related activities must be endorsed by the *gram sabha* before the work is approved and carried out. Besides, the responsibility of organising the *gram sabha* meetings should not be left to the *sarpanch* only, the ward *panch* should play an active role part in inviting people of his own ward.

*Accountability*

Elected representatives are usually accountable to their electorate. Their chance of re-election is a reflection on their performance. Thus, performance of *gram panchayats* is open for scrutiny before the electorate. Saxena (2001) revealed that the strategic linkages between the *panchayats* and people are often weak, which essentially is responsible for growing disillusionment of the electorate towards political leadership. Even after a decade of the 73rd Amendment, no substantive changes have occurred in the nature or extent of financial devolution or bureaucratic control. Some of the field observations made were:

1. In the formal sense, *gram panchayats* have a limited but important role in the various stages of planning and implementation of several developmental programmes, especially anti-poverty programmes. However, there was no evidence that the *gram sabhas* were involved in any of the roles assigned to them.
2. Often meetings of the *gram sabhas* were held under some external compulsion. For practical purposes, the *panchayat* is identified with the office of the *pradhan* and the role of the *pradhan* is itself subsidiary to the bureaucratic functionaries.

3. The poor have often been sidelined in the planning and decision-making process of the *panchayats*. But there were also periods when enlightened *pradhans* or even bureaucrats have been able to accelerate the implementation of these programmes firmly in the direction of the poor. Benefits from programmes accrue to a group of people who are close to the *pradhan* or the official machinery. Some of them acquire multiple benefits.
4. Devolution as implemented has reinforced unequal access to power. References to the works are often accompanied by sneering remarks about the money that has gone down the drain, or has disappeared into the pocket of the *pradhan* and the block officials. Much of what comes from the government is often snatched away by the important people.

However, the study concludes that negative assessment of omissions and commissions does not imply that *panchayats* and local level planning have lost their attractiveness for the villagers. On the contrary, the field survey revealed that an overwhelming 80 per cent of all respondents felt that the responsibility of village level development should be reposed with *panchayats*, against 9 per cent favouring the government officials. Of the respondents, when asked to choose between a variety of arrangements for evolving and implementing schemes and programmes at the village level, 79 per cent favoured stronger *panchayats*, but with more accountable *pradhans*, and 17 per cent favoured stronger *panchayats* and stronger *pradhans*. The verdict was clearly against the Block Development Officers and government officials who received only 4 per cent support.

Selection of beneficiaries is often regarded as discretionary, usually nearness to *pradhan* or officials is the only criterion besides bribes, that can facilitate entitlement to the government benefit. For instance, out of a total number of 95 beneficiaries in a *panchayat* of Rajasthan, only 52 per cent belonged to vulnerable categories.[10] Thus, the benefits flowed to almost 50 per cent of undeserving cases.

It is evident that though the ordinary village people feel optimistic about the potential of *panchayats*, they think that it has not brought

10. Saxena (2001).

the fruits of development to them. Corruption is singled out as the most important cause for the ineffective functioning of these institutions. Control, which is exercised by the sarpanch and Block Level officials over the Village *Panchayats* and *Gram Sabhas* has not only buttressed corruption, but it has also led to pessimism. The general feeling prevailing among villagers is that on their own and at their level it is almost impossible to change or improve things because of heavy dependence on elected functionaries and Block officials. Thus, the present system is seen to have actually reinforced dominance and unequal access to power, besides rendering the villagers helpless and alienated.

*Sustainability*

The overall functioning of *panchayats* reveals both positive and negative trends. *Panchayats*, by and large, have been able to maintain the periodicity while calling their general body and standing committees meetings. Lack of awareness, knowledge and experience have become impediments to their effective functioning and sustainability. The Constitution Amendment Act itself has certain provisions that adversely affect the sustainability of *Panchayati Raj* Institutions. For instance, while there are reservations for women and scheduled castes/scheduled tribes, these seats are to be allotted by rotation to different constituencies. In practice, this implies that a woman or a scheduled caste/tribal elected to a *panchayat* will normally have a term of five years, with no prospect of re-election (In Karnataka the term is only for 20 months). This goes against the spirit of democracy as people work hard for their constituencies in the expectation that they would be returned to power in the next elections. The existing provisions provide no incentive for the elected persons to deliver on their promises; on the contrary, self-interest would dominate, with little concern for the community at large.

The three tiers also compete for funds and powers. The lower tiers are normally the losers in this process. This would make decentralised development, within a district plan, infructuous and non-sustainable. It is imperative in the given framework that the State legislatures clearly delineate the work to be done by each of the three tiers in each of the sectors which fall within the purview of *panchayats*, in order to ensure that the *panchayats* at the village level can be effective institutions for local governance.

One of the imperatives of decentralisation is that it would ensure 'cost-effectiveness' in implementing development programmes. That is with the active participation of elected members, local organisations and people. The immediate effect would be seen in the reduction of corruption. There are reported cases of collusion between the elected representatives and official agencies in distributing benefits, especially in terms of awarding contracts. In order to check this, the Sen Committee, constituted by the Kerala Government, has strongly recommended the establishment of an Ombudsman. Further, the Act has also made a provision for 'social audit', which envisages more tranparency in the system. Every citizen will have the right to have a look at the estimates, list of beneficiaries, muster rolls, bills, vouchers, accounts and obtain photocopies of the same. This is a bold way of strengthening accountability and openness in the system, which will further improve the sustainability of the PRIs in the Indian polity.

## 2.8 Centrally Sponsored Schemes and Panchayati Raj Institutions

There is a plethora of Centrally Sponsored Schemes (CSS) being implemented by different Ministries and Departments of Central Government. As per the Constitutional mandate, in respect of 29 items of the Eleventh Schedule, funds have to be devolved to the Panchayati Raj Institutions for planning and implementation of schemes pertaining to the particular sector. In reality, the involvement of Panchayati Raj Institutions with respect to these 29 items has been minimal in most States. They continue to be implemented departmentally.

**Box 5.14**

*Centrally Sponsored Schemes*

- National Old Age Pension Scheme
- Annapurna Yojana
- Indira Awaas Yojana
- Samagra Awaas Yojana
- Credit-cum-Subsidy Scheme
- Accelerated Rural Water Supply Programme
- Drought Prone Area Programme
- Sampoorna Grameen Rozgar Yojana

- Swaranjayanti Gram Swarozgar Yojana
- Pradhan Mantri Gram Sadak Yojana
- Pradhan Mantri Gramodaya Yojana
- Employment Assurance Scheme
- Integrated Rural Development Programme
- Rashtriya Mahila Kosh
- Innovative Scheme for Housing & Habitat Development and Rural Building Centres
- Desert Development Programme
- Integrated Wasteland Development Programme
- Central Rural Sanitation Programme

*Panchayats* play an important role in implementation of the centrally sponsored programmes mentioned in the above box. For instance, the objectives of the SGRY are to provide additional employment in the rural areas, as also food security, alongside the creation of durable community, social and economic infrastructure in the rural areas. The programme is self-targeting in nature with special emphasis to provide wage employment to women, SCs, STs and parents of children withdrawn from hazardous occupations. This programme is being implemented at two levels, namely - it will be implemented at the District and Intermediate level *Panchayats* and at the *Gram Panchayat* level. In the former case, 50 per cent of the funds are available under the SGRY and distributed between the District *Panchayat* and the Intermediate *Panchayats* in the ratio of 40:60. In the latter case, 50 per cent of the SGRY funds are released to the Village *Panchayats* through the DRDAs/District *Panchayats*.

Various research studies have critically examined the implementation mechanism through *panchayats* and the evidence reviewed here suggests the following general lessons:

- Schemes having a large component of individual subsidy, or large individual transfers, attract the attention of politicians and officials bent on diverting funds away from their intended purposes and on allocating benefits to those outside the intended beneficiary group.
- By contrast, small, regular payments are generally seen as not worth the trouble of embezzling or diverting, and schemes offering these are generally robust in implementation.

- The schemes that were implemented by NGOs appeared to be less corrupt than those administered by government or by *panchayats*, but such examples are rare and may not be accepted as a robust finding.
- Corruption in schemes involving payments in kind (such as foodgrains) appears to be concentrated at fewer points than in those involving financial payments (such as the siphoning off of grain by fair price shops).
- Involvement of the private commercial sector in any aspect of implementation requires close monitoring, the evidence suggests widespread collusion between middlemen and local officials in falsifying invoices and in a range of other malpractices.
- The creation of sufficient local ownership of capital assets to ensure adequate maintenance and sustainability is exceptionally difficult for technical departments in the public sector to achieve (as in the case of water pumps under the ARWSP). Whilst recent public sector approaches (*e.g.* in DPAP) have attempted to break old top-down moulds, much remains to be done to break embedded patterns of corrupt behaviour.
- Equally difficult for government is the identification of the types of productive assets and opportunities that have the potential to enhance the livelihoods of the poor in sustainable ways. The negative experience of the IRDP is particularly instructive in this regard, though much the same applies to assets created under the EAS or SGRY.

However, it is also evident that the programmes of the Ministry of Rural Development are designed to have some involvement of the PRIs in the implementation, monitoring and review of their programmes. But CSS implemented by other Central Ministries, often ignore the involvement of PRIs. In case the role is identified, it is either non-existent or minimal.

## 2.9 Parallel Organisations and PRIs

In some sectors, people's involvement through parallel institutions like the Joint Forest Management (JFM) Committees, Village Education Committees (VEC), Water User Groups, *etc.*, transgress the

## Table 5.10

*Parallel Bodies and Panchayati Raj*

| *State* | *Parallel Body* | *Area of Overlap/Substitution* | *Institutional links with PRIs* |
|---|---|---|---|
| Uttar Pradesh | Water User Groups (WUG)/ Site Implementation Committee (SIC) | Formulating, developing and approving plans of the area covered by the WUG. Selection of farmers (beneficiaries) Construction, maintenance & management of links & main drains. Policy decisions like decision on rates of water charges. | Village *pradhan* may be the ex-officio Chairperson of the SIC. |
| Haryana | *Gram Vikas Samiti* | Supervision of construction of work out of the funds released by Haryana Rural Development Fund Board, decentralised planning or any other state government scheme. | *Samiti* consists of four members of *gram panchayat* - Chairperson, *Sarpanch*, elected members - one *panch* each from SC and OBC. One woman *panch*. |
| Kerala | Expert Committee | Preparation of *panchayat* development plan. | Technical and advisory body to the *panchayats* regarding the plans prepared by the *panchayat*. |
| Andhra Pradesh | *Janmabhoomi* Scheme | Planning and implementation of development programmes at the local level. | *Sarpanch* and the concerned ward member finds representation in the Habitation Level Committee of *Janmabhoomi*. |
| Gujarat | Joint Forest Management | Cultivation, collection and sale of minor forest produce. Conservation & maintenance of common property resources. | A representative of *gram panchayat* will serve as one of the members of the committee. *Gram panchayat* itself may become a *mandal* for the purpose of JFM. |
| Rajasthan | Watershed Management | Minor irrigation | *Panchayats* can become Project Implementing Agency (PIA) for watershed projects on priority basis. |
| Himachal Pradesh | Vigilance Committee | Supervision of *gram panchayat* of works costing up to Rs. 50,000. | Supervisory body within *gram panchayat* of the works, schemes and other activities of *gram panchayats*. |

*Source*: PRIA (2001)

mandate of PRIs. It is argued that a multiplicity of committees is a means of getting more benefits from the Government. On the contrary, it is perceived by many as dilution of the mandate of the 73rd

Amendment Act and duality in functions and resources. Part of the village population views it as an opportunity to ensure the development of their village through the involvement of a large number of government departments. But at the same time, others feel divided responsibility, multiplicity of function, and duality in the system results in distracted efforts and wasteful expenditure. The bureaucracy too favours such parallel bodies, as it is able to have a greater say in the implementation of the programmes through these committees. Committees also create a broader leadership base and provide an opportunity for more people to be involved in decision making through membership.

However, benefits from user committee-managed natural resource projects, such as forests and watershed management, are not sustainable in the long term. After the source of funds from the project dries up, plantations disappear, committees are disbanded or abandoned and the livelihood base of the poor remains only marginally improved, if at all. Perhaps in some cases they create some sustainable social capital by raising awareness amongst the poor. However, evidence suggests that most of the social capital created by projects is held by the rich and that in fact most projects have contributed to a further entrenchment of powers of the rich. Part of the reason given for involvement by NGOs is to ensure the sustainability of the project by threading it into the fabric of the local social and economic structure. Some NGOs have ensured the sustainability of some projects by creating participatory development and negotiating conflicts before leaving the village. Such successful cases are rare, but not problem-free either. The civil society organisations or community groups involved in such parallel bodies do not appear to have reached the stage yet where external support, whether operational or institutional, is no longer required.

Therefore, in the light of conflicting arguments on both sides, there is an urgent need for studying the institutional links between political decentralisation through *Panchayati Raj* and administrative decentralisation in the form of user committees promoted by external donor projects. This is important because in several development projects (*e.g.* drinking water, health, watershed development and primary education) the government has relied upon committees that are independent of *panchayats*. Often, in the same region, such as

Uttar Pradesh hills, the World Bank has promoted different committees, one for forests, a second for drinking water and a third for education and all these may be distinct from *panchayats*.

Thus, the present approach through user committees raises several questions about the links that exist and should exist between those committees and the PRIs. What should be the role of PRIs once natural resource management programmes become a broad rural development effort rather than a narrowly designed technical programme? Should the involvement of PRIs be more effective in implementing such programmes than committees constituted by government or multilateral institutions? Although it is too early to reach a conclusion, but whether parallel institutions will ensure the sustainability of development programmes is an area for further exploration.

One needs to understand that *panchayats* are responsible for development planning for a particular geographical territory and would be the natural apex body for linking several development programmes into other objectives. Besides, *panchayats* are democratically elected and hence reflect local needs and priorities better. Cost effectiveness is a critical issue. PRIs are better placed to be the apex linking body to effectively implement a development programme. The infrastructure support is available, *panchayats* have legislative mandate to raise revenue and the labour will be cheaper through wider participation.

On the contrary, the committees enjoy better relations with the bureaucracy and government *vis-à-vis panchayats*. Besides such groups are smaller than the *panchayats* and function on consensus rather than legal authority.

It is amply clear that three broad sets of issues hamper the development of effective *Panchayat Raj* Institutions in India. First, it is the resistance and non-cooperation from bureaucracy and the existing institutions of governance, which translates into, for instance, inadequate financial devolution, the framing of rules contradicting the spirit of *panchayats*, and red tapism and corruption. The second set of factors relates to the inherent resistance from the political class and the socio-economic and political elite of rural India, who view PRIs as a serious threat to their interests and hegemony. These include patriarchal forces or the feudal caste forces disturbed by the election of women and dalits to positions of dominance. The third set of factors are lack of capacities at grassroots level, lack of information among common people about *Panchayati Raj* and lack of political education among the ordinary people whose political role is critical for effective *panchayat* functioning. For example, despite the functioning of the *panchayats* for several years, Karnataka, Rajasthan, Madhya Pradesh, among others, have not been able to build capacities among elected representatives to allow them to keep financial records, or implement development plans. Thus, by default the real decision-making arena is left to the official agencies and affluent class.

One outcome of these shortcomings is that *panchayats* have refused to be accountable downwards, for instance to the *gram sabhas*. Indeed, the continuing weakness of *gram sabhas* is a major cause for concern and these need massive strengthening if they are to hold elected local government officials and the public administration to account. Although the *panchayati raj* system in India is confronted with multifarious problems, it is also evident that the *panchayat* movement has been successful in empowerment of the marginalised and inculcating participatory democracy in rural India. The cases of empowerment of women, *dalits*, collective community decision-making, and altering development priorities in favour of people's needs and aspirations are all very significant examples and raise hopes from the *panchayat* system, despite its shortcomings. These achievements in the context of a largely unequal non-democratic social and political order are extremely significant.

In tune with this perspective, a large number of civil society actors have identified the problems and successes of *panchayats* and are working to consolidate the gains from the *panchayat* system for people centric development and effective democratic self-governance. Due credit has to be given to the State governments for sincerity, openness and commitment to democratic decentralisation. Most State governments have been extremely receptive to ground realities about the inadequacies of the *panchayat* system and have put concerted efforts to devise strategies for making *panchayats* effective institutions of local self-governance.

States like Kerala, Madhya Pradesh and Uttar Pradesh who have had little experience of decentralisation, have made the most fundamental changes in this regard. Further, it is imperative that the

PRIs have resources to match the responsibilities placed on them. While State Finance Commissions have submitted their recommendations, very few States have taken the necessary steps to ensure fiscal viability of the PRIs. Yet, one can be hopeful that the experience of some States and some PRIs within States would provide the necessary impetus for greater devolution in other parts of the country.

# 6

# *Panchayati Raj*: Women's Empowerment

P.D. KAUSHIK

## Introduction

Eminent political scientist of the last century, Harold Laski, pointed out that *"the existence of a decentralised State is important for the realisation of rights"*. The concept of local government is better placed to take decisions for the improvement of public amenities for local citizens. Decentralisation signifies the transfer of certain powers and responsibilities and their devolution from one authority to another. The decentralised system of elected governance has certain inherent advantages. The value of decentralisation is well argued, as it is expected to provide greater efficiency, transparency, accountability, responsiveness and opportunities for people's participation. For instance, increased efficiency is because the decision makers who live locally are likely to know more about local conditions, thus they should be able to match resources and needs more precisely. When the decision-makers live and work in close contact with the users, they are exposed to more effective scrutiny and are under greater pressure to deliver goods, thus building transparency and accountability within the system. There are more opportunities for local people to participate in planning services and pay for them through local taxes. Experience also shows that local governments tend to give more priority than central government to human development.[1]

"The power brokers have established their vice-like grip only because democracy has not functioned at the grassroots. Once the people have their own elected representatives from the electorates as

1. Nirvikar Singh, *Governance and Reform in India*, 1996.

small as a hundred to five hundred persons, the source of power lies only as far as the *Panchayat Ghar*, not some distant state capital or even more distant capital of the country."[2]

### Box 6.1

*Economic Decision-Making Facts and Figures*

- Only 1 per cent of the world's assets are in the name of women.
- Men in the Arab States have 3.5 times the purchasing power of their female counterparts.
- 70 per cent of people in abject poverty—living on less than $1 per day — are women.
- Among the developed countries, in France only 9 per cent of the workforce and in the Netherlands 20 per cent of the workforce are female administrators and managers.
- Among the developing countries, in Ecuador and the Bahamas, 33 per cent of the workforce comprises women administrators and managers.
- Women's participation in managerial and administrative posts is around 33 per cent in the developed world, 15 per cent in Africa, and 13 per cent in Asia and the Pacific. In Africa and Asia-Pacific these percentages, small as they are, reflect a doubling of numbers in the last twenty years.
- There are only five women chief executives in the Fortune 500 corporations, the most valuable publicly owned companies in the United States. These include the CEOs of Xerox, Spherion, Hewlett-Packard, Golden West Financial, and Avon Products.
- In Silicon Valley, for every 100 shares of stock options owned by a man, only one share is owned by a woman.

According to Mahbub ul Haq (1996), equity and empowerment are essential components of human resource development. Equity in access to opportunities demands a fundamental restructuring of power in many societies. This includes equalisation of political opportunities through voting rights reform, campaign finance reform, and other actions aimed at limiting the excessive political power of a feudal minority. In a country with a heterogeneous population, a danger is that decentralisation may further marginalise the interests of weaker segments of the population, notably women, SCs and STs. To ensure their fair share, the 73rd Amendment required that a fraction of seats

2. Rajiv Gandhi, *Rajiv Gandhi: selected speeches and writings*, Publication Division, Vol. V.

at all levels be reserved for women, SCs and STs. While reservations for SCs and STs are in place in other elected bodies (national and state legislative assemblies), the Constitutional Amendment is the first one in India that mandated women's reservation, and this made it a landmark piece of legislation. This decision, therefore, reflects the challenges in achieving gender equity in rural India.

The demand for reservation for women was based on shared ideals and goals. Political representation was essentially seen as an instrument of social and economic transformation. Issues of women's representation not only raised a set of questions about citizenship, women's rights and feminist politics, but clearly demonstrated how social and economic inequalities combined with cultural values made it harder for women to challenge dominant ideologies and structures. Political participation is an exercise of power, reservation for women in political spaces is a direct form of empowerment. Two sets of issues affect women's participation - the first relates to the nature of representative democracy and the second relates to the status of political equality and citizenship. Women grapple with both issues in a multi-party democratic system.

Women's empowerment essentially implies progressive elimination of gender disparities at the grassroots level. As such, a perspective on women's empowerment differs from ideas about women's development in some important ways. Women's development is primarily a socio-economic concept while women's empowerment is essentially a political project. It is often argued that women's empowerment is indeed a precursor to women's development. The Constitution ensures equal rights to both men and women and has special provisions for the welfare of women to enhance their status in society. But women representation in politics has remained negligible. To fill this vacuum, the Government of India amended the Constitution to empower women at local levels. The purpose behind this move was to provide political space to women for decision-making.

Gender discrimination has been identified as one of the pervasive forms of institutionalised deprivation. *Panchayati Raj* assumes particular importance as a means of producing democratic functioning and decision-making through decentralised governmental power, thereby restructuring political institutions. The recent Constitutional amendment prescribes a structured form of decentralised governance and decision-making by emphasising statutory participation of women at grassroots level organisations.

### *Panchayati Raj*

The 73[rd] Amendment provides reservation for thirty-three per cent of seats for women in *panchayats*. The purpose behind this move is to provide more opportunities for women to participate in decision-making and thereby to increase the possibilities of accruing more benefits of development to rural areas. Reservation of 33 per cent seats for women in local bodies was building a case in favour of attainment of 'threshold level' or 'critical mass', ensuring that women's concerns will be adequately addressed. In 1988, Drude Dahlerup, in her study on the relevance of the concept of 'critical mass' in Scandinavian politics, established a threshold of 30-33 per cent when women start influencing the institutions.

Women are virtually excluded from political power all over the world. Although women constitute half of the population, only 3.5 per cent of the world's cabinet ministers are women, and women hold no ministerial positions in 93 countries. All political systems, regardless of ideology or form, routinely deny women formal political status. As a writer and researcher Maxine Molyneux (1994) observed, "Politics, more than any other realm, has remained largely a monopoly of men because its condensation of power and authority mainly lies in the hand of this gender". The facts of this statement can be easily observed by looking at the miniscule percentage of women occupying political power in every country of the world. As per HDR (1999), women hold only 12.7 per cent of the world's parliamentary seats and only 8.7 per cent of those in the least developed countries. As a consequence, political women are seen as the deviants, the trespassers or the guests in a terrain, which does not fundamentally belong to them.

**Box 6.2**

*Global Status of Women in Politics*

- Women ministers remain concentrated in social areas (14 per cent) compared to legal (9.4 per cent), economic (4.1 per cent), political affairs (3.4 per cent), and the executive (3.9 per cent).
- 7 per cent of the world's total cabinet ministers are women.

- There are nine women ambassadors to the United Nations. They are from Finland, Guinea, Jamaica, Kazakhstan, Kyrgyzstan, Liberia, Liechtenstein, Somalia, and Turkmenistan.
- In the United Nations system, women hold only 9 per cent of the top management jobs and 21 per cent of senior management positions, but 48 per cent of the junior professional civil service slots.
- In 1893, New Zealand became the first nation to grant women full voting rights.
- Among the countries in the developing world that were the earliest to grant women the right to vote were: Finland (1906), Albania (1920), Mongolia (1924), Ecuador (1929), Turkey (1930), Sri Lanka (1931).
- Some of the latest countries to grant women suffrage are: Switzerland (1971), Iraq (1980), Namibia (1989), Kazakhstan (1994).
- In the $21^{st}$ century, some countries still do not have universal suffrage. Among them are Brunei Darussalam, Kuwait, Sultanate of Oman, Saudi Arabia, and United Arab Emirates.
- Among the developing nations who have not ratified the Convention on the Elimination of All Forms of Discrimination Against Women (CEDAW) are: Bahrain, Palestine, Qatar, Saudi Arabia, Sultanate of Oman, Syrian Arab Republic, United Arab Emirates.
- The United States is the only industrialised nation that has not ratified CEDAW.

*Panchayati Raj*, as a system of grassroots governance, has been rightly conceived as the most viable and proper mechanism of realising goals of democracy and decentralisation. The empowerment of women, through a well-devised system of reservation, has not only brought about a change in socio-political culture, but has also led to a virtual transformation of the rural scene where people have increasingly become aware of their rights and have started demanding their share in power. As a result, rural India today has become the embodiment of a new revolution, which has broadly mobilised women.

## Status of Women in Indian Polity

In India electoral politics continues to remain a male preserve, both empirically and symbolically. Male voters have consistently out numbered women voters by 11 per cent over the last five elections, although this gap is narrowing. Sociologists consider that only 30 per cent of female voters are 'aware voters' in India.[3] In fact, when women

3. Chowdhary (1994).

cast their votes in India, there is a *de facto* pattern whereby women first take advice from male family members, or follow the instructions of male members in the household, suggesting that they are incapable of arriving at a reasoned decision on their own.

Fewer women contest political positions than do men. On average, there have been three women candidates for every 100 male contestants in past elections. Only 200 of the 9,107 candidates contesting in the 1989 Parliamentary elections of India were women. Though major political parties now promise to reserve 33 per cent of their seats for women, their record shows otherwise. In the 1999 elections, women comprised 9.9 per cent of Congress party candidates, 6.6 per cent of BJP candidates, 5.5 per cent of Communist Party candidates, and 3.4 per cent of Janata Dal candidates. Lower participation ensures that women remain under-represented in politics at all levels. Before India's Independence, women constituted 10 per cent of those jailed for protesting British Rule, the pivotal form of political activity at that time. Since then, women have never held more than 8 per cent of seats in Lok *Sabha*, even though in absolute terms the number of women Members of Parliament has risen from 22 in 1951 to 45 in 1999.

## Retrospective

If women were marginalised in politics at national and state levels, they were practically absent in erstwhile village committees and *gram panchayat*s. All-women *panchayat*s at the village level are clearly an anomaly in a country where women have so little political power. The importance of creating women's *panchayat*s at the village level received formal recognition in the mid 1970s, when the *Committee on the Status of Women in India* recommended the establishment of statutory women's *panchayat*s at village level. It is worth mentioning that women in Karnataka, Andhra Pradesh and Maharashtra had begun contesting elections, occupying reserved positions and actively participating in *panchayat*s. This was seen as a transitional measure to ensure greater participation by rural women in the political process.

In India, the women's movement has given little priority to women's participation in electoral politics until relatively recently. The movement has yet to evolve a coherent position or a coordination strategy on this issue, but there have been a few isolated regional initiatives in this area. Some groups, including the National

Commission for Women had earlier called for the reservation of seats for women. A few women's groups such as the voluntary organisation 'Vimochana' located in the city of Bangalore, were active in campaigning against politicians in the 1989 general elections, and many women's groups in various cities like Mumbai, Delhi and Bangalore prepared manifestos in the 1980s.

Thus, the theme of 'Women and Politics' has emerged as an important issue only in this decade. This theme was discussed at the 1990 National Conference held at Kozhikode in the State of Kerala. The possibility of forming a woman's party was also touched on. A few networks have since been formed around the issue of women's political participation. But autonomous women's groups still remain uncertain whether a continuing struggle within the formal political structures is more effective than the struggle for women's rights from outside the system. In this vacuum, government enactments have provided the greatest fillip to the issue of women's participation in electoral politics. Although both Karnataka and Maharashtra reserved seats for women at the local and State levels, it was not until 1992, with the constitutional amendment, that the issue of women's political participation has been brought sharply into national focus.

### Box 6.3

*Constitutional Provision*

- Balwant Rai Mehta Committee suggested provision for the co-option of two women members in *panchayats*.
- Ashok Mehta Committee recommended two women securing the highest number of votes among the women candidates take the seats reserved for them in *panchayats*.
- Only one or two women were co-opted in *panchayats* before 1992 in a group of 15 to 19 members.
- 33 per cent reservation in all the three tiers of panchayati raj institutions for women.

The present *Panchayati Raj* differs from the early pattern of women's *panchayats* at the village level. One, the earlier *Panchayati Raj* was not a political institution, but only an implementing body. Elections to *panchayat* bodies were held on an individual basis, and the contesting candidates were not nominated by the political parties. The

73rd Amendment Act allows political parties to enter into the election fray. Second, the present *Panchayati Raj* is not an implementing body to the development programmes. It is a decision-making body and rules over the governance of the village. A very important aspect of the new *Panchayati Raj* is that it empowers women and weaker sections of villages in the wielding of power.

## Current Status

Women are changing governance in India. They are being elected to local councils in unprecedented numbers as a result of amendments to the Constitution, which mandated the reservation of seats for women in local government. The women whom PRI has brought into politics are now governing, be it in one village, or a larger area such as 100 villages or a district. The sheer number of women that PRI has brought into the political system has made a difference. By 1998, about 3,30,000 women had entered politics as a result of PRI and many more have been elected in the last two years. The percentage of women at various levels of political activity has shifted dramatically as a result of this constitutional change, from 4-5 per cent before the Amendment to 25-40 per cent after the Amendment. But the difference is also qualitative, because these women are bringing their experience in governance of civic society into governance of the state. In this way, they are making the state sensitive to issues of poverty, inequality and gender injustice.

Madhya Pradesh was the first State in India to conduct and complete elections to all the three tiers in 1994. Between 1994-95, several other States including Tripura, Punjab, Haryana, Rajasthan and Uttar Pradesh conducted elections under the new Act. The *panchayat* elections across the country brought over 700,000 women to *panchayati raj* institutions. With the exception of a few States, most have met and some have even exceeded the one-third quota for women's reservation at *gram panchayat* level. The States, which have failed to meet the quota requirement, includes Assam and Punjab (only 30 per cent of women were elected to the *gram panchayats*). Others who failed to meet the quota include Sikkim (1.48 per cent), undivided Uttar Pradesh (25.55 per cent), and Chandigarh (20.18 per cent). On the other hand, Karnataka has 43.79 per cent women representatives at the *gram panchayat* level, which not only exceeds the

## Table 6.1

*Number of Elected Women Members in PRIs (All India)*

| *States* | *Gram Panchayats* | *Panchayat Samitis* | *Zilla Parishads* |
|---|---|---|---|
| Andhra Pradesh | 78000 | 5420 | 363 |
| Arunachal Pradesh (a) | — | — | — |
| Assam (b) | 5469 | 66 | — |
| Bihar (c) | — | — | — |
| Goa | 468 | — | — |
| Gujarat | 21351 | 1275 | 254 |
| Haryana | 16704 | 858 | 182 |
| Himachal Pradesh | 6015 | 858 | 84 |
| Jammu & Kashmir (d) | — | — | — |
| Karnataka | 35305 | 1343 | 335 |
| Kerala | — | — | — |
| Madhya Pradesh | 156181 | 3169 | 31 |
| Maharashtra | 101182 | 1174 | 587 |
| Manipur (e) | 555 | — | 22 |
| Meghalaya (f) | — | — | — |
| Mizoram (f) | — | — | — |
| Nagaland | — | — | — |
| Orissa | 27036 | 1754 | 284 |
| Punjab (g) | 26939 | — | — |
| Rajasthan | 33566 | 1740 | 33 |
| Sikkim | 326 | — | 28 |
| Tamil Nadu | 31548 | 2295 | 22 |
| Tripura | 1809 | 67 | 24 |
| Uttar Pradesh | 120591 | 13865 | 634 |
| West Bengal | 17883 | 2997 | 243 |
| | **Union Territories** | | |
| A&N Islands | 229 | 25 | 10 |
| Chandigarh (h) | — | — | — |
| D&N Haveli | 46 | — | 4 |
| Daman & Diu | 25 | — | 5 |
| NCT Delhi (i) | — | — | — |
| Lakshadweep | 30 | — | 8 |
| Pondicherry (j) | — | — | — |
| **Total** | **681258** | **37109** | **3153** |

*Notes:* (a) Arunachal Pradesh *Panchayati Raj Act* not yet passed. (b) Figures not current. Fresh Elections due since Oct, 1997. (c) Post 73rd Amendment elections not held in the State. Election issue *sub-judice*. Figures not available. (d) 73rd Amendment not applicable in the State, proposes to adopt 73rd Amendment. (e) Fresh elections held but latest data not available. (f) Traditional Councils perform duties of local govt. 73rd Amendment not applicable in these States. (g) Elections due in Punjab. (h) Current figures not available. (i) NCT government proposes to conduct *Panchayat* Elections. (j) Current figures not available. Post-73rd Amendment Elections not held in the State.

*Source: CSO, Statistical Abstract India, 2000.*

requisite quota, but is also the highest among all States and UTs. Other States that substantially exceed the 33 per cent quota include Goa, Kerala, Manipur, West Bengal and Daman & Diu.

At the intermediate level, Assam, Punjab and undivided Uttar Pradesh fall below the quota, while Karnataka (with 40 per cent women representation) again exceeds the prerequisite. At the district level or *Zilla Parishad*, Uttar Pradesh (25.40 per cent) remains the major defaulter to the set norms, besides States like Sikkim and UTs like Chandigarh and Dadra & Nagar Haveli.

The number of women *sarpanch* (Chairpersons) at the various levels of *panchayati raj* reveals that only Karnataka, Maharashtra, Orissa and Tamil Nadu meet the quota at all the three-tiers. West Bengal's record in this respect is surprisingly low - 4.62 per cent at the third-tier, 3.0 per cent at the middle-tier, and nil at the top-tier.

State Election Commission's figures pertaining to Madhya Pradesh and Rajasthan reveal that less than 1 per cent of the seats in *panchayats* remained vacant, and these seats were not reserved for women. In Madhya Pradesh, many of such vacant seats fall in districts with substantial tribal populations. Some of such seats in Rajasthan also fall in tribal districts. A research study covering three States and 850 women representatives highlighted that 45 per cent of the representatives got elected without contest. Most of these were at *gram panchayat* level, but such unopposed elections were also visible in the other tiers of *panchayati raj*. However, the incidence of unopposed elected representatives was significantly high at lower levels, especially election of members. But election for coveted position of women *sarpanch* or *pradhan* did not go unopposed.

There are also instances of women getting elected from unreserved constituencies at *panchayats* in Madhya Pradesh, Tamil Nadu, Karnataka, Maharashtra, *etc.* A study of two districts in Tamil Nadu, highlighted that 88 per cent of women got elected from reserved for women constituencies, and 7 per cent from constituencies reserved for SCs, which was open for both men and women[4]. However, the districts in Tamil Nadu chosen for the fieldwork had a fairly successful mass literacy campaign. Likewise, another study carried out at Angul district in Orissa revealed that 33 out of 53 women ward members were

4. Athreya *et al.* (1998).

elected unopposed, and two were elected from unreserved constituencies.[5] It needs to be mentioned that the amended *Gram Panchayat Act* of Orissa makes literacy mandatory for the representatives.

Bringing these women into politics was an act of positive discrimination. It was the pressure of law, combined with the political imperative of winning elections that changed political parties' perception of women's limited capacity for public office. But, crucially, PRI has helped to change women's perceptions of themselves. Women have gained a sense of empowerment by asserting control over resources, officials and, most of all, by challenging men. PRI has also given many women a greater understanding of the workings of politics, in particular the importance of political parties. On the other hand, some women's involvement in PRI has helped them affirm their identity as women with particular and shared experiences. This self-perception arises from two sources, namely from women's own sense of their shared experience and from attitudes and imagery imposed on them by the men. It appears that gender can supersede class and party lines.

The constitutional provisions ensure the representation of women in PRIs both as members and as functionaries, but it must be kept in mind that merely becoming members does not ensure their effectiveness. Secondly, even though the representation is based on an elective process, it is not always the case that capable and active women come through these reservations. In some cases, the women who are relatives of the existing local leaders may get elected to fill up these reservation seats. Somehow this system appears to discourage competent women from contesting the elections. The conservative nature of rural areas, the lack of education and access to media, poor exposure to the outside world, the patriarchal nature of the family, economic dependency on men *etc.* make the women of rural areas powerless and unequipped to participate effectively in the political process. Though the reservation appears to be the only way to ensure the presence of women in PRIs, having secured their presence there, an agenda for action must evolve to ensure their effective participation in the PRIs and through them, in the process of decision-making at the grassroots level.

---

5. ISED (1998).

## Social and Economic Characteristics of Women Representatives

Social and economic characteristics of women representatives are not different from any other women in the Indian society. Empirical works on women issues have focussed on variety of aspects of women empowerment. Murthy (1994) outlined five key aspects over which women's control has to be assessed, namely their labour, resources (economic, health, education and political), their reproduction, sexuality, (their physical integrity and freedom from mental and physical violence), and their mobility. The outcomes of historical subordination of women, although stark and visible, present themselves in such complex ways that many perceive them as natural, immutable and even correct social arrangements. However the social and ideological roots of gender subordination are continuously being unearthed in different studies carried out on women issues.[6]

### Box 6.4

*Profile of Elected Women Representatives*

- **Age**: Most of the women who stood for the elections and won were in the age group of 35-55 years.
- **Political experience**: Less than 20 per cent of the women, compared to 80 per cent of men, had previous political experience.
- **Caste**: Caste still plays a major role during elections. Almost 60 per cent of the elected members whether men or women, were from the dominant caste. However, reservation for the "downtrodden" castes added a margin of representation for these groups.
- **Education**: Literacy is one of the crucial factors for effective leadership and functioning of women and *dalit* representatives. Here too, the variations were striking between men and women, with 20 per cent of men being professionally educated, compared to less than 5 per cent of women.
- **Occupation**: The majority of women representatives were engaged in domestic work, including child rearing, field working, fetching water, and looking after the old members of the family. This put limits on the time they could spend in political affairs.

*Source:* PRIA (2001)

6. Kabeer N (1994).

The concept of equality has been significant to the explosion of the term 'women's empowerment' as evidenced in writings of many feminists.[7] What constitutes power, what the gender determinants of power are and what is involved in the process of empowerment give credence to the meaning of the terms 'advancement of women' and 'enhancement of women's status in the society'. The current focus has thus been increasingly on the language of rights. The concept of human rights has brought into focus the responsibility of the nation-state in creating and sustaining conditions that enable the achievement of gender equality.

### Box 6.5

*Pakasma* Panchayat, *Rohtak District*

Lakshmi Devi, *sarpanch* of Pakasma *Panchayat* belongs to the dominant Jat community. She is illiterate. She was persuaded by her family members to contest the elections, since this seat was declared reserved. Prior to being declared as a reserve constituency, her husband was the *sarpanch*. This time, her husband contested on a member seat and won. He has been now elected as *Up-sarpanch* and in effect, the *sarpanch*. All *gram panchayat* meetings and *gram sabha* meetings are conducted by him. He goes to the Block Office for information on government schemes and carries out all other *panchayat* related activities.

Women's powerlessness stems from the lack of resources - human, material, and intangible.[8] When gender relations are examined as power relations, it is evident that men are favoured by the rules of the institutions within which gender relations occur, and that they enjoy and exercise power in commanding these resources. Gender inequality is therefore an outcome of asymmetry in power, where men are in a position of privilege and women of subordination. These power relations often remain unchallenged because the ideology of subordination is accepted as given. Men are meant to dominate and women to subordinate. The ideology of subordination is also self-perpetuating, as the norms, rules and practices of social institutions in which gender relations occur, ensure its reproduction in time.

---

7. Gita Sen and Caren Grown (1987).
8. Kabeer and Subrahmaniam (1996).

**Table 6.2**

*Women Leadership in Panchayats*

| *Inhibiting Factors* | *Enabling Factors* |
|---|---|
| Illiteracy | Training |
| Ignorance | Awareness Generation |
| Lack of Confidence | Training and Awareness Campaign |
| Hesitation | Exposure |
| Apathy at personal level | Personal interest, involvement and commitment |
| Family | Family Support |
| Mobility | Family Support and Economic Support |
| Patriarchy | Family, Community and Community Based Organisations Support |
| Poor Economic Status | Self Help Groups and other Income Generation Programmes |
| No-confidence Motions | Governmental and NGO support |
| Male Officials | Gender sensitive administration |

Thus, being elected to the office is of course a major step taken by women to enter the political arena, but it is just a first step. The real test of women's empowerment begins when they start exercising their rights and responsibilities, especially participating actively in the decision-making processes of their village, developing their confidence and establishing their qualitative presence in the power structure. Thus, the general view is that women in *panchayat*s are showing signs of political awakening. But inhibiting factors, such as illiteracy, domestic pressure, and dependency on men hinder their progress. By and large, a few women who have emerged significantly into political prominence are those who are 'economically well off' and who belong to the upper strata of society. Perhaps, it is because the higher stratum of the society is usually endowed with the enabling factors *de facto*.

## Literacy Level

The majority of women entering the PRIs are illiterate or barely literate. This limitation is a major impediment in overseeing the responsibilities of elected representatives. A study[9], conducted in Haryana, Madhya Pradesh and Rajasthan, confirms this observation,

9. Kaushik (1998).

where 25 per cent of the elected women surveyed were illiterate. However, the same study also confirms insignificant share of illiterate women representatives in Tamil Nadu and Orissa.

### Table 6.3

*Distribution of Women by Education Status (1998–99)*

*(Education Level in per cent)*

| *State* | *Illiterate* | *Literate (<Primary School Complete)* | *Primary School Complete* | *Middle School Complete* | *High School Complete* | *Higher Secondary Complete and Above* |
|---|---|---|---|---|---|---|
| Andhra Pradesh | 63.8 | 5.2 | 15.4 | 4.8 | 6.8 | 4.0 |
| Assam | 53.9 | 11.9 | 10.5 | 14.1 | 5.4 | 4.2 |
| Bihar | 76.6 | 3.0 | 8.1 | 3.8 | 5.7 | 2.7 |
| Goa | 28.6 | 10.9 | 16.3 | 12.5 | 15.4 | 16.3 |
| Gujarat | 50.3 | 6.1 | 14.7 | 8.7 | 9.2 | 11.0 |
| Haryana | 55.2 | 2.4 | 14.3 | 8.1 | 10.8 | 9.2 |
| Himachal Pradesh | 36.3 | 4.3 | 23.6 | 12.6 | 15.2 | 7.6 |
| Jammu & Kashmir | 69.8 | 1.5 | 7.9 | 8.9 | 6.5 | 5.4 |
| Karnataka | 55.2 | 4.4 | 14.3 | 6.6 | 11.0 | 8.5 |
| Kerala | 12.6 | 9.3 | 20.9 | 17.1 | 24.6 | 15.6 |
| Madhya Pradesh | 68.5 | 5.3 | 11.0 | 5.7 | 3.5 | 5.9 |
| Maharashtra | 44.6 | 8.8 | 18.1 | 10.8 | 9.8 | 7.9 |
| Manipur | 42.9 | 7.6 | 9.3 | 17.1 | 8.6 | 14.5 |
| Meghalaya | 38.1 | 28.4 | 12.6 | 11.6 | 4.6 | 4.6 |
| Mizoram | 10.0 | 25.7 | 25.4 | 22.8 | 10.3 | 5.8 |
| Nagaland | 39.8 | 11.3 | 22.2 | 15.1 | 6.8 | 4.7 |
| Orissa | 59.5 | 9.6 | 16.5 | 6.9 | 4.4 | 3.1 |
| Punjab | 38.8 | 2.9 | 18.3 | 10.5 | 16.8 | 12.7 |
| Rajasthan | 75.5 | 2.8 | 8.6 | 5.9 | 3.7 | 3.5 |
| Sikkim | 49.4 | 11.8 | 15.8 | 11.2 | 6.5 | 5.2 |
| Tamil Nadu | 47.5 | 4.5 | 18.7 | 13.4 | 8.2 | 7.6 |
| Uttar Pradesh | 70.2 | 2.7 | 9.1 | 6.8 | 4.3 | 6.9 |
| West Bengal | 50.0 | 14.4 | 14.9 | 10.1 | 5.1 | 5.5 |
| Arunachal Pradesh | 52.7 | 9.4 | 14.5 | 13.8 | 5.5 | 4.1 |
| Delhi | 29.1 | 2.7 | 12.5 | 11.5 | 15.4 | 28.7 |
| **India** | **58.2** | **5.9** | **13.4** | **8.2** | **7.4** | **6.8** |

*Source:* International Institute for Population Sciences, *National Family Health Survey*, 1998-99.

It is imperative to understand that the overall literacy level among women in India is quite low, which is also a reflection of the educational level of women representatives in the country. In the same study, it was highlighted that 23 per cent of the women elected representatives were educated up to primary school level. In other words, almost one-fourth of women representatives had barely reading and writing skills. Less than 10 per cent of women representatives had college education.

**Box 6.6**

*Dhangarh Panchayat, Sidhi District*

Kunti Devi is the *pradhan* of Dhangarh *panchayat*. It is a tribal village. Her husband is known as the *pradhan* in the village and conducts the *gram sabha* and *gram panchayat* meetings. Only when money has to be withdrawn from the bank, does Kunti Devi go to the bank to sign. But both husband and wife are illiterate, thus have no knowledge of financial matters. The financial matters and other *panchayat* related work are handled by the Village Secretary (a government appointee) and *panchayat karmi* (an educated person from the village nominated by the *gram sabha*).

## Income and Occupation

A CWDS study, conducted in Haryana, Madhya Pradesh and Rajasthan, revealed that 40 per cent of the women representatives belong to families with income that place them below poverty line. Around 14.2 per cent of the elected women representatives belong to landless category, 19.5 per cent had marginal land holdings and 20.6 per cent have small land holdings. Only 33 per cent of all those surveyed had an annual income over Rs. 20,000. The occupational background was more or less similar across all the three States, *i.e.*, 50 per cent of the women representatives are cultivators, while 40 per cent describe themselves as housewives, essentially including support to the dominant household occupation, agriculture or business.

Reflecting on the occupation, the caste pattern is evidently lopsided and favours the OBCs. According to the CWDS study, the highest percentage in terms of caste for members and *pradhans* is that of the OBCs, 28.9 per cent for *panchayat* members and 30.3 per cent for *pradhan*. Kaushik's field survey also revealed a similar pattern, showing women representatives were mostly from the OBC category.

However, another study revealed the dominance of higher castes (*Thakurs* and *Brahmins*) in hill regions of Uttar Pradesh and Haryana (where *Yadav* caste is closer to higher caste). Another district level study[10] on *Panchayats* in Karnataka revealed dominance of the landowning upper castes, the *Vokkaligas*.

## Table 6.4

*Distribution of Women by Employment Status (1998-99)*

| *State* | *Working in Family Farm/Business* | *Working for Someone Else* | *Self Employed* | *Not Worked in the Past 12 Months* |
|---|---|---|---|---|
| Andhra Pradesh | 17.9 | 35.6 | 5.2 | 41.3 |
| Assam | 4.8 | 10.8 | 4.5 | 79.8 |
| Bihar | 9.1 | 11.6 | 5.7 | 73.6 |
| Goa | 12.0 | 28.1 | 7.3 | 52.6 |
| Gujarat | 23.4 | 22.8 | 4.6 | 49.2 |
| Haryana | 3.3 | 8.5 | 0.8 | 87.4 |
| Himachal Pradesh | 11.8 | 8.6 | 0.4 | 79.2 |
| Jammu & Kashmir | 30.1 | 7.8 | 4.6 | 57.6 |
| Karnataka | 16.6 | 29.6 | 5.8 | 47.9 |
| Kerala | 2.4 | 16.9 | 5.7 | 75.0 |
| Madhya Pradesh | 26.2 | 27.4 | 3.6 | 42.8 |
| Maharashtra | 20.7 | 28.7 | 6.3 | 44.3 |
| Manipur | 22.9 | 18.6 | 28.4 | 30.1 |
| Meghalaya | 18.6 | 20.1 | 8.8 | 52.4 |
| Mizoram | 23.5 | 19.2 | 7.2 | 50.1 |
| Nagaland | 37.3 | 14.8 | 11.7 | 36.1 |
| Orissa | 7.2 | 15.95 | 7.5 | 69.4 |
| Punjab | 0.4 | 8.0 | 1.0 | 90.6 |
| Rajasthan | 30.3 | 8.9 | 4.4 | 56.5 |
| Sikkim | 4.2 | 14.0 | 3.9 | 77.9 |
| Tamil Nadu | 10.4 | 39.2 | 4.2 | 46.2 |
| Uttar Pradesh | 12.5 | 7.2 | 3.5 | 76.6 |
| West Bengal | 5.5 | 14.9 | 8.1 | 71.5 |
| Arunachal Pradesh | 37.7 | 7.9 | 13.9 | 40.4 |
| Delhi | 3.5 | 13.4 | 3.9 | 79.1 |
| **India** | **14.4** | **19.7** | **5.0** | **60.8** |

*Source:* International Institute for Population Sciences, *National Family Health Survey, 1998-99, India Introductory Report*, Bombay.

10. Vidya (1997).

As regard age profile, PRIA, CWDS and Kaushik, among others, have similar observations, revealing that 74 per cent of women representatives belonged to 20-40 years age group. This observation sharply contrasts with the pre-Amendment period *panchayats*, where the women representatives belonged to much higher age groupings, free of their child-bearing and domestic responsibilities. All the three studies also found that an overwhelming percentage (over 90 per cent) of women representatives was married. The information on age is corroborated by evidence from Bangalore Rural District in Karnataka[11] and Karnal district of Haryana.[12] In fact, for all such socio-economic profile assessments on *gram panchayats*, one has to depend on micro studies due to non-availability of information on *panchayats*, especially at intermediate and *gram panchayat* levels.

On the issue of family background, past or existing political family associations, there was wide contradiction among the research studies. Many studies showed that the elected women representatives belonged to locally influential families with political connections. However, Kaushik's study contradicted such findings, showing that only 30 per cent of the women representatives surveyed came from politically connected families. The CWDS study showed that the majority of women elected to the *panchayats* are first timers, with only 3 per cent having any previous experience of participation in *panchayats*. Other studies showed that elected women candidates had a history of involvement with *Mahila Mandals*.

In fact, various studies on women's participation in the PRIs have shown a wide variety of factors, which lead women to contest in elections. The first and most common factor is the mandatory provision for reservation, in the absence of which only a few women considered or like to consider, contesting elections. The provision for reservation made women's representation possible because it compelled the men in the community to take the initiative in persuading the women in their families to contest. The objective can be either to keep the seat in the family till rotational system caused the reservation to lapse or to retain control over *panchayat* resources.

---

11. Vidya (1997).
12. MARG (1998).

A study on Karnal district documents pressure and/or support from family and community as being the main reason for contesting elections. The only exception reported in the study is the case of one woman who took her own decision to contest for the *panchayat* elections, she was subjected to verbal and physical abuse from her husband and family. On the election campaign, the male members dominate the organising and running of the election campaign. The women canvassing mainly among women of their constituency, leaving the task of mobilising male votes to their husbands and other male members of the household.

### Box 6.7

*Kalva Panchayat, Kurnool District*

Fatima Bi is an illiterate woman but she was good enough to bag the United Nations Development Programmes's (UNDP) Race Against Poverty Award for the Asia - Pacific Region. She was an ordinary housewife when she became a proud *sarpanch,* a seat declared reserved for women in her village. In the very first session, Fatima Bi showed grit and scrutinised the village records. The *Mandal* officials promptly promised to bring all the records over. Then, she called a meeting of the village women and asked them to join hands with her in developing the village. During her term, a metalled road was laid, check dams were built, a new school building was raised and the old school building was renovated. Under the '*Janmabhoomi*' programme, Fatima Bi helped the village women to raise Rs. 30,000. A scheme was taken up at a cost of Rs. 2 lakh to dig a 5 Km. irrigation drain and clear 500 acre of fallow land for paddy cultivation.

Fatima Bi led the womenfolk to join the '*Podupu Lakshmi*' groups and urged them to save a small amount of money every month. Within a year, 40 Thrift and Self-Help Groups with 300 women members saved Rs. 2 lakh. The UNDP was impressed by this achievement and granted Rs. 12 lakh as an interest-free loan to the Village Development Organisation (VDO). A women committee consisting of representatives of SHGs with Rs. 20 lakh as capital now runs the VDO. The loans granted by VDO have helped many families to undertake small businesses and improve their living conditions.

Once a poor and backward, Kalva is now a completely transformed village with happy faces all around and modern amenities in almost all houses. Child marriages are a thing of the past. The women who have suffered social injustice all along now stand by the side of their daughters. All credit to the hard-working woman *sarpanch* who rightfully won the title of "*Uttam Sarpanch*" and received an award on Independence Day.

But increasing the representation of women has not automatically led to a more gender-focussed analysis of the issues confronting local government. Nor has it necessarily raised the profile of women's needs and interests in the policy agenda, given that elected women often act as proxies for men's views at the councils, being advised by their male relatives. But there is now a minority of women who are in politics because of their leadership qualities or feminist consciousness and visible changes in the articulation of ideas and leadership qualities exhibited by this minority have been noted in the different priorities and different values espoused by women in politics.

## Functioning of *Panchayats* and Women Representatives

The enormous expansion of women's representation in decentralised government structures has highlighted the advantages of proximity, namely the redress of grievances and the ability to mobilise struggle at a local level, where it is most meaningful. Thus, women are helping to radically improve governance at a local level. Some of the ways in which women are changing governance are evident in the issues they choose to tackle, like water, alcohol abuse, education, health and domestic violence. Women also express different values. Women value proximity, whether it be to a drinking water source, a fuel source, a creche, a health centre, a court of justice or an office of administration.

Are the women representatives aware of their duties as *panchayat* functionaries? Perhaps this is the most researched topic on *panchayat*s. CWDS (1999), Kaushik (1998), MARG (1998), Verma (1998), among others, have shown that awareness of *panchayat* issues among rural women is directly dependent on the literacy and educational level of women. Another important observation made by these studies is that levels of awareness about *panchayat*-related matters do not vary significantly according to gender. Thus, the awareness level on *panchayat* matters in general is dependent on education and literacy levels, for both men and women. Thus, it could be safely concluded that awareness level on *panchayat* matters is abysmally low among rural women. Likewise, it is important to understand that when few women from the same segment are elected, how are these women representatives placed to carry out their *panchayat* responsibilities effectively and efficiently? Kaushik in her study revealed that women representatives are not aware of the basic functioning of *panchayats*. But as a rider, she mentioned that even their male counterparts, both members and *sarpanch*, have been found ignorant on the matters of *panchayats*. Therefore, such ignorance about the foundation of the entire pyramidal structure of local democracy is surely a matter of concern. Perhaps, this also serves to explain the ineffectiveness of the *gram sabha* as an instrument of direct democracy, which records a fairly poor presence of rural women.

## Attendance at the *Panchayat* Meetings

The CWDS had constructed a comprehensive index of participation that includes, attendance at the *panchayat* meetings, efforts to carry one's own viewpoint in *panchayat* meetings, weekly time devoted to *panchayat* work, petition and problems received and attended to, and efforts to overcome difficulties that are encountered. The CWDS survey revealed that 65.5 per cent women representatives regularly attended the *panchayat* meetings, with attendance being higher among women *sarpanch* and lower among women members.[13] The reasons for absence pertain to domestic work or livelihood concerns, with a small fraction citing inconvenience of distance or seclusion. The results of other studies are not vastly different. A few studies have indicated that often husbands or male members of the household mark the proxy attendance for women representatives. However, these studies have also observed a steady decline in the proxy phenomenon, but do not deny the presence of male members as escorts. This is attributed to distance, poor public transport facilities, and meetings that do not always end before nightfall.[14]

Information about the meetings is often improperly communicated, like information on the meeting is communicated at the last minute, resulting in the absence of women representatives. There are significant variations between research studies and States. For instance, in Madhya Pradesh it is commonly observed that information about the meetings is communicated well in advance, but often agenda papers are missing. In many States the date of meetings is statutorily fixed, however the schedule is not necessarily followed. On the contrary, the study on

13. This survey was conducted in Uttar Pradesh.
14. Athreya (1998).

Haryana showed that the dates of the meetings are fixed, the schedule is not followed and meetings are held as and when the *sarpanch* or the Village Secretary deems it necessary. The mode of communication for *panchayat* meetings is the village *chowkidar*, who invariably informs the husband or son of the woman representative. Since acute factionalism exists in some areas on caste basis, often such information is withheld.

Sometimes, even if the date of the meeting is communicated well in advance, it may be postponed for lack of quorum. Such unpredictability in the functioning of *panchayat* meetings often becomes the cause of disenchantment of women representatives. Sometimes to attend the meeting, one has to forego a day's livelihood. At higher levels, political differences have been a major reason for absence. In Garhwal, one *Kshetra Panchayat* (intermediate tier) woman member complained that the *pramukh* invariably tampers with the post to force her exclusion from the meetings because she belongs to the rival political party.

Different studies use different measures of participation. But the most commonly observed phenomenon is that the women representatives, especially women *pradhan/sarpanch*, lobby with fellow-members, and outside, mobilise friends and family members to gain support on their viewpoints. Women *pradhan*s have also boycotted *panchayat* meetings to stress their viewpoints. The CWDS study revealed that almost 60 per cent of the women representatives devote no time at all to the *panchayat* work, and only 27 per cent women representatives in Madhya Pradesh, Uttar Pradesh and Rajasthan devote more than three hours per week to such work. The study also reveals that about 50 per cent of the petitions received by the women representatives relate to land (land disputes, distribution of land), employment and government assistance for basic needs.

**Box 6.8**

*Women's Participation: Some Field Observations*

- Caste polarisation is prevalent when submitting petitions to PRI representatives, women representatives work closely with their own caste group.
- Women representatives depend heavily on their husbands and other male members of their households to resolve the problems presented to them, especially when interacting with officials.

- Women representatives at higher tiers are often educated and experienced in PRI functioning, they are more vocal and participative in the meetings as compared to women members in *gram panchayat* meetings.
- Women members, irrespective of their caste background, sit separately from their male colleagues in *gram panchayat* meetings, though men and women sit in mixed fashion at *Zilla Samiti* and *Zilla Parishad* level.
- Deep divide between women members on caste lines at *gram panchayat* level, higher caste women members refuse to eat with low caste women members.
- There are no or negligible representation of women members on *panchayat* committees, many women members at *gram panchayat* level are not aware of *panchayat* constituted committees.

Various studies have shown sharp divide between women representatives along caste lines in the *gram panchayat*'s functioning. In one instance, the woman *panchayat pradhan*, belonging to SC community, sat on the floor while the high caste *panchayat* members sat on the *charpoys*.[15] Another study on *panchayats* in Orissa revealed that non-political background of women members was an asset in arriving at unbiased decisions on community matters, such as construction of community hall, selection of beneficiaries, water supply and work under SGRY. In overall terms, there are significant variations in the participation of women representatives, especially –

(a) between the three tiers, with greater involvement as they climb up the ladder of PRIs;

(b) between members and *sarpanch*;

(c) women members prefer to address vital needs like education, health, *etc.*, against the male counterparts preferring construction of roads, community halls, *etc.*; and

(d) active in the implementation of government schemes like drinking water, inspection and monitoring of nutrition centres under ICDS scheme, *etc.*

The women representatives have been also found taking innovative ways to intervene in disputes related to family and matrimonial

15. Kaushik (1998).

matters. Often the women representatives provide counselling services to abusive or alcoholic husbands and settlement of land disputes.[16]

## *Panchayati Raj*: Gender Exclusion

Obstacles to the realisation of PRI's transformative potential are many. There continues to be a resistance to really devolving power and funds from centres of (male) power to the periphery. Women still face considerable handicaps in their involvement in politics, for instance, inadequate education, the burden of reproductive and productive roles, a lack of self-confidence and the opposition of entrenched cultural and religious views. Therefore, exclusion takes many forms and is effected in a variety of ways. Some of the common gender exclusions could be broadly divided into two categories, namely social constraints and institutional constraints.

## Social Constraints

Social constraint is essentially the result of the patriarchal order of the Indian society that includes commonly observed phenomena of tokenism and surrogate representation. Such constraints also include illiteracy, which makes it impossible for the women to participate in the process of decision making that are dependent on the written word and the legalese of agenda, minutes and signatures. Caste is also a form of social constraint, as it mandates seclusion or places women members of low castes at twin mercies of patriarchy and caste position. Social constraints vary considerably, depending on the nature of local society, rather than territorial boundaries. Wherever structure of patriarchy and castes are more oppressive, the empowerment of women through *panchayati raj* institutions faces a formidable task. At places, where the caste structures are relatively less oppressive and patriarchy is weaker due to male migration, the participation of women members is less constricted.

The MARG study collected suggestions from women representatives on how to overcome seclusion in *panchayats*. One of the suggestions was to have a separate forum for women members where they could sit and share their opinion on issues related to the *panchayat* meeting. Once a consensus is reached between the women members on the issue, then it could be placed before the entire

16. CWDS (1999).

*panchayat*. Undoubtedly, it is evident that women representatives hesitate to participate as individuals, without undermining their strong desire to participate and have their voice heard.

**Box 6.9**

*Social Constraints: Field Observations*

- Lack of confidence among women members from low castes.
- '*Purdah*' or veil is a remnant of the patriarchal system and inhibits participation of women.
- Uneducated women representatives have been reticent on the issue of '*purdah*' or veil.
- Male members attempt to dominate the meetings without giving any space to women members to participate.
- Often the suggestions, opinions, petitions and recommendations of the women representatives are taken up negatively by the male members and usually ignored by the *pradhan*.
- Social customs do not allow women to speak before men, which seriously inhibits women representatives from mixing with the other male members and speaking in the *panchayat* meetings.
- Physical violence in *panchayat* elections and meetings often impedes women's participation in *panchayati raj*.

The exclusion of women representatives from effective decision making in *panchayat* institutions has been well documented. Several research studies have concluded that the attempt to empower women through quota based representation has resulted in tokenism. There is plenty of evidence of surrogate or proxy representation by husbands and other male members, who not only canvass for their women, but also receive notices to attend meetings in their place. For instance, the husband of a woman representative in Alwar district not only canvassed for his wife's election, but also had the banners printed with his name and picture on them. Husbands of women *pradhans* are often referred to as the *pradhan*, as they assume the authority of the *pradhan* and discharge the functions of the office. Given the patriarchal system of Indian society, surrogate representation is common across the country, with variations. Lieten (1996) observed that after the Amendment, there has not been any significant change in the functioning of *panchayats* - still there were large numbers of surrogate representation, rigging of elections through capture of polling booths, extensive corruption in developmental works, and an agenda that is devoid of social concerns because it reflects only the interests of the dominant local elite, represented by *pradhan*.

**Box 6.10**

*Surrogate Representation: Field Observations*

- General impression about *panchayat* election is that women stand a better chance of becoming a member of *panchayat* if they are illiterate, frail of body and of mind and rather old - Lieten (1996);
- Women *pradhans* are often for namesake, the real power lies with the husband or male member of the household - Pai (1998);
- Government of UP issued orders that husbands of women *pradhans* will not be allowed to enter their wives' offices (except for urgent work or to take part in meetings of village *panchayat*) to accept memoranda from villagers, and to travel in official vehicles - *Panchayati Raj Update* (1998);
- Some female *gram panchayat* members were not aware of their membership to the *panchayat* in Rajasthan, Uttar Pradesh and Himachal Pradesh - Kaushik (1998);
- Government officials are indifferent towards women representatives, but they respond immediately to male representatives - Athreya (1998);
- Ms. Mayawati, ex-Chief Minister of UP and the first *dalit* woman Chief Minister has set an example for the *dalits* to push their girl child for education. This phenomenon may be called proto-empowerment, as *dalit* women representatives have started actively participating in the *panchayat* meetings.

Literacy is another reason for seclusion. Without exception, every field survey on this issue has recognised that women representatives would have been better able to contribute to the *panchayat* proceedings and activities had they been educated. Women representatives find lack of education as a major shortcoming, especially to deal with government officials (block office and police). Women representatives also seek greater knowledge on the law and procedures of *panchayati raj* institutions. However, a study in Tamil Nadu contradicts the usual belief, where graduate women members feel that they are ignored and not taken seriously by the male counterparts in the *panchayat* meetings. The government officials often adopt dismissive attitude towards women representatives.

**Box 6.11**

*Lack of Education: Field Observations*

- Lack of education and knowledge about law and procedures of PRIs are major impediments for women representatives to deal with officials - MARG (1998);
- Almost 12 per cent of the surveyed women representatives in Rajasthan link their ineffectiveness to illiteracy - CWDS (1998);
- Male members and government officials adopt a dismissive attitude towards educated women representatives - Athreya (1998);
- Illiterate women representatives are often asked to collect their travel and daily allowance and leave, the resolutions are not read out and they are asked to put the thumb impression - Kaushik (1998);
- Often women representatives ask for besides education, training in leadership, legal literacy and gender justice - PRIA (2001).

Training to women representatives remains woefully inadequate and ineffective. Even the training provided lacks creativity and innovativeness, thus whatever benefit is imparted through the existing training programmes depends on the eagerness of the women to learn. More importantly, the training must address the need to create a consciousness about patriarchy and the social and cultural practices that adversely affect the performance of women representatives. Another issue that needs to be taken up is the process of organising and building networks and alliances. In fact, training programmes that impart gender-sensitivity to men hold the key to a more enlightened policy, even at the micro-level.

**Box 6.12**

*Other Constraints: Field Observations*

- More violence was reported in women reserved constituencies than in others in Uttar Pradesh, Madhya Pradesh and Rajasthan - CWDS (1998);
- Rival camps frequently resort to intimidation and violence towards the family members of the contesting women representatives - MARG (1998);
- After election, the elected women representatives for some time fear to move alone without escort due to fear of violence - Kaushik (1998);

- In Uttarkhand, a *panchayat* member accused government officials of sexual exploitation for granting approval to the proposed developmental work - Verma (1998);
- In Khandwa District, the elected women *sarpanch* was gang raped by the defeated rival party members - Kaushik (1998);
- In Pipra *Panchayat*, the *Yadav* community (OBC) resorted to violence towards the *dalit* woman *sarpanch*, for attempting to hoist the national flag as part of Independence Day celebrations - Sainath (1998);
- In Rajasthan, a *dalit* woman *sarpanch* was beaten up along with her family members by the higher castes for refusing to abide by their proposal - Matthew (1996).

Physical violence or threat of it, as well as many shades of intimidation and outright coercion, are not uncommon in Indian polity. Violence in *panchayat* elections is a routine occurrence, even much worse than State or Parliamentary elections. Apart from the familiar range of electoral malpractices, *panchayat* elections have also experienced intimidation, booth capturing, rigging and snatching of ballot papers and boxes, *etc*. Instances, such as mentioned, restrict wider women participation in PRIs.

Sexual abuse is also not uncommon. It is the most common form of punishment meted to erring women representatives acting against the demands of higher castes. However, there has been ample evidence of women representatives resorting to such insinuations to downplay the rivals for coveted *panchayat* positions. In many States, there have been attempts to intimidate women into withdrawing from the election by alleging affairs with men. Often *panchayat* meetings are held till late night, which also increases the chances of non-participation by women representatives.

Despite reservation of seats for women and members of *dalit* community, it is clear that the domination of the upper caste endures. In intra-family disputes and similar conflicts, it is the upper caste leaders that village folk tend to approach, rather than the *gram panchayat*. These castes also tend to influence the choice of candidates for elections, as well voting patterns. Hence to expect PRIs to work in a way that is insulated from the inequalities of local society may be Utopian.

## Institutional Constraints

Respective Conformity legislations specify the procedures for no-confidence motions against *sarpanch* and *up-sarpanch* at all the three tiers of the *panchayati raj* system. Many of these require two-thirds majority of elected members or maintaining the quorum, but such provisions are found to have been ingeniously used to effectively de-reserve a reserved seat. In many States, it was observed that there is a pattern in the use of such provisions, which are systematically used by male members to unseat women *pradhans* and *up-pradhans* and take control of the *panchayat* themselves. Although there are safeguard provisions within the State legislations[17] against misuse, these provisions are often bypassed. For instance, a *Zilla Panchayat* president in Saharanpur was actually thrown out by invoking this procedure. Likewise, a *pradhan* of a *gram panchayat* in Dehradun was threatened with a no-confidence motion, only because she refused to surrender the bank passbook to them. An inter-State comparison of no-confidence motions suggests clearly intersection of caste, class and gender.

### Box 6.13

*Surbaya Panchayat, Madhya Pradesh*

Bhakti Bai, an illiterate *adivasi* woman, was elected unopposed to serve as a prop for the influential *up-sarpanch* Anil Sharma. Bhakti Bai, heavily dependent on Sharma, initially functioned as his rubber stamp. This soon changed. In a land feud between Sharma and an *adivasi* (Narpat), Bhakti Bai favoured the *adivasi* Narpat. She also began chairing the *panchayat* meetings in the presence of Sharma. Insulted by this power play, Sharma used his influence and instituted a no-confidence motion against her, citing her illiteracy as the reason. Even Bhakti Bai signed the no-confidence motion against herself, ignorant of its content. Matters followed routinely and the date for re-election was fixed on the day when Bhakti Bai was attending the last rites of her son. Another *adivasi* woman, Sajende Bai was chosen as *sarpanch*. Ironically, Sajende Bai had no idea how she became the *sarpanch* or even who appointed her.

*Source: Women Leaders in Panchayat*, PRIA (2003).

17. In Rajasthan and Uttar Pradesh, the legislation prohibits a no-confidence motion in the first two years after elections, and again for a whole year after an unsuccessful no-confidence motion.

There are wide variations across States in the quorum required for a meeting, with some requiring one-third quorum, and others half. But no State provides for the mandatory presence of women representatives or members of SC/ST community. This makes it possible for the *sarpanch* to conduct meetings with his own community members and other male members to take decisions. The absence of women is quite evident at the *gram sabha* level. The *gram sabha* is precisely the level at which the invisibility of women is highest. Any initiative for democratisation is bound to be less than effective if mobilisation is enforced rather than spontaneous.

Another recent development is the two-child norm, which is in fact a legal provision rather than norm. The Rajasthan government issued an ordinance barring those who have more than two children from contesting *panchayat* elections. If a third child is born to a member after the election, the person will have to forfeit the seat. Under this provision, 450 persons were disqualified, out of which 112 were women, mostly at the *gram panchayat* level. Other States have also contemplated introducing such a norm. The High Courts of Rajasthan, Haryana and Orissa have upheld its validity, when approached by various agencies on grounds of incompatibility with *the Representation of the Peoples Act* and Muslim Personal Law. Such a provision clearly discriminates against individuals, especially women, because Indian women have little or no control over reproductive decisions.

## Key Issues: Women's Empowerment through PRIs

1. There is a lot of resistance from the male members of the village, due to their loss of power and significant positions in the affairs of the village. Often they adopt obstructive practices and create difficulties for the woman *sarpanch*. They also take advantage of women's ignorance regarding the procedural matters.

2. Women resisting the new concept, after the initial hesitation and indecision, were able to conduct meetings of the village council effectively. They secured support from some of the well-meaning members and thereby have their effective say in decision making.

3. Women members have their own agenda and priorities which include provision of drinking water, sanitation facility,

immunisation for children, implementation of mother-child care programme, primary education to ensure that females complete school, construction of roads, repair of *choupals*, arrangement of street lights *etc.*

4. Women have been found successful in dealing socially more effectively than their male counterparts, especially the menace of alcoholism, domestic violence, *etc.*, by passing resolutions in the '*Gram Sabha*'. They also became aware of and attempted to limit the sources of corruption at the village level.
5. Women members sought assistance from the male members in their families to overcome their functional difficulties. Inadequately placed with respect to household chores and dependent on men in their families for guidance and economic support, often women representatives avoided attending *panchayat* meetings and giving time to *panchayat* work.
6. Although women are elected representative of *panchayats*, they feel neglected. Male *pradhans* and husbands of some women *pradhans* did not allow the women to attend the training camps for social reasons. There are instances when invitation letters for attending the meetings were not distributed among the elected women representatives of *Panchayati Raj* Institutions (PRIs).
7. Women of higher castes realised that they were merely place holders because, although elected, the *de facto* power rests with the male members of the family and on the contrary, the lower caste women representatives enjoyed more freedom for attending meetings and training camps.
8. The bureaucracy has remained hostile to women representatives. The women representatives find the government officers intimidating and unresponsive. Besides, whenever they visit the district or block office, they rarely find female employees to deal with them.
9. Women representatives seem to be determined to bring about comprehensive development of their villages and to overcome the difficulties created by their male counterparts. The male members are slowly reconciling to the fact that women *sarpanches* are a reality.

10. Rural women show a keen interest in learning more about *panchayat* administration and community development. These changes among women brought respectability for them in the community. The women acquired confidence to share the experiences and also to learn from their peers.

In sum, there is a growing realisation among the women that local elections are a means of bringing positive change in their lives. They are motivated to change the traditions. These women seemed determined to bring about comprehensive development of their village and to overcome the difficulties created by their male counterparts. The male members had to reconcile to the fact that women *sarpanches* is a reality and they are capable of shouldering the responsibilities. In a nutshell, we can say that the empowerment and participation of women in the affairs of villages bodes well for the development of the village community.

## Women in *Panchayats*: Capacity Building and Systemic Improvements

There is also a need for a more enabling environment, which would allow PRI to become a process for the empowerment of women, not to mention other social groups who have been left out of participation in representative governance. Such an environment would include legal frameworks and services, as well as packages of technical support.

## Training

Once the election is over, women who are elected to the PRIs should receive training for their new office. Training should be a participatory process. The participants should be encouraged to draw political ideas from their own experiences as well as those of others. Ultimately, women will need to acquire a new set of values, behaviour patterns, attitudes, and methods of work and begin to make qualitative decisions about themselves, their homes and their communities. Stifled by oppressive and controlling patriarchal relations, rural women are often burdened by heavy work and encouraged to think not about themselves but about their husbands and families first. The programme must also impart essential information to women to carry out their responsibilities as *panchayat* leaders. Effective participation of women in the PRIs and its usefulness for women's rights and development will not materialise if the *'Panchayati Raj'* system itself does not operate in a democratic and meaningful way.

## Political Participation

The willingness of the people to participate in the political process is a basic requirement for a democracy. However, low literacy rates and limited mass communication alienate a large sector of the populace and need to be increased to help draw a larger number of women into the political mainstream.

"Political participation" means the involvement of citizens in activities aimed at influencing the government's decision, directly or indirectly. Political participation aims at pressuring the *panchayat* to maximise the allocation of resources for the benefit of women.

The central purpose of the participatory process is the awakening of women *panchayat* members' dormant energies and unleashing of their creative powers. The process of conscientisation, or the emerging awareness of one's previously stifled creativities, should also be an objective in women's political participation. Conscientisation leads to self organisation as means of undertaking initiatives.

## Organising Self-help Groups

*Panchayat* members can play the role of change agents, facilitators, group organisers and catalysts. Such groups, perhaps comprised of women from shared socio-economic backgrounds, would provide a forum for dialogue, analysis and reflection, thereby contributing to the capacity of the members to understand and find solutions to their problems. Second, membership in a group would reduce individual insecurities and dependencies and build confidence. Third, the groups could provide a mechanism for discussion, choice and elaboration of social and economic activities to be undertaken on individual or joint bases. Fourth, groups serve as one mechanism for the poor to transform their individual weaknesses into collective strengths, thus enhancing their bargaining power *vis-à-vis* other economic groups and exerting countervailing pressure against the local power structure.

Small group meetings are ideal forums not only for developing collective strength, unity, bargaining capacity, support and confidence, but also for the socio-economic, political and legal advancement of rural poor women through women's own efforts. Removing ignorance by dissemination of information and raising general awareness among the toiling villagers is possible through group meetings. The realisation of their capabilities, potentialities and role in society would strengthen their self-image and would foster them with confidence to take action in life on their own.

Thus, there is a need to provide women with specific kinds of support systems, which go beyond technical training. They need support to build solidarity amongst women, through strengthening links between women's organisations and elected bodies. They need information about innovative organisations, which enhance women's lives, such as health providers and credit institutions. It is also necessary to strengthen women's sense of common identity by articulating the elements of a proactive consciousness and presenting it as the special quality of women's leadership.

## Conclusions

If permanent changes are to take place in the status of women that give them control over their income, autonomy and self-confidence, women must have access to intervention programmes (such as micro-credit organisations). Alternatively, they themselves can organise to run income-generating activities on their own, but they must be supported by structural and institutional changes that allow them access to skill, leadership, decision-making and economic independence.

PRI reminds us of a central truth: power is not something people give away. It has to be negotiated, and sometimes wrested from the powerful. Enshrining political change within the law has forced both the pace and direction of such change. Democratic politics is, in reality, the interplay of vested interests and PRI's great achievement has been to mandate a vested, and mutual interest, between women and the political process. The lesson of PRI is clear: if the wisdom of grassroots organisations, especially the courage and clarity of women, is to become policy, it will not be through the art of intellectual persuasion, but by the arrangements made within a political system for their voice to have power. Bringing women into power is thus not only a matter of equity, of correcting an unjust and unrepresentative system. Many believe that the removal of poverty, the achievement of full employment and social integration cannot be effectively addressed without the democratisation of the representative process.

The above evaluation reflects on the difficulties that women power wielders have to face owing to the obstructionist attitude of the male folk and their dependence on them, owing the lack of experience. However, after assuming power, the women office bearers learn fast the rules of the game. In a decade after the amendment, women are performing their duties independently. They are also determining priorities in their villages. There is a wind of change in the *panchayat*s as these women act as "agents of change". These are excellent prospects for women to play a significant role in *Panchayat*i *Raj* of India in the years to come.

# 7

# The Working of Agricultural Cooperatives in India: Is there any Lesson to learn from the Chinese Experience?[1]

MOHAMMED SAQIB
DEBASHIS CHAKRABORTY

## Introduction

The co-operatives are defined by ICA as "an autonomous association of persons united voluntarily to meet their common economic, social, cultural needs and aspirations through a jointly-owned and democratically-controlled enterprise".[2] The co-operative movement did not originate in India on its own, but gained momentum from government regulations to save the farmers from exploitation of moneylenders. The major advantages enjoyed by the co-operative over individual farmers originate from efficient utilisation of economies of scale. While an individual farmer has to concentrate on each and every aspect, starting from obtaining credit to marketing of the final produce; a cooperative is capable of augmenting the income of the members through division of labour in production efficiently and bringing professionalism in marketing of the final produce. Stating this alternatively, cooperatives are a major source of market power to the members. Cooperatives can exist in two forms, either through horizontal organisation among producers or co-operatives (for selling of products at the primary stage), and vertical integration into value-added processing and distribution (for selling of products at the primary stage).

Co-operatives being a decentralised economic unit have distinct forward and backward linkages in the economy, where individual

1. For considering the status of cooperatives in India, the current analysis drawn from Dutta (2004).
2. Taimni (1998), p.56.

members have a say in the operation (exercised through voting rights). Their relevance in the Indian village economy is all the more important, owing to the land-holding structure prevalent here. Most of the farmers are placed under the category of marginal and small farmers (*i.e.*, with farm-size lower than one hectare). In Kerala the proportion of marginal farmers is maximum (48.77 per cent), followed by West Bengal, Uttar Pradesh, Bihar, Tamil Nadu and Tripura respectively. Owing to the small farm-size, the average small farmer is not in a position to purchase quality inputs, generate sufficient volume of marketable surplus and undertake risky projects (*e.g.* – diversification to cash crops). Given this scenario, the cooperatives have a tremendous potential in enhancing the economic condition of the members, by contributing in all of the above-mentioned areas. Datta and Singh (1998) have pointed out the following important functions of the cooperatives:

- Safeguarding the interests of a vast number of small and marginal farmers from the imperfections of the input market, production and agro-processing conditions and marketing framework.
- Controlling unfair treatment of the producers by private enterprises and setting up quality standards and norms of behaviour in the market place.
- Ensuring mass empowerment in general and empowerment of women, and weaker communities in particular, at the grass root level through a close link with the lowest tier of governance, *panchayats*. The point draws support from the experience of the successful sugar and milk cooperatives.[3]
- Bringing people below or near the poverty line back to the mainstream market structure through initial formation of self-help groups (SHGs) and producer cooperatives in the next phase, through provision of gainful employment.
- Guaranteeing environment-friendly quality products.

These projected advantages and functions of the cooperatives are supported by the spread of formal cooperatives in India, as well as the

3. "Suitable strategic alliance with local bodies (and not political subordination, as for example is the case in states with too powerful local bodies) can not only provide grass root level political support base to co-operatives, but also a steady source of demand for their services." Dutta (2004), p. 98.

informal ones like the self-help groups.[4] Although co-operatives developed as credit-sharing institutes, they have successfully diversified into other businesses as well, of which sugar (Maharashtra, Gujarat, Karnataka and Tamil Nadu) and milk commodity systems (Gujarat, Maharashtra, most southern states and parts of Rajasthan and Madhya Pradesh) deserves special attention. Cooperatives are also operational in other fields, which include marketing of oilseeds, spinning and weaving of cotton and other yarns and fabrics, leather products, handicrafts *etc.* The steady spread of the cooperatives in India as well as their effectiveness could be explained with the help of the following statistics:

- The total number of credit societies has increased from 124083 in 1950-51 to 140347 in 1999-2000.
- The total number of membership (in '000) has increased from 7785 in 1950-51 to 147482 in 1999-2000.
- The membership per primary agricultural credit society has increased from 46 in 1950-51 to 1072 in 1999-2000.
- The membership per primary non-agricultural credit society has increased from 279 in 1950-51 to 505 in 1999-2000.
- The total deposits and working capital per member has increased from Rs. 127.66 and Rs. 260.60 in 1950-51 to Rs. 27388.66 and Rs. 50149.19 respectively.

The steady increment in select variables for cooperatives portrays a rosy picture about their functioning. However, the situation is not that colourful for a formidable section of the vast number of cooperatives spread all over the country. In the current analysis, we briefly study the evolution of the legal framework for the cooperatives, and the inherent weakness in their mode of functioning. The scenario in rural India and the structure of the rural workforce is focused on next. The neighbouring country China also has a major section of the population living in the countryside, and they tried to improve the condition of the village and small towns through the network of Township and Village Enterprises (TVEs). A brief account

4. "In fact, in the state of Andhra Pradesh, many thrift groups continue to remain as SHGs, when they were not allowed to be registered under the traditional Co-operative Societies Act of that state; they became formal co-operatives, when they came forward for registration under the new and parallel Act instituted in 1995." Dutta (2004), p. 59.

of the TVE policies and realised success is presented. Finally, comparing the scenario in the two countries, certain policy conclusions are drawn.

## Evolution of Laws Related to Cooperatives in India

During late nineteenth century several laws, *e.g.* – *Deccan Agriculturists' Relief Act (1879), the Land Improvement Loans Act (1883)*, and *the Agriculturists' Relief Act (1884)* were passed to facilitate the co-operative movement, primarily to help credit-availability to farmers. *The Co-operative Credit Societies Act (1904)* was a major step, but the non-automatic nature of registration approval remained a problem area. Members were also not free to dissolve the cooperative, once formed. Although cooperatives were allowed to raise deposits from members without restrictions, borrowings from non-members as well as utilisation of the fund was subject to regulations and restrictions. *The Co-operative Law (1912)* tried to ease the regulatory nature of the 1904 Act, as its objective was changed from controlling the societies to the role of facilitator. The definition was expanded to include any form of cooperatives, and the concept of secondary co-operatives was also introduced. However, the power of the Registrar was still very much there. In later years, co-operative legislation became a provincial subject once *the Bombay Co-operative Societies Act (1925)* was passed. *The Co-operative Law (1932)*, though enhancing the power of the Registrar in certain respects, the registration provision was freed from his permission, and an appeal against refusal to register was placed. Two other important policy changes enacted in the 1932 Act need to be quoted. First, government aid to cooperatives in various forms (*e.g.* - shares, loans or other financial assistance) was allowed. Second, net profits were allowed to be divided among members, after keeping a portion of it for reserves. The second policy became instrumental in attracting participation of average Indian farmers.

Given the path of a planned economy chosen by the country since Independence, various laws and policies were introduced from time to time. While these laws enabled smooth functioning of the cooperatives in certain respects, the powers that the Registrar enjoyed over cooperatives and of certain other administrative bodies were also increased. Among the important laws enacted after independence, *Hyderabad Co-operative Societies Act (1952)* and *the Multi-State Co-operative Societies Act (MSCS Act, 1984)* deserve special mention. The second law is applied to co-operatives with members from more than one State, and this should have been instrumental for the vertically integrated cooperatives. However, the law failed to deliver much. In 2002 the Act was amended by Parliament, and afterwards in several other States across the country. It is expected that the cooperatives located in neighbouring States/various parts of the country would take advantage of the improved policy framework in the future.

In recent years, qualitative concerns in cooperative performance have been very important. Several years back, *the Andhra Pradesh Mutually Aided Co-operative Societies Act (MACS Act, 1995)* was passed for facilitating the operation of the co-operatives without having any share capital from the government. The registration process was simplified, and many rights of the registrar were taken away. Dutta (2004) has commented that instead of concentrating on the Registrar, as in the case of earlier Acts, the new law was drafted keeping the farmer member in view. In recent years, two major policy changes have taken place. *National Policy on Co-operatives (2002)* has recognised the constraints of their functioning, and recommended policies to enable them to witness professionalisation and democratisation of operation. The policies have been targeted to foster their development as self-reliant and economically viable units. On the other hand, section 581J of *the Companies (Amendment) Act, 2002* has enabled any inter-State co-operative society with objects not confined to one State to make an application to the Registrar for registration as Producer Company, which is likely to benefit the cooperatives in the long run

## The Weakness of Cooperatives in India

As noted by Dutta (2004) the major weaknesses of the cooperatives in India include the following:

- *Non-Harmonised Policy Framework*: Before announcement of *the National Policy on Cooperatives (2002)* and amendment of *the Multi-State Co-operative Societies Act* and *Companies' Act (2002)*, there was no appreciable policy thrust on the meaningful working of cooperatives as self-sufficient units in the market economy. Only a handful of State governments came forward to undertake the much-required step of liberalising cooperatives. The Central Government has also failed to implement the proposed *Model Cooperative Act*, which has been pending for a long time. Clearly, the cooperatives functioning as separate islands in the market economy, without vigour, failed to achieve much success.

- *Absence of a Comprehensive Taxation Policy*: A large number of cooperatives are financially not self-sufficient and suffer the problem of inefficient funding. The taxation policy adopted by the government should aim to facilitate the working of such cooperatives so that they can prosper with the help of suitable financial incentives. Unfortunately, inadequately equipped and unevenly applied tax laws of private and co-operative enterprises tax policy and its implementation creates more bias against working of cooperatives than it solves. The cooperatives have often been subjected to an ambiguous status in assessment of income and other taxes, which imposes arbitrary and disproportionate tax burdens on them. In addition, the prevailing situation encourages higher-tier co-operatives to save tax burden by distributing all surplus earnings rather than building up reserves for future expansion. The existence of multiple agencies dealing with co-operatives has resulted in a multiplicity of controls, procedures and guidelines that need to be followed, and a harmonisation in the functioning of various funding agencies is the need.
- *Variation in State Laws*: Since, agriculture and co-operatives are State subjects, a number of rules, regulations, policies as well as political interests dominate the working of cooperatives at the State level. However, the extent of this problem has declined in these days owing to introduction of parallel Co-operative Acts being introduced in one State after another.
- *Utilisation for Government Planning*: The government involvement in ensuring smooth operation of the cooperatives practically turned the latter into quasi-government organisations for implementation of social development programmes. Consequently, cooperatives often ended up functioning as government target-meeting instrument for disbursement of cheap loans, grants

and other benefits rather than performance-based independent units.[5]

- *Excessive Government Control*: The cooperatives are supposed to function with local participation on the basis of democratic principles. Although government participation in equity, *i.e.*, in guaranteeing the debt of a co-operative brings certainty, excessive powers in the hands of the Registrar severely constrained the principle of democratic control, apart from practically lowering the stakes, which in turn affected innovative activities within the cooperatives. However, after implementing the parallel Co-operative Societies Act in a number of States, this constraint is gradually declining in importance.
- *Problems in Undertaking Right Decisions*: The management decision is often driven not by market demand or qualitative concerns, but by the existing regulations cited by the bureaucracy. Because of the excessive stress on maintaining the institutional framework, co-operatives suffer from poor forward and backward linkages. Ironically, the working of co-operative promotional activities often end up hurting the cooperatives more than consequent gains, and causes a poor co-ordination across tiers and also within a tier.
- *Poor Quality of Management*: A vast majority of cooperatives are severely cash-constrained, and therefore fails to attract leading professionals in management. To make things worse, most of the co-operative boards consist of government-nominated Directors, who are generally averse to the idea of adopting innovative strategies, and prefer to operate along traditional lines instead. They never properly appreciate the business potential of the raised deposit, utilisation of the credit, and disposal and reinvestment of the revenue generated. In most of cooperatives, the farmer members are still considered as depositors or borrowers, and not as integral part of the business unit, as the case should be. In this background, the modest performances of the majority of the cooperatives are quite natural.

---

5. *Khusro Committee* pointed out the problems faced by the cooperative movement: 'The co-operatives have been subject to undue governmental interference and the elected bodies have been superceded frequently. They have thus been prevented from developing steadily as a self-reliant and resilient credit system. The secretary of the PACs barring exception, is a badly chosen, ill-equipped, non-professional and low-paid functionary with little motivation'. (Khusro 1989, p. 7), Dutta (2004), pp. 129-130.

Dutta (2004) has noted that the condition for the cooperatives is yet to change, as the new credit planning mechanism is often more restrictive for their activities. As a result, the loss-making cooperatives are compelled to rely more on the officials of the State cooperative departments (who are the prosecutor, judge and the executor in those situations according to State laws). The bureaucratic controls further lower the efficiency of the cooperatives.

The difference in performance of two distinct groups of cooperatives needs to be highlighted. Wherever producer farmers have taken the membership of the cooperative, the performance remained more than satisfactory, as the system is run in that case in a businesslike fashion. For instance, the case of the milk producers and sugarcane growers in Maharashtra should be quoted. In all these cases, a clearly discernible production enhancement effort preceded and adequately matched the output marketing efforts, and in the later years, the co-operatives played a key role for development of the member-farmers in particular and village communities in general. In particular, the experience of Amul, set up in the sixties is worth mentioning, which has immensely influenced the lifestyle of the persons under its coverage. Proper planning matched by efficient marketing strategies has ensured their success.

In order to change the scenario, the *Pant Committee* recommended initiation of business development planning (BDP) in cooperatives, and the National Co-operative Union of India (NCUI) started BDP training programmes for cooperative managers and leaders from various States since 1991. However, studying the government initiatives to promote BDP in Indian co-operatives, various studies have concluded that their effectiveness till date is quite modest. On the basis of a survey in Maharashtra, Gujarat and West Bengal, Dutta and Kapoor (2000) commented, "The conspicuous absence of the process part of BDP gets amply manifested in two case studies. Even though both societies are very serious about implementation of BDP and doing everything possible to promote members' interests, because of past traditions and the present level of understanding of BDP, they seem to have taken a rather narrow, mechanistic and static view of BDP so that its presence or absence does not make much difference".[6]

---

6. Dutta and Kapoor (2000), pp. 18-20, quoted in Dutta (2004).

## The Rural Scenario

In Tables 7.1 and 7.2, we compare the changing composition of the rural workforce in India. Before going into further details, we define the professions quoted here first. For Census purposes, a cultivator is defined as a person who is engaged either as employer, single worker or family worker in cultivation of land owned or held from private persons or institutions for payment in money, kind or share. An agricultural labourer is defined as a person who works in another person's land for wages in money, kind or share, without any right or claim on the land. The persons engaged in rural non-farm activities are placed in the other two categories. Also the Census classifies the working population in two categories, main workers and marginal workers, with respect to the duration of their work. The main workers are defined as those persons whose main activity was participation in any economically productive work by his physical or mental activities and who has worked for 183 days or more. The definition of work includes not only actual work, but also effective supervision and direction. Similarly, marginal workers are defined as those persons whose main activity was participation in any economically productive work by his physical or mental activities for less than 183 days. Although the reasons behind the structural changes in employment pattern are an area of extensive research, a few brief comments are made.

From Table 7.1, it is seen that the proportion of cultivators and agricultural labourers among main workers are slowly declining in most of the States, the rate of change being very high for States like Kerala and Punjab. Other States are not far behind. However, the situation has not changed much in Madhya Pradesh, Maharashtra, Rajasthan and certain North-Eastern states. The relative shift towards rural non-farm activities is a welcome move, which should be strengthened through the cooperative movement.

In Table 7.2, the similar trend in case of marginal workers is shown. It seems the shift towards the industry and the service sector is even stronger as compared to the same for main workers. The network of value-added cooperatives is, *i.e.*, the cooperatives involved in vertical activities should be made stronger for utilising this workforce transformation.

## Table 7.1

*Sectoral Trends in Employment from the Census Data*

| *States* | *Cultivators* | | | *Agricultural Labourers* | | | *Household Industry Workers* | | | *Other Workers* | | |
|---|---|---|---|---|---|---|---|---|---|---|---|---|
| | *1981* | *1991* | *2001* | *1981* | *1991* | *2001* | *1981* | *1991* | *2001* | *1981* | *1991* | *2001* |
| Andhra Pradesh | 38.39 | 33.42 | 31.79 | 42.01 | 47.38 | 41.42 | 4.49 | 4.66 | 4.42 | 15.11 | 14.54 | 22.38 |
| Arunachal Pradesh | 75.04 | 67.46 | 68.15 | 2.57 | 5.31 | 2.93 | 0.24 | 0.61 | 0.96 | 22.15 | 26.62 | 27.96 |
| Bihar | 47.95 | 47.66 | 34.88 | 38.71 | 40.39 | 46.21 | 2.28 | 2.27 | 3.34 | 11.06 | 9.68 | 15.57 |
| Gujarat | 50.34 | 46.10 | 41.55 | 29.62 | 30.68 | 26.28 | 2.31 | 1.99 | 1.67 | 17.73 | 21.23 | 30.49 |
| Haryana | 55.80 | 50.63 | 48.08 | 19.68 | 24.16 | 12.81 | 2.57 | 2.33 | 2.07 | 21.95 | 22.88 | 37.03 |
| Himachal Pradesh | 73.14 | 70.76 | 61.66 | 2.86 | 3.72 | 2.01 | 1.82 | 2.07 | 1.84 | 22.18 | 23.45 | 34.50 |
| Karnataka | 47.81 | 43.99 | 44.56 | 32.37 | 35.71 | 26.37 | 3.53 | 2.35 | 3.59 | 16.29 | 17.95 | 25.47 |
| Kerala | 15.31 | 15.29 | 9.37 | 32.46 | 30.77 | 15.84 | 3.86 | 3.76 | 3.36 | 48.37 | 50.18 | 71.43 |
| Madhya Pradesh | 59.95 | 61.20 | 58.51 | 27.45 | 27.00 | 25.21 | 3.04 | 2.54 | 3.20 | 9.56 | 9.26 | 13.08 |
| Maharashtra | 47.86 | 46.33 | 45.59 | 35.14 | 36.80 | 33.32 | 2.22 | 2.40 | 2.02 | 14.78 | 14.47 | 19.07 |
| Manipur | 72.02 | 64.78 | 53.69 | 4.90 | 9.19 | 6.75 | 8.41 | 6.10 | 5.60 | 14.67 | 19.93 | 33.96 |
| Meghalaya | 71.80 | 64.64 | 60.03 | 11.12 | 14.99 | 14.63 | 0.72 | 0.87 | 1.92 | 16.36 | 19.50 | 23.42 |
| Mizoram | 82.86 | 80.95 | 81.66 | 1.32 | 2.27 | 2.01 | 0.44 | 0.57 | 0.73 | 15.38 | 16.21 | 15.60 |
| Nagaland | 80.74 | 77.18 | 74.88 | 0.78 | 5.22 | 1.89 | 0.22 | 1.40 | 1.57 | 18.28 | 16.20 | 21.65 |
| Orissa | 51.78 | 49.30 | 42.03 | 30.14 | 31.64 | 25.49 | 3.26 | 3.47 | 4.46 | 14.82 | 15.59 | 28.03 |
| Punjab | 47.73 | 45.10 | 34.88 | 28.52 | 30.53 | 18.74 | 2.27 | 2.09 | 2.82 | 21.48 | 22.28 | 43.56 |
| Rajasthan | 73.13 | 71.47 | 67.38 | 8.36 | 11.67 | 6.92 | 2.74 | 2.11 | 2.27 | 15.77 | 14.75 | 23.43 |
| Sikkim | 69.96 | 63.45 | 53.05 | 3.77 | 8.67 | 4.74 | 0.81 | 1.52 | 1.53 | 25.46 | 26.36 | 40.67 |
| Tamil Nadu | 38.28 | 33.06 | 30.90 | 40.27 | 44.52 | 36.39 | 3.81 | 4.04 | 4.82 | 17.64 | 18.38 | 27.89 |
| Tripura | 47.71 | 44.09 | 33.45 | 26.29 | 26.25 | 22.20 | 1.45 | 1.90 | 2.36 | 24.55 | 27.36 | 41.99 |
| Uttar Pradesh | 68.41 | 62.63 | 57.95 | 17.91 | 21.85 | 18.14 | 2.83 | 3.17 | 4.53 | 10.85 | 12.35 | 19.37 |
| West Bengal | 40.20 | 37.95 | 27.92 | 33.58 | 32.17 | 27.60 | 3.55 | 4.88 | 6.74 | 22.67 | 25.00 | 37.74 |
| **India** | **50.95** | **48.22** | **44.22** | **30.09** | **32.29** | **26.41** | **3.07** | **3.10** | **3.63** | **15.89** | **16.39** | **25.74** |

*Source:* Census Data

## Table 7.2

*Sectoral Trends Among Marginal Workers from the Census Data*

| *States* | *Cultivators* | | *Agricultural Labourers* | | *Other Categories as a % of All India Figure* | | *Marginal Workers* | |
|---|---|---|---|---|---|---|---|---|
| | *1991* | *2001* | *1991* | *2001* | *1991* | *2001* | *1991* | *2001* |
| Andhra Pradesh | 27.59 | 8.74 | 60.41 | 74.43 | 11.98 | 16.83 | 5.32 | 6.43 |
| Arunachal Pradesh | 81.69 | 70.49 | 15.68 | 12.37 | 2.62 | 17.15 | 0.02 | 0.08 |
| Bihar | 47.52 | 21.21 | 49.23 | 64.98 | 3.23 | 13.81 | 7.87 | 8.22 |
| Gujarat | 36.38 | 27.83 | 51.32 | 53.15 | 12.28 | 19.02 | 9.07 | 4.80 |
| Haryana | 68.55 | 40.64 | 28.87 | 33.40 | 2.56 | 25.96 | 1.40 | 2.39 |
| Himachal Pradesh | 94.82 | 85.10 | 3.86 | 5.65 | 1.41 | 9.25 | 1.60 | 1.25 |
| Karnataka | 50.48 | 18.69 | 41.88 | 64.16 | 7.62 | 17.15 | 5.65 | 4.54 |
| Kerala | 24.70 | 7.90 | 41.66 | 33.29 | 33.62 | 58.81 | 2.60 | 2.07 |
| Madhya Pradesh | 56.36 | 34.10 | 38.29 | 55.71 | 5.33 | 10.19 | 12.25 | 7.58 |
| Maharashtra | 50.49 | 29.69 | 43.91 | 56.08 | 5.59 | 14.23 | 9.91 | 6.70 |
| Manipur | 41.99 | 37.21 | 48.04 | 25.89 | 9.96 | 36.91 | 0.17 | 0.28 |
| Meghalaya | 73.82 | 43.07 | 22.54 | 37.23 | 3.63 | 19.69 | 0.14 | 0.24 |
| Mizoram | 84.76 | 78.02 | 12.78 | 10.33 | 2.44 | 11.65 | 0.07 | 0.07 |
| Nagaland | 72.84 | 66.42 | 24.35 | 13.80 | 2.79 | 19.78 | 0.01 | 0.16 |
| Orissa | 29.59 | 17.84 | 62.23 | 63.45 | 8.17 | 18.71 | 5.51 | 5.59 |
| Punjab | 41.91 | 15.10 | 55.25 | 36.92 | 2.82 | 47.97 | 0.58 | 1.38 |
| Rajasthan | 71.98 | 59.62 | 25.45 | 24.96 | 2.56 | 15.43 | 11.55 | 7.30 |
| Sikkim | 69.52 | 62.15 | 22.73 | 16.37 | 7.73 | 21.48 | 0.01 | 0.06 |
| Tamil Nadu | 28.15 | 10.91 | 63.97 | 71.38 | 7.86 | 17.70 | 4.69 | 4.05 |
| Tripura | 52.06 | 25.89 | 36.94 | 45.48 | 10.99 | 28.63 | 0.20 | 0.29 |
| Uttar Pradesh | 59.98 | 27.16 | 34.47 | 54.07 | 5.53 | 18.76 | 12.26 | 16.63 |
| West Bengal | 43.48 | 18.82 | 32.65 | 48.34 | 23.86 | 32.84 | 4.73 | 7.16 |
| **India** | **51.08** | **28.94** | **42.61** | **51.89** | **6.30** | **19.17** | **100.00** | **100.00** |

*Source:* Census Data

## Township and Village Enterprises (TVEs) in China

Owing to the diversity in ownership and management, it is not possible to provide a unique definition of TVEs. *The Law of Township and Village Enterprises* of China does not help much in clarifying this issue either, where they are defined as any enterprises located in the rural area and funded by the collectively owned rural economic organisations or rural residents to engage in agriculture-related economic activities.[7] Weitzman and Xu (1994) and Li (1996) emphasised the ambiguous nature of TVEs' property rights arrangements, arguing that TVEs are coalitions of local governments and private entrepreneurs. Chang and Wang (1994), Naughton (1994), and Che and Qian (1998) have considered them as organisations assigned to control rights to the local government and distributing benefits to the government, nominal owners of TVEs and the rural residents in these towns and villages.

A TVE can be defined as a (typically industrial) community enterprise belonging to all residents of a rural community, where it is also usually located, with a governance structure controlled by the community government. A rural community can be either a township (about 3,500 households) or a village (about 200 households), with each community usually having a number of such enterprises. The collection of TVEs in a community can be viewed as one firm, since the community governments rather than the enterprises themselves exercise most strategic control rights. Functionally, community residents, community government and individual TVEs represent the major beneficiaries of the firm, the board of directors and management at the headquarters of the firm, and divisions, branches, or subsidiaries within the firm respectively. In other words, the three-tier structure resembles that of conventional, publicly held multi-divisional corporations.

## Evolution of TVEs in China

The TVEs' operations can broadly be divided into three groups, (i) pre-1979 period, (ii) 1979-1993, and (iii) the period since 1994. The community-owned enterprises were first explored since 1958, but the small-scale industrial enterprises run by communes, eventually

7. TVEs functionally include the privately owned enterprises within its purview. A circular issued by the State Council of China (1984) clearly stated that TVEs include four types of enterprise: (i) enterprises owned by townships; (ii) enterprises owned by villages; (iii) cooperatives formed by groups of rural residents; and (iv) private family businesses. While the first two are closer to collectives operational in communist regime, the last two closely resemble the private firms in a market economy. Despite considering TVEs as non-state sector, a substantial proportion of their output is produced by enterprises collectively owned by township governments and villages, and not by privately owned enterprises.

collapsed. The Ministry of Agriculture (MoA), through its Township Enterprise Bureau (TEB), took the initiative for TVEs and the exercise was initiated in the 1970s. In early years, farmers' collectives ran the units and the produced items included agricultural inputs, farm machinery, agro-products and other low value-added goods (Wong, 1991). In the eighties, a change was noticed when a number of urban enterprises, in a cost-cutting bid, shifted part of their production units to TVEs, which was encouraged by the government.[8] The community enterprises, known as "commune and brigade enterprises" then (predecessor of TVEs), fast emerged as sub-contractors of SOEs in nearby urban areas. The total output value of these units increased from 9.25 billion Yuan in 1970 to 27.2 billion Yuan in 1976, with an average annual real growth rate of 25.7 per cent (p.10, Byrd and Lin 1990). By 1978, their total output value increased to 49.3 billion Yuan (pp.389-390, *Statistical Yearbook of China,* 1992), of which 38.5 billion Yuan was for industrial output, accounting for 9 per cent of the national industrial output (p.1, *Xiangzhen Qiye Tongji Ziliao,* 1992).

During 1979-1993, TVEs grew at great speed, especially after abolishment of the commune system in 1984, when commune and brigade enterprises were formally renamed as township and village enterprises. This period coincided with replacement of the commune production scheme in agriculture by the household responsibility system and rural industrialisation received a big push.[9] Between 1978 and 1993, the share of industrial output of TVEs increased steadily from 9 per cent to 27 per cent. Although the government issued many encouraging policy directives to help the TVEs, the county governments were entrusted to supervise their functioning.

Since 1994, the changing atmosphere turned more favourable for TVEs. Organisational efficiency was brought through selling of shares to employees and managers or community residents (as "joint-stock cooperatives"), partial privatisation through sales of control rights to

---

8. However, evasion of strict pollution control norms and other environmental regulations were also part of the driving motive for the firms to move to the rural belt. On the other hand, the government found this move favourable for reducing the growing rural-urban inequality.

9. At the end of 1992, China had 48,200 townships and 806,000 villages. On average, each township with a population of about 18,000 had 8.2 township enterprises with 66 employees per enterprise, and each village with a population of about 1,000 had 1.4 village enterprises with 23 employees per enterprise (p.15 and p.395, Statistical Yearbook of China, 1993).

managers and employees or to foreign investors *etc.* Although the community governments continued to hold a minority stake in the partially privatised former TVEs, they mainly concentrated on investing in infrastructure (*e.g.*, power supplies, roads and harbours) and other conventional public works, which immensely benefited the units. Also it is argued that the direct election of village leaders by village residents played a key role in efficient management of TVEs as well.[10] In short, by 1998, the traditional family-style management in the enterprises was replaced by collectively owned, individually run, joint stock cooperatives or foreign-funded firms, turning them into proper business ventures.

## Legal Regulation on the Governance of TVEs

China adopted a law on TVEs at the 22nd Meeting of the Standing Committee of the Eighth National People's Congress on October 29, 1996, which was later promulgated by Order No. 76 of the President of the People's Republic of China, dated October 29, 1996. The law, with 43 articles, became effective from January 1, 1997 onwards.

This Law is enacted for the purpose of facilitating and guiding the sustained development of enterprises, which were established in townships (including the villages under their jurisdiction) with the bulk of their capital being invested by rural economic collectives or farmers, with obligations to support agriculture. The objectives of TVEs included:

- Developing production of commodities in light of market demands;
- Providing service to the public;
- Increasing the supply of marketable products;
- Absorbing surplus rural labour;
- Helping in raising farmers' income;
- Supporting agriculture, advance agricultural and rural modernisation.

10. By 1995, about one-third of the villages had already formulated "village self-governing charters", more than one-half of the villages had established "village resident congress", and more than 90 per cent of village residents had participated in the elections. It is also reported that to promote direct election in villages, China has established model villages in 63 counties, in 3,917 townships and in 82,266 villages (*People's Daily*, November 15, 1995).

It is broadly seen from various provisions of the law that the State restricted its activity to provision of support to TVEs in terms of planning and guidance in various forms, although management was TVE responsibility. The TVEs were free to undertake re-registration under a different name, breaking up or merger with other TVEs. The Law explicitly stated the property right provisions in this case, and the same, depending on categories, was either owned collectively by all the farmers who contributed in establishing the enterprise, or by the investors in proportion to the amount of their shares. The TVE has full responsibility for its own profits and losses. In case of close down of firms, the employees coming under a labour contract receive some social insurance. The governments at or above the county level can also create development funds for TVEs in accordance with the relevant regulations of the State Council, which also advises on the use and management of this. The TVEs are free to enter into economic and technological cooperation and exchange with other countries, by building export-oriented commodity production bases, subject to fulfillment of certain conditions. They also need to pay a close attention to quality control as well as quality improvement and adoption of environment-friendly production techniques. The government approves certain benefits to the TVEs in terms of tax treatment. However, if any TVE refuses to undertake its obligations for supporting agriculture, and fails to do so even after warning, it will not receive the benefits any more. However, three major issues, as seen from the regulations, need special mention.

First, the TVE assets are legally owned by the residents of the township or village, not by enterprise employees or residents outside the community. The provisions, are as follows: "Assets (of a TVE) are owned collectively by the whole of rural residents of the township or village who run the enterprise; the ownership rights over the enterprise assets shall be exercised by the rural residents' meeting (or congress) or a collective economic organisation that represents the whole of rural residents of the township or village. The ownership rights of the enterprise assets will not change when the enterprise is under a managerial contract responsibility system, leasing, or joint operations with enterprises of other types of ownership".[11] In other

11. Zhonghua *et al.* (1990), Article 18, Chapter 3, p.81.

words, the local population has a considerable interest to ensure smooth working of the TVEs.

Second, the owner has the control rights over economic decisions, which could also be delegated or shared with an agency representing the community. The purview of the owner includes, "The owner of a TVE, according to the law, determines the direction and formats of its business operations, selects managers or determines the method of such selection, determines the specific distribution ratios of after-tax profits between the owner and the enterprise, and has the rights over the enterprise concerning its spin-off, merger, relocation, stop operation, close-down, application for bankruptcy, *etc.*"[12]

Finally, the regulation restricts the use of revenue and distribution of after-tax profits of TVEs strictly for two purposes – reinvestment and provision of local public goods. The regulation states, "The part retained by the enterprise should be no less than 60 per cent of the total and should be arranged under the enterprise's autonomous decision. The retained after-tax profits for the enterprise should be mainly used for the increase of the funds for production development in technological transformation and expansion of reproduction, and also for the appropriate increase of welfare funds and bonus funds." In addition, the law requires, "the part remitted to the owner of the enterprise should be used mainly for the support of construction of agricultural infrastructures, agriculture technology services, rural public welfare, renewal and transformation of enterprises, or development of new enterprises".[13]

## TVEs: The Fact Sheet

Over the last 20 years of China's reforms, the development of township and village enterprises enabled the national economy to advance at a healthy rate. Through adjustment of the ownership structure, they significantly contributed to the establishment of an industrial and city civilisation to vast rural areas, enabling farmers to improve their caliber as a whole. The remarkable development of the non-state sector, and the changes in industrial and employment structures in rural areas led to the development of small towns and

12. Zhonghua *et al.* (1990), Article 19, Chapter 3, p. 84.
13. Zhonghua *et al.* (1990), Article 32, Chapter 5, p. 137.

villages, by effectively improving the production conditions of agriculture, stimulating the transformation of traditional farming to a modern one, apart from promoting the national economy. The direct export permit to select TVEs through four permissible channels was another major policy initiative, although a formidable section of TVEs still faces substantial barriers to export.[14] For instance, out of a total number of 24.53 million TVEs in 1993, only 156 TVEs were granted direct export privileges, although the excluded ones had the right to be subcontractors for firms with export orders. The broad achievements of TVEs are the following:

- In 2001, there were 21.15 million township enterprises, which increased by 19.63 million compared with that in 1978.
- The proportion of non-farming industries in the rural economy climbed from 30.5 per cent in 1978 to 67.2 per cent in 2001.
- In 1997, TVEs in China produced an output value of 1800 billion Yuan (nearly 30 per cent of GDP), and rural secondary and tertiary industries accounted for 75.6 per cent of the whole rural economy, by employing 130 million rural surplus labourers.
- The revenue, value added and profit for the TVEs in the first half of 2004 was as high as 8,261.3 billion Yuan (around 995.3 billion dollars), 2,018.6 billion Yuan (around 243 billion dollars) and 470.6 billion Yuan (around 57 billion US dollars) respectively.[15] The official expectation is that the high growth rate would continue.[16]
- The TVEs have been instrumental in transferring around 29 per cent of China's 480 million rural labourers from farming to non-farming activities.
- In 1998, the townships achieved 2,400 billion yuan of value addition, 750.2 billion yuan of export, and 644 billion yuan of profit and tax.

---

14. The export channels available for TVEs include, (i) the traditional channel through state-owned foreign trade companies, who purchase TVE's' products to export them, (ii) through joint ventures formed with the state-owned foreign trade companies, (iii) through joint ventures formed with foreign enterprises, and (iv) through direct export if TVEs are considered large enough to obtain export licenses.

15. Bureau of township enterprises, Government of People's Republic of China, recent issues.

16. The bureau predicts Chinese Township businesses will realise a 12 per cent growth in value added over the whole year (*xinhuanet*), dated 29th July 2004.

- TVEs' export reached US$ 25 billion in 1993, accounting for more than 41 per cent of China's total exports of US$ 61 billion.

## The Role of Community Government

Since the community governments[17] of townships and villages enjoy full autonomy over both government and business activities within the community, because of the decentralisation exercise (Wong 1992, Qian and Xu 1993, Qian and Weingast 1996), they undertake a wide variety of government activities, ranging from maintaining social order to providing basic living conditions (*e.g.*, sanitary facilities), and building local infrastructure (*e.g.*, roads) to implementing family planning policy. In addition to these traditional government functions, the community governments in China are engaged in organising local business as well. However, as the lowest level of government in rural areas, the community governments have limited power in dealing with state financial institutions and the rural sector has not been incorporated into the state industrial system (Byrd and Lin 1990, and Ma *et al.* 1994). Therefore, instead of ordering a bank to provide funds, the community governments are forced to negotiate the terms of financing with banks. In other words, the TVEs are financially more constrained than the SOEs.

Studying the role of community government, Byrd and Lin (1990) and Oi (1994) had found that although most TVEs enjoy a considerable degree of enterprise autonomy, it is largely restricted to daily operational decisions or management. Stated alternatively, the community government reserves the right to undertake three types of strategic decisions – in the areas of (i) investment and finance, (ii) selection of managers, and (iii) the use of after-tax profits for public expenditure.

**Investment and finance:** Both studies found that most projects set up by TVEs have to be approved by community governments, which play a key role in internal fund raising (either from collective accumulation or from individual contributions), securing loans (from either the Agriculture Bank of China or Rural Credit Cooperatives) or

17. It is worth mentioning that the governmental hierarchy in China has six layers: central, provincial, prefecture, county, township and village (a municipality is assigned a level of provincial, prefecture, or county depending on size).

provision of several levels of service *etc.* The township and village governments may provide loan guarantees for TVEs, or initiate the process of bargaining and borrowing from the banks for them. TVEs are also permitted to use the community assets (which could be assets of other enterprises in the same community) as equity or collateral. Finally, in some cases, the community governments shoulder the responsibility for repayment if the borrowing TVE cannot pay it back.[18] Without the community government's involvement, it is usually very difficult, if not impossible, for TVEs to obtain loans directly from either the ABC or RCCs.

**Selection and rewarding of TVE managers:** Although managers are employed by TVEs through contract, specifying tenure and compensation schemes, the community government represents the owner of TVEs in negotiating the form of contracts (*e.g.*, fixed-wage, profit-sharing, or leasing contracts) and signs the contract with the managers.

**Use of after-tax profits for public expenditure***:* The community government has direct control over two parts of after-tax profits from TVEs; the first part is remitted directly to the community government ("management fees"), and the second part, although retained by TVEs, is earmarked for public expenditures. The remaining portion is used for reinvestment under community government surveillance, and an increasing trend has been noticed.[19]

## Recent Policies

Various policies have been introduced in China from time to time to help the TVEs, of which a few noteworthy ones are mentioned in brief:

- A new government policy has been introduced, where all commercial banks were told to establish Small Enterprise Credit Departments to supply loans to profitable small firms.

18. The repayment of bad loans by community governments are usually done through their fiscal budgets, or from after-tax profit remittances, or by arranging for other TVEs to repay them.

19. In 1985, about 46 per cent of TVEs' after-tax profits were reinvested and 49 per cent was used for local public expenditure, including 12 per cent for welfare. In 1992, 59 per cent of TVEs' after-tax profits was reinvested and 40 per cent was used for local public expenditure, including 9 per cent used for welfare. *Statistical Survey of China*, 1992, p.67; *Statistical Survey of China*, 1993, p.67.

- The government promised to increase investment in high-tech firms, in infrastructure and the development of small cities, as a support measure to TVEs.
- For developing the less prosperous western provinces, local governments in those parts were encouraged to adopt more favourable policies regarding credit, land use and taxation in order to attract investment, qualified personnel and advanced technology. They were also encouraged to develop border trade with neighbouring countries.
- For raising the competitiveness of non-agricultural TVEs, technical innovations in 3,000 promising medium and large TVEs, 500 top agricultural processing TVEs, and funding of new technology has been promised.
- Also for revitalising the TVE sector as a whole, the government declared that the weaker ones could be sold, annexed, declared bankrupt or turned into cooperative shareholding or joint-stock companies, taking care not to erode collective funds. On the other hand, viable TVEs were encouraged to expand their economies of scale and explore market opportunities.
- To increase financing, 40 TVEs were allowed to list on the Shanghai and Shenzhen stock exchanges since 1993, but the number declined to 29 by October 1999.

The Township Enterprise Bureau (TEB), for revitalising TVEs, has called for the lifting of illegal fines and arbitrary quotas imposed on them. They are also working on optimisation of TVE potential by upgrading their technology, enhancing enterprise management, attracting urban talent, preferential policies on taxes, loans and development funds and better enforcement of Township Enterprise Law by recommending specific regulations to support the law's enforcement. Also, alternate financing for TVEs were being sourced, as competition with SOEs turned out to be harmful for them. The TEB is asking for more support to the sick TVEs, in the form of clearing of bad debts by banks, and merger of bankrupt TVEs with SOEs, where competition would be uneconomic to both.

## Conclusion

Various studies have come out with policy prescriptions to enhance the performance of the cooperatives in India from time to time. Citing the lessons learnt from the experiences of the Prawara

Sugar Cooperative in Maharashtra, the Amul Co-operative Dairy in Gujarat and some experiences from a few South-east Asian countries, Gupta and Gaikwad (1985) recommended that marketing of farmer-members' produce should be the central activity of co-operatives. They also advised against limiting the basic unit of planning for agro-processing cooperatives by traditional geographical boundaries – village, block and district approach. The study suggested that the determination should be based on the command area needed to supply requisite quantity of raw material as determined by the installed capacity of the processing unit.

Dutta (2004) has suggested the following policies for the cooperatives in the future:

- Adoption of progressively input-intensive agricultural policy, with greater emphasis on high-value crops, leading to a favourable demand situation, both in terms of quantity and quality.
- Displaying greater degree of self-reliance for mobilisation of resources and functioning with autonomy.
- Reorientation for serving the original purpose of creation – building commercially viable alternative institutions to meet the demands of the disadvantaged sections.
- Building timely and adequate recoveries of dues and ensuring a climate that encourages income generation from borrowings and repayment through additional income.
- Ensuring increasing focus on building of strategic alliances and partnerships for business development planning for co-operatives.
- Ensuring active participation by the marketing cooperatives in marketing of agricultural produce. In addition, the capital formation and R&D expenditure in them needs to be enhanced.

A number of studies have focused on the role of information technology in enhancing the performance of the cooperatives. Bhatnagar and Schware (2000), Patil (1999), Singh *et al.* (1996) and Chattopadhyay (1996) stress the role of IT in cooperatives' future. The cooperatives stand to gain not only from the information about various policies and procedures available over Internet, but also through e-commerce as well. The products of the cooperatives would be available over Internet, which could be accessed by anybody in the world. This would actually benefit the cooperatives engaged in production of value-added products.

While the above recommendations are very important, after comparing the state of cooperatives in India with the working of the TVEs in China, we feel that the Indian laws and procedures on cooperatives should take note of the following five provisions for better functioning:

- First and foremost, the TVEs are owned by the community, and hence the community has always been concerned towards success of the initiatives. Unfortunately, in India, such community rights are absent, and therefore, the functioning of cooperatives suffers from their indifference towards success.
- Second, the management and credit allocation by cooperatives in India is subject to monitoring. Although there exist various provisions related to credit in China, the monitoring of management is much weaker, thereby enabling them to undertake innovative initiatives. In addition, the management of TVEs could be remunerated in case of outstanding performances. This performance-based incentive structure has never taken off in India, as a result of which, the main aim of the management was to minimise losses rather than maximise profits.
- Third, the regulation on TVEs clearly stipulated that a part of the profit earned has to be earmarked for public expenditure. As a result, although the money was not directly with the TVE concerned, it resulted in improved physical infrastructure for the next period.
- Fourth, the community governments played a key role in ensuring the success of the TVEs. For instance, their role in ensuring credit inflow to the TVEs is indispensable. Without the community government's involvement, it is usually very difficult, if not impossible, for TVEs to obtain loans directly from financing institutions. Their involvement is duly acknowledged and paid back by remitting a part of the profit to them. This stimulates the community governments also to maintain a weak monitoring on the working of the TVEs, so

that the latter can earn positive profits. However, in India we do not have any similar power and incentive structure delegated to the *panchayats*.

- Fifth, the Chinese government encourages urban talent in the management of the TVEs. However, in most of the cases, the management structure of cooperatives in India does not come with proper management backgrounds, and the cooperative members' training and education has never reached the expected level.

It is not possible to remove or alleviate rural poverty to keep the villages as self-sufficient, primary-sector reliant economic units. In order to break the jinx of poverty, the secondary and tertiary activities have to be promoted in the rural belt. The Chinese success in this regard is worth mentioning. Although the importance of rural non-farm activities has increased in India in 2001 as compared to the 1991 figure, cooperatives in association with *panchayats*, are capable of ensuring the transformation at a faster rate. The policymakers should take note of the lessons learnt from the Chinese experience while formulating any policy for cooperatives in future.

# 8

# *Panchayati Raj* - Civil Society and ICT Initiatives

P.D. KAUSHIK

## Introduction

After more than five decades, India is the largest democracy in the world. To sustain this democracy and freedom, it is necessary to ensure economic empowerment and better quality of life for all its citizens. Despite significant progress in industrial development, the Indian economy is still largely dependent on agriculture. Over 65 per cent of the population living in rural areas is primarily dependent on agriculture for livelihood. A majority of these families spend over 90 per cent of their earnings on basic needs such as food, fuel and health care. Over 35 per cent of the rural families being poor, tackling their problems is the national priority to ensure social justice and better quality of life. Unemployment and under-employment are the major reasons for rural poverty. The other factors are small land holdings, harsh agro-climatic conditions, poor infrastructure and limited opportunities for rural industrial development, poor health care, illiteracy, social suppression, addiction to alcohol and exploitation by vested interests.

Apart from inadequate income generating opportunities, rural India also suffers from poor health arising from starvation, lack of immunisation, hygiene and sanitation. Over 25 per cent villages do not have year-round supply of drinking water and about 75 per cent of the potable water sources are polluted. Most villages have no adequate sanitation facilities. Medical and immunisation services do not reach remotely located villages. Illiteracy in rural areas is high, particularly among women, varying from 55-75 per cent. This has a direct bearing on population growth, child health and education. One of the major limitations of India's stunted progress is the centralised form of governance. Realisation of this failure provided impetus to the issue of decentralisation, leading towards participatory and responsive local self-government. The 73rd Constitutional Amendment established the foundation for *'Panchayati Raj'* or governance based on direct democracy in India.

The experience and operationalisation of *Panchayati Raj* have serious implications on governance, democracy and modernity. *Panchayati Raj* is a system of local self-governance at the three-tier level, namely village, *taluka* and district levels, moving from indirect to direct democracy. It is based on the premise that the local population should represent the views, aspirations, needs and interests of the people. The new system intends to give power to the elected representatives. To built-in accountability, *Gram sabha* or village assembly was entrusted with the job of identification of beneficiaries and development projects, monitoring, *etc*. An analysis of the past decade on the functioning of *Panchayati Raj* in the States clearly indicates that despite several attempts by the respective stakeholders, the Panchayati Raj Institutions (PRIs) could not truly emerge as people's institutions. Unfortunately, the distortions of the existing political systems at the State and Union levels were replicated at the *Panchayat* level and a new class of elite and power centres led by the elected representatives emerged within the *Panchayati Raj* system, undermining the spirit of democratic decentralisation.

Given this background, this paper is on two countervailing initiatives. In Section 1, we look at the role of civil society, insofar as it impacts on *panchayati raj* institutions (PRIs). In Section 2, we consider the evolution of various ICT (information and communication technology) initiatives.

## SECTION 1

## CIVIL SOCIETY

The voluntary sector emerged as a powerful stakeholder in the rural society due to its broad-based presence in education, health, natural resource, employment generation, empowerment, *etc*. Lately, the voluntary sector has taken up the responsibility of capacity building of PRIs. Civil society has made significant efforts in the strengthening of people's institutions. However, it is important to note that the results have been mixed. Often these initiatives of the third sector have only been able to influence some *Panchayats* at the micro level to perform effectively, but have had little influence at the macro level. At the macro level, voluntary organisations have succeeded to a limited extent in creating a supportive environment for a progressive *panchayati raj* system through their advocacy efforts with the government. In this context, the relatively small size of the voluntary sector as compared with the requirements of the *Panchayat* system need to be taken into account. In the beginning, as the Act came into force, civil society had no prior experience, time, space or resources to prepare for a meaningful response. Voluntary agencies found themselves unprepared to promote economic development and social justice through PRIs.

## Voluntary Sector

"A voluntary organisation is interpreted broadly as a self-governing body of people who have joined together to take action for the betterment of the community and are established otherwise than for financial gain." Clark (1995), Diamond (1993), Renshaw (1994), Ritchey-Vance (1996) among others commented that non-governmental organisations (NGOs) are increasingly promoted as the panacea for correcting all the inequities and problems encountered when governments in the developing regions of Asia, Latin America, and Africa pursued objectives of rapid economic growth. Economic transition in many of these countries has been characterised by a withdrawal of the government from many sectors of the society, thus fostering a civil society between government and market that embraced many types of voluntary organisations included as NGOs. Participation in these voluntary organisations is believed to promote citizen involvement and help create a political culture and social capital necessary to sustain democracy. Many governments, impacted by structural adjustment and economic uncertainties, see NGOs as low-cost providers of services they themselves are unable or unwilling to provide. Even in China and Vietnam, international NGOs work through government institutions to provide services for the people, such as micro-credit schemes for the rural poor in Vietnam or services for the disabled in China. Further, rapid economic change often redirects or undermines earlier systems of social support, thus increasing the need for additional services for women-headed households and urban slum-dwellers.

Edwards and Hulme (1996), Rustam (1996), among others, suggested that willingness of NGOs to assume this task of service provision raised concerns that the dependence on official funding will co-opt the NGOs and undermine their legitimacy as instigators of democracy. Yet some corporate-driven countries, such as Mexico, Indonesia, or Egypt, which have tried to provide for the needs of their citizens through governmental or party institutions, have tended to view such service providers as oppositional. Today, under international and economic pressure, the space in which NGOs are allowed to operate in these countries is also increasing.

In contrast, in countries where the tradition of charitable service to the poor is centuries old, as in India, voluntary groups renewed their efforts to provide basic human needs to the disadvantaged throughout the country as the socialist model faltered in the late 1960s. Today, the Government of India sees NGOs as part of the poverty alleviation strategy. International development agencies and the global network of international non-governmental organisations encourage this emphasis on NGOs because they believe such organisations are closer to the people and therefore more able than an elite patrimonial bureaucracy to determine the types of services needed. They argue that interaction with the recipients also fosters participation in solving local problems, that in turn empowers local leadership and enhances prospects for local decision-making.

As the number and strength of NGOs increase, they begin to assume the role of loyal opposition, questioning programmes and regulations that interfere with their projects and challenging policies that damage the environment or restrict free speech. This shift from the role of service provider to an advocacy or policy role forces many NGO leaders to wonder about their own moral stance when the bulk of their funding comes from outside the country. As NGOs venture into advocacy and criticism, governments in many developing countries feel a loss of control. When appeals to government go unheeded, NGOs frequently take their complaints to international bodies and to the global media. While such advocacy is read by western democracies as an indication of the health and independence of the civil society that is a prerequisite of democracy, governments often interpret such action as an interference with national sovereignty. These concerns, and the increase in sheer numbers, have resulted in more stringent government regulations that attempt to control NGO funding and actions in such soft dictatorships as Indonesia.

'Civil society' or 'social capital' refers to the myriad tissues of association and cooperation that make for a resilient and self-governing society[1]. Broder (1996) argued that "civil society" may be equated with democracy. Various views on civil society converge on one issue - poverty isn't just the lack of material goods. It is also distance from decision-making and a sense of being devalued that manifests itself as apathy, anger, and a weakening of the civic culture. Agents in bringing decision-making to the people may be found in the myriad of new voluntary organisations that are appearing throughout most of the world. Many arise in response to dire need, others because of concern for vitally important issues, such as environment or human rights abuse. But others are formed because funds are available from sources both in their country and outside. Such an amorphous set of organisations tends to be lumped together under the residual term NGOs.

During the nineties, NGOs have emerged as important players in the development arena, especially in India. On one hand, the voluntary sector made significant contributions to the UN sponsored meetings at a global level, and on the other, they worked for the empowerment of the poor at the grassroots level. The role of civil society was particularly recognised at *the United Nations Conference on Environment and Development* held in Rio de Janeiro, Brazil in June 1992. Thereafter active presence of civil society continued at all important global international fora, such as *the Cairo Population Conference 1994, the Copenhagen World Summit on Social Development 1995, the Beijing Conference on Women 1995,* and so on. In the coming years, it is expected that the voluntary sector would be playing significant role not only in social sectors, but also in other sectors.

## Voluntary Sector: Indian Scenario

Voluntary Organisations play a vital role in the shaping and implementation of participatory democracy. Their credibility lies in the responsible and constructive role they play in society. They have been contributing immensely for quite some time towards various

1. Robert Kuttner (1996).

development programmes. They work at grassroots level even in remote areas and, therefore, their reach is much wider. They are closer to ground realities and know the needs of the communities. Their approach with target groups is direct, emphatic and therefore they are able to draw more contexualised plans of action. They also manage to develop intimate contacts with the people and develop confidence among them.

The IYV[2] ensured that the full potential contribution of the voluntary sector is realised with the fullest possible communication and cooperation between national, State and local governments. This led to the inclusion of the voluntary sector in the Indian planning process. Keeping in view the strategic role of civil society, the Tenth Plan constituted a Steering Committee for facilitating and improving the working of the voluntary sector in India.

India has a rich tradition of voluntary action. Before Independence, civil society imbued with the Gandhian philosophy, was playing a significant role mainly in social welfare activities and now, the range of spheres covered by the voluntary sector has expanded considerably, covering almost all development related activities. Some of the reasons put forward for increase in the number and activities of NGOs are the decline of socialism and an increased national and international funding for the voluntary sector. In a number of developmental activities, NGOs are working as supplements or complements to governmental efforts.

The origin and development of the voluntary sector in India has been shaped by two major influences - one rooted in indigenous traditions and value-systems, and the other a product of the interface between Indian society and the western world. The Indian traditions and value-systems are in turn rooted in religion that prescribes a code of ethics for the individual and the principles governing social life. A noteworthy feature of all major religions has been the emphasis they place on charity and sharing wealth with others, especially the poor.[3]

---

2. The UN General Assembly in its 52$^{nd}$ session declared the year 2001 as *International Year of Volunteers (IYV).*

3. In Hinduism, serving the poor is considered equivalent to serving God. Philanthropy and individual acts of social service have, historically, been the main forms of voluntary activity in India. Institutionalised social service activities existed largely within the domain of religious institutions - *Ashramas* and *Maths* among Hindus, *Waqfs* and *Khanqahs* among Muslims and *Gurudwaras* and *Deras* among Sikhs.

In the Post-Independence period, there was general awareness that development, to be meaningful, requires mobilisation of resources, public cooperation and creation of social capital. It was established that no development strategy can be successful unless a shared vision of the public sector, the private sector and the voluntary sector is created. The process of social mobilisation and development of people's initiatives cannot be achieved without the active support and involvement of the voluntary sector.

**Box 8.1**

*Voluntary Sector in India: Types*

**Traditional Associations** - A social unit either defined by a tribe, ethnicity or caste, *e.g.*

**Religious Associations** - Charity service to the poor and *daan* have been uniformly recommended by all religions and sects in India, *e.g. Vishwa Hindu Parishad, Majlis-e-Musilmeen*, YMCA, *etc.*

**Social Movements** - Social movements trying to reform society, institutions and governance and act as harbingers of social change, *e.g.* Green Peace, Amnesty International, *etc.*

**Membership Associations** - Organisations set up to represent the opinions and interest of a particular category of citizens, *e.g. Nehru Yuvak Kendras*, MCC, IHF, *etc.*

**Intermediary Associations** - Social unit functioning between individual citizens and macro State institutions, *e.g.* CARE, Rajiv Gandhi Foundation, Action-Aid, *etc.*

Diversity of the activities of the voluntary sector can be gauged from large number of schemes being implemented through the voluntary sector by various Ministries. Rough estimates suggest existence of 250 such active government-sponsored schemes. A suggestive list is given in the Annex. *The Mid-Term Review of the Ninth Plan* identified many inadequacies in governmental delivery systems, especially at the implementation and monitoring levels, like existence of hospitals/dispensaries but absence of personnel, existence of school buildings but teachers remain absent, *etc.* To rectify these anomalies, the voluntary sector deserves encouragement to ameliorate at least some of the above-referred problems, because of its following comparative advantages:

- NGOs are much closer to the poorer and disadvantaged sections of the society.
- Staff of voluntary sector is normally highly motivated and altruistic in their behaviour.
- Voluntary sector can easily stimulate and mobilise community resources and have access to volunteers.
- They are more effective in bringing people's participation.
- NGOs are less rule-bound and are non-bureaucratic, non-formal and flexible in their structure and operations.
- Voluntary sector has greater potential for innovations.
- NGOs prefer to work in a multi-sectoral framework.
- Voluntary organisations are catalysts for creating social cohesion.

The voluntary sector has a strong presence in influencing the life of rural poor, especially in areas like land, water, livelihood, human development, linking producers and consumers, *etc.* However, certain disadvantages or shortcomings of the voluntary sector are also well-known, namely, their inability to cooperate with each other in a way which would allow for coherent policymaking, their accountability and transparency is not perfect and their operations are smaller in scale. Therefore, there is a need to improvise the working of the voluntary sector by scaling up their operations and by making them transparent and accountable.

## Voluntary Sector: Land, Water and Livelihood

Access to land and water resources is critical for improving the economic status of the poor and the marginalised. Part of the land and water problem is the increasing demand for these resources for domestic, industrial and agricultural purposes - a direct response to an ever increasing population and more intensive use and consumption. In India, 70 per cent of the water usage is for crop irrigation. Land and water shall remain a major constraint in the future for improving productivity in agriculture. The voluntary sector has a strong presence in the coordination of the management of land and water resources. It is actively taking up issues like—establishment of secure land and water property rights, where they do not exist, reorganisation of policies at the river basin level, introduction of concepts of shared and equitable water use, and alternatives to the use of marginal land.

## Integrated Watershed Development: Rajiv Gandhi Watershed Management Mission, Madhya Pradesh

The links between poverty and environmental degradation have been identified as being crucial to improving the productivity and income of the people residing in rural areas. The Rajiv Gandhi Watershed Management Mission, initiated in 1994, aims at improving the land and water resources in environmentally degraded villages.

### Figure 8.1

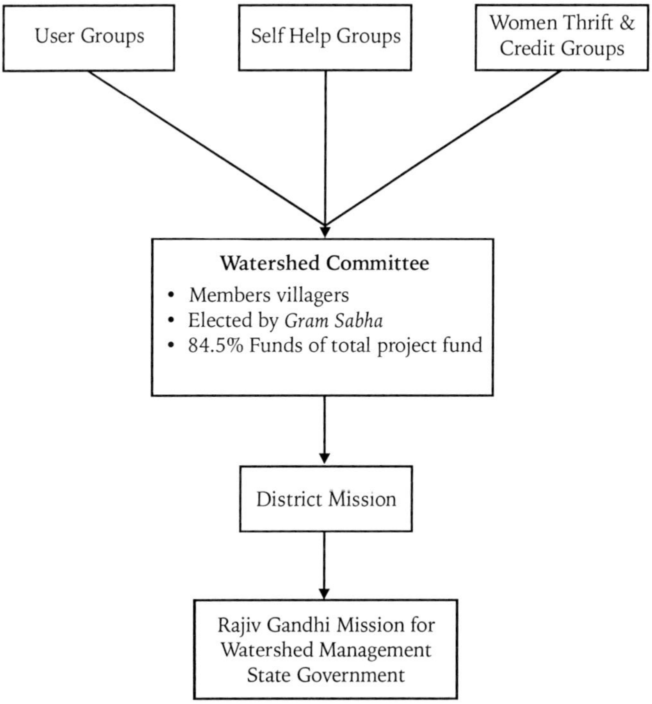


The larger goal is to move watershed management from being a techno-centric programme to a people's movement. RGWMM has, therefore, adopted direct people's participation as a core element of its strategy. The institutional arrangements are geared to a participatory bottom-up approach, in which communities exercise control over programme activities at each stage and government and non-government agencies play catalysing, facilitating and coordinating roles. An easily accessible repository of inter-disciplinary inputs drawn from the departments, NGOs, sectoral experts and research and academic institutions has been prepared to inform planning and implementation.

The programme is mandated to coordinate the watershed development efforts of various line departments in the State, pool resources and expertise readily available to create synergy and lend focus to interventions and work towards building an appropriate environment for sustainable people-centred interventions. There are institutions for watershed development at the three levels - the State, district, and village. Participatory Rural Appraisal (PRA) is instrumental in identifying programme activities at the village level, as well as beneficiaries, who are organised into groups. Villagers have to make a certain minimum contributions, in the form of cash, labour or material, to the programme activities.

The programme has led to substantial improvements in environmental conditions, irrigation facilities and land use patterns, which have led to an improvement in overall agricultural productivity. The direct wage employment opportunities provided through the RGWMM have provided immense relief to the landless and small and marginal farmers. These opportunities have made a significant contribution to household income, addressed immediate concerns at the household level and checked daily movement to urban centres in search of work.

One of the major achievements of RGWMM has been the emergence of leadership and management skill pool at the village level, which can potentially challenge established power structures and complement the *Panchayati Raj* agenda of the Government of Madhya Pradesh. Land-use changes and improved water availability, as reported in some project villages, may be expected to affect livelihood favourably, especially agriculture. On the other hand, there remain project villages where changes have been witnessed on a lower scale. Some of these can be ascribed to reasons that cannot be addressed in the current RGWMM framework, such as encroachments, migration, grazing and the declining stakes of small and marginal farmers in agriculture.

**Box 8.2**

*Rajiv Gandhi Watershed Management Mission: Jhabua*

Jhabua district of MP is endowed with great variations in social conditions, terrain and resource endowment. While parts of it through which the Narmada flows are reasonably well endowed in terms of soil quality, water resources and settled agriculture, the rain shadow region is extremely underdeveloped, largely due to soil erosion.

As a result, agriculture gives way to seasonal migration in search of livelihood for the small and marginal farmers. The emergence of canal-irrigated areas in the neighbouring regions and States has created pull effects that reinforce the push effect from degrading and marginal holdings in rainfed areas. The net effect of these phenomena is the increasing marginalisation of agriculture and high fluctuations in agricultural productivity in the rainfed areas of Jhabua. A significant proportion of the small and marginal landholders' time is spent away from the village, leading to low stakes in land improvement. With agricultural income deemed uncertain, it is indeed a daunting task to check seasonal migration, especially among small and marginal farmers.

Given this situation, it is remarkable that the Jhabua experience in watershed management has been widely hailed as a success story. The RGWMM has transformed the arid and semi-arid region, now the region has improved water levels, cropping patterns and intensity.

*Source*: Planning Commission & UNDP (2000).

There are, however, other issues related to competing land-use claims, funding delays and adequacy of allocations, planning and efficacy of water-harvesting structures and the scale and protection of afforestation and fodder development interventions that the RGWMM is in a position to address. Terrain and land ownership patterns admittedly are key constraints for RGWMM interventions and would require development of location-specific technologies and interventions over time through constant experimentation. These assume importance in the light of limited impacts in select locations, particularly with respect to increase in cropped, non-crop biomass and irrigated areas. A more direct approach to ensure increased control of women over household resources and decision-making has been in the form of WTCGs. These WTCGs, much like SHGs, have suffered from myriad problems, notwithstanding isolated successes in Jhabua and elsewhere.

The Rajiv Gandhi Watershed Management Mission has succeeded in highlighting the following features for its success:

- Creation of a right environment for the people to participate and take adequate interest in the activity.
- Involving people from different fields, including politicians, bureaucrats, technical experts, NGOs and the beneficiaries, thus lending credibility and accountability to the programme.
- Ensuring equity by involving and addressing the specific needs of different groups like the landless labourers and women.
- Emphasising transparency through robust monitoring mechanisms like periodic reporting and accounting systems.
- Stressing the need for continuous training and capacity building activities.
- Empowering people by generating awareness and developing leadership.

### Involvement of Women in Agriculture: TANWA, Tamil Nadu

Rural agricultural households are characteristically dependent on the income of the male members. Women were rarely involved in decision-making regarding the crops to be grown or the agricultural techniques to be adopted. A striking feature of the Tamil Nadu Women in Agriculture (TANWA) project initiated in Tamil Nadu is aimed at training women in latest agricultural techniques. It is an innovative scheme that aims at improving the living standards of small and marginal farm households and inducing women in such households to play an active part in agriculture, thereby raising agricultural productivity and family income. It is a project wherein both the trainer and trainee are women and it relies on its multiplier effect.

The long-term objective of the project is to increase the productivity of small and marginal holdings and to ensure full utilisation of the potential of farm-women. Small and marginal women owning a minimum size of land holding (2.5 acre of irrigated land or five acre of unirrigated land or less) and engaged in cultivating their land, form the first stage target group of the project. The trainees are selected on the basis of a set of criteria specified for the purpose:

**Box 8.3**

*Objectives of TANWA*

- To introduce the farm-women to a package of 10-12 skills of relevance to them in crop production and related activities and to enable them to choose and adopt relevant agricultural practices.
- To spread agricultural knowledge and skills from TANWA trainees to non-trained fellow farm women.
- To improve access to existing agricultural extension services for women belonging to small and marginal holdings.

- Wife of small or marginal farmer cultivating own land.
- Female head of the small or marginal holdings.
- Women in the age group of 20 to 45 years.
- Women possessing leadership qualities.
- Women interested in improving agricultural practices.

TANWA is a DANIDA assisted project. The success of the programme can be assessed from various surveys and evaluation reports. The Monitoring and Evaluation Unit of the State Directorate of Agriculture has periodically brought out study reports on the impact of training and skill demonstration given to farm women on technology adoption, skill acquisition, development of communication skills, increase in yield of crops *etc.* As per the *14th Monitoring and Evaluation Report of the Directorate of Agriculture* (April 1999), the adoption of technology exceeds 50 per cent in almost all districts and there is a productivity increase in paddy, *cholam, ragi* and groundnut. A critical assessment of the impact of the project revealed a significant increase in the total number of farm women trained under the project (from 5,350 women in 1998-1999 to 7,775 in 1999-2000) and an increase in plan allocation from Rs. 507 lakh in 1998 to Rs. 626 lakh in 1999-2000.[4]

The training strategy has been devised to suit the needs of the farm women in different agro-climatic conditions. It comprises imparting agricultural skills, demonstrating skills and encouraging the trainees to practice the skills on their own. In each VBT session, the

4. *18th Evaluation Report*, DANIDA (2000).

trainees are exposed to a combination of about 10 skills relevant to three or more crops, depending upon the location and cropping pattern. The package of skills includes a wide spectrum of activities such as seed selection, seed treatment, nursery management, planting, application of the fertilisers, pest management *etc.* that lends itself to replication in other States and to other crops as well. Being a woman-to-woman programme, there is no restriction on learning and follow-up; gender bias is ruled out. The women farmers adapt into their existing farming methodology and the skills imparted to them. This results in increased productivity of different crops due to improved technology.

**Box 8.4**

*TANWA Success Stories*

- A Farm Women's Group in Trichy run by Anthoniammal is successfully making and selling vermicompost and earning money from this business venture.
- A farm woman, who has come to be known as *Jhansi ki Rani* of Mesiapuram, Tirunelveli district, has bagged the Rs. 1 Lakh award from the Aspee Foundation for her exemplary work in dairy farming in her Women's Self Help Group.
- Menaka of Tiruvarur and Kannagi of Cuddalore have become famous for promoting mushroom cultivation in their SHGs.
- Many other farm SHGs are creating savings in their group by functioning like mini banks through micro-credit systems. With the savings earned, they promote small-scale household activities like soap manufacture, doll making or other income generating activities.

*Source*: Planning Commission & UNDP (2000).

An evaluation of 530 sample trainees under TANWA-I, made by the State Directorate of Evaluation and Research (DEAR), revealed the following results:

- ***Selection of farmers for the programme:*** Wives of small/marginal farmers constituted 95.3 per cent (505) of the sample trainees.
- ***Ownership of land:*** About 87 per cent of trainees (462 women) were engaged in own cultivation and 7.7 per cent (41 women) in tenant cultivation, in addition to own cultivation.

- ***Leadership qualities in community activities:*** 46 per cent (244 women) actively participated in community activities.
- ***Interest in improving agricultural practices:*** The adoption rate of improved agricultural practices by the trainees after the completion of TANWA training would broadly indicate the extent of keenness shown by the trainees in improving agricultural practices. About 94.5 per cent (501 women) trainees adopted one or more of the skills in their farming operations and a small percentage (5.5 per cent) did not adopt any skill.
- ***Ability and commitment to share knowledge with other farm women:*** The DEAR study indicated that 98.3 per cent (521) had contacted other farm women at the rate of 10 per trainee and conveyed TANWA messages.
- ***Educational status of the trainees:*** The DEAR study showed that 9.8 per cent (52 women) were illiterate, 30.2 per cent (160 women) had studied up to class V and 60.0 per cent (318 women) had studied up to class X and above.
- ***Community status:*** A vast majority of trainees in the project belonged to backward and most backward classes (82.3 per cent), followed by scheduled castes (16.4 per cent).

## Voluntary Sector: Human Development and Social Services

Education is the basic building block of human development. It is an enabling tool in expanding the range of opportunities, choices and capabilities of an individual for sustained improvement in well-being. Improvement in educational attainments translates into increased productivity and hence increased economic growth. The issue of health, especially in the Indian context, is important for more than one reason. From a purely economic point of view, the nexus between poverty, under-nutrition, morbidity and fertility implies low productivity of human resources.

## Education – Lok Jumbish Project

Community participation is the only means of undertaking any civil works in improvement of school facilities under the *Lok Jumbish* Project. Experiments in community participation under *Lok Jumbish* in many States have been very encouraging. The *Sarva Shiksha Abhiyan* aims to mobilise resources under the Rural Employment Programme and other developmental schemes for constructing school buildings. The rural community provides maintenance of school facilities. An annual support to the community for repair and maintenance is envisaged under the SSA. The upper ceiling is Rs. 5000 per year, based on the actual need and the willingness of the community to contribute. The *Lok Jumbish* Project has had significant success by adopting this procedure.

Elementary education is an obligation of the State (including the local government), the *Panchayats* are directed to prioritise construction of school facilities wherever it does not exist. The participation of the community in all civil work activities is mandatory in order to ensure a sense of ownership and a departure from the contractor driven approach. Engagement of contractors is not allowed under the *Sarva Shiksha Abhiyan.* School Management Committees/ Village Education Committees/*Gram Panchayat* Committees on Education carry out the civil works activities through a transparent system of account keeping. The DPEP and *Lok Jumbish* Project have developed effective community-based approaches for civil works in all the *Sarva Shiksha Abhiyan* identified districts.

The principle of social audit is accepted for minor repairs. The Village Education Committee certifies the maintenance and repair work undertaken in a school. For larger repair and maintenance, as well as new construction, specified technical provisions are followed under the *Lok Jumbish* project. Efforts to improve the school environment by addition of a few inexpensive internal and external elements are made. New building designs developed in *Lok Jumbish* and DPEP are adapted to promote child-centred learning. Use of local materials and cost effective technologies are encouraged. A civil works innovation fund is set up in each State/UT to encourage experimentation with design. Repair and maintenance of buildings is given the top most priority.

A large number of (more than 100) building designs for schools have been developed in DPEP districts. These designs, apart from being attractive, are child-centred, functional and in tune with the new pedagogical concepts. The publication called "Building Rural Primary schools" published by the EdCil and the building construction manuals developed by the *Lok Jumbish* Project are utilised by all the States/districts to develop their civil work plans. The States may make use of designs already developed under DPEP/*Lok Jumbish* Project in their specific local contexts. Incorporation of child-friendly internal and external elements is mandatory in all the new construction and repair works.

There is need for school-wise compilation of physical and monetary requirements. Local community makes an assessment of minimum money required to provide adequate infrastructure to each school, including repairs, toilets, drinking water, boundary wall, *etc.* Provision of additional classrooms is considered only after exploring possibility of repairs and double shifts. Once the total requirement for the district is obtained, one needs to find out how much of this requirement can be funded through the ongoing schemes and therefore what is the gap that is required to be funded through SSA. Often, it is the engineering department in the district, which manages all funds related to school construction. All school infrastructure works are executed by the single agency.

## Health – Family Planning Association of India

The Family Planning Association of India is the country's leading voluntary family planning organisation. Composed of volunteer members and staff, it has 40 Branches, eight Integrated Rural Projects spread across the country. Its aim is to promote knowledge of family planning as a basic human right, as well as population policies that can help to bring about a balanced development of the resources of the country, as a means towards raising the quality of life. FPAI is deeply committed to all aspects of planned parenthood. Its activities include population, family life and sex education programmes for young people; clinical and non-clinical services for reproductive health, including family planning and MCH; training and research. Its rural projects utilise innovative community participation approaches to integrate reproductive health with youth concerns and women's empowerment. The FPAI's people-centred focus for promoting health and improving the quality of life at the grassroots is in accordance with the ICPD Programme of Action. The FPAI plays a strong catalytic role by assisting other NGOs to make reproductive health, including family planning, an integral part of their work.

*Activities*

- Information dissemination and awareness creation on health issues at the grassroots level.
- STDs/AIDS prevention education is an intrinsic component of the IEC programme.
- Providing quality reproductive health services through 93 static and mobile service facilities and other distribution outlets in different parts of the country.
- Social marketing through project outlets and 114 condom vending machines at branch level.
- Promoting population, family life and sex education programmes to develop responsible attitudes among youth.
- Providing specialised services and training in family life, marriage and sex counselling through 36 centres.
- Stimulating community participation in reproductive health and family planning through various developmental activities.

In 2002, the FPAI workers organised 53,139 educational and motivational events for 1.39 million men and women and made 1.23 million interpersonal contacts. It also held over 1,340 conferences, seminars and workshops at the village, district, State and national levels. During the year, 215816 new acceptors were served at FPAI centres. Of these, 70 per cent opted for spacing methods, and 30 per cent adopted permanent methods. There were 15,693 MTP and MR cases and 2,257 infertile couples. About 128,011 mothers and 169,446 children benefited from FPAI's maternal and child health services. In addition, 133,838 men and women were served for reproductive health services. The population and family life education programme covered 10,215 students in schools and colleges, as well as 2,195 teachers, teacher-trainees and other youth workers. These programmes were also organised for 14,392 out-of-school youth and 1194 medical and non-medical professionals, village leaders, *etc*. The SECRT Centres served 23,554 new clients and organised educational and training programmes for over 59,836 health providers, social workers, teachers and youths.

As a National NGO, FPAI supports 121 FNGOs under the Government MNGO scheme in eight districts of Madhya Pradesh. They are provided technical assistance and funding to integrate RCH with their other activities. To date, six FPAI Branches, namely Ahmedabad, Madurai, Manipur, Mohali, Lucknow and Trivandrum have been accorded Mother NGO status. The FPAI's Small Family by Choice Project (*Parivar Pragati Pariyojana*) was launched in 1995 in three of the 90 low performing districts in India - Bhopal, Sagar and Vidisha in Madhya Pradesh, which has extended to the neighbouring district Raisen (covering a population of 4.35 million in 3,901 villages). The project aims at bringing about social transformation, increasing access and excellence in reproductive health, including family planning education and services. The Project, which has won two global awards for innovative women's empowerment and community participation strategies, has been selected by the International Committee of Expo 2000 Hannover, Germany, as one of the outstanding sustainable development projects from among 800 entries.

## Voluntary Sector: Linking People to Markets

Since the planned development of India, several development programmes and schemes have been implemented. With liberalisation, there is a paradigm shift at the State level, with the government playing the role of facilitator. At the same time, there remains a large area of direct public interface with the government, and small improvements in the functioning of these areas are likely to contribute significantly to public well-being. Better governance and implementation of programmes, within the pro-poor framework, are needed for effective results on the ground that visibly benefits the people.

The domination of the middlemen in agricultural markets in India has reduced the producer-consumer relationship to the weakest link in the marketing chain. Lack of market information, credit facilities and *ad hoc* marketing techniques have reduced the benefits of marketing of agricultural produce for the farmers. The consumers are often dissatisfied with inferior quality, spiralling prices and market malpractices. Both government and voluntary sector have realised these problems and initiated steps to bring the producers closer to markets.

### *Rythu Bazar*

*Rythu Bazar*s were conceptualised to provide better marketing avenues for agricultural produce, as well as to bridge the gap between the farmers and the consumers. The Horticulture Department of

Andhra Pradesh Government identifies farmers from a cluster of 10-15 predominantly vegetable-growing villages, who are willing to participate in the *Bazar*. *Rythu Bazar*s help to reduce variations in prices and protect the interest of the consumers. A system of price fixation has been put in place in *Rythu Bazar*s, which is done through a Committee and Estate Officer. The Estate Officer conducts meetings with farmers once a week to assess the functioning of the *Bazar*.

*Rythu Bazar*s are located on government-owned land that is identified by the District Collectors and a location that is convenient for both farmers and consumers is chosen. The criteria for the opening of a new *Rythu Bazar* are the availability of at least one acre of land in a strategic location, and identification of 250 vegetable growing farmers, who are willing to participate in the *Bazar*. The establishment of marketing linkages between buyers and sellers is critical to the successful functioning of a *Rythu Bazar*. Infrastructure facilities are provided for all *Rythu Bazar*s through funds from the Agricultural Market Committees. Temporary structures, such as vegetable containers and vending stalls, have been replaced by semi-permanent structures in *Rythu Bazar*s to provide adequate protection against sun/rain to both producers and users alike.

*Facilities at the Rythu Bazar*

- Adequate number of sheds for farmers to store and sell their produce.
- Adequate arrangements for supply of drinking water and proper sanitation facilities.
- Proper arrangements for parking of vehicles.
- Arrangements for periodic removal of garbage and regular cleaning of the market.
- Facilities for storage of unsold produce, including refrigeration facilities like Zero Energy Cool Chambers.
- Provision of tamper-proof weighing scales for all the farmers.

The Horticulture Department identifies the vegetable-growing farmers, each farmer is issued with an identity card. These cards help identify sellers in the market and prevent unauthorised personnel from misusing the facilities that are provided to the registered farmers. Price setting is also a unique feature of the *Rythu Bazar*. The price difference between the wholesale market and the retail outlet in perishables is sometimes more than double. To combat this variation in price and to protect the interests of consumers, a system of price fixation is done through a committee of farmers and the Estate Officer. Every day's wholesale market and local retail market prices are collected and the prices fixed in the *Rythu Bazar* are kept between the wholesale and retail rates. Usually the prices at the *Rythu Bazar* are kept 25 per cent higher than the wholesale prices and 25 per cent lower than the retail prices.

The cost of the entire operation is met through funds provided by the Agricultural Market Committee and the Horticulture Development Department. The Agricultural Market Committees, from their own funds, provide infrastructural facilities in the *Bazar*. *Rythu Bazar*s generate sufficient income for their sustenance through auction of parking space, lease of private nurseries and profits from the market canteen. Government officials look after the auctioning and leasing of space. The money realised through auction is credited to the *Rythu Bazar* funds and can be used for provision of sanitation, drinking water facilities, purchase and repair of weighing scales, and general maintenance of the *Rythu Bazar*.

Table 8.1

*Profile of Rythu Bazars in Andhra Pradesh*

| *Indicators* | *1999* | *2000* | *2001* |
|---|---|---|---|
| No. of Rythu Bazars | 92 | 97 | 97 |
| Permanent Rythu Bazars | 7 | 28 | 34 |
| No. of Farmers | 4500 | 4888 | 5871 |
| Weekly Arrivals (quintals) | 51142 | 75389 | 101111 |
| Computers | 12 | 29 | 34 |

Some facts

- About 97 *Rythu Bazar*s are functioning in Andhra Pradesh, where one lakh quintals of vegetables are sold per week.
- About 6000 farmers are availing the benefits of *Rythu Bazar*s.
- Total turnover of vegetable and other essential commodities is about Rs. 7.5 crore per week.

- *Bazars* have facilitated direct marketing, cutting short marketing channels by eliminating middlemen.
- Producers of perishable goods around the cities and urban towns are able to get the benefit of direct selling to the consumers.

Tamil Nadu and Orissa have already replicated the *Rythu Bazar* model in their respective territories. At the National level, the Agriculture Division of the Planning Commission envisages promoting the concept of *Rythu Bazars* as an innovative example of creating a viable alternate market structure.

*Bharatiya Agro Industries Foundation (BAIF)*

BAIF is a Public Charitable Trust. Considering the challenges in rural areas, BAIF has set its mission to create opportunities of gainful self-employment for the rural families, especially disadvantaged sections, ensuring sustainable livelihood, enriched environment, improved quality of life and good human values. This is being achieved through development research, effective use of local resources, extension of appropriate technologies and up-gradation of skills and capabilities with community participation, presently operating in 12,000 villages in India.

BAIF has been promoting people's participation through formation of Self Help Groups and Local Planning Committees to discuss their problems and find out suitable solutions. The members of these groups are trained in various agro-based skills to develop them into local resource persons. The training emphasises on selection of appropriate technologies, optimum use of resources and management aspects of project implementation.

The Cattle Development Programme, operated through 725 centres covering 10,000 villages in seven States, is providing breeding services to cattle and buffaloes, at the doorsteps of the farmers. The programme has helped over one million farmers to upgrade their livestock and to increase their income through milk production. Dairy husbandry has been providing an excellent opportunity for women and small farmers to earn a sustainable livelihood, while promoting eco-friendly practices such as organic farming, bio-gas production and stall feeding.

The dairy development programme has a gestation period of 3-4 years, till the newly born calf comes into milk production. In land-based development programmes the gestation period may vary from 2-6 years, depending on the type of farming systems practiced by the farmers. In case of arable crop production, the gestation period is short due to short rotation crops, while the fruit and tree crops take 5-6 years to generate income. While promoting these income generation activities, there are two critical factors that affect the success of the programmes. Firstly, the programme should be well planned to generate substantial income to enable the participating families to come out of poverty. Generally, small farmers having poor quality land and livestock, may not be able to earn substantial income with only one intervention. Hence multi-disciplinary programmes have the advantage. Similarly, small interventions such as kitchen garden, vermi-composting, homestead horticulture in isolation will not help the poor. These interventions can be helpful as a part of an integrated programme.

The other important aspect is to provide support during the gestation period. Many of the poor who do not have any resources even to procure their daily ration, are likely to neglect their development work, if no support is available in the form of assistance or wages to ensure their food security. Hence different short-term income generation activities need to be designed till the income starts generating from the major interventions.

Development of wastelands through tree based farming and water resource management is being implemented in about 1000 villages by providing technical guidance and critical inputs to convert 0.5 to 1.0 ha degraded lands owned by poor families into productive orchards. They are encouraged to plant multipurpose tree species on the bunds and borders of the orchard to serve as wind break and a source of green manure, herbal medicine, fodder, fuel and timber. The inter-space used for growing cereals and vegetables has been generating regular income while ensuring food security.

A tribal development programme covering these components in Dharampur block of Valsad district in Gujarat has rehabilitated over 16,000 families in the recent past. This programme is being widely replicated in other parts of India with necessary modifications to address the local problems. Community health, an integral part of the overall development strategy, focuses on improved health status of the families through promotion of safe drinking water sources, hygiene and sanitation facilities, nutritious diet, immunisation, mother and child health care, nutrition gardens and health education. Use of traditional health practices with a wide range of home-grown herbs and alternate methods of garbage disposal are also being popularised. BAIF has been emphasising on the formation of people's organisations in all its development programmes for ensuring sustainable development.

## Voluntary Sector and *Panchayat*s

Voluntary and community activity is fundamental to the development of a democratic, socially inclusive society. Voluntary and community groups, as independent, not for profit organisations, bring unique value to society and fulfil a role that is distinct from both the State and the market. They enable individuals to contribute to public life and the development of their communities by providing the opportunities for voluntary action. They also make a major contribution to the development of society and to the social, cultural, economic and political life of the nation. The voluntary and community sector also makes an important direct contribution to the strengthening of local bodies like the *panchayat*s.

The importance of local organisations and institutions in rural development is widely recognised and has become a part of the development policy in India. Despite this, the actual integration of these institutions and organisations in development practice has often been ineffective, especially in building linkages with the *panchayati raj* institutions. Perhaps, there are two main reasons for this. In some cases, the real commitment of State governments and official agencies to serious recognition of and support of local *panchayat* organisations has been very limited. The second reason is that *panchayat* representatives fail to recognise and support the local voluntary sector. Besides, there is limited understanding of the sociological basis for effective voluntary sector organisations.

One of the primary strategies of voluntary agencies' work with respect to PRIs comprises capacity building. This entails direct strengthening of the capacities of the local population, other local voluntary sector organisations, support organisations and building strong coalitions of such organisations. To promote democracy at local level, a variety of local civil society organisations have played a vital role in strengthening PRIs. In many areas, successful conscientisation, group building and promotion of local leadership among marginalised sections have already been achieved through the efforts of voluntary organisations and social activists. As a result, these voluntary agencies and social activists have played a dominant and a more direct role in the promotion and strengthening of PRIs. Therefore, the voluntary sector's critically important and strategic intervention for PRIs is targeted at building capacity and encouraging participation of local population in *panchayati raj*. For instance, PRIA, a voluntary sector organisation, is an international centre for learning and promotion of participation and democratic governance. It promotes people-centred development initiatives within the perspective of participatory research.

The voluntary sector active participation in rural areas principally revolves around the following set of principles:

- Voluntary and community activity is fundamental to the development of a democratic, socially inclusive society and fulfils a role that is distinct from the State and the private sector.
- PRIs must recognise and support the independence of the voluntary sector, including its right within the law to campaign, to comment on their working, and to challenge their policy, irrespective of any funding relationship that might exist, and to determine and manage its own affairs.
- Government has a responsibility to create and promote a favourable tax and fiscal environment in which the voluntary sector can flourish.
- Central, regional and local government must recognise that where they work, or want to work, in partnership with the sector, those partnerships must benefit all stakeholders and that the government has a responsibility to invest time, skills and capacity to make them work.
- Government should ensure that the cost of engagement in partnerships for voluntary organisations is met, particularly at a local and community level.

- It is essential that local institutions and government provide the voluntary sector with a long-term commitment of support.
- PRIs and official agencies must strive to ensure that there is consistency in their dealings with the voluntary sector.

A coordinated approach between all the stakeholders results in effective and efficient functioning of the PRIs. Three most important contributions of voluntary organisations in rural India are:

**Innovations** – The voluntary sector has been experimenting with new ways of promoting more sustainable, people-centred development. Through flexible and risk-taking experimentation, they have been able to develop methods, models and equipments that have been widely adopted by the State and national government. In making these contributions, the voluntary sector requires flexible resources and a process-oriented approach which is not weighed-down by rules and procedures.

**Empowerment** - Another important contribution of the voluntary sector in India has been promotion of the concept of empowerment of the socio-economically marginalised and exploited sections within the rural society. Most significant contributions can be seen on issues of minimum wages, bonded labour, child labour, access to government schemes, land *patta*, ration cards, housing rights, access to customary rights on forest and water by tribals, *etc*. However, it is important to recognise that such efforts of empowerment by voluntary organisations create conflicts and tensions. In a hierarchical and patriarchal society, any attempt on empowerment of women, *dalits*, tribals *etc*. is likely to challenge the vested interest of the local elites. The government needs to find peaceful ways of dealing with such conflicts.

**Research and Advocacy** - Many intermediary voluntary organisations in India have also undertaken public education and policy advocacy through their sustained research. This has brought many issues on the agenda of public discourse and national policy in India. For example, the issues of women, tribals and *dalits*, environment, education, human rights have gained visibility and policy response largely due to the work of voluntary organisations. What is important is listening to and acceptance of different voices from the voluntary organisations and a willingness to share new knowledge generated by them.

Voluntary organisations like PRIA and MSSK, have also contributed towards making *Panchayati Raj* and municipal bodies effective institutions of local self-governance. For the last five years, these organisations have undertaken strategic interventions to strengthen PRIs in many States of India, like Andhra Pradesh, Himachal Pradesh, Kerala, Madhya Pradesh, Maharashtra and Uttar Pradesh, almost accounting for about two-thirds of the rural population of India. The broad framework adopted for the strategic intervention targeted at PRIs was based on the following principles:

- The PRIs are to be viewed as institutions of local self-governance, not as mere implementers of centrally determined development programmes.
- Bottom-up planning, based on micro-planning, is to be the basis of self-governance.
- The PRIs should not be allowed to become the third-tier of development administration.
- The emphasis must be placed on active participation in decision-making by women (and other weaker sections), with a view to enhancing their role, status and leadership in local self-governance.
- Interventions in strengthening PRIs should focus on building, promoting and empowering new leadership by women, SC/ST and *Dalits*.
- The PRIs should assert their access to and control over natural and human resources, as well as other development resources available with the State and the national government.
- Strengthening PRIs will entail clarifying their roles, systems of governance, accountability, transparency and inter-linkages.

The rationale for these interventions is to enhance the potential for community participation and responsibility in development, that is, people-centred and people-controlled development. The constitutional provisions provide new opportunities and possibilities for building up leadership from among women and *Dalits* (SC/ST). The PRIs can also become the basis for further elaboration and strengthening of civil society in the country. The voluntary sector believes that only a strong, participatory, responsive and accountable government at local level can fulfil people's aspirations and their needs.

**Box 8.5**

*Strengthening People's Participation:*
*Kehar Panchayat, Mandi District*

PRIA initiated micro planning in Kehar with the help of RTDC, a local voluntary agency (VA). Being active in the area, RTDC had close linkages with community and community organisations of Kehar. With the help of RTDC the Village Development Committees (VDCs) for each ward of the *Gram Panchayat* were constituted. These VDCs comprise 15-20 members from different groups of the *Gram sabha*. Local population was mobilised to prioritise community problems, prepare a list of resources available and ask the *panchayat* to draw up a plan. The planning was facilitated by the involvement of local organisations and community groups like youth and women's groups, which allowed local people to scrutinise and judge the performance of their *panchayat*.

The PRIs have to be supported by strong voluntary actions. The people's bodies like *Gram sabhas* have to be strengthened. There should be healthy cooperation between community organisations and *Panchayats*. Finally, governmental policies should create an enabling environment for PRIs to act as vibrant and thriving institutions of local self-government.

## *Panchayats* and Voluntary Sector: Successful Interventions

### *Mobilising Community Groups*

In every village there are a number of functional groups like Self Help Groups (SHG), Community Based Organisations (CBO) and Village Development Committees (VDC). Their interaction, co-operation and conflict with local bodies are areas of current debate in India. Besides statutory bodies like the *gram panchayats* and *gram sabha*, there are a number of non-statutory participatory groups in almost every village. These groups may be of two types. One emerging from the community's own needs and initiatives, that is, community-driven groups like Youth Groups, *Mahila Mandals* (Women's Groups) or even Caste *Panchayats*. Other types of groups are those that are created by external agencies/projects/programmes, usually for a specified period. These groups possess specialised expertise and have a close linkage with their creators (external agencies). For example, the Government of India's project District Primary Education Programme (DPEP) has created Village Education Committees (VECs). For effective collaboration between community organisations and PRIs, the *gram sabhas* should be made aware, active and strong. In every *gram panchayat,* there are sector-specific standing committees like a Health Committee, Education Committee, Social Justice Committee, *etc*. The *Sarpanch* or a member of the *gram panchayat* heads the committee. An institutional mechanism may be developed so that these specialised organisations have close interaction with specialised standing committees of *gram panchayats*. In this regard, project-based committees should be strengthened to be more effective, autonomous and participatory.

### Box 8.6

*Linkages between a Gram Panchayat and a VEC*

Kaliram is a village in Kaithal block of Haryana. The *Sarpanch,* an educated man, is a member of the VEC. The Headmaster of the village primary school, local voluntary organisations and the *Sarpanch* took the initiative in enhancing the enrolment of children in the school. The *Sarpanch* and others took the initiative to organise a competition for school-going children and also sponsored a *Ma-Beti Mela* (Mother-Daughter Fair), organised at the school. Both the events were successful in enhancing community participation in village education. The *Sarpanch* monitors the attendance of teachers and teachers are not resentful of this fact. They feel that this monitoring should be adopted in all schools.

*Source*: PRIA

The public and policy environment for people's participation in governance is inadequate, if not downright hostile. Positive support from Union and State governments is required for genuine and functional devolution of financial resources and authorities to PRIs. This requires intense advocacy efforts to influence policy changes at Union and State levels. Policy advocacy entails influencing policies from the vantage point of enabling the participation and empowerment of the marginalised. It comprises systematic and ongoing monitoring of existing policies, their implementation and reform.

PRIA promotes citizen advocacy, not just professional advocacy. To advocate changes in government policy, in addition to public pressure, macro-level well-documented 'proofs of ground reality' become imperative. So, PRIA and other voluntary agencies are engaged in systematic documentation of different processes. Participatory research aimed at building the capacity of the people are regularly undertaken as a move to strengthen *Panchayati Raj* in rural India. For instance, PRIA conducted a study on the *Status of Functions and Finances of Panchayati Raj Institutions in India* for sensitising the citizens, media, NGOs, bureaucrats, ministers and political parties about the rather weak status of finances of PRIs.

True democracy emphasises decentralisation of governance. The institutions of local self-governance should be strengthened to be participatory, responsive, transparent and accountable. For this, citizens should be educated and people's bodies like *Gram sabha*s must be strengthened to act as custodians of grassroots democracy. The capacities of PRI members should be enhanced through training and workshops. The government officials who are used to the top-down model need to be sensitised to the new realities of local self-governance. NGOs have played a very effective role in making people more and more conscious of their roles and rights. Through processes like micro-planning, special emphasis on weaker sections of the population, participatory research studies and advocacy, people's participation has been greatly enhanced in 'intervened' areas. However, sustained and more aggressive interventions are needed to deepen democratic local self-governance. Research and policy advocacy has to be promoted on an extensive and sustained basis to improve different aspects of local self-governance. And creative individual and collaborative efforts by civil society and the Government to strengthen local self-governance need to be scaled up.

## PRIA: Capacity Building and Advocacy

PRIA is a civil society organisation, undertaking development initiatives to positively impact the lives of poor, weak, marginalised and excluded sections of the society, by encouraging and enabling their participation in the processes of their governance. It strives for achievement of equity and justice, through a people-centred approach, focusing on 'Citizens'- 'their participation and inclusion', 'awareness and empowerment' and 'their democratic rights'.

It recognises the value of people's knowledge, challenges traditional myths and concepts, raises awareness of people's rights and promotes experiential learning. PRIA applies a multi-dimensional strategic approach of creating knowledge, training and capacity building of stakeholders, public education and policy advocacy and intervenes at various levels of the demand and the supply segments, to reach out locally, nationally and globally. It engages itself in strengthening of *panchayati raj* institutions and municipalities, promoting environmental and occupational health, facilitating a network of strong civil society organisations, promoting citizen leadership, monitoring policies and programmes of bilateral, multilateral and government agencies, to achieve an agenda of 'Governance where People Matter.' PRIA proactively involves and engages a range of stakeholders, including academia, media, donors, bi-lateral and multi-lateral agencies, civil society organisations, trade unions, industry, corporate and government institutes in its efforts and provides a platform for a multi-stakeholder development approach. Ongoing grassroot level research, studies and analysis provide inputs and directions to its interventions.

The fact of the local bodies beginning to be treated as the third tier of implementation of development policies and programmes designed by higher tiers of government negates the essence of local bodies as institutions of local self-governance. Needless to mention, the lack of information flow, funds, lack of transparency in functioning, coupled with bureaucratic procedures and non-accountability of line department officials are constraints. The growing concern of transparency, accountability, self-management and self-governance in the PRIs has drawn civil society's attention to PRI.

## Civil Society: Focus Areas in *Panchayati Raj*

1. The issue of the *panchayat* having control over management of all resources (natural, physical and human) within their ambit would imply accountability of line department ministries at the provincial and national levels to the local level. Strong participation of civil society organisations made this possible in several instances.
2. Increasing participation, especially of women and marginalised sections of the community, is another arena that civil society has influenced through various programmes.

3. Promotion of citizen participation also requires sustaining authentic and timely information. The role of civil society in assuring timely information through *Panchayat* Resource Centres (PRCs) has contributed towards informing the local bodies and those who form the electorate.
4. In collaboration with civil society, various awareness programmes have been organised with innovative means of communication to reach the marginalised sections of society.
5. Another area of important contribution of civil society organisations in effective functioning of the PRIs has been building the capacity of new local leadership, especially in the case of women, *dalits*, tribals and other weaker sections of the society. Building their confidence, enhancing their skills and creating opportunities for continuous learning are some of the contributions that civil society organisations have made and will make in the future as well.
6. Ongoing support through training, printed materials and involving them in awareness programmes, have been provided by civil society organisation to other voluntary organisations and community-based organisations interested in strengthening *Panchayati Raj* Institutions.
7. Continuous support is also given to the *Gram sabha*s in rural areas to make them effective. Support in the form of awareness programmes, identifying need-based issues and prioritising them for discussion are addressed through capacity building sessions. Follow-up plans are undertaken in collaboration with civil society to liaison with the government bodies to further the needs of the people.

There are cases where the media and civil society have worked hand in hand, in awareness building and spreading of information. However, for a large country like ours, such efforts need to be supported by all. Attempts should be made to bring local self-governance on the agenda for all institutions and as an issue of concern for all citizens. Sustained public education is needed to build a commitment towards local self-governance. The media and civil society could play a supportive role in this aspect in the form of awareness programmes, training, news slits, documentaries and others. Using new information technology as well as conventional means, authentic, timely and easily accessible information about institutions of local self-governance should be made available to concerned citizens on a sustained basis.

## Voluntary Sector: Issues and Concerns

Broadly, several factors influence the operations and effectiveness of the voluntary sector. One of the major stakeholders that influences the voluntary sector operations is the government, both central and State levels. Although most interventions seek to mobilise community and its people, often schemes and interventions of the government and voluntary sector are targeted at the same deprivation. Lack of communication links between the government agencies and the voluntary sector consequently results in duality of efforts and duplication of resources. In such circumstances, voluntary agencies confront the hostile/non-cooperation attitude of the officials. Besides, the increased community involvement in the planning and implementation stage have further stressed on the need for close cooperation between all the stakeholders in the rural society. Some of the issues and concerns in the effective operations of the voluntary sector are as follows:

### *Simplification of Procedures/Guidelines for Involvement of NGOs*

There is a lot of variation in the procedures/guidelines of the government for involving the voluntary sector in different programmes. In most cases, government assistance is available only through straitjacketed schemes. Moreover, most departments have not played a pro-active role in establishing partnership with the committed voluntary sector. Government has often confined its attention to only those who apply for funds to their offices. It has, on its own, not requested established NGOs to come to their fold and begin a relationship. Often government subjects all proposals, including those from established NGOs, to a uniform appraisal procedure, inhibiting sensitive or well-established organisations from the voluntary sector. Generally, it is difficult for the government to properly examine a large number of proposals and monitor activities of the sprawling voluntary sector. Often there are considerable variations in vetting procedures also, which dissuades the voluntary sector from cultivating strong relations with the government.[5]

*Capacity Building in the Voluntary Sector*

Traditionally, capacity building interventions have focused on strengthening State and public sector institutions. However, due to the growing importance of civil society, there is a need now to find ways to strengthen the capacity of these organisations. Capacity building means development of both individual workers and the organisation. It is essential to focus not only on the individuals in an organisation, but also organisation itself. It is essential to address the issue of institutionalising capacity in an organisation, which is a long term and gradual process[6]. It was recognised that there is an urgent need to build the capacity of the voluntary sector to act as a balancing force between the State and market institutions by imparting training to make them effective agents for good governance, service delivery and managing newer challenges of development.

*Facilitating Inter-Sectoral Partnerships*

One of the major challenges facing the world community, as it seeks to replace unsustainable development patterns, is the need to activate a sense of common purpose on behalf of all sectors of society. Forging such partnerships successfully is the emerging new *mantra* of the new millennium. Some steps have been initiated to fortify the collaborative relationship between government and the voluntary sector, but still a lot needs to be done to increase the existing partnership levels between the voluntary sector and the private sector and local bodies. It is essential to explore possible ways to nurture genuine partnerships and dialogue, while recognising the independent roles, responsibilities and special capacities of each sector.

*Galvanising the 'Spirit of Volunteerism'*

The UN sponsored International Year of Volunteers - 2001, provided a unique opportunity to highlight the achievements of the

---

5. Suggestions of some of the earlier reports of Government of India, such as the *Report of the Expert Group on Simplification of Procedures Dealing with Voluntary Organisations (1987)*, *Action Plan to bring about Collaborative Relationship between Voluntary Organisations and Government (1994)* and *Study Report on Monitoring of Government Aided NGO Projects (1997)* made a recommendation to simplify procedures on the existing methods/procedures for selection of NGOs, release of funds and monitoring of their work, *etc.* But no action was taken.

6. IFCB (2000).

millions of volunteers worldwide and to encourage more people globally to engage in volunteer activity. Volunteerism is related to the part time or full time work done by any person on his/her own free will for the welfare and development of people and society. It appears that over the years, increased dependence on the State has reduced the volunteering spirit amongst the people, which needs to be revived.

*Monitoring and Evaluation of Schemes Implemented through Voluntary Sector*

Like the existing variations in case of procedures and guidelines of various Departments for seeking proposals from the voluntary sector, there is a lot of variation in the methodologies adopted for monitoring and evaluation. The concern for proper monitoring and evaluation of the work of voluntary sector has been raised from different quarters.

A potential problem with the role of the voluntary sector in rural development is that the entire emphasis is on excluding the PRI framework. An integration of all the stakeholders can easily turn into an emphasis on decentralised planning, which works more efficiently for decision-making at local levels. But inherent weaknesses of the local bodies present a real dilemma for the government, especially in building strategic partnerships. Perhaps, the only way out of the dilemma is for governments is to think in terms of setting up platforms in which various local organisations and stakeholders can negotiate solutions on local development and resource management issues. Rather than setting specific objectives for local level development and resource management, governments (supported by NGOs and other organisations) can play essential roles such as providing technical support, assisting with capacity development and providing mediation and facilitation between competing interests.

Some of the key lessons, which could make effective local organisations and institutions are as follows:

- Organisations and institutions for common property resource management need to involve all mutually recognised users.
- Where effective local institutional and organisational arrangements exist, these should be recognised, supported and strengthened, rather than replaced.

- Establishing sponsored organisations on the basis of standard structures should be avoided.
- Effective local organisations are often concerned with a single function. While interests may sometimes expand to involve other activities, it is not advisable to impose multiple functions.
- Where new organisations are being established, processes for developing institutional arrangements (vision, agreed rules/ norms and practices) are more important than organisational structure and should come first.
- Effective local organisations need to have the capacity (and right) to make meaningful decisions about objectives and implementation, rather than having these imposed from above.

## SECTION 2

## INFORMATIONAL POWER TO RURAL SOCIETY – ICT INITIATIVES

Having discussed the role of civil society, we now turn to a consideration of ICT initiatives.

India had realised long back that devolution of empowerment to the poor could facilitate alleviating the sufferings of millions. This initiative of decentralisation was motivated from the fact that delivery of public goods and services is most effective when the responsibilities of discharging these functions are shouldered by the institutions that are closest to the people. As a result of this, the 73rd Constitutional (Amendment) Act aimed to revive and strengthen the *Panchayats*, a third tier of governance with a major role in rural development and poverty alleviation. It conferred constitutional status on the *Panchayats* under a three-tier structure - village, block and district levels in each State. In fact, this body aimed at empowering the rural poor to effectively participate in decision-making processes at the village level primarily to combat absolute poverty.

The literature on the size and trends of rural development and poverty in India is sizeable and controversial. Much of the theoretical literature makes an attempt to address the aggregation problem (notably Sen, 1976, Greer *et al.* 1984). Other works have tried to review other issues, such as direct anti-poverty interventions (*e.g.* land reforms, rural public works, rural credit programmes, *etc.*).[7] The striking commonality emerging from these works is that isolated, piecemeal interventions are not likely to make a dent on rural poverty. Instead, a whole package of simultaneous and well-coordinated interventions in land, labour and credit markets is necessary. Besides, two studies, namely World Bank (1990) and FAO (1991) emphasised that the failure to reduce poverty is not so much because of government inaction or indifference towards the poor, but stems from inappropriate implementation of anti-poverty measures. Concomitantly, sufficient empirical evidence has accumulated on the weakness of anti-poverty measures. A common observation of most studies is that the onus largely lies in the institutional mechanisms responsible for implementation of anti-poverty programmes, leading to mis-targeting of benefits. For example, inaccuracy of targeting allows leakage of benefits to those who are not poor. However, scattered empirical evidence has emerged on the impact of technology in poverty alleviation.

Stiglitz (2000), among others, has made an attempt to derive a relationship between informational power with market imperfections. *The World Development Report* (1998) has made an attempt to highlight information as an intangible input to combat against poverty. Some available works focusing on technology have made an attempt to highlight rural public works in connecting villages to markets and related benefits, but these are isolated works.

The two basic questions with respect to rural development and poverty alleviation are:

a) What does it all mean?

b) How do we take advantage of ICTs?

*The World Development Report* (1998) states that mechanisms for aggregating and dissemination of information are inadequate for targeting the benefits to the poor. Mis-targeting of benefits to the poor could be attributed partly to the poor information and communication facilities in rural India. Thus, leading to poor monitoring and evaluation of poverty alleviation programmes. Modern info-communication systems have considerably improved the

7. Relevant works include Burgess and Stern (1989) on the role of government in poverty alleviation; Ravallion (1989), Lipton and Van der Gaag (1991) on land reforms; Dreze, Lanjouw and Sharma (1992), Gaiha (1991) on rural credit interventions; *etc.*

collection and collation of information. Besides, it has also improved the monitoring and evaluation process in order to suitably plan and design anti-poverty interventions for the poor. The pervasive deprivation and misery - largely in rural areas - calls for quick and effective remedial action.

India has emerged as a software giant in the last decade. But information continues to remain a scarce resource for common masses. Partly the blame lies on low literacy levels but more on the flow of information, which usually remains with the power centres in rural society, namely official agencies and the rich class. Whether information and communication technologies (ICTs) can contribute to rural development beyond the obvious income effects generated by software exports, depends on how pervasive are ICT's impacts on the economy, ranging to improving the efficiency of existing delivery mechanisms. Policy initiatives to bridge the digital divide in India may considerably help in directly reducing the deprivations associated with poverty. For example, empowerment, gender equity, better access to agricultural market information or to government services may be relatively more valuable for poor people who cannot afford to use traditional communications media, or to pay for the services of traditional facilitating intermediaries.

## *Gram Panchayats* and SGRY: A Case Study

*Sampoorna Grameen Rozgar Yojana* (SGRY), previously known as *Jawahar Rozgar Yojana,* is one of the important centrally sponsored anti-poverty schemes. The objective of the SGRY is to provide additional employment in the rural areas, as also food security, alongside the creation of durable community, social and economic infrastructure in the rural areas. The programme is self-targeting in nature, with special emphasis to provide wage employment to women, SCs, STs and parents of children withdrawn from hazardous occupations. The basic framework for the SGRY comprises:

a) Identification of rural needs.

b) Identification of beneficiaries.

c) Disbursement of benefits.

d) Monitoring and evaluation of SGRY projects.

e) Auditing of financial accounts.

The SGRY is implemented at the grassroot level by the *gram panchayats*, the lower most tier of self-governance, under the supervision of government agencies, like the DRDA. However, there are inherent inadequacies in the overall framework of the *Panchayati Raj* system.

**Box 8.7**

*Panchayati Raj Institutions: Structural Inadequacies*

- *The dominant role of official agencies either remained intact or became stronger. A detailed analysis of the new structure in UP revealed that, out of all areas assigned to the panchayats in the State Act, only rural sanitation was assigned to them.*
- *Reallocation of responsibilities within the panchayat system - Zilla Parishad or Taluk Panchayat monopolise majority of the anti-poverty schemes at the implementation stage. Gram Panchayat has a minimal role in the implementation of these programmes.*
- *State Conformity Act lays emphasis on accountability of Panchayats to higher authorities/bodies, it is not matched by a concern for accountability of the Gram Panchayat to the village assembly, commonly referred as the Gram sabha.*
- *Legislative shortcoming in the reporting of Gram Panchayat to the village assembly, without any mandatory requirement of gram sabha's approval.*
- *Overlapping of areas, functions and responsibilities amongst the government agencies in general, and the three levels of Panchayati Raj Institutions.*
- *Act fails to narrow down the areas of responsibility at different levels of PRIs in accordance with their comparative advantage.*

The structural framework of the *gram panchayat* provides strict guidelines on sharing of information. It is mandatory on the part of the *gram panchayats* to hold a *gram sabha* meeting twice in one year. The date and time of the meeting is to be communicated to all the residents of the constituency in advance. The identification of projects and beneficiaries in the village is to be made by the *gram sabha* with the approval of the *panchayat* members. It is also mandatory for the *gram panchayat* to clearly display the development fund sanctioned for the current year and the break-up of the expenditure incurred during the previous year. Besides, the *panchayat* is also responsible for communicating new welfare schemes launched by the government for the rural poor. All such forms of information are an integral part of the structural framework. Field observations indicated various forms of informational inadequacies that restrict effective implementation of SGRY at village level.

- *Gram panchayats* rarely held the village assembly. Even if the meeting was held, then the date and time of the meeting was communicated to a few residents who belonged to the Chairperson's group to conduct business to fulfill formalities. **(Information for Transparency)**
- None of the interviewed poor households and *panchayat* members were aware of how SGRY operated, the name of beneficiaries of the previous year, amount allocated and spent on them or on village development and the last *gram sabha* meeting held. **(Information for Decision Making)**
- The *Panchayats* under the SGRY Scheme received an average amount of Rs. 17,000 during 1996-97 and these funds were utilised mostly for constructing *khiranja* (brick roads). The criteria of selection for construction of brick laden streets were highly discriminatory and largely based on the discretion of the Chairperson. **(Information for Utilisation of Benefits)**
- In the reserved constituencies, especially women representatives, the Chairperson remains as a nominal head and the actual power is enjoyed by her husband or son or near relatives. In the case of SC/ST constituencies, there is evidence of capture of *panchayats* by the higher castes. **(Information for Empowerment)**
- The official agencies enjoy complete authority over the decisions of the *Panchayat* through *Panchayat* Secretary and Village Development Officer. The *Panchayat* Secretary maintains the financial accounts and the Village Development Officer is a co-signatory to the *Panchayat* funds. **(Information for Monitoring and Evaluation)**
- The poor were primarily concerned about lack of access to drinking water, primary health care facilities, non-functioning schools, unhygienic conditions and public toilet facilities, *etc.* **(Information on Actual Needs of the Poor)**

Field observation forms a strong basis for suggesting that dominance of locally powerful groups over the rehabilitation of the rural poor could be partly attributed to the informational power. Poor monitoring has resulted in stifled flow of information at all levels, thus seriously violating the established operational framework of the *panchayati raj* system designed to provide relief to the rural poor.

## Informational Imbalances

The *gram sabha* meeting is the foundation of self-governance to raise the accountability of the decision-makers. The fundamental objective of the village assembly is to build a strong coalition of the poor and empower them to highlight their requirements. The *gram sabha* meetings inculcate transparency in the operating system. However, the flow of information from the official agencies to the *gram panchayats* is on a need-to-know basis. Likewise, the flow of information about the beneficiaries and identification of projects, from the Chairperson to the *Panchayat* members and the *gram sabha* is no more than minimal.

### Box 8.8

*A Gram Panchayat in Hathras District*

The *gram sabha* meeting was not held since the *Panchayat* elections. Some of the village elders from the poor section of *Balmiki* caste approached the Chairperson (*Jatav* caste) to provide a tap for drinking water in their area as they were not allowed to use the village well at times. Their request was turned down due to shortage of funds. A local retired school teacher raised this issue in the presence of the District Magistrate and made a request to arrange a *gram sabha* meeting in 1996. On the orders from the official agency, the Chairperson convened a meeting and also mobilised support from his community. This led to wide scale violence in the village assembly, deterring other groups from supporting the cause of the *Balmiki* community. Besides, some from the *Balmiki* community were implicated in false police cases. The *Balmiki* community still awaits their tap connection.

The JRY guidelines stipulate that the Action Plan should be thoroughly discussed in the village assembly and, subject to approval, implemented by the *Gram Panchayat*. If the village assembly meetings are publicised, held regularly, well-attended and their minutes are systematically maintained and prominently displayed, collusive/ arbitrary decision making may be checked. Besides, the official agencies are also required to oversee that such meetings are regularly held. However, poor monitoring by the official agencies and collusion between the local officials and the Chairperson, lead to such a state of affairs. Absence of adequate communication channels between the poor and the official agencies has adversely affected the formation of a strong coalition of the poor. Effective communication involves listening as well as talking - a simple truth too often overlooked in development work carried out by the official agencies.

Info-communication systems are not limited to the communication of knowledge. Access to a telephone for the poor could considerably ameliorate their living conditions.[8] A poor person can get advice from a doctor or a veterinarian with barely minimal time lag - or attract the attention of the authorities to the poor quality of health services or the venality of local officials. In the mentioned example, the village has no telephone connection and the nearest telephone connection is about 8 kms on the State Highway in the Sasni *Tehsil*. Lack of adequate communication channels had led to the vulnerability of the *Balmikis* to voice their grievances against the Chairperson. Besides, the violence at the village assembly would be considerably controlled with the timely intervention of the local authorities. It would also benefit the official agencies to monitor the operations of rural institutions. In fact, the info-communication system ensures that the poor have the means to speak for themselves and induces them to participate in local self-governing institutions.

**Box 8.9**

*A Gram Panchayat in Gautambudh Nagar*

The brick road was constructed by making voluntary contributions in terms of labour, material and finances by the residents along the adjacent sides of the road to avoid water-logging in residential areas. A few residents contributed land-filling from their agricultural land and others provided free labour (*Shram Daan*). The bricks were supplied from the financial contributions made by the residents. All households interviewed denied receiving wages. However, the Chairperson claimed that about 200 persons participated in this activity for 7-10 days and the road was constructed by JRY funds. It was also established that the brick laying activity was undertaken in busy months for agricultural labourers, resulting in their virtual exclusion.

8. The *Grameen* Mobile Telephone Experiment in Bangladesh provides evidence of the benefits of info-communication systems. This experiment has generated additional income opportunities for the poor and enabled the poor to gain an instrument of "power" that connects the village to market places and local authorities.

In the absence of village assembly meetings, the Chairperson in collusion with local officials, selects SGRY projects on an arbitrary basis. Lack of transparency provides rent-seeking and siphoning of fund opportunities.[9] By controlling access to information, the colluding parties take all the important decisions without any involvement of *Panchayat* members or the local community. Higher authorities are powerless under the new legislation, as the procedure for removing the Chairperson requires a no-confidence motion. Under such circumstances, the chances of different sections combining in a highly stratified community are of course quite remote. What makes it even harder for the poor is the fact that they are trapped in interlocking transactions with the affluent in land, labour and credit markets. As a result, the rent-seeking behaviour and siphoning of SGRY funds by such groups remain largely unchecked.[10]

*Gram Panchayats*, including official agencies, have a special obligation to disclose information about their operations. The official agencies enjoy considerable influence on the *gram panchayats*' decision making because of their sole proprietorship over information. The stifled flow of information creates lack of transparency that leads to corruption and weakening of the structural framework. It is also used to conceal mistakes and incompetence, limiting the ability of the villagers to monitor the official agencies and to choose effective leaders. In the mentioned example, the self-interest of the residents has allowed the colluding parties to siphon off SGRY funds. However, the collusion is evident from the fact that none of the *Panchayat* members knew anything about the scheme - financial outlays, nature of activities and number of beneficiaries. In another case, it was discovered that brick-laying activity was completed well before the SGRY grant was received.

Literacy levels have a considerable impact on creating a transparent working environment. The info-communication system benefits the poor by educating them about the various State-run

---

9. Nepotism and corruption is confirmed in a study of Jaunpur District in UP. "The order for supply of bricks was placed with an owner of a brick kiln located at 35 kms away, though there were several brick kilns within a radius of 5-8 kms. These kilns were ignored in favour of the far away brick kiln because the official agencies, contractor and Chairperson colluded to siphon *Panchayat* funds. The bricks in required quantity and quality never reached the work area." (H. Singh, "Constitutional Base for *Panchayati Raj* in India: The 73rd Constitutional (Amendment) Act", *Asian Survey*, Vol. XXXIV, 1994).

10. Gaiha, Kaushik and Kulkarni (1998).

welfare programmes. The classroom TV programme could be used to educate the poor in the remotest villages. Besides, the government needs to communicate on wide-scale basis all the welfare programmes for the poor. An adequate awareness among the people of their rights and duties could facilitate in building a positive environment and reduce such corrupt activities considerably. Rapid technological developments in info-communications have resulted in widespread availability of Internet connections. Convergence of information with communications technology could enable faster and accurate flow of information to the end-users. Once the poor are made aware of the welfare schemes and required procedures, they are bound to form a strong coalition to air their grievances and actively participate in the local decision making body.

### Box 8.10

*A Gram Panchayat in Bulandshahar District*

The *Panchayat* Chairperson is a woman and for all purposes, her nephew shares the mantle of Chairperson in the village. Higher caste population dominates the village and agriculture is their main occupation. About 500 Muslim families live in this village in absolute poverty and their occupation is as agricultural labourers. Their primary requirement is public toilet facilities. According to some Muslim households, they have to finish their daily chores by 4 A.M., otherwise they have no alternative other than to use the open areas near their dwelling units. Their women folk experience a difficult predicament, as they cannot use the open space in the daytime. Besides, about 200 Muslim families share a drinking water tap in the village against seven taps provided at the temples under the JRY scheme. None of the streets in their area have been identified for laying bricks under JRY and round the year, their streets are water-logged. In the same village, the lower caste dwelling units have brick roads.

The severity of deprivation is more pronounced for some communities due to acute stratification of rural society. However, the requirements of weaker sections and poor exhibit a stark commonality in terms of basic needs. They were primarily concerned about lack of access to drinking water, primary health care facilities, non-functioning schools, unhygienic conditions and public facilities, *etc*. For instance, the SGRY programme aims at reducing poverty through creation of supplementary employment opportunities for the rural poor during agricultural slack periods. Other objectives are creation of social assets and a positive impact on agricultural wage rates. Over the period 1992-1995, total allocation of the SGRY funds registered an increase of about 18 per cent. Person days of employment generated rose from 782.10 million to 894.72 million, implying a growth of 14.40 per cent.

All *panchayats* during the fieldwork associated SGRY funds with the construction of brick roads in villages. The SGRY scheme is known among the locals as "*khiranja* laying scheme". In fact, there are various other urgent needs of the poor, such as adequate drinking water facilities, sanitation facilities, primary health care facilities, *etc.* Most *Pradhans* interviewed in the reserved constituencies have barely minimal educational background and therefore are dependent on the advice of the local officials or affluent class. Though they are aware of the problems of their village, they tend to ignore their real needs in view of the vested interests.

## Illustrations of Informational Inadequacies

Although some useful insights into the functioning of the *panchayats* have been elaborated, data limitations precluded an analysis of rent-seeking behaviour of *Pradhans*, officials and locally powerful groups. Rent-seeking behaviour was pervasive in all *panchayats*, resulting in large-scale diversion of resources. The benefits of SGRY or other welfare schemes to the poor were barely minimal, if any. Given the local power structure (*i.e.* domination of upper castes), and lack of awareness and organisation among the poor, rent-seeking behaviour remained unchecked. Regardless of whether the *Pradhans* belonged to upper or lower castes, there was little variation in the method and pattern of domination by the locally power groups. Excessive pessimism and fear of violence among the poor and other vulnerable sections virtually eliminated any prospect of organised protest or resistance. The reasons which could be attributed for poor results are multiplicity of objectives, duplication of efforts, inherent hesitation of bureaucracy to hand over financial autonomy to *panchayats*, monopoly over information, *etc.* Besides, political influence on the *gram panchayats* had also adversely influenced performance at the village level.[11]

11. *Report of the Task Force on Panchayati Raj*, "Revitalisation of *Panchayati Raj* in India–Problems & Prospects", Rajiv Gandhi Foundation.

In one of the villages, the cremation ground for weaker sections is situated four kms from the village and there is no provision of water. People carry water in earthen vessels along with the dead body in order to perform the last rites. During the interview, the *sarpanch* agreed that it is an urgent need of the poor, but the local officials do not recommend disbursement of SGRY funds for such activities. Poor knowledge of the *gram pradhans* on rules and procedures put them completely at the mercy of official agencies. Well-informed people in the village could considerably influence the *Panchayat*'s decision making. This is possible only through use of modern info-communication systems.

The dominant role of governmental agencies in lieu of their informational power in the decision-making of *panchayats* has led to ignoring the basic needs of the rural poor. Besides, financial paucity of civil society makes them critically depend on the government funds, which are inordinately delayed. Thus, different poverty alleviation programmes run under the *panchayat*'s jurisdiction suffer from poor coordination between major rural institutions. The *gram panchayats* identify the beneficiaries and government functionaries release the funds. However, on most occasions the identified beneficiaries are small landholders and not really poor. Severe political influence and caste-based domination in the governing bodies tend to favour the dominant groups rather than the actual poor within their jurisdiction. Besides, collusion between the government agencies and legislative bodies leaves ample scope for rent-seeking in the disbursement of benefits.

It is indeed an irony that despite a drastic overhaul of *Panchayats*, following the 73rd Amendment, large segments of the rural population continue to be dominated by a handful of powerful groups. In fact, the Act was primarily designed to ensure greater participation of the weaker sections and poor. Thus, it is not enough to design organisations, such as the *Panchayats*, responsive to the needs of the poor. What is crucial is that conducive conditions must also be created for them to act in their favour[12]. It is all the more important that such conditions should facilitate formation of a strong coalition of the poor. This could only be attained through free flow of information by integrating modern info-communication systems with anti-poverty

12. Gaiha, Kaushik and Kulkarni (1998).

programmes. Adequate diffusion of knowledge can improve people's lives in myriad ways, besides higher income.

## Digital Divide and Rural Needs

Digital divide is pervasive in the Indian context. A narrow definition of the digital divide focuses on access to computers and the Internet. But access alone does not bridge the technology gap. To realise the potential of today's information tools, people need the skills to operate them to better their lives and the health of their communities. Access to info-communication technologies (ICT) is definitely a major impediment, which widens the technological gap further. But the number of people connected to telephones or the Internet is low primarily because of low public investments in ICT, resulting in high access cost. Comparison of select indicators attempts to present the extent of wide ranging disparities in India in terms of technology intensity with other countries.

**Table 8.2**

*Divide in Selected Countries (2000)*

| *Country* | *Population (million)* | *Adult Literacy (%)* | *GDP Per Capita* | *Telephone (per 1000)* | *Cellular Phones (per 1000)* | *Internet Hosts (per 1000)* |
|---|---|---|---|---|---|---|
| USA | 280.4 | 99.9 | 31,872 | 682 | 312 | 179.1 |
| UK | 59.3 | 99.9 | 22,093 | 575 | 463 | 57.4 |
| Singapore | 3.9 | 92.1 | 20,767 | 482 | 419 | 72.3 |
| Brazil | 168.2 | 84.9 | 7,037 | 149 | 89 | 7.2 |
| China | 1264.8 | 83.5 | 3,617 | 86 | 34 | 0.1 |
| **India** | **992.7** | **56.5** | **2,248** | **27** | **2** | **0.1** |
| Bangladesh | 134.6 | 40.8 | 1,483 | 3 | 1 | 0 |
| Mozambique | 17.9 | 43.2 | 861 | 4 | 1 | — |
| Malawi | 11.0 | 59.2 | 586 | 4 | 2 | 0 |

*Source*: UNDP (2001)

Poor infrastructural facilities, like electricity, in the developing region also dampen the potential of harnessing the full benefits of the digital medium. Pohjola (2000) among others observed that investments in ICTs have a strong influence on economic growth in OECD countries. But his observations also confirm that requisite benefits have somehow eluded the developing countries as a result of poor stock of physical infrastructure in these countries. However, the developing region can ill afford to delay transformation into an information society due to perennial infrastructural limitations.

## Rural Society

A closer look at Indian rural society shows that almost half of the population lives below the poverty line, the majority of the population is deprived of basic civic amenities like primary health care, drinking water facilities, housing and education. On other aspects, rural society is riddled with illiteracy, exploitative market forces, caste and class break-ups, poor governmental delivery systems, *etc*. An ICT based strategy for economic development of rural society is bound to confront all such barriers. But the essential aspect of an ICT based developmental strategy is the understanding of information-related needs of people.

### Figure 8.2

*Rural Society, Informational Services & Requirements*

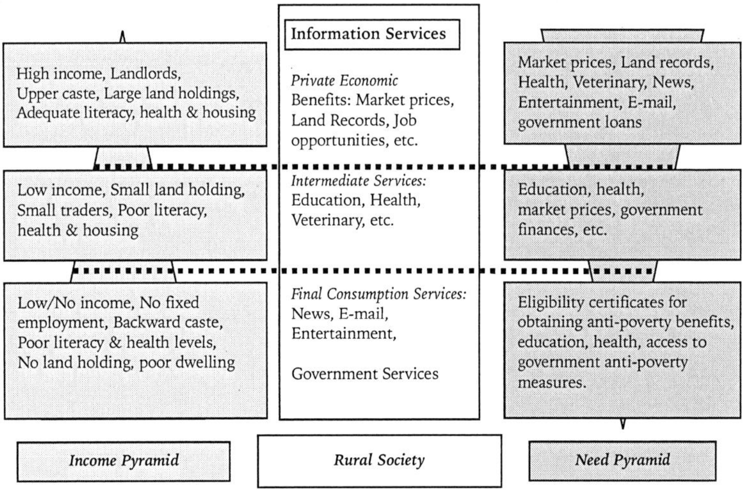


Rural society is exhibited in the form of an income pyramid. The base is comparatively the largest segment, comprising majority of the population, which is poor, landless and vulnerable. Sociologically, this segment houses a considerable proportion of backward and economically weaker sections of the society. Unlike urban society, the mid-section of the pyramid is narrow, mainly constituting low income and small landholders, comprising a mix of both higher and lower castes. The apex segment of the pyramid constitutes higher caste population with considerable influence, large landholdings and high income. The lower and middle segments of the pyramid are deprived of basic services like education, health care, housing, *etc.* faring badly in terms of human development indicators. In terms of needs and accessibility, each segment exhibits a distinct feature in their requirement patterns. The lower segments, for which all government sponsored anti-poverty measures are targeted, require efficient and effective delivery of government services, for example subsidised food, free education, healthcare facilities, *etc.* In the mid-section, especially the small-entrepreneurial class further widens the need requirements to government finances and market prices.

Although all segments have the need for private economic benefits, intermediate services, final consumption services, *etc.*, deprivation supercedes such requirements and government services become their primary requirement. On the other side, the influential class of large landholders, have a different set of requirements, like government loans, market prices of farm inputs and produce, entertainment, quality education and health care facilities, *etc.* In terms of accessibility, the lower segments confront a variety of impediments in accessing these services. Illiteracy and other forms of deprivation make them dependent on the influential and educated class, which considerably increases their opportunity cost for consuming government services. To obtain anti-poverty benefits, lack of information paves the way for rent-seeking amongst the official agencies. A few observations at the *panchayat* level in the districts of Uttar Pradesh reveal the criticality of information in day-to-day governance[13].

The higher class is more politically and economically active, therefore it has easy access to information, law enforcement and other official agencies. Info-communication technology is a medium to

13. Kaushik (2000).

provide improved accessibility without any class or caste distinction. Therefore, the segment confronting barriers to access traditionally, may shift to ICT for getting their required services. Thus, the market determined product mix must include the type of services required by such segments. The product mix offered by the respective ICT initiatives must satisfy these needs for sustainable revenue generation stream. Undoubtedly, information services are designed to suit the rural needs, which may have a considerable impact on the quality of life of the people in the long run. But sustainability of the initiative rests on satisfying consumer needs. These needs are essentially concerned with private material economic benefits, participatory governance and building civil society.

**Table 8.3**

*Information-related Services*

| *Private Economic Benefits* | *Intermediate Services* | *Final Consumption Services* | *E-governance* |
|---|---|---|---|
| Market prices | Education | E-mail | Eligibility Certificates |
| Employment | Health | Entertainment | Licenses |
| Government Benefits | Veterinary | News | Complaints |
| Land Records | Training | Weather Forecast | Law & Order |
| Railway booking | Child care | Horoscope | Empowerment |

Private material economic benefits are concerned with information related to enhance income opportunities and other benefits. This may include market-related information on the prices of farm produce or inputs, employment opportunities in the lean seasons, *etc.* In terms of rural needs, market information is critical for income generation amongst small farmers and traders. Similarly, intermediate services like education and health are primary needs of the rural society. Increase in public investments in primary health care and education is becoming more and more difficult. Distance education and tele-medicine have emerged as an ICT-based alternative to outreach remotely located rural population. Other aspects of informational needs are related to final consumption, like news, entertainment, personal communication, *etc.*

In real terms, rural society remains almost insular to the contemporary chain of events taking place.[14] Nevertheless, information is power. Very little of relevance is available in the print medium for rural society. Other forms of communication systems that are gaining wider acceptability are radio and television. But these are primarily catering to the needs of urban populace than rural. The use of ICTs has made it possible to have news of local relevance. Indubitably, this may mean content development with an eye on the local needs.[15] Similarly, one can obtain weather forecasts for any remotely located part of the country in advance. Large sections of the rural society seek various government services, like land records, birth and death certificates, *etc*.

It is evident that information scarcely percolates down to the man waiting last in the queue for receiving benefits. In the last decade, various stakeholders, like government, civil society, *panchayats*, and private sector, within the rural society have initiated ICT-based experiments to connect the rural population to government and markets. The primary objective being establishment of shortest and efficient channel of communication between the government and its people, keeping in mind the last man in the row. An attempt is made to critically analyse select ongoing ICT-enabled experiments in rural India.

## ICT Initiatives in Rural India

Information and Communication Technology (ICT) in the Indian spectrum is believed to be the answer to all the ills of poor governance, which is far from the truth. A closer look at the rural society exposes wide-ranging disparities at all levels, be it a State, district or village. Some States, like Andhra Pradesh, Maharashtra, Karnataka and Tamil Nadu, have successfully attempted to bridge the digital divide at the State level through proactive State government

---

14. It is understandable that a villager may not expect that lowering of production capacities by OPEC may lead to increase in prices in commodity markets.

15. For example, Pondicherry is situated on a rough coastline frequently experiencing cyclonic storms and rough weather. Swaminathan Foundation is obtaining weather forecast conditions for the coastal region in advance from the US Navy website, it translates the information in local language and announces it in the evening on the loudspeaker situated in the heart of the village. The local fishing community, after listening to this weather forecast, plans out their next day's outing in the sea. In fact, it has become a daily ritual for the local fishing community in Pondicherry.

policies.[16] States like Madhya Pradesh and Rajasthan have initiated a few public-private partnership experiments in reaching people at the village level.[17] The results may vary from region to region, however, successful experiments in a few districts have paved the way for others to replicate. Such public-private partnership experiments have been currently adopted by two progressive States in Northern India, namely Punjab and Haryana. However, there is a strange paradox that two most progressive States of India tending to adopt ICT experiments are carried out in what are regarded as the *BIMARU*[18] States, namely Madhya Pradesh and Rajasthan. But perhaps these *BIMARU* States felt a more urgent need for experimenting with ICT as a tool for sustainable economic development and efficient governance than States that were already performing well.

These initiatives seek to mark a paradigm shift in government delivery systems by using ICT for rural people. Besides, it raises the awareness levels of the rural population, especially in terms of government schemes, developmental fund outlay for the district, *etc.* Another advantage of such initiatives is creating the links between the farmers and markets. Although the objectives of all the ICT-based initiatives are similar, there are stark differences in their product mix and characteristics of main collaborator.

## Government Sponsored ICT Initiatives

State governments have been proactively adopting ICT-based initiatives to connect the government offices with the rural population through information kiosks. The government-sponsored initiatives reflect certain basic features, which are as follows:

a) The State government owns the project.

b) Government is responsible for handling all types of back-end operations.

---

16. Andhra Pradesh and Karnataka have put their district centres online. Maharashtra is currently connecting via network all sales tax circles at district level. Tele-centre experiment in Tamil Nadu has connected most villages at the district level.

17. *Gyandoot* project by Government of Madhya Pradesh in Dhar District has emerged as an economically viable form of government-to-citizen e-commerce activity. This project gives affordable access to the rural community to government services and market information.

18. Bihar, Madhya Pradesh, Rajasthan and Uttar Pradesh

c) Government, in association with *panchayats*, identifies appropriate locations in the rural areas, identifies beneficiaries, provides funds to start info-kiosks.

d) Select government services are provided online at the info-kiosks.

Some of the successful government initiated ICT projects are:

*Gyandoot*

*Gyandoot* is a form of Government-to-Citizen (G2C) e-commerce activity *via* closed network (Intranet), which is giving the rural population in Dhar district affordable access to various government services and market information. *Gyandoot* has been operational since January 2000 and has 21 multimedia kiosks or cyber cafes spread over the entire district of Dhar, covering five blocks in a district. Each kiosk provides public services to 20-30 villages, almost 20,000-30,000 people. *Gyandoot* received international recognition when it was named as a joint winner in the Public Services and Democracy category of the Stockholm Challenge Award in 2000.

Each kiosk caters to about 25 to 30 villages. The entire network of 31 kiosks covers 311 *Panchayats*, over 600 villages and a population of around half a million (nearly 50 per cent of the entire district). Kiosks have been established in the village *Panchayat* buildings. Information kiosks have dial-up connectivity through local exchanges on optical fibre or UHF links. The server hub is a Remote Access Server housed in the computer room in the District *Panchayat*. User fees are charged at the kiosks for the services provided. Local rural youth act as entrepreneurs, running these information kiosks along commercial lines.

The following services are now offered at the kiosks:

1. **Agriculture Produce Auction Centres' Rates**: Prevailing rates of prominent crops at the local and other recognised auction centres around the country are available on-line for a nominal charge of Rs. 5. The volume of incoming agricultural produce, previous rates, *etc.*, are also provided on demand.

2. **Copies of Land Records**: Documents relating to land records including *khasra* (record of rights) are provided on the spot at a charge of Rs. 15. All of the banks in the district have agreed

to accept these kiosk documents. Approximately 0.2 million farmers require these extracts at every cropping season to obtain loans from banks for purchasing seeds and fertilisers.

3. **On-line Registration of Applications**: Villagers had to make several visits to the local revenue court to file applications for obtaining income/caste/domicile certificates. Now, they may send the application from a kiosk at a cost of only Rs. 10. Within ten days, notification about the readiness of the certificate is sent *via* e-mail to the relevant kiosk. Only one trip is needed — to collect the certificate.
4. **On-line Public Grievance Redress**: A complaint can be filed and a reply received within seven days for a cost of Rs 10. These can include complaints regarding drinking water, quality of seed/fertiliser, scholarship sanction/disbursement, employee establishment matters, functioning of schools or village committees, *etc*.
5. **Village auction site**: This facility began in July 2000. It makes auction facilities available to farmers and villagers for land, agricultural machinery, equipment, and other durable commodities. One can put one's commodity on sale for a charge of Rs. 25 for three months. The list of salable commodities can be browsed for Rs. 10.
6. **Transparency in government**: Updated information regarding beneficiaries of social security pension, beneficiaries of rural development schemes, information regarding government grants given to village committees, public distributions, data on families below the poverty line, *etc*. are all available on the Intranet, which makes the government functioning more transparent.

Other services offered at the kiosks include on-line matrimonial advertisements, information regarding government programmes, a forum for school children to ask questions, ask an expert, e-mail (free for information on child labour, child marriage, illegal possession of land belonging to Scheduled Tribes, *etc*.). Some kiosks also have added photocopy machines, STD PCO, and horoscope services. Twice each day, the person managing the server prints the complaints, applications, and e-mails that have been received and sends them to the appropriate authority. The collector responds to certain queries and complaints. If a complaint cannot be addressed, a reply is forwarded to the kiosk manager. The action necessary to address the problem in the field is expected to be taken within 7-10 days. A reply is received at the server room, which is forwarded to the kiosk manager. The district is in the process of putting up a LAN connecting major departments (health, education, tribal development, revenue, food, agriculture, public health engineering, District Council and District Magistrate) to the *Gyandoot* server.

The architecture of the *Gyandoot* project rests mainly on official agencies. The District Rural Development Agency (DRDA) acts a main collaborator with the village *panchayat* (village council) as the local collaborator. The village *panchayat* recommends a local resident for running the kiosk to the DRDA, which reviews the applications and selects the person to run the kiosk in the village. The kiosk owner takes a bank loan to purchase requisite hardware, while the local *panchayat* covers the cost of the phone line. The NGOs have played an active role in raising the awareness of local residents about the services offered by the info-kiosks. Rural population use *Gyandoot* to keep track of market prices, making government services easily accessible, reducing the opportunity cost for local villagers considerably. The revenues from the kiosk are shared between the kiosk owner and the *panchayat*.

*Bhoomi Project*

The Department of Revenue in Karnataka has computerised 20 million records of land ownership of 6.7 million farmers in the State. Previously, farmers had to seek out the Village Accountant to get a copy of the Record of Rights, Tenancy and Crops (RTC) — a document needed for many tasks such as obtaining bank loans. There were delays and harassment. Bribes had to be paid. Today, for a fee of Rs.15, a printed copy of the RTC can be obtained online at computerised land record kiosks (*Bhoomi* centres) in 140 *taluk* offices. The *Bhoomi* centres were opened in remaining 37 *taluks* in 2002. In the next phase, all the *taluk* databases are to be uploaded to a web-enabled central database. RTCs would then be available online at Internet kiosks, which are likely to be set up in rural areas.

Today, from a computerised land record kiosk (*Bhoomi* centre) at *taluk* level, a farmer can obtain a copy of an RTC online by paying a

Rs.15 fee. A second computer screen faces the clients to enable them to see the transaction being performed. Copies can be obtained for any land parcel in the *taluk* by providing the name of the owner or the plot number. A *patwari* is designated for *Bhoomi* centres to authenticate the copy of the land record.

When a change of ownership takes place through sale or inheritance, farmers can file for a mutation of the land record at the *Bhoomi* centre. Each request is assigned a number by the computer. The number can be used to check the status of the application on a Touch Screen provided on a pilot basis in three of the computerised kiosks. The computer automatically generates notices, which are then handed over to the Village Accountants. Most *patwaris* are not stationed at *taluk* offices, but they visit the central *taluk* office every 2-3 days to pick up these papers. The process of issuing notices by Village Accountants to the interested parties remains the same.

With the computerised system, administrators can quickly determine the number of approved and overdue mutation orders. Information collected from one urban *taluk* indicates that earlier 3,000 mutations were handled annually. After computerisation, there is an almost 50 per cent jump in the number of mutation requests. This change would seem to indicate a level of approval of the new system by the population, and willingness to update changes in land ownership that were previously left undocumented.

*e-Seva*

*e-Seva* is built on the success of Hyderabad's Twin Cities Network Services Project (TWINS). TWINS was launched in November 1999 to focus on Hyderabad and Secunderabad. It was renamed *e-Seva* with the Andhra Pradesh government plans to extend the services to major towns and municipalities of the State. The *e-Seva* centre is a one-stop-shop for more than 30 government-to-consumer (G2C) and business-to-consumer (B2C) services.

Online services of various kinds, including payment of utility bills, reservations of train tickets, getting birth and death certificates, vehicle permits, driving licenses, transport department services, sale and receipt of passport applications, telephone connections, collection of small savings, ATM (cash withdrawal and deposits and issue of statement of accounts), mutual funds (collection of applications and transfer of shares), receipt of complaints or requests in connection with citizen services, cell phone bill payments, *etc.*, are made available at *e-Seva* centres.

Before the launch of the *e-Seva* project, these services were available at separate offices and were normally time-consuming because of slow processing and often, large crowds waiting for the services. The goal of *e-Seva* is to simplify the delivery of city services by providing a wide spectrum of citizen friendly services that will save citizens the bother of running around various departments. The Andhra Pradesh government has plans to integrate both the State government and some central government-centric services through the *e-Seva* centres. The system used in *e-Seva* is not sophisticated. It is a client/server model relying on Web browsers on the front end, an Oracle relational database on the back end, and an Oracle Web application server and connected through reliable ISDN lines. There are 19 *e-Seva* centres with 200 service counters spread across Hyderabad and Secunderabad.

Because of the innovative idea undertaken by the *e-Seva* project, it has been able to attract the attention of customers and suppliers of services. Various public and private organisations are providing their services through *e-Seva* centre. For instance, the Industrial Credit and Investment Corporation of India (ICICI), Housing Development Finance Corporation Project (HDFC), Unit Trust of India (UTI) are some of the banks with whom *e-Seva* has tied up to facilitate banking services. *E-Seva* has shown phenomenal growth rate in terms of number of transactions conducted as well. By September 2001, Andhra Pradesh government served more than 500,000 citizens through *e-Seva* centres. Before September 2001, Rs. 5 was being charged for each service such as payment of property tax, registration, electricity bill, *etc.*

The resistive forces originating from low-income and poverty-ridden groups were overcome to some extent by making the services provided by *e-Seva* free. Since low-income people in the State cannot afford PCs, availability of free services encourages higher level of uses. Similarly, to overcome the barriers of illiteracy and hence to extend the services to the illiterate population, touch-screen kiosks are being commissioned. To extend the services to farmers, in another experiment, 82 agricultural marketing committees have been linked together and with the organisation's headquarters. The objective is to make available market prices at the *mandis* and wholesale markets.

*JanMitra*

*JanMitra* is an ICT based initiative of '*JanMitra*' society, registered under the Societies' Act. It is an integrated e-platform through which the rural population of Rajasthan gets desired information and avails services related to various government departments at information kiosks within its reach. It is an initiative of the Government of Rajasthan, supported by the UNDP's "Improving Citizens Access to Information". This initiative is currently operational at Jhalawar, a backward district of Rajasthan. Currently, *JanMitra* has opened 19 information kiosks at various locations in the district.

*JanMitra* is an ICT integrated platform, which facilitates communication and information interchange within a localised Intranet between village kiosks and district centres. The kiosk is connected to the network through a 'dial up' connection. This initiative has been successful in building efficient management and decision support systems for district level officers, beside efficiency and transparency in government delivery systems. The major stakeholders in this initiative are - the State Government as service provider, the District Collector as the systems in-charge, Department of Information Technology as the nodal agency, the kiosk-owner as a contact point for service delivery.

*JanMitra* provides a wide variety of government services like Public Grievance Redressal, Online Applications, Land Records, Public Information and Awareness Services, Market Information, Village-to-Village (V2V) services, *etc.* The following services will be shortly put online - status of court cases, status of old age pension applications, tenders for government procurement, reservation of seats on Rajasthan roadways buses, *etc.* This is a local language (Hindi) interface, which is easy to comprehend and use. The entire content for the network is designed by the government to ensure State-level integration, especially with the use of census codification patterns and database linkages between intra- and inter-departments.

The information kiosks provide user-charge-based services to rural people. Each kiosk is equipped with a computer wired through an Intranet network connected with the district headquarter. These kiosks cater to 25 to 30 surrounding villages or 15 *gram panchayats*, providing information services to a population of around 20,000-30,000.

## ICT Initiatives of Civil Society

Civil society has established its presence in delivering a variety of services, like education, health, low-cost housing, management of natural resources, capacity building for income generation, empowerment of weaker sections of the society, *etc*. Lately, the civil society has introduced ICT-enabled services for the rural population. The common features of such initiatives are:

a) The NGO is the main promoter, with possibilities of the government as joint partner.

b) The NGO floats a company and operates on franchisee terms, *i.e.* annual franchisee fee or revenue sharing basis.

c) Kiosk owners are selected on the basis of their capital investment capabilities and entrepreneurship skills.

d) The promoters provide training and assist in the establishment of the kiosk.

e) Often the range of services is limited, if the promoters fail to rope in the district administration.

f) The thrust areas are computer education, vocational training, *etc*.

Some of the successful initiatives are:

### *TARAhaat*

The *TARAhaat* project was launched with financial assistance and inputs of content from its promoter Development Alternatives, an NGO focusing on sustainable rural development in India and its marketing arm, Technology and Action for Rural Advancement (TARA). *TARAhaat* uses a franchisee-based business model to bring computer and Internet technology to rural India. Its business model is based on B2B, B2C and C2C, which attempts to create revenue streams using ICT technologies, leading to financial viability for itself and its franchisees. It is a horizontal portal, but several domains such as medical services, commodity trade, distance education, *etc.*, appear as strong vertical elements. The portal displays information in the local language. For a majority of the illiterate rural population, the portal uses animated pictures, self-explanatory diagrams and voice-over. *TARAhaat*'s central core is built around the information needs of the end-user. It has been operational in Bhatinda district since January 2001.

**Box 8.11**

TARAhaat: *Integrating Services*

| | |
|---|---|
| TARAdhaba- | provides connectivity |
| TARA*Bazar*- | access to products for rural households, farmers, SSIs |
| TARAvan- | deliver ordered goods at remote locations |
| TARAdak- | connects rural population with their distant relatives |
| TARAgyan- | education and training modules for rural youth |
| TARAguru- | decentralised university for mentoring & consultancy |
| TARAscouts- | collect information to be put on the portal |
| TARAvendor- | runs the *Bazar* and caters to products at TARA*Bazar* |
| TARAcard- | allows people to consume goods on credit |

*TARAhaat* has been operational in Bhatinda District of Punjab. It has opened eight TARA*kendras* with assistance from Bhatinda DRDA. All franchisees are located at the focal points identified by the Government of Punjab and have been operational since early 2001. The TARA*kendras* have been currently linked to the Internet by dial-up connections. *TARAhaat* has segmented the rural market into five different habitats based on population size[19]. Each *kendra* has a catchment area of five kilometers radius, depending on the habitat type. Rough estimates of *TARAhaat* reveal that each *kendra* serves the needs of four-six villages, almost a population of about 10,000-15,000. *TARAhaat* plans to open 47,000 such *kendras* in the country by 2006.

*Drishtee*

*Drishtee* is a revenue-generating platform for rural networking and marketing services that enables e-governance, education, and health services. It is a project replicated from the *Gyandoot* project in the form of a commercial initiative. *Drishtee* is currently associated with Digital Partners for logistic support. It has developed a software package which facilitates communication and information interchange within a localised Intranet between village kiosks and the district centre. The *Drishtee* website offers a variety of rural informational

19. These habitats are cities (pop. below 500,000), block towns (pop. 15,000-50,000), large villages (pop. 5,000-15,000), medium villages (pop. 2000-5000), and small villages (pop. <2000).

services covering land records, mailing software, market information, matrimonial services, on-line grievance postings, and a host of other customised services. The objective of the project has been to establish community-owned, innovative and sustainable information technology projects in the most poverty-stricken and tribal-dominated rural areas. It addresses the socio-economic developmental needs of the villagers through a G2C (Government-to-Citizen) based model.

**Figure 8.3**

*'Drishtee' Business Model: Connecting Village-by-Village*

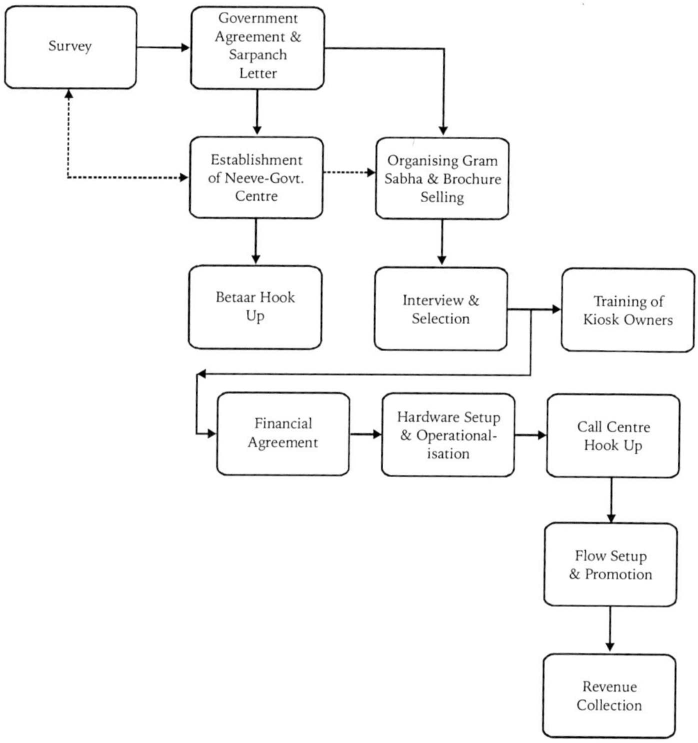


Source: www.*Drishtee*.com

*Drishtee* is currently installing low cost, self-sustaining, and community owned rural Intranet projects in various districts, Seoni and Shahdol in Madhya Pradesh, Sirsa in Haryana and Jallandhar in Punjab.

Information services are provided through *Drishtee's soochanalaya* in a village (or a group of villages). These kiosks or *Soochanalayas* provide user-charge-based services to rural people. Each kiosk is equipped with a computer wired through an Intranet network connected with the district headquarter. These *Soochanalayas* cater to 25 to 30 surrounding villages or 15 *gram panchayats*, providing information services to a population of 20,000-30,000. With the help from the local DRDA, *Soochanalayas* are established in the buildings of *Gram Panchayats*, which are located either at block headquarters or at prominent *bazaar* (weekly marketplace in tribal areas) or on major roads (*e.g.* highways).

Each ICT-based initiative is offering more or less similar types of information services. Although the approach strategy in the rural market may differ, broadly the initiatives have a wide range of service offerings. However, all the services are not fully operational for diverse reasons, like no telephone connectivity (Sirsa) or poor quality telecom services (Bhatinda), delay on the part of main collaborators in launching new services, lack of initiative on the part of main collaborators to ascertain rural needs, *etc.* An appropriate market strategy and product mix offering must be commensurate to the rural needs. At a micro-level, rural society's needs are barely minimal, primarily concerned with incremental improvement in the quality of life. The ICT-based initiatives (*TARAhaat* and *Drishtee*) have designed their marketing strategy and product mix offering to suit their own requirements.

## ICT Initiatives promoted by Industry

Very recently, the Indian industry has realised the untapped potential of rural markets. Traditionally industry looks at rural areas as markets for products. But the ICT-enabled business model has provided an opportunity for industry to have a two way business channel - one, directly procuring farm produce from the farmers, and two, pushing their products in the rural market. The two prominent ICT based initiatives are ITC's *e-choupal* and Parry's Corner of EID-Parry. Both companies produce farm inputs and process agricultural produce.

### *e-choupal*

*e-choupal* is an initiative of ITC (a large agricultural processing company in India) to link directly with rural farmers for the procurement of agricultural and aquaculture produce like soya, coffee, and prawns. The *e-choupal* was conceived to tackle the challenges posed by the unique features of Indian agriculture, characterised by fragmented farms, weak infrastructure and the involvement of numerous intermediaries. Traditionally, these commodities were procured in '*mandis*' (major agricultural marketing centres in rural areas of India). ITC has now established computers and Internet access in key rural areas where the farmers can directly negotiate the sale of their produce with ITC. The PCs and Internet access at these centres enable the farmers to obtain information on *mandi* prices, good farming practices and place orders for agricultural inputs like seeds and fertilisers. This helps farmers in improving the quality of produce, and also helps in realising a better price.

Figure 8.4

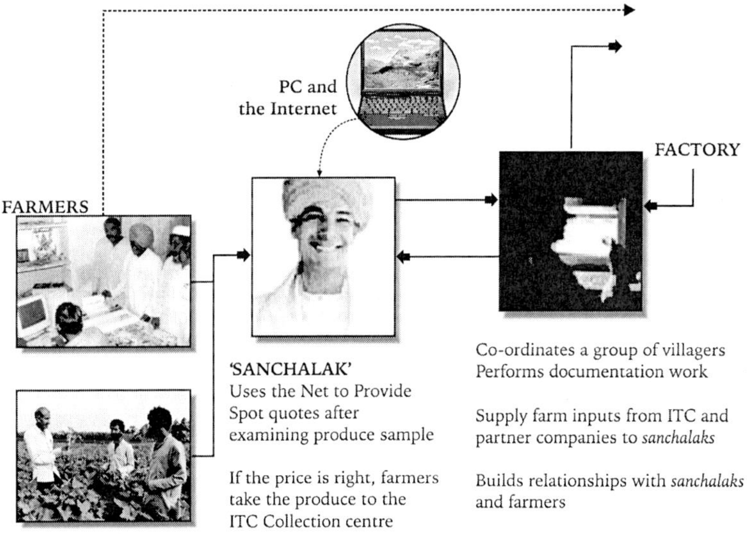


Each ITC kiosk having an access to Internet is run by a *sanchalak*—a trained farmer. The computer is housed in a farmer's house and it is linked to the Internet *via* phone lines or by a VSAT connection and serves an average of 600 farmers in ten surrounding villages within about a five km radius. The *sanchalak* bears some operating cost, but in return gets commissions for the e-transactions done through his *e-choupal*. The warehouse hub is managed by middlemen called *samyojaks*. The *samyojak* acts as a local commission agent for ITC.

Due to the *e-choupal* services, farmers have seen a rise in their income levels because of rise in yields, improvement in quality of output and a fall in transaction costs. Even small farmers have gained too. Customised knowledge is offered to the farmers despite heterogeneity. Farmers can get real time information despite their physical distance from the *mandis*. The system saves procurement costs for ITC. The *e-choupal* model is quite different from the other models, as the farmers do not pay for the information and knowledge they get from *e-choupals*. The *e-choupal* model runs without any subsidy. There is no government money involved in this project.

ITC has extracted value in four steps:

(a) elimination of non-value adding activities;

(b) differentiating product through identity preservation;

(c) value added products traceable to farm practices;

(d) e-market place and support services to future exchange.

One of the success factors is ITC's managerial competence to execute a complex project and manage cost. The ITC bottom line is—roll out, fix it, and scale it up. The principle of the *e-choupal* is to inform, empower and compete.

## Challenges in Scaling up

- Developing entrepreneurial capacity of the rural community to take up the role of *sanchalaks* and *samyojaks* is difficult and plenty of training is required. Also, there is a need to enhance management capacity of ITC frontline by developing a new cadre of agricultural graduates.
- Lack of infrastructure, such as power and broadband.
- Slow policy reform (*e.g.* modification of the *Agricultural Marketing Act*).

ITC has invested $ 22 million to set up 3,500 *e-choupals* serving 20,000 villages and 1.8 million farmers in five States of India. Transactions worth $100 million were carried out through these *choupals* in the first year. ITC is adding seven new *e-choupals* a day and plans to scale up to 20,000 *e-choupals* by 2010 covering 100,000 villages in 15 States, servicing 25 million farmers. Transactions through these *e-choupals* may rise to about US $ 2.5 billion by 2010.

*Parry's Corner*

The bane of Indian agriculture is not lack of technology, R&D efforts or credit availability. It is inadequacy and inefficiencies in the dissemination of relevant information to the farming community – including, but not limited to the right cultivation practices, correct post-harvesting techniques, and up-to-date information on market prices of commodities. The farmer is thus caught in a vicious cycle of sub-optimal use of farm inputs, higher cost of credit and lower price realisations on his produce, leading to insignificant disposable incomes for him and his family.

The rural community today needs:

- Instant dissemination of market and commercial information.
- Constant education on the latest developments in agri-science and post-harvest technology.
- Access to the right markets (for both the farm and the non-farm produce) through affordable credit and transportation solutions.

While the agriculture universities, research stations, Department of Agriculture and other agencies have developed several solutions and technologies for the farming community, the dissemination of the same has not been possible on a large scale because of the country's size. The Internet, however, is a tool that can be leveraged to reach out to a much wider base literally at the click of a mouse.

EID Parry (I) Ltd. is closely linked to the farming community through its Sugar Division (100,000 registered sugarcane growers) and its Farm Inputs Division (about 3,000,000 end-users). The Company operates in three industry segments:

1) Producing and selling farm inputs such as fertilisers, pesticides, and seeds, which are sold primarily in the interior of south and east India;
2) Producing and selling sugar from four factories in Tamil Nadu; and
3) Producing and selling Sanitary-ware across the country.

The Agri Portal has been designed to address the specific needs of the rural farming community and is an attempt to catalyse e-commerce in agricultural and non-farm products by offering a network of partnerships in the areas of Content, Connectivity and Commerce. This content has been developed by using in-house expertise (EID Parry's Sugar and Farm Inputs Division and Corporate R&D Lab) and working with the Tamil Nadu Agriculture University and its Research Stations, Tamil Nadu University for Veterinary and Animal Sciences, National Horticulture Board, AMM Foundation, Murugappa Chettiar Research Centre, other players in agriculture related media and publishing houses.

The content is in Tamil language for ease of use. There is also a Web-based application for the registered sugarcane growers of EID-Parry to access and maintain their transaction records with the Company. An application for the dealer channel and the sales force of the Company is also under development. To make the experience richer and navigation easier, the site is equipped with mouse-overs and voice-overs and has been designed with touch-screen panels in conjunction with an offline web-room to make downloads faster.

Several other utilities such as a farming calculator and farming calendar, as well as farm advisory services, are also under various stages of development and will soon be launched on the portal. Discussions with commerce and logistics players are also taking place to help the farmers and users reach the right markets with their produce. The connectivity in rural areas is provided through reliable and low-cost CorDECT Wireless in Local Loop technology. It can provide 35/70 kbps simultaneous Internet and telephony within areas of about 25-30 km radius.

The EID-Parry kiosks are known as Parry's Corner. These Parry's Corners have the potential of becoming the business hub of villages (as the Parry's Corner in Madras did over the past 200 years). The first 16 "Parry's Corners" have been set up using the franchisee scheme. These owner/operators have been trained to use PCs and surf the Portal and the Net and assist users coming to the kiosks. About 150 farmers have been trained on the use of the Net and the portal and especially the special application built for them to view their transaction record with the company. Following the pilot at Nellikuppam, Parry plans to roll out another similar initiative in

Tiruvallur district in Tamil Nadu. The Nellikuppam model will be replicated in three other sugar factory areas (of EID Parry) in Tamil Nadu soon.

Understandably, many new initiatives at various levels have come up across rural India. But in their first phase of operational strategy, the franchisee business model is the most popular. Rural society has also responded well to such initiatives and related developmental benefits are evident in terms of response of end users and a growing number of info-kiosks in the districts. However, there exist inherent weaknesses in the initiatives, which have considerably affected the sustainable revenue stream of such initiatives in the long run.

## Impact of IT Initiatives on Developmental Objectives

Today, the major dilemma is whether ICT is a vehicle for growth for the privileged class or does it have a spillover effect on the deprived sections too? But so far it is suggested that PC penetration has virtually skipped rural India, strengthening the arguments of ICT revolution skeptics. Some argue that technology is a reward of development, making it inevitable that the digital divide follows the income divide. But on the contrary, empirical findings have shown that ICT has enabled people to increase their incomes, enjoy a better standard of living, improve the quality of life by greater transparency in governance and build communities for creative[20]. A perception of ICTs as a fundamental developmental tool rests on certain assumptions. At the macro-level, the introduction and use of ICT will improve the efficiency of rural infrastructure, enhance economic performance and strengthen competitive capacities in the market[21]. At the level of human development, ICTs contribute to improvements in provision of basic social services, help to disseminate valuable information on production and conservation, improve the efficiency of governments, and enhance the provision of education and health services[22]. In other words, global networks have reorganised production and channels of distribution. Networks have reduced distances to the markets and considerably influenced the markets themselves. The concept of good governance or smart governance has

20. UNDP (2001).
21. Braga (1996), Kenney (1995).
22. World Bank (1996).

emerged, which provides greater transparency in the government distributive channels.

Thus, ICT's role in economic development is gaining more visibility in the present context and contributing towards strengthening democracy, increasing social participation, and removing barriers to modernisation. The following conclusions are drawn from the field studies of the respective ICT-based initiatives:

**Income Generation:** Exploitative market forces prevailing in the rural society are a major impediment for income generation. By lowering the transaction cost, ICTs may enhance the economic efficiency and encourage the spread factor and product markets in developing countries[23]. Furthermore, empirical work has suggested that the spreading of markets and reduction of information monopolies provide impetus for institutional change. *The World Development Report* (1998) points out that in rural Costa Rica, small farmers use ICTs to obtain information on international coffee and cocoa prices from the city. Similar experiences are shared for Sri Lanka, Mexico, Bangladesh, *etc.* The field survey in Madhya Pradesh, Punjab and Haryana revealed that market intermediaries tend to push prices down while procuring directly from the farmers and inflate transaction costs considerably to charge better prices in the market.[24] In the entire market procurement and delivery system, producers remain ignorant of the prevailing prices of produce in the market, as well as about the price of the inputs. The intermediaries keep the accounts for producers, which is adjusted against the procurement of the next consignment. There is evidence of mobile phone use by a few progressive farmers to know the prevailing market price of their produce for negotiating a better deal with their commission agents. The market negotiation depends primarily on the opportunity cost for the commission agent and the search cost for the producer. Use of ICTs considerably lowers search and opportunity costs. In the event of reduction in the opportunity and search costs, market information

23. Norton (1992).

24. For instance, Bhatinda is a major farm produce market in the North. But farmers tend to sell their entire produce to the commission agents, who sell the produce in the market. There is no exchange of money physically between the intermediary and the farmer. But the intermediary's outlets take care of all material needs of the farmer. For diesel, the intermediary issues a receipt to the farmer for a particular diesel depot, from where the farmer collects the diesel by handing over the receipt. The intermediary makes the payment directly to the diesel depot and deducts the amount from farmer's accounts.

improves the producer's capabilities in obtaining a significant share of the savings on mutually agreed terms. Thus, market information has a considerable influence on the income opportunities for the rural society.

**Human Development and Entertainment**: Education, healthcare, access to basic amenities, *etc.*, remain as the weakest link for human development in developing countries. The distance education programme has emerged as a major benefit of ICT in the present context. Communication networks have exhibited great potential in taking education to communities for whom access to quality education is difficult. Educational content developed and put at one place, made accessible to all locations without physical travel, is the concept behind distance education. Innovations in multimedia have paved way for distance education learning, especially primary and secondary education[25]. Currently, the best medium for the delivery of multimedia is the CD-ROM. For example, Microsoft and many other institutions have developed educational CDs for all levels. But the scope of CDs is limited in terms of limited capacities (almost 640 MB) for storing text, video and audio. The delivery of such multimedia services on the Internet circumvents this shortcoming. This is likely to improve further with the increase in the bandwidth of communication channels and establishment of platforms independent of execution environment like Java[26]. TARAgyan module is providing such services in rural Punjab. Multimedia is also good for reference works like encyclopedias and dictionaries. Such intermediate services also open newer opportunities for educated youth in developing and providing relevant educational content for the rural society.

Likewise, ICT has a similar role to play in delivery of health and veterinary services at remote locations.[27] Indubitably, isolated cases of ICT-based interventions in health and veterinary services cannot determine the overall impact on the rural society. But field surveys

25. Open University in UK has a new course, THD204, for students stationed at remote locations such as oil rigs, active military service, *etc.*, through which lessons and a students' library are sent on CD-ROM, replacing the earlier practice of sending reading material by postal delivery.

26. Hall (1996).

27. For example, telemedicine services are provided using teleconferencing and other forms of advisory services *via* computer networks. A pilot project in Tamil Nadu, local Veterinary Institute, with logistic support from Cornell University (USA) is providing veterinary services in rural Tamil Nadu.

reveal that rural society in the respective districts, which depended on far flung public health and veterinary services in the past, is now using telephones, health based portals of academic institutes, and other means of communications, to access information and services of medical practitioners. Besides, the concept of telemedicine has also given a boost to barefoot technicians.[28] There is ample evidence on the use of telephones by barefoot technicians in providing basic health and veterinary services in the rural areas.

Personal communication *via* e-mail is an important service for the rural society. There are reported instances of labourers sending e-mails to their families at a nominal fee from the info-kiosks in Punjab[29]. Similar experiences have also been reported from urban centres like Bombay. Frequent use of e-mail facilities by taxi drivers hailing from Uttar Pradesh and Bihar working in Bombay have further broadened the scope of ICTs in rural society. Besides personal communication, ICTs also provides a novel method of leisure and entertainment. In the absence of cinema halls and other means of entertainment in rural environs, multimedia kits provide an efficient medium of entertainment, like computer games for children, movies, *etc.* Another aspect of consumption services is horoscopes. Though horoscopes are usually treated as any other use of computers in western societies, the horoscope plays an important role in Indian society. Whether it is match making for marriage, birth of a child, opening a business establishment or buying a house, horoscopes and placement of stars are deeply etched in the Indian psyche, be it urban or rural.

**Good Governance**: No one can ignore government, whether for any benefit or maintaining the law and order situation. Such

---

28. The barefoot technician is a novel concept in rural India, where NGOs train educated youth in the villages to supply basic health care and veterinary services. In cases of emergency, they are trained to provide immediate relief to allow the patient to reach the nearest government hospital for specialised treatment.

29. A large number of economically active population migrates from Bihar and Uttar Pradesh for gainful employment in richer regions like Punjab and Haryana during the harvesting season. These agricultural/menial labourers are away from their homes for long periods and letters are the only means of personal communication. Private courier service is almost unaffordable and public postal service is highly unreliable. E-mail has emerged as a boon to this community, which is reliable and fast. It is reported during another field survey that labourers from Uttar Pradesh and Bihar send their e-mail messages at charges varying between Rs. 7-10 in Hindi fonts to an e-mail address of the public info-kiosk in their region. The kiosk owner in their home region takes a printout and delivers at their residence or family members collect the printout from the kiosks themselves at a nominal fee of Rs. 2.

experiments, if looked at from the supply-side, shift the focus on another benefit of ICTs, commonly known as smart governance or electronic governance. E-governance is not only about bringing transparency and accountability in the government, but also about efficient delivery of government services.[30] Empirical analysis and other related works validate breakdown in the communication process, that results in poor governance and ineffective implementation.[31] Land records of the village are kept with the village *patwari* (government official who maintains land records). But maintenance and updating of land records are done manually. This method of keeping land records is time-consuming, less accurate and discretionary. But as far as the use of this information is concerned for the village community, it is vitally important because the land revenue is fixed on the basis of ownership of agricultural land.[32] There are multifarious other forms of information needed to plan and implement economic development plans and anti-poverty measures. Population size, demographic data, human development indicators, *etc.*, are a few among others, which could be essential for planning and implementation.[33] In fact, information on disbursement of benefits is essentially required to control and monitor all government sponsored programmes, like identification of people below poverty line, beneficiaries for old age pension, *etc.* Besides, there are other scores of services provided by the government departments, like issuance of driving license, bona fide residence certificates, issuance of passports, *etc.* Likewise, supply of essential commodities through the Public

30. For instance, if one person from the village needs a below the poverty line certificate to get government sponsored anti-poverty benefit, the option available before him is to travel from his village to the district centre to file his application. This is a costly and time-consuming process. The use of ICTs for filing such applications at a nominal cost at the village info-kiosk saves time and results in considerable reduction of opportunity costs. In another instance, rarely are people aware of the respective official dealing with BPL certificates. Identification of the right person is difficult under the existing governmental system. This results in intermediaries/touts, which increases opportunity costs considerably because of ignorance.

31. Gaiha *et al.* (2000).

32. For example, the agricultural land may have a small section of rocky land or a small pond, which is not used for agriculture. If the *patwari* has ignored to put such observations in the land record, the revenue assessment will be made for the use of full land, thus end up farmer paying more than what he is required to pay to the government.

33. The Government of Madhya Pradesh had released *the Madhya Pradesh Human Development Report, 1999*. This further strengthens the argument that relevant information exists at various levels, it is a question of maintaining and updating a database.

Distribution System (PDS) is another type of benefit for the rural community.

Monitoring and controlling are an essential act of governance. The monitoring agency has to discharge overlapping functions of a controlling agency. The information requirement depends on the nature of work.[34] For instance, it could be about the date and time of *gram sabha* meetings, project progress, *etc*. Thus, the information requirement is more or less similar to those required for information on disbursement of benefits. Perhaps this is the third aspect of electronic governance, which focuses on performance appraisal. Smart governance is all about efficient delivery of services, but these services cannot be delivered efficiently without proper collection, collation and validation of information. Introduction of IT at governmental level paves the way for smart governance or e-governance.

**Empowerment:** The Bangladesh *Grameen* Mobile Phone Experiment has further strengthened the role of communication systems in empowerment of the poor because it was observed that mobile phones not only brought them nearer to the markets, but telephone connectivity brought them nearer to the government administration.[35] It is already established that info-communications have closed the knowledge gap. Literacy is critical in helping the poor to absorb and diffuse knowledge within the community. But information is important for giving voices to the poor. Largely, the past experience has emphasised that poor have no voice in the actual decision making of the implementing organisations. As the awareness increases among the poor about their own circumstances and comparison is made against possible alternatives, they are bound to make a choice. It benefits them in terms of discovering possible ways to overcome the obstacles they face.

---

34. For example, the official agencies would like to know whether the benefits are reaching the targeted beneficiaries or whether the allocation of funds to beneficiaries was approved in the *gram sabha* meetings or how many villagers were present at the meetings. Information like these helps the official agencies in ascertaining that anti-poverty benefits are appropriately targeted.

35. *Human Development Report (1998)*. Also, the Director General of Police (DGP) in Uttar Pradesh launched his personal website for receiving complaints of erring police officials in the State. In first month of its operation, the DGP received variety of complaints against his department relating to corruption, extortion, harassment, refusal of filing FIR by the police station in-charge, *etc*. This experiment assisted the DGP in streamlining the functioning of his department. (As narrated by the DGP-U.P. at the 2-4 Dec. 1999 meeting on *Equity, Diversity and Information Technology.)*

Increased awareness generates the ability to voice concerns, desires suggestions and complaints. Ultimately, it leads to airing of voices among the poor. This inference strengthens the rationale for public action to ensure that poor have access to education and information. The net impact of info-communications on social inequalities is positive. Access to IT also strengthens the voice of the poor, whether in terms of marketing their goods or in advocating policies that address their needs. It brings with it an increase in communication across the country, and will help to reduce narrow differences on grounds of region, caste and worship. Increasing accessibility into remote rural and backward areas with the help of a computer and a telephone line could be used to promote education and bring these areas closer to the urban, more prosperous areas of the country. The cause of ethnic differences largely rests in ignorance and lack of information. A well-informed and educated society could not be easily misled for individual interests. Most ethnic differences emerge from illiteracy and ignorance.

The *Gyandoot* and *Drishtee* initiatives have emerged as a means to establish equity in the society. Some of the services offered in these initiatives are primarily directed at the weaker sections of the society. Traditionally, pervasive effect of gender, caste and economic disparity did not provide an opportunity to women, poor and backward castes to interact with official agencies. But an info-kiosk in the village has emerged as great leveller in equity in the rural society. The *Gyandoot* and *Drishtee* kiosks at different locations receive the maximum number of visitors applying for below poverty line (BPL) certificates and old age pensions, both categories are primarily Centrally Sponsored Schemes directed at the weaker sections of rural society.

## Employment Generation

It is difficult to estimate the impact of ICT initiatives on employment generation in rural areas. But directly, the respective ICT initiatives provide self-employment opportunities to unemployed educated rural youth. The proportion of beneficiaries under the initiative may be a very small fraction, but indirectly these initiatives inform and train people in improving their job prospects. *TARAgyan* imparts computer education to the rural population, resulting in the upgradation of skills of rural youth, thus improving their job prospects. Besides, *Gyandoot* and *Drishtee* inform people about the various schemes of the government for self-employment. These initiatives improve the job prospects for rural youth. For instance, the *Gyandoot* portal displays the details of public works carried out at various places in the district. Besides, it also displays the list of formalities for getting employment under PMRY, Employment Guarantee Scheme, *etc*. Information such as these indirectly improves the job prospects.

Although no empirical evidence is available on the number of beneficiaries from these initiatives, but surely these initiatives are instrumental in changing the employment pattern in the rural society. For instance, the *Drishtee* initiative has opened new opportunities in content development. People with adequate computer skills in Sirsa district are hired on piece-meal basis to develop content for local population. The *TARAgyan* initiative launched a scheme known as "learn and earn", which allows students of advance computer courses to teach in the computer familiarisation courses. These students are compensated in the form of significant discounts in fees.

It is evident from the case study of SGRY that information is power. Lack of access to information results in domination of bureaucracy on *panchayats*, mis-targeting of benefits, rent-seeking for disbursement of benefits, collusion of stakeholders to siphon off government funds, *etc*. The marginalisation of "have-nots" remains a common feature of implementation of all the government sponsored welfare programmes. *Panchayat* functionaries are also hamstrung due to inherent deficiencies, such low literacy levels, first-time *panchayat* leadership's non-exposure to general administrative functions, *etc*.

The ICT initiatives provide an important insight into the dynamics of rural society. Understandably, the information revolution taking place in rural India has become an integral part of the development strategy, especially focusing on improving the quality of life in rural areas. Rural society in the respective districts is beginning to understand the benefits of the initiatives.

Each initiative has highlighted certain critical elements for success, especially validating the successful attempts in building public-private partnership. The critical elements of success remain - designing the architecture, selecting a right kind of product mix, integrating interest between strategic partners, making a concrete marketing strategy in line with the rural needs, and establishing optimal market size for each info-kiosk. Alone government or private initiative is not in a position to cater to the local informational needs. A balanced product mix comprising primary needs like education, health care, *etc.*, along with public services like land records, various types of eligibility certificates, *etc.* is a must for broadening the impact of the initiative on the life of the people. The role of the government also becomes vitally important in reaching people, especially the last man in the row for disbursement of benefits, which he is entitled to get.

Thus, the government needs to focus its attention to integrate info-communications within the operational framework at the grass oot level to effectively implement effective and responsive governance. Indubitably, the impact of the respective ICT initiative is direct in some cases, but a major impact is observed as part of the spin-off benefits. ICT initiatives have a direct influence on raising awareness levels, income generation, human development and good governance. But at the same time, the impact is more profound, though not in direct terms, but indirectly in changing the employment pattern and implementing anti-poverty measures. In fact, ICT initiatives have proved that it is a great leveller and tool for empowerment. Some immediate measures could be adopted along the following lines:

a) Increase the knowledge base of the poor through the digital medium, especially about their rights and available alternatives.

b) Communicate with deprived to understand their real needs.

c) Expand their income generation capabilities, with primary focus on women participation.

d) Coordinate the efforts of the rural institutions, especially by bringing NGOs near to the information.

e) Develop info-communication infrastructure with primary aim to increase the penetration ratio in the rural sector.

Such measures facilitate dissemination of information to a larger section of the deprived population. Information inculcates transparency in the system, expedites decision-making, optimises utilisation of benefits, leads to better monitoring and evaluation. Poverty is multifaceted and often self-perpetuating in rural society. Lack of basic education, inadequate health care facilities, access to credit and such basic assets like land, is a pervasive phenomenon in rural India. Most of the problems are linked to gaps in knowledge and imperfections in information. The rural institutions are the key actors to raise the general awareness of the rural poor. Appropriate partnership between these institutions and main collaborators provides a strong base for creating an information society in the rural environs of India.

# 9

# Attracting Private Capital in Pursuit of Social Goals: A "Social Investing" Approach to Indian Micro Credit

RAJIV LALL

## What is Social Investing

There is growing interest around the world in what is being termed "social investing" or investing for objectives that are not purely financial. Official donor agencies as well as private foundations have become increasingly drawn to the notion of social investing because of a growing concern about effectiveness of aid and charitable giving. In their quest to demonstrate results and quantify the impact of their interventions, donors both public and private, previously focused on measuring non-financial returns to their grant making activities, are increasingly also targeting financial returns. Thus, within the community of private philanthropists, including amongst members of the Indian diaspora, the idea of "investing for social purposes" rather than merely "giving" is catching on. At quite another level, financial markets are also beginning to design and offer products to investors in pursuit of objectives that are not purely financial. Hence the growth of "green funds", for example, which offer investors the opportunity to signal their support only to environment-friendly companies.

There is, however, considerable confusion about the terminology used to describe these new types of initiatives. Before we elaborate on this phenomenon and what role "social investing" could have in the Indian micro-finance sector, it might be useful to define more clearly the terminology used in the discourse.

## The Public Goods Supply Chain

To put it in economics speak, the pursuit of a social goal involves the delivery of a public good or service. Prices of such goods are, by definition, not set purely by market forces. Therefore investing for a social goal *necessarily* implies the subordination of the pure profit motive to some other objective(s).

For example, providing credit to women from low-income households is a service that has an important "public good" aspect to it. The market, left to its own devices, does not serve this segment of the population. Or if it does, it does not do so in a manner that is socially unacceptable. Village based moneylenders do provide credit to low-income households, but they do so at rates that are usurious and predatory. Capital needed to build formal channels of credit delivery to this segment of the population at "reasonable" interest rates will most likely have to be satisfied with sub-market rates of return, at least initially. In this sense, investing to build micro-finance institutions can be regarded as social investing.

Investing in the delivery of public goods and services pre-supposes what might be called a whole supply chain. The "public goods supply chain" links three essential functions: namely, ***Financing***, ***Intermediation*** and ***Delivery***.

***Financing*** is the originating point of the supply chain. It involves sourcing the capital needed to fund the production and delivery of public goods. There can be multiple sources for capital spanning the continuum between ***purely for-profit or market driven investors on the one hand, to entirely not-for-profit providers on the other***. The former would provide capital strictly in order to maximise their financial return (for a given level of risk). This would include commercial debt and equity markets. The latter source type would provide capital entirely for achieving some non-financial objective. It would include private sources, as in philanthropists, or public sources, as in governments or bilateral donors. In between, there lie a growing number of investor types that would be satisfied with different combinations of financial and non-financial returns. These would include both private sources (such as philanthropist looking for some level of sub-market financial return) and public sources (such as government contributions to the non-concessional lending though bi- and multi-lateral aid agencies).

***Delivery*** lies at the other end of the supply chain. Like the sources of finance, agents that deliver public goods and services to the ultimate client too span the spectrum from purely not-for-profit agents at one end to entirely for-profit service delivery channels at the other. We can term the for-profit delivery agents as ***Corporate.*** Not-for-profit agents can be private, as in Non-Government Organisations or ***NGOs or*** public, as in ***Government agencies.***

***Intermediation*** is the link in the supply chain that channels capital from various sources to the delivery agents. So far the task of intermediation in the public goods supply chain has been dominated by not-for-profit public and private organisations. Multilateral agencies such as the World Bank and the Asian Development Bank would be examples of public intermediaries. Private foundations, trusts and charities would be examples of private intermediary organisations.

## The Smart Subsidy as Catalyst

It was noted earlier that pursuing a social goal, by definition, involves subordinating the pure profit motive to other objectives. **Said another way, the financing and delivery of public goods necessarily involves some kind of implicit or explicit subsidy somewhere along the supply chain.**

Given that the fundamental objective of market driven sources of private capital is pure profit, it follows that the only way in which such capital can be attracted to the pursuit of social goals is if there is some other party in the supply chain that is willing and able to absorb the cost of the subsidy involved. It is quite unrealistic to expect debt and equity capital markets to provide financing for micro-credit without the involvement of some not-for-profit source as well.

However, this subsidy need not be financial in nature. Nor does the subsidy have to be permanent. Sometimes, a market failure can be corrected by removing information gaps. Market participants can, for example, be persuaded to make investments in activities previously considered too risky if regulatory uncertainty is removed, or if better information about the opportunity is disseminated to market participants. Micro-credit is a case in point. Commercial banks in India are increasingly interested in lending to the poor thanks in part to the efforts of not-for profit credit rating agencies to collect and disseminate data on the portfolio quality and risk return profile of lending activities of micro-finance institutions (MFIs) across the country.

Hence, the notion of a "smart subsidy". A smart subsidy applied to the public goods supply chain is one that acts as a catalyst to what should then become a self-sustaining flow of private capital to fund the delivery of a public good or service.

In attracting private capital to help finance Indian MFIs, our challenge is to (a) design the supply chain in such a way that the subsidy involved is smart, *i.e.* that the flow of private capital to the sector is self-sustaining; (b) that the ultimate clients, *i.e.* low income households are well served from a social or public policy point of view; and (c) that this call be done on a large scale.

## The Development of the Microfinance Sector in Asia

It is well recognised that access to financial markets is important for poor people. Like all economic agents, low-income households and micro-enterprises can benefit from credit, savings and insurance services. Such services help people take advantage of profitable business opportunities and increase their earnings potential, manage risk and smooth consumption. In many developing countries, as much as 60 per cent of households are low income. Access to financial services can be extraordinarily powerful for spreading economic opportunity and fighting poverty.

There is also plenty of evidence to suggest that the impact on poor households is substantially greater through the empowerment of women. Women are the primary custodians of family unit's welfare. Providing women with access to finance has a huge impact on levels of educational attainment by children in poor households, on quality of health and nutrition in the households and on the pace of accumulation of household assets. Women from low-income households have also proven to be systematically better credit risks than male borrowers from similar households. By directing loans to poor women micro-finance has been shown to be an extremely effective and economical way to attack poverty.[1]

Microfinance is defined primarily as the provision of unsecured, short-term loans, typically less than Rs. 10,0000, to individuals or

1. See for example, M. Pitt and S. Khandker, "Impact of Group Based Credit Programmes in Poor Households In Bangladesh: Does the Gender of the Parties Matter?" *Journal of Political Economy*, 106, 1998.

groups of mostly women borrowers and/or to microentrepreneurs from low-income households. The term is also increasingly applied to the provision of other financial services to low income clients (*e.g.*, savings accounts and insurance).

Microfinance provides the working poor with access to more affordable capital. Studies of the development impact of microfinance are compelling. For example, a recent study on the impact of microfinance programmes in India covering schemes across 11 states concluded that within the households that participated in the study, income per household rose 33 per cent, average employments in person-days per year rose 18 per cent, the proportion of households below the poverty line declined from 74 per cent to 57 per cent; average value of assets per household increased some 72 per cent from Rs 6,843 to Rs. 11,800, with almost 60 per cent of all households reporting an increase in the value of their assets. Other reported benefits include a marked decline in family violence.[2]

The origins of modern microfinance can be traced to the mid-1960s, when a number of multilateral institutions, government agencies and non-profit organisations began to analyse and develop credit programmes to assist the world's poor to achieve sustainable economic development. It was noted fairly early on that local moneylenders and middlemen were able to achieve high repayment rates from loans to poor households relying on peer-based, non-collateral borrowing and repayment. So development organisations began experimenting with the creation of affordable credit programmes applying a variety of operating techniques.

In an unsecured lending business, borrower information quality and monitoring techniques are critical. Micro credit programmes developed a variety of methods to minimise and manage credit risk. Three principal lending techniques evolved: (i) group lending; (ii) village banking; and (iii) individual micro-lending. Group lending programmes, pioneered by Grameen Bank of Bangladesh[3], involve the cross-guaranteeing of loans within a group of mostly women from low-income households. The rationale behind group lending is that

2. Puhazhendi and Satyasi, 2001, *Impact Assessment of Self Help Groups-Bank Linkage Programme*, NABARD, Mumbai.

3. Todd, Helm, 1996, *Women at the Center: Grameen Bank Borrowers After One Decade*, Dhaka University Press Ltd.

peers have better information on the economic activities of their neighbours. That they are able to put more pressure, and a different kind of pressure, on borrowers than institutional staff are willing and able to do — reputation among peers is a stronger motivator then the potential loss of physical collateral. In addition, borrowers feel more obligated to repay when the members of their immediate community of friends stand to lose rather than a faceless institution.

Micro credit programmes employing the "village banking" model make loans to a community group, which then on-loans the funds to within their community. The rationale for this model is an extension of that for the group-lending model.

Individual lending, as the name implies, provides credit to borrowers on an individual basis. On-site visits to the borrower's place of business are standard operating procedure for such micro-credit programmes. An on-site visit can confirm the existence of the business and is the most reliable way to obtain a sense of the scale and profitability of the borrower's business activities. Peer review is another important information gathering technique for individual micro-credit programmes. As part of the peer review, lenders interview friends, neighbours, relatives, and long-time business associates to verify and obtain additional information about the prospective use of borrowed funds. Group lending, village banking and individual lending continue to be the core operational models for microfinance today.

## Commercial Viability of the Microfinance Sector in Asia

Many leading MFIs have achieved operating cost self-sufficiency (defined as covering operating costs) for over a decade. Micro credit programmes have surprised economists and conventional finance professionals with their high loan repayment rates, which are often above 95 per cent. Academic studies have sought to explain the surprisingly high repayment rates given the perceived risk level for this type of credit investment. Many of the studies conclude that because, outside of micro credit, there is such a shortage of capital amongst this borrower class, the borrowers believe that they cannot afford to default, because a default would likely result in a permanent loss of access to this source of capital.

Table 9.1 provides an illustrative example of the revenue and cost structure of a sample of ***self-sufficient*** MFIs in Asia[4], with all numbers expressed as a percentage of the MFIs' gross loan portfolio:

**Table 9.1**

*MFI Business Model as a Percentage of Average Gross Loan Portfolio*

| | |
|---|---|
| Interest & Fee Income | 33.5 |
| Loan Loss Provisions | 1.8 |
| Interest Expense(1) | 8.1 |
| Net Interest Income | 23.6 |
| Operating Expenses | 22.5 |
| Income Before Taxes | 1.1 |
| Taxes | 0.3 |
| Net Income | 0.8 |

(1) Assumes Portfolio is 67 per cent financed with liabilities paying a blended rate of 12 per cent.

As Table 9.1 indicates, the interest rates charged by typical MFIs are quite high relative to bank loans (30-35 per cent compared to 9-13.5 per cent for the banks). But as we will argue below, banks by-and-large are unable to reach the poor clients that MFIs reach and some forms of bank financing have some form of subsidy implicit in them. Moneylenders are the only alternative source of credit for low income households and they charge interest rates that range anywhere from about 40 per cent to 20 per cent, with an average rate of close to 60 per cent[5]. That is why there is in fact great demand for MFIs credit from poor households.

One of the reasons why self sustaining MFIs do need to charge rates that are higher than typically charged by banks is that their operating expenses are high relative to more conventional financial institutions. This is principally because microfinance is a labor-intensive business: a typical MFI has thousands of loans outstanding with thousands of borrowers, resulting in significant monitoring and administrative costs. Moreover, MFIs provide the convenience of at-

4. Based on data from M-CRIL, *Microfinance Review, 2003*, Micro Credit Rating International Ltd., Gurgaon.

5. P. Basu and N. Verma, *Improving Access to Rural Finance in India: An Overview*, World Bank, 2003.

the-doorstep-banking to their clients. MFIs are mobile banks in that they deliver credit and service their portfolio at the domicile of the client (typically the village) – they do not require for clients to make their way to a branch. A fairer comparison of rates charged by MFIs *versus* banks would adjust the latter rates for transaction costs (number of visits to the bank, documentation, and in some cases also bribes) incurred by borrowers. So adjusted, the cost of average bank loans in India, for example, is closer to 22-23 per cent.[6]

In addition to covering operating costs, an increasing number of non-commercial MFI investors have required MFIs to earn a return on invested capital. The rationale for this is to improve accountability, cost efficiency, and to continue the evolution of the sector toward commercial viability, and to demonstrate to commercial investors that the sector can earn a return on capital. As shown in the Table 9.2, a review of 10 leading MFIs in Asia suggests that over recent years the best MFIs are paying debt investors an annual return of close to 10 per cent, and are earning an average (unrealised) return on accounting equity of over 10 per cent.

### Table 9.2

*Return on Capital of a Sample of Asian MFIs Based on Most Recent Rating Conducted by M-CRIL (US$ in Millions, Unless Otherwise Indicated)*

| *Portfolio Characteristics* | |
|---|---|
| Average Gross Loan Portfolio | $1.3 |
| Average Annual Portfolio Growth Rate | 34% |
| Average Number of Clients | 32,100 |
| Aggregated Number of Clients | 528,000 |
| Average Loans in Arrears (>60 days)/Portfolio | 2.8% |
| Return on Capital | |
| Average Return on Assets (ROA) | 2.1% |
| Average Return on Equity (ROE) | 10.0% |
| Average Interest Expense/Debt Outstanding | 10.0% |

Notes: Data covers top 10 MFIs from a sample of Asian countries. Averages represent "weighted-averages" of each category for the 10 MFIs. Source: *M-CRIL Microfinance Review 2002*, Micro-Credit Ratings International Ltd.

6. Vijay Mahajan and Bharti Ramola Gupta, *Microfinance in India, Banyan Tree and Bonsai,* World Bank, 2003.

The indicators above do not include data from the four giant and enormously successful MFIs in Bangladesh, namely Grameen, BRAC, Proshika and ASA, that each have 1-3 million clients because these are not rated by M-CRIL. It also excludes Bank Rakyat Indonesia, a government owned community bank that has also achieved very significant outreach with commercial viability. What all of this suggests is that there is enormous room for microfinance to grow and that prospects for creating commercially viable MFIs that are also capable of delivering financial services to large communities of poor people at affordable rates are quite promising.

## The Indian Micro-finance Sector[7]

Although access to financial services can be a very effective anti-poverty instrument, because of their special features, financial markets often serve poor people badly. Lack of collateral and high transaction costs means that the poor are most often excluded from financial markets. On the face of it, India has a deep financial system. Financial assets amounted to about $430 billion or about 93 per cent of GDP in India compared to 68 per cent of GDP in Mexico, a country with a per capita income that is ten times higher ($4,440 vs. $440). India also has a very large network of commercial bank branches – 66,500 of which almost half are in rural areas. As a result, India compares favorably in terms of branch density (average population served per commercial bank branch) of 12,800 *vs.* a similar number for Mexico. However, India's financial system has been relatively unsuccessful in allocating resources to the country's private sector. Private credit as a share of total bank assets is only 36 per cent compared to about 50 per cent in Mexico. In particular though, despite all the infrastructure of rural bank branches and rural cooperative banks, the Indian financial system has failed to provide access to the poor, especially the rural poor. Almost 60 per cent of households do not have access to a bank account; only 20 per cent of rural households have access to credit from a formal source; 87 per cent of marginal farmers do not have access to any formal credit.[8] It takes between 4-7 months for a formal loan to be approved. Bribe-taking by personnel of rural

---

7. This section draws heavily from World Bank, Priya Basu and Niraj Verma, 2003.
8. World Bank-NCAER, *Rural Finance Access Survey*, 2003.

financial institutions is rampant with bribe amounts varying from 10-20 per cent of the loan amount.[9]

An estimated 260 million Indians live below the poverty line, of which about three–quarters live in rural India. What this implies is that about 42 million households in India do not have access to credit. If households living near the poverty line are also included, it is estimated that about 60 million Indian households do not have access to credit today. Various studies have found that the average annual potential credit usage of poor households varies from Rs. 3000 to 9,000. This would suggest an unmet demand of between Rs. 175 – 535 billion rupees per annum.[10]

Faced with this problem of insufficient outreach of the financial system to the poor, the government of India, NGOs and financial institutions have all made attempts to bridge the gap.

***Self-Help Group—Bank Linkage Programme*** is an important initiative in this regard. The SHG programme involves organising the poor (mostly women) into groups of 15-20 persons that are encouraged to save collectively. These groups are then linked to the mainstream banking system, thus allowing them access to credit. The SHGs is essentially a variation on the village-banking model described earlier – the groups at the core of this model, save, borrow and repay collectively. Once the group is formed, the tasks of credit evaluation, loan monitoring and collection are all left to the group itself. The success of this model thus depends critically on the quality of the groups. Here the programme has relied heavily on NGOs and Regional Rural Banks (RRBs) to promote, nurture and strengthen SHGs. This involves inculcating the savings habit amongst group members, teaching group members book-keeping skills, keeping the group members cohesive and then introducing them to a bank.

The number of SHGs has grown very rapidly from just 500 or so in the early 1990s to over 800,000 in 2003. SHG-Bank Linkage Programme today reaches about 12 million women and their households. It has cumulatively over the past decade provided about Rs. 22 billion in loans, with loans outstanding amounting to about Rs. 11 billion. It has in effect become the dominant mode of micro-

9. World Bank, Priya Basu and Niraj Verma, 2003.

10. V. Mahajan and B.R. Gupta, *Micro Finance in India, Banyan tree or Bonsai*, World Bank, 2003.

credit in India. But even so, this programme meets only 2.0-6.2 per cent of the estimated annual demand for credit from low income households in the country.

The great merit of the programme is that it reduces the transaction costs to the banks because the bulk of the underwriting and loan monitoring responsibility is transferred to the group itself. But although the banks offer loans to SHGs at 12-13.5 per cent, the on-lending cost to ultimate borrowers who are the group members is still about 24 per cent.[11] Moreover, this cost does NOT include the full costs of promoting and supporting the SHGs, a task currently outsourced to NGOs and RRBs. It is estimated that if these costs were properly accounted for, the effective lending rate from the banks to SHGs would be in the 22-28 per cent[12] range, and consequently the cost to the ultimate borrower would be closer to 34-40 per cent.[13]

Second, scalability and sustainability are matters of serious concern. A sample of 61 SHGs surveyed in India had an average return on assets of (–)2.5 per cent, with over half the sampled groups showing returns worse than (–)15 per cent on assets.[14] The evidence suggests that as the SHG-Bank Linkage Programme has caught on, quantitative targets set by government for group creation have begun to take priority over the quality of the groups promoted. A recent survey by the *Andhra Pradesh Mahila Abhivruddhi Society* (APMAS) showed that only 17 per cent of groups created in Andhra Pradesh (a state that is a leading proponent of the programme) were of adequate quality to be linked to banks.[15] Indeed this finding is also reflected in the M-CRIL survey, which indicates that the share of the portfolio at risk (more than 60 days overdue) for SHGs was over 19 per cent, more than six times that for *Grameen* type MFIs in the portfolio.[16]

***Grameen Type and Other Specialised MFIs.*** Outside of the SHG programme, there have been a number of initiatives to promote

11. Basu and Verma, *op. cit.*
12. S. Sinha, 2003, "The Outreach Conundrum: Can India's Regional Rural Banks Really Serve Low Income Clients", M-CRIL, Gurgaon.
13. According to the Ministry of Rural Development, promotion costs about Rs. 10,000 per group.
14. M-CRIL *op. cit.*
15. Mahajan and Gupta, *op. cit.*
16. M-CRIL *op. cit.*

*Grameen* type MFIs and other specialised MFIs that follow the individual lending model. None of these initiatives, however, enjoys widespread government support and overall their outreach remains very limited. According to M-CRIL, the largest 49 such MFIs had total outstanding loans of about Rs 3.6 billion in 2003, and reached less 1.4 million borrowers in total.[17] The bulk of the MFIs, with some notable exceptions, continue to be run on a not-for-profit basis by a variety of NGOs. Most operate on a sub-optimal scale, heavily dependent on grant financing, with no assurance sustainability.

The lack of debt financing is NOT a constraint to the development of these MFIs. Indeed, there is an abundance of debt capital available. Domestic commercial banks have shown an increasing willingness to lend to MFIs as a cost-effective, and even profitable way, of meeting their priority sector targets (targets set by government to meet certain social objectives). To the extent that there is a shortage of capital, it is equity capital that has been short supply. Because they are run as not-for-profit entities, no equity financing is forthcoming to adequately capitalise these MFIs. Hampered by skewed capital structures, a lot of MFIs are unable to access debt financing from commercial banks.

The biggest hurdles to the scalability of non-SHG type MFIs in India are (i) the philosophical and attitudinal resistance of most NGOs and MFIs themselves to functioning in a more commercially focused manner, (ii) the acute shortage of managerial talent and institutional bandwidth in this sector and (iii) the maze of regulations that restrict the operation of foreign donors and/or investors in India's financial sector.[18]

The bulk of Indian MFIs see themselves as providers of development assistance to the poor. The dominating perspective is one that regards the poor as unable to carry debt on commercial terms and/or unable to make productive use of credit without training/advice or some form of technical assistance. As a result, the overwhelming majority of Indian MFIs are high cost, small-scale operations that struggle to survive on a self-sustaining basis and rely heavily on uncertain on government/donor support. One of the big problems in this regard is the lack of commercial orientation of the

17. M-CRIL, *op. cit.*

18. For a description of the regulatory hurdles, particularly to equity investment in the MFI sector see Basu and Verma, *op. cit.*

NGOs that operate these MFIs. Government intervention in the sector is often politically motivated and tends to be infected with a subsidy culture. This has served to further corrupt the institutional culture of the MFI sector and undermine its financial viability.

***Summary Diagnostic.*** The MFI sector is surprisingly under-developed. The commercial viability of the micro credit sector in India has been established in only a few and mostly small-scale programmes in the country. The full potential of the sector remains unexplored. The Indian Government's interventions in this sector have had moderate success and, even with a growing number NGOs venturing into micro finance, the reach and scale of these initiatives remains very limited compared with the estimated demand for micro credit.

Perhaps the single biggest obstacle to scalability in this sector is not a shortage of financing, but rather a lack of commercial orientation. Most Indian MFIs now have access to some debt financing if not from commercial banks, then from public sector intermediaries. Although many are still constrained by the lack of equity capital, almost all MFIs suffer from an acute shortage of management talent and perspective.

To use the vocabulary of the public goods supply chain, the Indian MFI sector has so far attracted capital from mainly not-for-profit **financing sources** in the form of government sponsored schemes with implicit subsidies and grants from the donor community. The **intermediaries** have overwhelmingly been government owned financial institutions (state owned commercial banks, RRBs, NABARD), none of which operate for a purely for-profit motive. And the **delivery agents** have also been mostly not-for-profit players including and variety of community managed MFIs (such as the SHGs), or NGO managed MFIs (such as the *Grameen* type MFIs and individual banking type entities). The real bottleneck to the growth and sustainability of the MFI sector in India comes at the level of intermediaries and delivery agents. The intermediaries are mostly intermediating credit to low income households on a non-commercial basis – this segment of their business operations is not sustainable and would become even less so if they were to be burdened with the task of really scaling up their interventions in the MFI sector. At the level of the delivery agents, there is very limited absorptive capacity. NGO delivery channels are tough to scale up. For one, being grant financed, NGOs often run into funding fatigue after they reach a certain size. But more importantly, their institutional culture and mind-set is often ill-suited to create service delivery organisations of scale – NGOs are very effective in serving the needs of small communities of clients, but are unable to serve large populations efficiently. Because of its not-for-profit orientation the MFI delivery channel in India risks becoming a growing source of bad debt creation.

The challenge is how to attract for-profit financing sources to fund the delivery of affordable financial services to the poor but in a way that is commercially viable and scalable.

## *Lok Capital*: A Model for Creating Large Scale, Commercially Viable MFIs in India

Given the above diagnostic, we concluded that any intervention intended to help the MFI sector should aim to (i) mobilise for profit equity and debt capital (in an environment in which there does not appear to be any shortage of debt financing); (ii) back and nurture MFI managerial talent; and (iii) contribute to institution building. These three aims being very similar to the objectives of investors in early stage companies, we believe that a **"venture capital approach"** suits the needs of the Indian MFI sector. The idea is to create an appropriate entity/platform or a venture fund that would allow persons with venture capital experience to invest in a selection of suitable Indian MFIs with the objective of bringing equity capital to the table and nurturing these "investee companies" to grow and evolve along commercial lines.

However, venture funding by itself is unlikely to yield results for two reasons. First, the rates of return required by venture investors are probably too high to create MFIs capable of being self sufficient at lending rates that are affordable (say 25-30 per cent). Second, venture investors by themselves cannot resolve the problem of the lack of management capacity and skills. They need a pool of skilled managers to back and to nurture. The development of such a pool of skills has a strong public good element to it and so requires financing from not-for-profit sources of funding. A parallel **capacity building facility** financed through grant financing is therefore also required to help deliver long term technical assistance and training support to those MFIs that would be the recipient of equity investments from the venture fund.

The *Lok Capital* initiative was launched in 2001 with the objective to (a) mobilise and direct private (mainly equity) capital to fund micro-finance activities first and foremost in India, but eventually also elsewhere in the world; (b) fund/provide long term management and technical support for the development of commercially sustainable MFIs; and (c) disseminate information about, and inform the public policy debate on, innovative ways of empowering the poor, especially poor women and the rural poor. Lok Capital is raising the first India focused venture fund managed by local professionals, with a significant on-the-ground presence, capable of making long-term equity investments in, and delivering effective non-financial local assistance to, MFIs in India.

***The Lok Capital Group*** comprises several entities: Lok Foundation, Inc., a New York based, not-for-profit corporation operating as a charitable foundation; Lok Fund, LLC, a New York based limited liability company, and a New Delhi based services company, Lok Capital Services Pvt. Ltd., and its affiliate, EDA Rural Systems Pvt. Ltd., a Gurgaon based management-consulting company focused on delivering technical assistance to MFIs and NGOs in India and elsewhere in Asia. Together the various entities of Lok Capital function like a U.S. style venture firm (financed through the Fund), supported, however, by a strong capacity building function (financed through the Foundation) and delivered through LCS and EDA Rural Systems, two on-the-ground services companies based in India.

***The Foundation***, which is the Managing Member of the Fund, is organised to (i) act as a catalyst for directing private capital to MFIs in India and possibly elsewhere in developing Asia, (ii) fund and provide long term management and technical support to these MFIs and (iii) act as a platform for disseminating knowledge and encouraging debate on innovative ways of empowering the poor, especially poor women and the rural poor.

The Foundation will pursue objective (i) by acting as the Managing Member of the Fund. The Fund is to be a receptacle for mobilising patient capital from social investors, both institutional and individual, that are willing to participate as Members and entrust the Foundation with the task of directing/managing equity investments into MFIs in India, and possibly elsewhere in developing Asia.

In pursuit of objective (ii), the Foundation will mobilise grant financing from institutions and individual contributors worldwide. These funds will then be deployed through LCS, a New Delhi based service company intended to facilitate the investment activities of the Fund, EDA Rural Systems, an India based management-consulting company with whom the Foundation and Fund have a renewable service contract, and/or other appropriate service providers that are able to deliver long term capacity building services to MFIs that the Fund has invested, or may invest, in.

In pursuit of objective (iii), the Foundation will seek to share *Lok Capital*'s experience in applying venture techniques to supporting MFIs and to forge partnerships with other NGOs, Foundations, or commercial organisations that are willing to experiment with new approaches to empowering the poor across South and South-East Asia.

Contributors to the Foundation would be eligible for a tax deduction for United States income tax purposes to the extent permitted by law. In addition, they can expect to take satisfaction from acting as a catalyst (through the Foundation's capacity building activities and its role as Managing Member of the Fund) for attracting private risk capital to MFIs.

***The Fund*** will be the first India-focused venture fund managed by local professionals, with a significant on-the-ground presence, capable of making long-term equity investments in, and delivering effective non-financial local assistance to, MFIs in India. The Fund's investment objective is to provide capital appreciation by making selected equity investments in MFIs located in India. The Fund's activities are also to be overseen by the Foundation's directors and executive officers.

***LCS,*** incorporated in New Delhi, is a wholly owned subsidiary of the Fund. LCS's function is to provide "venture services" to the Fund. LCS will identify potential investments; conduct due diligence on potential investee MFIs; help execute transactions on behalf of the Fund, once the investment decision has been made by the Investment Committee; supervise and monitor investments that have been made; and assist with "exit" strategies to liquidate investments. LCS's budget will be financed in part by the Fund and in part through a contractual arrangement with the Managing Member.

***EDA Rural Systems*** is a private limited company incorporated in Gurgaon that provides management-consulting services and delivers technical advisory support to NGOs and MFIs in India and elsewhere in Asia. Its function would be to deliver long- term local management and technical advisory support to MFIs that the Fund has invested, or may invest, in. In addition, EDA Rural Systems will work to forge partnerships with community level NGOs to encourage them to move out of the credit delivery business and focus on their core competence, *i.e.* the targeted delivery of services such as vocational training, and preventive health care advice for example to members of their focus communities. EDA Rural System's services would be important to the Foundation's capacity building efforts and to the long-term scalability and sustainability of MFIs that might form part of the Fund's investment portfolio.

***In summary,*** the Lok Capital model is an attempt to **forge a constructive partnership between for-profit and not-for-profit sources of capital and for and not-for profit delivery agents to provide a "public good",** *i.e.* affordable financial services to women from low-income households on a large scale and in a commercially sustainable manner.

In effect, the not-for-profit capital source in this model would be funding the cost of the "**smart subsidy**", which in this case would be to absorb a portion of the cost of capacity building both at the MFI and the community levels, such that (i) the interest rates charged to the ultimate client remain affordable (sub-30 per cent); (ii) private commercial banks are persuaded to provide debt financing in bulk and at market rates; and (iii) the providers of equity capital are able to reap some reasonable return on their investment. This subsidy (which is to be delivered in kind in the form of training and or community support activities) would reduce the time and losses to break even and therefore improves the economics of investments from the Fund. The not-for profit Foundation thus acts as a catalyst for market driven financing through the Fund at the financing end of the supply chain. And EDA Rural Systems and partner NGOs provide not-for-profit support to the investee MFIs, the for-profit credit delivery agents.

## Some Concluding Observations

- Attracting market driven equity capital to fund the delivery of affordable financial services to the poor in India will require partnership with not-for-profit financing sources that are willing to cover the cost of the subsidy implicit in the process.

- This subsidy must not be seen to be benefiting the private source of capital, but is the cost that must be borne by some not-for-profit entity in order that the poor may gain access to financial services currently denied to them.
- This subsidy can be funded through private sources of grant funding provided it is designed appropriately.
- Mobilising market sources of financing is only part of the challenge. An equally big issue is ensuring that the service delivery channels *i.e.* the MFIs are efficient, have sufficient absorptive capacity, and are scalable.
- This will require creating for-profit MFIs as the main delivery channel for credit and other financial services to the poor. But there is room for such MFIs to work in partnership with not-for-profit agents such as NGOs. But must be taken to ensure that functions of each are assigned according to their respective objectives and strengths and opportunities for complementary action are fully exploited.
- In short success requires "unbundling" the financing and delivery chain of the public good called "affordable financial services to the poor" into discrete components to be assigned to market driven as well as not-for-profit players working in partnership with one another.
- *Lok Capital* is an innovative attempt to apply these principles in practice in the Indian context.

# 10

# Rural Development: Decentralisation and Rural Markets

P.D. KAUSHIK

## Introduction

There are no universally accepted approaches to rural development. It is a choice influenced by time, space and culture. The term rural development connotes overall development of rural areas to improve the quality of life of rural people. In this sense, it is a comprehensive and multi-dimensional concept, and encompasses the development of agriculture and allied activities, village and cottage industries and crafts, socio-economic infrastructure, community services and facilities and, above all, human resources in rural areas. As a phenomenon, rural development is the end-result of interactions between various physical, technological, economic, social, cultural and institutional factors. As a strategy, it is designed to improve the economic and social well being of a specific group of people—the rural poor. As a discipline, it is multi-disciplinary in nature, representing an intersection of agriculture, social, behavioural, engineering and management sciences.[1]

In the Indian context rural development assumes greater significance as 72.22 per cent (according to the 2001 census) of its population still lives in rural areas. Most of the people living in rural areas draw their livelihood from agriculture and allied sectors (60.41 per cent of total work force), and poverty mostly persists here (27.1 per cent in 1999-2000). At the time of independence around 83 per cent of the Indian population was living in rural areas. Accordingly, from the very beginning, our planned strategy emphasised on rural development and shall continue to do so in future. Strategically, the

1. Kartar Singh (1999).

focus of our planning was to improve the economic and social conditions of the underprivileged sections of rural society. Thus, economic growth with social justice became the proclaimed objective of the planning process under rural development. It began with an emphasis on agricultural production and consequently expanding to promote productive employment opportunities for rural masses, especially the poor, by integrating production, infrastructure, human resource and institutional development measures.

Strategic changes made in the Ninth Plan (1997-2002) to promote the process of nation building were through decentralised planning. Greater role of private sector was also ensured in the development process. It laid stress on a genuine thrust towards decentralisation and people's participation in the planning process through institutional reforms. Decentralisation process, which began in the 90's, aimed at removing prevalent anomalies from the government delivery systems. The reorganisation of *panchayats*, after the 73rd Constitutional Amendment, has completely changed the nature of local governance in India, especially by adopting a bottom-up approach for rural development programmes. This emphasised strengthening of the *panchayati raj* and civil society groups for promoting transparency, accountability and responsibility in the development process.

Although rural development in India has a long past, but its implementation has always remained a source of concern and subject of criticism. In the absence of well-planned rural development programmes and efficient delivery systems, most of these resources do not benefit the target groups. It has been reported that only 18 per cent of the rural development budget reach the target families, while the rest is wasted due to inefficient delivery systems or pilfered out.[2] As a result, the pace of progress has remained stunted and the poor continue to suffer. However, Mukarji (1999) commented that decentralisation in India is confronted with variety of limitations. In other words, the ambiguity surrounding the concept of 'self-government' and the substantial power that still rests with the state governments have prevented most states from devolving any substantive power to the *panchayats*. Such findings are also consistent

---

2. Nayak *et al.* (2002)

with wider literature on the problems most commonly associated with decentralisation in India.[3]

## Decentralisation: Theory and Practice

Johnson (2003) explained decentralisation as a political process whereby administrative authority, public resources and responsibilities are transferred from central government agencies to lower-level organs of government or to non-governmental bodies, such as community-based organisations (CBOs), 'third party' non-governmental organisations (NGOs) or private sector actors.

**Box 10.1**

*Decentralisation: Some Explanations*

**Deconcentration,** in which political, administrative and fiscal responsibilities are transferred to lower units *within* central line ministries or agencies- Crook and Manor (1998); Rondinelli *et al.* (1989); and Meenakshisundaram (1999)

**Devolution,** in which sub-national units of government are either created or strengthened in terms of political, administrative and fiscal power- Blair (2000); Crook and Manor (1998); Rondinelli *et al.* (1989)

**Delegation,** in which responsibilities are transferred to organisations that are 'outside the regular bureaucratic structure and are only indirectly controlled by the central government- Meenakshisundaram (1999)

**Privatisation,** in which all responsibility for government functions are transferred to non-governmental organisations (NGOs) or private enterprises independent of government- Meenakshisundaram (1999)

Such transfers can involve the power to decide the allocation and distribution of public resources, the power to implement programmes and policies and the power to raise and spend public revenues for these and other purposes. These three powers are classified broadly as political, administrative and fiscal decentralisation.[4]

- **Political decentralisation** transfers policy and legislative powers from central government to autonomous, lower-level

3. See also Crook and Manor (1998); Jha (2000); Mathew (2001); Mukarji (1999); Oommen (1999); Vyasulu (2000); World Bank (2000).
4. World Bank (2000).

assemblies and local councils that have been democratically elected by their constituencies.

- **Administrative decentralisation** places planning and implementation responsibility in the hands of locally situated civil servants and these local civil servants are under the jurisdiction of elected local governments.
- **Fiscal decentralisation** accords substantial revenue and expenditure authority to intermediate and local governments.

However, decentralisation implies more than the downward delegation of authority. It entails a system of governance in which citizens possess the right to hold local public officials accountable through the use of elections, grievance meetings and other democratic means. On these lines, the *Panchayati Raj* or democratic decentralisation can be defined as meaningful authority devolved to local units of governance that are accessible and accountable to the local citizenry, who enjoy full political rights and liberty. A defining feature of any democratic system is that decision-makers are under the 'effective popular control' of the people they are meant to govern.[5] The four effective popular controls are:

- Regular elections and accountability to social interest groups;
- Institutionalisation of all adult citizens in voting (*i.e.* one person, one vote);
- Political freedom in the eyes of the state;
- Policy decisions made on the basis of majority rule.

Beyond these very basic principles, democracy also implies a wide range of rules, norms and customs through which citizens can exercise 'effective popular control' through an independent judiciary, a free press, systems of transparency, and freedom of association and speech.

Decentralisation in India was aimed at improving the quality and reach of government services, particularly ones aimed at rural development and improving the lives of rural poor.[6] In the context of poverty reduction, access to the resources and benefits that governments provide is associated with systems of governance that

5. Mayo (1960)
6. de Souza (2000)

empower poor and vulnerable groups in society. Although there is great variation among cultures and regions, but a number of roles that governments typically play in poor and predominantly rural areas are:

- Provision of public goods, such as universal education and healthcare;
- Provision of divisible goods, such as irrigation, agricultural extension and credit;
- Determination and enforcement of laws regulating key economic inputs, such as land, labour and capital;
- Recognition and protection of rights allowing for organisation, association and entitlement in the eyes of the state.

However, all these roles are problematic in the context of India because they require systems of governance, which ensures that public resources are being delivered efficiently and effectively.[7] Studies on decentralisation have shown that devolution of authority can improve systems of local governance in a number of ways.

1. The establishment and empowerment of local resource user groups (delegation or privatisation) can improve the ways in which local people manage and use natural resources, thereby improving the resource base on which rural poor are often disproportionately dependent. Such arguments are generally made in relation to the provision of local public goods, such as common pool resources or local credit organisations.[8]
2. Collaboration between public agencies and local resource users can produce 'synergistic' outcomes, in which citizens and civil servants cooperate to provide goods that would be unobtainable were they acting alone. Classic examples of this would include joint forest management,[9] fisheries co-management[10] and participatory watershed management.[11]
3. Democratisation and empowerment of local administrative bodies can enhance participation in decision-making fora,

7. Johnson & Start (2001).
8. See Agrawal & Gibson (1999); Baland & Platteau (1996); Johnson (2001).
9. IFAD (2001).
10. Pomeroy & Berkes (1997).
11. Farrington *et al.* (2000).

particularly among groups that have traditionally been marginalised by local political processes.[12]

Studies from Africa, Asia and Latin America have shown that the introduction of elections, systems of transparency and rights of association can significantly transform the rural settings and empower poor, enhancing their ability to participate in local decision making and encouraging them to hold public officials to account[13]. But decentralisation in India, especially in the light of the 73rd Amendment, is looked upon with inherent weaknesses. The World Bank's study of Indian decentralisation ranks India 'among the best performers' internationally in terms of political decentralisation, but places India 'close to the last' in terms of administrative decentralisation. Most States have held at least two rounds of elections since 1993. Reservations allowing the participation of women, scheduled castes and scheduled tribes have been respected. Finally, voter participation has been high. In its study of 53 villages in Rajasthan and MP, the World Bank[14] found that voter turn out in *panchayat* elections was well over 90 per cent for all categories (defined in terms of gender, class and caste).

But the study goes on to argue that Indian States and the Union government are unwilling to vest them with sufficient "administrative control over functions or fiscal autonomy". In most States, *panchayats* have been handed a wide array of responsibilities, especially rural development and poverty alleviation, without the necessary fiscal and administrative resources. Confirming the World Bank's observations, the *Task Force on Devolution of Powers and Functions upon PRIs*[15] found that 'most of the States' had satisfied only the basic requirements relating to the transfer of functions, functionaries, funds and financial autonomy to the *panchayats*.

Oommen's (1999) comparison of 12 Indian States concluded that the Conformity Acts have generally 'been an exercise in amending existing *panchayat* legislation for the sake of satisfying the mandatory provisions. In particular, he raised following concerns:

---

12. See Blair (2000); Crook & Sverrisson (2001); Crook & Manor (1998).
13. See Crook & Manor (1998); Drèze & Sen (1996), Rondinelli *et al.* (1989).
14. Alsop *et al.* (2000).
15. Ministry of Rural Development (2001).

- Village *panchayats* have been delegated functions 'without adequate administrative, financial and technical support'.
- With the exception of Kerala and West Bengal, *panchayats* lack discretionary powers over spending and staff.
- Insufficient clarity and differentiation of functions among *panchayats* and other levels of government.
- States reserve the right to assign or withdraw functions to and from the *panchayats* by 'executive fiat'.
- *Panchayats* at all levels have inadequate powers of taxation.
- *Panchayats* lack autonomous budgeting powers.

Such form of hesitant and resistant decentralisation in India has further marginalised *panchayats* in rural development process and in improving the lives of rural poor. Although there are some isolated examples of *panchayats* performing well in terms of developmental works, but most *panchayats* have been stifled due to acute resistance by the bureaucracy and inexperience of *panchayat* representatives in local governance. One of the positive outcomes of the decentralisation process in rural India is the example of 'Malan Village Panchayat'.

### Box 10.2

*Malan Village Panchayat*

Malan is a large village and the *panchayat* has access to more resources. Nearly half of its revenue is raised through taxes and about 30 per cent through donations. The *panchayat* also has under its control 130 acres of pastureland and auctions timber and firewood from this land to generate additional revenue.

The *panchayat* in Malan has undertaken several tasks related to building infrastructure in the village like, 5000 ft. of concrete road, four rooms in the village school, four crèches, a primary health centre, public bathrooms and toilets, and a tubewell. In addition, the *panchayat* has focussed on providing drinking water supplies in the village. A water tank was constructed and the main water supply pipes have been installed. The *panchayat* provides water connections to individual houses on the condition that the applicants bear the cost of delivery pipe from the main pipe and arrange drainage facilities. In 1998, about 17 per cent of all households had water taps in their houses. Apart from the connections to the houses, the *panchayat* has installed public taps in most localities from where households not having private taps can take water.

The evidence on functioning of new institutions of local governance has indicated vast potential of using these institutions to generate local resources. The findings from various studies broadly support this body of evidence. The *panchayats* have undertaken several activities for village development. These activities can be strengthened by further devolution of resources and powers to these institutions. In particular, the *panchayats* have shown exemplary performance in several states in respect to implementation of rural development programmes. Effectiveness of these programmes has been found to be markedly better in states where *panchayats* were closely involved in both planning and implementation of these programmes.

Active involvement of the *gram sabha* in various development programmes is a strategic move to ensure accountability within the system. However, the difficulty lies in motivating the villagers to attend the *gram sabha* meetings. In most of the backward villages, the vested interests considerably influence the proceedings, which may not be in the interest of the community. Therefore, the office bearers of various village level organisations such as schools, colleges, cooperative societies, banks, *mahila mandals*, youth groups, farmers' associations and voluntary agencies must take part in the meetings as these institutions are expected to safeguard the interests of the community. Some of these institutions can also assume the role of facilitators of the *gram sabha* and form a link between the *Gram Panchayat* and *Gram Sabha*.

There are instances where the members of the village SHGs monitor the attendance of teachers and *Anganwadi* and Health Workers. Such groups have prevented vested interests from mismanaging the *Gram Panchayats* and have elected new members and therefore ensured transparency. In Maharashtra, several farmers' groups involved in milk marketing are able to independently hire the services of veterinarians to avail of livestock breeding and health care services, while the farmers in many other states are still dependent on government assistance for similar services. Such group activities are able to sustain the development programme without external assistance. Thus motivation and training of the target groups to build leadership through local organisations can play a vital role in poverty alleviation and sustainable development in India.

## Rural India: An Introspection

Any strategy for rural development must involve the people themselves and their institutions at all levels. The need for revatilising PRIs has been recognised as an instrument for participative planning and implementation of various developmental programmes at grassroots level.

**Figure 10.1**

*District Legislative and Administrative Structure*

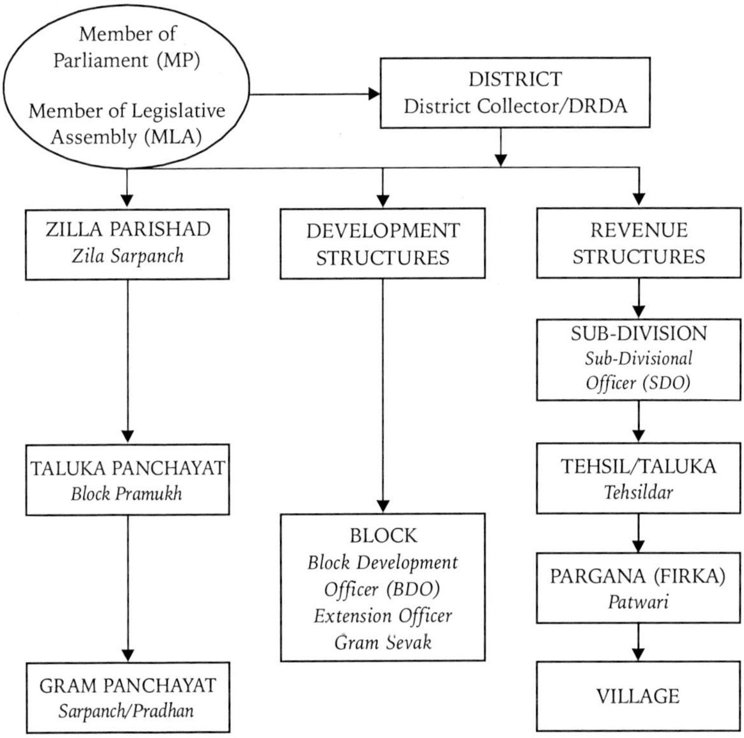


In order to improve the quality of life of the rural poor and to ensure equal and effective participation of the people, rapid restructuring of the programmes is required in order to assist functionaries at various levels of local self-government. Studies have been too critical of the existing government delivery systems, especially on the district administrative structure. The district as an administrative unit, assumes a lot of significance in the context of decentralised planning and implementation of development plans and schemes.

The district is the principal sub-division within the state. There are 593 districts in India with almost six lakh villages. The districts vary in size and population. The average size of a district is approximately 4,300 square kilometers, and the average population numbered nearly 1.8 million in the early 1990s. The district collector is the senior most executive official in the district. The collector's role in most states is confined to heading the district revenue department and coordinating the developmental activities and social welfare in the district. A district is sub-divided into *talukas* or *tehsils,* revenue areas that contain from 200 to 600 villages. The *taluqdar* or *tehsildar,* who serves in much the same capacity as the collector, is the chief member of the *taluka* revenue department. Economic development and social welfare departments are also likely to have offices at the *taluka* level. Although the revenue department may have village representatives, generally known as *patwaris,* to maintain land records, the development and welfare departments generally do not have offices below the *taluka* level.

## Population

India crossed one-billionth mark at the turn of the millennium, the first nation to cross this mark after China. It is estimated that India is a home for 1,049,700,118 (2003), at an average annual growth rate of 1.47 per cent. Medinipur district in West Bengal is the largest district in India in terms of population size (9.64 million), which is higher than population of 16 States and Union Territories of India. However, Medinipur has 10,603 villages with almost 90 per cent of rural population. Yaman in Pondicherry is the smallest district with a population of 31,362. This district essentially comprises urban population with no identified village. The 2001 Census figures show that almost 72 per cent of the total population reside in rural India.

The Census-2001 figures reveal that there is highly skewed distribution across the country with large concentration in relatively smaller areas. The population size and its distribution have serious implications on the economic development and environment. It also has influence on the political, social and cultural fabric of the country to a large extent. Largely the uneven distribution is due to changing patterns of urbanisation, topography, lack of employment opportunities in local areas and frequent occurrence of natural calamities that forces the population migration even within the state. However, the figures also suggest that the decline in population growth rates is spreading and encompassing larger geographical areas in the country.[16]

## Table 10.1

*Top Five – Bottom Five Districts (Population-wise) in India (2001)*

| *District* | *State* | *Males* | *Females* | *Total* |
|---|---|---|---|---|
| *TOP* | | | | |
| Medinipur | West Bengal | 4929000 | 4709473 | 9638473 |
| North-24 Pargana | West Bengal | 4635262 | 4295033 | 8930295 |
| Mumbai (Sub) | Maharashtra | 4702761 | 3884800 | 8587561 |
| Thane | Maharashtra | 4377806 | 3751027 | 8218833 |
| Pune | Maharashtra | 3768001 | 3456223 | 7224224 |
| *BOTTOM* | | | | |
| Yanam | Pondicherry | 15876 | 15486 | 31362 |
| Upper Siang | Arunachal Pradesh | 17844 | 15302 | 33146 |
| Lahul & Spiti | Himachal Pradesh | 18413 | 14811 | 33224 |
| Tawang | Arunachal Pradesh | 17676 | 17029 | 34705 |
| Mahe | Pondicherry | 17146 | 19677 | 36823 |

*Source*: Census, 2001.

## Human Development

With ever increasing population, demand for basic needs has been steeply rising. The growing populations need food, clothing, shelter, fuel and fodder for their livestock. In India, over 60 per cent of the rural population neither have adequate land holdings nor alternate service opportunities to produce or procure these commodities. In the absence of adequate employment opportunities, the rural people are unable to generate enough wages to sustain their livelihood. As a result, 40 per cent rural households are classified as poor, below the poverty line. Apart from lower income, rural population also suffers

16. *Census of India* (2001).

from lack of basic amenities like, clean drinking water, poor health care and illiteracy, *etc.*, adversely affecting the quality of life in rural India.

The *National Human Development Report* (2001) highlights that about 25 per cent of the villages do not have assured source of drinking water for about 4-5 months during the year and about 70-75 per cent of the water does not meet the standard prescribed by WHO for drinking purposes. Poor quality of drinking water is one of the major reasons for poor-health and high infant mortality in rural areas. Overall, human development as reflected in the HDI has improved significantly between 1980 and 2001. At the national level, during the eighties the index has improved by nearly 26 per cent and by another 24 per cent during the nineties. There has been an improvement both in rural, as well as in urban areas. Though the rural-urban gap in the level of human development continues to be significant, it has declined during the period. Inequalities across States on the HDI are less than the inequalities prevailing in terms of income levels as reflected in the per capita State Domestic Product.

Poverty is a major concern for rural development. The magnitude of human poverty, *i.e.* the head count ratio, the rural-urban ratio for the proportion of the poor on the HPI is nearly twice as high as that on the head count ratio of poverty. The HPI in terms of the broader aspects of deprivation, covers accessibility to basic minimum services, such large differences in rural and urban areas imply that the availability of basic amenities that are virtually taken for granted in urban areas are, in fact, quite scarce in rural areas. The inter-state differences in Human Poverty Index (HPI) are quite striking. Although the magnitude of HPI in the last decade has declined in all the States, but the relative positions of the States remained quite similar to the earlier period. The status of States in terms of head count ratio has not changed in the last decade. The worst-off states in the 80's continue to remain poverty-ridden states, like Orissa, Bihar, Arunachal Pradesh, Assam and Uttar Pradesh. Similarly, the better-off states in the 80's continue to perform better like, Kerala, Punjab and Himachal Pradesh. It was only in the smaller, predominantly urban areas of Delhi and Chandigarh that had an HPI in the range of 17-20 per cent. The HDI at national level has improved from 0.302 in 1981 to 0.381 in 1991. The improvement for rural areas is from 0.263 to 0.340 and in case of urban areas, from 0.442 to 0.511. Though the rural-urban gap continues to be significant, it has still declined. The ratio of urban to rural HDI has declined from around 1.7 in early 80's to 1.5 in the 90's.

### Table 10.2

*Inequality Adjusted Per Capita Consumption Expenditure (1999-2000)*

*(Figures in Rupees per month)*

| *States/UTs* | *Rural* | *Urban* | *Combined* |
|---|---|---|---|
| Andhra Pradesh | 345.83 | 533.73 | 402.76 |
| Arunachal Pradesh | 458.73 | 537.44 | 475.02 |
| Assam | 340.43 | 560.68 | 367.31 |
| Bihar | 304.58 | 410.37 | 320.40 |
| Goa | 653.58 | 842.44 | 750.20 |
| Gujarat | 423.09 | 634.88 | 502.06 |
| Haryana | 543.21 | 652.13 | 572.65 |
| Himachal Pradesh | 523.03 | 872.29 | 556.54 |
| Jammu & Kashmir | 552.42 | 740.17 | 599.89 |
| Karnataka | 379.18 | 618.29 | 460.01 |
| Kerala | 559.11 | 634.36 | 582.09 |
| Madhya Pradesh | 304.82 | 476.89 | 350.44 |
| Maharashtra | 368.50 | 637.24 | 481.65 |
| Manipur | 434.75 | 554.82 | 476.02 |
| Meghalaya | 479.43 | 772.93 | 533.58 |
| Mizoram | 585.91 | 806.74 | 727.08 |
| Nagaland | 795.30 | 986.08 | 835.77 |
| Orissa | 282.79 | 437.70 | 308.39 |
| Punjab | 566.10 | 638.43 | 589.07 |
| Rajasthan | 434.05 | 572.51 | 469.02 |
| Sikkim | 414.39 | 673.65 | 433.36 |
| Tamil Nadu | 370.52 | 584.71 | 448.87 |
| Tripura | 428.75 | 618.78 | 462.27 |
| Uttar Pradesh | 352.39 | 464.62 | 377.61 |
| West Bengal | 352.82 | 582.62 | 418.15 |
| Andaman & Nicobar Islands | 612.62 | 852.08 | 679.35 |
| Chandigarh | 740.12 | 985.66 | 956.77 |
| Daman & Diu | 717.76 | 748.97 | 761.95 |
| Dadra & Nagar Haveli | 399.73 | 875.56 | 455.40 |
| Delhi | 775.04 | 910.46 | 887.74 |
| Lakshwadweep | 712.87 | 779.06 | 759.39 |
| Pondicherry | 442.49 | 551.82 | 521.12 |

*Source*: *National Human Development Report*, 2001.

## Social Inequalities

Gender inequality feature across all parts of India, though in varying degree. The trend of low sex ratio in 0-6 age group is visible even in economically better off areas of India. However, rural areas, that tend to be poorer and more deprived, contain higher females per male ratio than males in urban areas. According to Census-2001, rural India has a sex ratio (0-6 age group) of 934 females per 1000 males, as compared to 903 females per 1000 males in the urban areas.

Education is by far the most potent means of enhancing human development, both in terms of economic well being as well as health of an individual and his family. Therefore, deprivation from education also reflects on the likelihood of improvement in other sectors of human development. While the average literacy rate in rural areas is around 50-65 per cent, it is as low as 20-25 per cent among women in backward areas. Illiteracy has also suppressed rural development due to lack of communication with the outside world.

**Table 10.3**

*Employment Pattern in India (2001)*

| | |
|---|---|
| Total Population | 1,028,610,328 |
| Total Number of Workers | 402,234,724 |
| Males | 275,014,476 |
| Females | 127,220,248 |
| Total Non-Workers | 626,375,604 |
| Work Participation Rate | 39.1% |
| Type of Workers: Main Workers | 77.8% |
| Marginal Workers | 22.2% |
| Category of Workers- Cultivators | 31.7% |
| Agricultural Labourers | 26.5% |
| Household industry workers | 4.2% |
| Other workers | 37.6% |

*Source: Census, 2001.*

The level of employment, its composition and the growth in employment opportunities is a critical indicator of the process of development in any economy. It is also an indicator that, in most cases, directly captures the economic attainments and hence the level of well being of individuals. During 1983-2000, the percentage of persons in the labour force at the national level declined from 66.5

per cent in 1983 to 61.8 per cent in 2000. For the males this declined from 87.1 per cent to 83.5 per cent and for the females from 44.4 per cent to 38.5 per cent during the period. It was observed that the labour force participation rates are expectedly higher in rural areas in comparison to urban areas, but in both cases there has been a steady decline. At the States level, except for Haryana, Andhra Pradesh, Himachal Pradesh and the North Eastern States of Mizoram, Meghalaya and Manipur, where a marginal increase was experienced between 1983-1994, but subsequently the overall trend followed a decline.

The proportion of households living in one room declined both in rural and urban areas, while those living in two or more rooms increased in each Census conducted since 1961. In 1981, at the national level, nearly 73 per cent of the households were living in houses with two or less rooms. The proportion was identical for rural and urban areas. In 1991, the proportion of households living in houses with two or less rooms declined marginally to 71 per cent, at the national level. This proportion was marginally higher in rural areas in comparison to urban areas. A majority of India's population does not have access to toilet facilities in their dwellings and lacks sanitation facilities for the disposal of waste. Apart from the availability of safe drinking water, lack of sanitation, particularly sewage and disposal of solid waste including 'night soil' has been observed as among the main reasons for prevailing ill health and morbidity levels in the country. As per the 1991 Census, less than one-fourth of the households in the country had toilet facility within the premises of their residence.

Rural population is slow in adopting new practices, which are essential with the changing times. Apart from lack of communication, social taboo has also hindered their progress. Several vested interests, both local and outsiders have exploited this situation. The rich landlords do not want any infrastructure development, which would benefit the poor, because of the fear that they would not get cheap labour to work on their farms. The local moneylenders do not want alternate financial institutions to provide cheaper credit needed by the poor. The traditional healers canvassed against modern medicine under the garb of religion and divine power. Thus, the rural poor continue to live in the clutches of the powerful, accepting it as their destiny and resulting in a voiceless and suppressed life. It is a vicious cycle and rural development programmes need to address such needs in a broader sense so that the rural poor can come out of the vicious cycle.

## Rural Market

The Indian rural market with its vast size and demand base offers great opportunities to producers. Almost two-thirds of Indian consumers live in rural areas and almost half of the national income is generated here. It is natural that rural market forms an integral part of the total domestic market of India. According to one study, if the rural income in India goes up by 1 per cent, there would be a corresponding increase of about Rs. 10,000 crores in the buying power. On the other hand, the urban sector has also shown little signs of growth. However, widespread rural poverty, large variations in income levels and human development, etc., dampened the growth of rural markets in India. Besides, accessibility, penetration, lack of infrastructure, long distances from nearest towns, further added reaching complexities to rural market network. While the rural market certainly offers a big attraction to producers, the major impediment is of penetration.

In the existing market structure the consumer is so distanced from the farmer by the layers of intermediaries that the farmer is hardly market responsive. A farmer is unable to anticipate the consumer demand and therefore often faces situations of glut and scarcity. Usually the rural business transactions are conducted in a non-transparent manner and pave way for restrictive business practices. The existing market structure provides no incentive for farmers to standardise/grade and sort produce or to grow better quality. Ironically the sorting/grading activities occur at the last link in the chain—retailer/consumer level, thereby adding inefficiencies and costs in the supply chain.

Rural India has at least one or more government-instituted *mandis* (market place) in each district for farm produce. On the last count, there are about 7161 regulated *mandis* (2001). These markets provide a convenient point for collection of large volumes of produce from different sources. It also acts as assortment centre to meet the needs of the retailers in the country. The procurement of agri-produce by various government agencies also takes place through these markets.

## Figure 10.2

*Key Players in Rural Market*

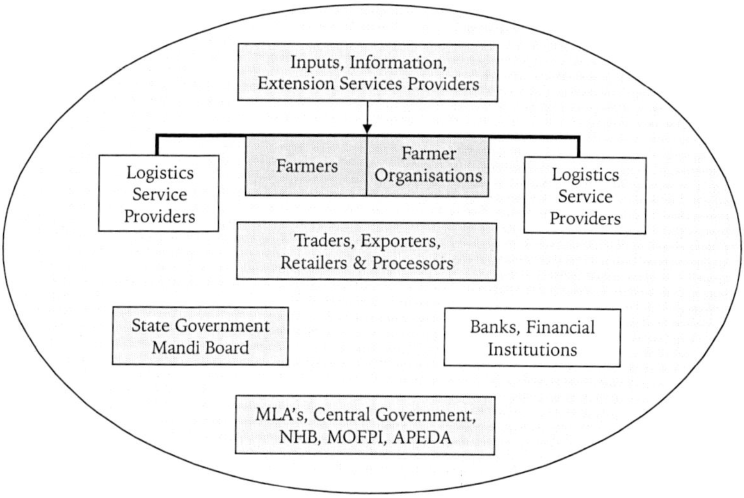


The volumes handled in these markets are much larger. These markets, therefore, require not only an elaborate physical infrastructure but also some kind of regulation to protect the interest of both the producer and the consumer. Most *mandis* are covered under the Agriculture Produce Marketing Committee (APMC) Acts and therefore called regulated markets. In major business hubs these markets perform dual function—transit market for supplies to the hinterland and distant markets and terminal market for supplies to the retailers for local consumption. The primary wholesale markets are located in important towns near the centres of production. The producers-farmers bring the major part of the produce for sale themselves in these markets. The secondary wholesale markets are generally located in district headquarters or important trade centres. The bulk of the arrivals in these markets are linked with other smaller markets. Major transactions take place between commission agents and wholesalers.

The *mandis* are spread over the entire length and breadth of the India, but clustering of market place in the North, West and South is quite distinct. It is imperative to mention that clustering of *mandis* is the result of locational advantage of product-specific market place, like grain, fruits and vegetable *mandis* in the North and West, *etc*. These markets have emerged as business hubs due to their nearness to the urban centres. But majority of them continues to struggle for survival. One of the major impediments to market development is widespread lack of basic infrastructure facilities, like poor roads and communication connectivity, absence of linkages with industrial consumers, *etc*.

The market intermediaries, *adhaatis* or *dalals*, play a major role in capturing the market place to suit their requirements. The intermediaries purchase the farm produce directly from the farmers and bring the farm produce to the market for selling.[17] In fact, small farmers find such arrangements with the middlemen more appropriate because the intermediary takes care of their material needs along with the supply risk,[18] market risk[19] and price risk.[20] Besides, the government *mandis* are out of reach of large number of farmers because of middlemen-procurement agencies nexus.

Unlike *mandis*, the *haats* are informally structured essentially a rural market place.[21] Despite development of permanent shops, *haats* play an important role in the rural economy. These markets provide an opportunity not only to purchase consumer goods but also to sell surplus agriculture and allied produce. The producers sell their produce directly to the consumers or to small rural retailers. Since both producers and consumers are local, therefore the volume of

17. Bhatindha is a grain *mandi* in the North. Field survey revealed that farmers tend to sell their entire produce to the "dalal" in advance. There is no physical exchange of money between the intermediary and the farmer. But the intermediary's outlets take care of all material needs of the farmer. For instance, if the farmer wants diesel, he is given a receipt for a particular diesel depot, from where the farmer collects the diesel. The intermediary makes the payment directly to the diesel depot and deducts the amount from farmer's accounts. Likewise, the intermediary has his own network of retail shops in the village from where the farmer obtains other products and services. At the end of the year, the intermediary informs the farmers about the balance, which is adjusted against the procurement of next consignment of his produce. In the entire market procurement and delivery system, the farmer remains ignorant of the prevailing prices of his produce in the market as well as about the price of the inputs. A farmer narrated that the middleman leaving a small share of produce for his own requirements lifts a major part of his produce. The farmer remains in debt for his entire lifetime. This practice is prevalent among large number of small farmers.
18. Ability to participate in the market as a seller of produce, *e.g.* climatic fluctuations.
19. Ability to establish linkages in the market.
20. Ability to negotiate on appropriate price at a particular time and location.
21. Periodic markets or *haats* are also known as *peta* or *angadi* in Telugu, *hatwara* in Rajasthan, *shandies* or *chindies* in Kerala and *painth* in Uttar Pradesh and fairs (melas, jatras) are the major rural market system in India.

business is low in such markets. Retailing in *haat* is direct selling in its pristine form.

These markets are largely unregulated and are generally held once in a week. Rough estimates suggest that there are about 47,000 *haats* in the country. Local bodies control the auctions of space and issues licenses and permits to the vendors. A market tax or fee is collected from each participant. Their main function is to provide the basic infrastructure for carrying out the transactions smoothly. Despite substantial revenue collection through annual auctions or through collection of fee from the participants, little effort has been made to provide the necessary infrastructure or to develop the rural market.[22]

The small farmer, with limited surplus, does not find it economical to go to wholesale markets or *mandis* located at distant places. A *haat* is a temporary market place, thus it is not equipped with basic facilities like platforms for sale or auction, electricity, drinking water, facilities for grading, sorting, traders' premises *etc*. The participants generally sit in the open air, thus exposing themselves and their products to heat, dust, rain, cold, *etc*. This in turn shortens the shelf life of their agri-produce and renders other food items unhygienic and unsafe for human consumption. Owing to these shortcomings, the potential buyers/traders do not operate in these markets and the producers do not get competitive prices for the sale of their produce. Although domination of large players cannot be denied in the *haats*, but small and marginal farmers and producers also get an equal opportunity to sell their produce. Rough estimates suggest that a *haat* usually conducts business of worth Rs. 3-5 lakh depending on the location and market size. Besides, there are established product-specific and farm produce markets.

Another business network, which is worth mentioning, is the establishment of more than 15,000 retail outlets of KVIC throughout the country. The functions of the KVIC are to plan, promote, organise and assist in implementation of programmes for the development of *khadi* and village industries. The KVIC operates through 30 State/UT KVI Boards, 4969 registered institutions and 30,129 cooperatives, and 188 departmental units. No private sector enterprise in the world today has such vast distribution network, covering a market in all the

22. Patnaik (2003).

593 districts in India. The KVIC is a major link between rural-based producers and markets. The objectives of the KVIC include skill improvement, employment generation in rural areas, transfer of technology, rural industrialisation and promotion self-reliance among the people and to build up a strong rural community base.

KVIC retail stores are old-timers in this business, with an entirely different business vision. Though extremely low-key they have surprisingly good business volumes. In fact, the KVIC promotes direct engagement of people, craft persons, *etc.* in the value addition activity. It acts as one of the major players in the government sponsored livelihood programmes, ranging from cottage industry to value adding activity on food products. One of the major shortcomings for the rural producers and small craft persons is brand name. The KVIC fills this gap and markets these rural products under their own brand name, thus establishing standards for rural products. It provides credible generic identity to Indian products, like handicrafts, handlooms, processed food items, etc. However, KVIC, being a government organisation, is also endowed with the similar problems of mis-management and accountability, red tapism in decision making, poor supply chain management, *etc.*

The clustering phenomenon on a region-wise basis is even more evident for the manufacturing sector. There is a large concentration of industrial clusters in small-scale and tiny sectors in select areas. This industrial concentration is visible in places, where the markets are clustered around the urban centres, *i.e.* location in the North (NCR Delhi), West (Maharashtra) and South (Tamil Nadu, Lower Karnataka & Kerala). Therefore, concentration of manufacturing sector along with the presence of established market place has been the cause of emergence of large business hubs at select locations in the North, West and South. The UNIDO has identified almost 300 industrial clusters across India and currently it is in the process of developing 200 more new industry clusters in India. Besides, the UNIDO and Government of India have also identified 1600 artisan clusters, which are spread over a large part of India, but still the concentration remains at select locations. Thus, it can be safely mentioned that a large business hub is more than a market place, it also constitutes economic activities like cottage industry and manufacturing/ processing activity.

Unlike the markets and industry clusters, the agricultural production centres are spread over evenly throughout the country. Government of India has identified more than 300 locations for agri-produce export development across the country on the basis of comparative advantage. For instance, the largely undeveloped business hubs in the central and eastern parts of India are also found to have comparative advantage in select farm produce. The vegetables and fruit production regions are scattered all over rural India, including the backward regions. However, the limitation of developing these vegetables and fruit growing regions into business areas is lack of infrastructure facilities and poor linkage with markets. More than 25 per cent of our vegetables and fruits perish due to absence of adequate storage facilities. But more than that the vegetables and fruit growing regions have yet to establish their supply linkages with processing centres and urban markets.

One of the reasons of emergence of the rural market recently is the rising income level of rural community. The income level phenomenon is increasingly percolating down to the middle-income group in the country. The NCAER Report reveals that the rural income in the (+) Rs. 90,000 category which has 17.8 per cent in 2001-02 is projected to rise to 36.9 per cent in 2009-10. The report also projects that the national average by 2009-10 will be a healthy 48.4 per cent against poor 28 per cent in 2001-02. In the rural segment, the percentage of households in the low income group (< Rs. 45,000) is also projected to decline to 20.6 per cent by 2009-10, against a high of 42.7 per cent during 2001. The lower middle category (Rs. 45,001-90,000) has also seen a sharp rise in the last decade from 23.9 per cent (1989-90) to 39.5 per cent (2001-02).

Table 10.4

*India: Distribution of Rural Household Income*

| *Annual Household Income* | *1989-90 (%)* | *2001-02 (%)* | *2009-10 (%)* |
|---|---|---|---|
| Below Rs. 45,000 | 67.3 | 42.7 | 20.6 |
| Rs. 45,001-90,000 | 23.9 | 39.5 | 42.5 |
| Above Rs. 90,000 | 8.8 | 17.8 | 36.9 |
| **Total** | **100.0** | **100.0** | **100.0** |

*Note*: Rs. at 2001-02 Prices

*Source*: *Hindustan Times* (29 September 2004)

Undoubtedly, the growth in agricultural production coupled with economic reforms has allowed percolation of benefits to the rural areas. The four factors that are going to have a considerably influence on the rural markets are structural changes in the product ownership, bridging the rural-urban divide, growing FMCG market and consumer financing. But Patnaik (2003) suggests that the existence of number of domestic market distortions are negatively impacting on rural consumers, for instance poor access to credit and insurance for rural consumers, lack of adequate communication systems, poor market regulation by government agencies, etc. All such deficiencies within the rural market stifle the consumer base of rural India. Although there are signs of revival in the rural economy with the entry of Indian corporate giants, but to facilitate growth in the rural market, policy instruments must eliminate the domestic market distortions.

## Box 10.3

*Changing Economy*

**Structural Changes in Product Ownership**

1. Both the ownership and purchase data on consumer durable products show that the product composition is getting transformed.
2. Households prefer high-priced products (Group III) to medium-priced durables (Group II) at an additional cost for increased product utility and feature values.
3. The ownership change has been faster in urban India than in rural areas.
4. The latent demand that surfaced during the mid-1990s has dampened.
5. These observations, supplemented by the fact that income distribution is rapidly and constantly transforming and that product penetrations have a long way to go before they saturate, assert that consumer demand will exist and rise in the future.

**Rural-Urban Divide**

1. The rural markets are growing. However, the level of infrastructural development (including that of the services sector) and performance of agriculture will determine their further growth.
2. Availability of electricity alone is a critical factor for durable ownership.

**The FMCG Market**

1. During the 1990s, the rural segment of the FMCG market has grown steadily at over 3 per cent p.a. The urban market has expanded faster.
2. The market dynamics for expendable products/FMCG (for 22 products) have been analysed in detail.
3. Different factors impacting the market growth in various product categories in the 1990s have been analysed.
4. Market size for products with lower penetration and consumption levels has grown at over 40 per cent p.a. during the later half of the 1990s. Significantly, such products also are at the higher side on the price line.
5. There are others such as washing materials and tooth paste/powders where substitution effect is observed to have taken place.

**Role of Consumer Finance**

1. Consumer finance is the key to future market growth, since (a) the income effect (boom) of the mid-1990s is over; (b) the latent demand of the mid-1990s has exhausted; and (c) there is no more "a readymade consumer market".
2. Consumer finance is taking shape with financial/banking sector reforms.

Although the realisation was slow, but the Indian corporate sector has now shifted its focus to rural markets as a strategic move to suit their plans of expansion. Pepsi Foods jumpstarted this phenomenon by establishing linkages for procuring agri-produce directly from the rural markets, which has paved way for the Indian companies to follow. Now the Indian corporate sector has started the process of consolidation on the supply side by establishing linkages with the farm producers directly. Such linkages between the producers and processing plants will eventually result in the establishment of a rural business hub in India.

## Central Government Programmes for Rural Development

The Ministry of Rural Development is striving to bring about rapid and sustainable development and socio-economic transformation in rural India with an integrated approach towards improving the quality of life of rural poor and ensuring equity and effective people's participation. The thrust of rural development programmes has been to make a frontal attack on poverty through special employment generation programmes, productive asset transfer through institutional credit and subsidy programmes and programmes of rural housing, drinking water and sanitation.

**Box 10.4**

*Rural Development in India: Chronological Highlights*

| | |
|---|---|
| 1952 | Community Development Programme launched (October). |
| 1958 | Three-tier structure of local self-governing bodies *(Panchayati Raj)* launched (October). |
| 1969 | Rural Electrification Corporation set up. |
| 1970-71 | Drought Prone Areas Programme started (December). |
| 1971 | A Joint Consultative Council on Community Development and *Panchayati Raj* constituted (December). |
| 1971-72 | Crash Scheme for Rural Employment introduced. |
| 1972-73 | Pilot Intensive Rural Employment Project (PIREP) launched. Accelerated Rural Water Supply Programme started. |
| 1977 | Food for Work Programme started (April). |
| 1977-78 | Desert Development Programme started (April). |
| 1978-79 | Integrated Rural Development Programme launched. |
| 1984 | NREP and RLEGP merged into one single rural employment programme to be known as Jawahar Rozgar Yojana (JRY). |
| 1985-86 | Indira Awaas Yojana started. |
| 1988-89 | Million Wells Scheme started. |
| 1992 | The Parliament passed the Constitutional 73rd Amendment Act to grant constitutional status to the Panchayati Raj institutions (December). |
| 1993 | Employment Assurance Scheme implemented (October). |
| 1995 | National Social Assistance Programme (NSAP) launched (August). |
| 1999 | Jawahar Gram Samriddhi Yojana launched (1 April), Swarnjayanti Gram Swarozgar Yojana launched (1 April), Innovative Stream for Rural Housing and Habitat Development Scheme launched (1 April). |

Strong thrust has been given to social security programmes for providing assistance to the destitutes and poor families. The Ministry has undertaken development of wastelands, desert and drought prone areas and land reforms in the country. Assistance and encouragement to voluntary agencies and training of functionaries of rural development forms part of the emphasis on accelerated rural development.

## Table 10.5

*Financial Outlays of Schemes of the Ministry of Rural Development*

*(Rs. Crore)*

| *Name of the Scheme* | *2000-2001* | *2001-2002* | *2002-2003***  |
|---|---|---|---|
| Sampoorna Grameen Rozgar Yojana | 2950* | 3250* | 4440 |
| Food for Work Programme | 0 | 0 | 600 |
| Pradhan Mantri Gram Sadak Yojana | 2500.5* | 2500 | 2500 |
| Rural Housing | 1710 | 1527 | 1725 |
| Swarnajayanti Gram Swarozgar Yojana | 1000 | 500 | 710 |
| DRDA Administration | 220 | 220 | 220 |
| Grants to National Institute of Rural Development | 5 | 5 | 5 |
| Training Scheme | 14.5 | 18 | 19 |
| Information, Education and Communication (IEC) | 10 | 10 | 10 |
| Assistance to CAPART | 30 | 30 | 30 |
| Monitoring Mechanism | 5 | 10 | 11 |
| NSAP@ | 715 | 835 | 0 |
| Annapurna@ | 100 | 300 | 0 |
| **Total** | **9260** | **9205** | **10270** |
| Drought Prone Areas Programme (DPAP) | 190 | 210 | 250 |
| Desert Development Programme (DDP) | 135 | 160 | 185 |
| Integrated wastelands Development Programme (IWDP) | 480 | 430 | 450 |
| Computerisation of Land Records | 50 | 45 | 55 |
| Strenghening of Revenue Administration & Updating of Land Records (SRA & ULR) | 25 | 30 | 35 |
| Others | 20 | 25 | 25 |
| **Total-Land Resources** | **900** | **900** | **1000** |

* Outlay for east while EAS & JGSY which have been merged with SGRY.

** Rs.0.50 crores for Roads in special problem areas.

@ NSAP & Annapurna are being transferred to States/UTs.

*Source*: Ministry of Rural Development, *Annual Report 2001-2002*.

However, a major weakness of the architecture of rural development programmes and anti-poverty programmes in particular is that they are conceived as having an isolated existence in "a self-contained universe of micro-oriented programmes and projects to specific groups of the poor." Such programmes remain incapable of generating the synergy needed to eliminate poverty and tend to degenerate into welfarism. As a result, they become unsustainable without continuing access to financial assistance.

The project approach detracts from the task of mainstreaming rural poverty and development agendas into the overall design of development, rather than hoping that the trickle down effect will do the trick if the growth impulse is strong enough. For instance, an important rural development programme—the Indira Awas Yojana (IAY), the largest housing scheme for the poor in India, is kept outside the regulation of the *panchayats* by some state governments. Even wherever the scheme is implemented under *panchayats*, often the contractors and the block-level bureaucracy supercedes the *panchayat* decisions.

Nayak *et al.* (2002) looked into select centrally government sponsored programmes and concluded that malpractice by lower-level officials has been pervasive in the implementation of programmes like SGRY, IRDP, *etc.* Surveys in some areas indicated that bank officials made 10 per cent deduction as informal 'charges'. In other localities, over 20 per cent of the subsidy component were charged in various ways as 'speed money'. Another common form of corruption was collusion of officials with local middlemen to provide the asset specified by beneficiaries, contrary to the regulations which require these to be provided by approved suppliers in exchange for cash payments by the beneficiaries. Working in collusion with administrators, the banks have also made illicit 'charges' on beneficiaries.

Other problems include:

- the limited capacity of government to identify investment opportunities resulting in excessive investment in one particular kind of asset, such as dairy cows, within limited areas, so that markets quickly become flooded;
- frequent loan moratoria instigated by politicians, so that few beneficiaries take seriously the obligation to repay;
- inadequate monitoring at activity or output levels so that problems of inappropriate assets, high risk levels and low returns are rarely detected;

- complex application procedures, which are, near impossible for low-income people to understand.

There is a large literature on the limitations of the IRDP in helping to create a sustainable productive asset base for the low-income self-employed. In many cases there is no insurance provision for assets such as livestock, so that their death will make it impossible for beneficiaries to repay loans.

Researchers have widely analysed the benefits and effectiveness of the "Employment Assurance Scheme". It was commonly observed that within-district responsibilities for storage, transport and distribution of food grains were contracted out to fair price shops and private contractors, which provided the opportunity for fraudulent practice because of price variations in the market place.[23] The use of foodgrains for payment in kind is minimal in the EAS, and EAS regulations prohibit the engagement of contractors or middlemen, but this provision is widely flouted, and has been accompanied by falsification of attendance lists and other irregularities. Some estimates suggest that, given the combination of malpractice among administrators and contractors, only 25 per cent of the wage funds to which beneficiaries are entitled actually reach them, the remaining 75 per cent disappearing through leakage of various kinds.

Likewise, Nayak *et al.* (2002) revealed existing malpractices in the implementation of some of the centrally sponsored schemes, like NOAPS and IAY, etc. She concluded that the pension and housing schemes exhibit contrasting design criteria- NOAPS disburses small amounts of money on a regular basis through relatively non-corrupt channels (mainly, the Post Office), whilst IAY allocates large lump sums on a one-off basis. The main difficulty for the poor in the NOAPS case is that of obtaining documented recognition of their age and destitution status. Often potentially eligible applicants have found their applications either rejected, or more commonly, lost in a bureaucratic maze, which they find impenetrable. Despite the small individual amounts of money involved, and the low-income status of applicants, these defects in the registration procedure are associated with some degree of corrupt practice on the part of bureaucrats. By contrast, politicians see the housing scheme as an important means

23. Prices of foodgrains at the PDS are much lower than the market price.

of patronage. The Rs. 20,000 lump sum payment is large enough to offer a significant reward to political supporters. There is clear evidence that a high proportion of the benefits of the scheme have been manipulated to this end. The size of individual payment also makes this scheme popular with local officials. It is large enough to withstand unofficial 'fees' running into several thousand rupees per application for the provision of forms, assistance in completing them, and the provision of signatures.

## Barriers to Rural Development

Land is a limiting factor, over 75 per cent owning less than 2 ha. As only about 28 per cent agricultural land is under irrigation and the rest under rainfed areas, a large number of people are seasonally employed, causing severe underemployment for over 250 days in a year. Even with good quality land and assured source of water, many farmers are not able to invest in necessary inputs to optimise their agricultural production. Lack of resources is the other reasons for lower crop yields. The average crop yield in India is 1.9 tonnes as compared to the world average of 2.5 tonnes/ha and 4 tonnes/ha in China.

Optimal utilisation of resources is a major drawback due to lack of education, awareness and confidence. This has resulted in neglect of various development schemes, which were introduced for sustainable use of these resources. Over 70 per cent of the rain water flows back to the sea causing flood and soil erosion. About 80-85 per cent of the livestock population is unproductive causing undue pressure on forest resources, while about 50-60 per cent of the rural population is underemployed. It is feasible to make sustainable use of these natural resources through application of appropriate technology and use of idle labour.

Despite many success stories, small and poor farmers are not confident about their ability to participate in development programmes. They are neither confident about the appropriateness of the technologies, nor convinced about the capabilities of the development agencies involved in launching these projects. Poor farmers, who have been receiving financial assistance in the past from the government and other donor agencies, lack adequate motivation and training. In the absence of their felt needs, they have been misusing these inputs for unproductive purposes or for mere survival without fulfilling the project goals. In this process, many poor farmers have developed a 'dependency syndrome' and expect outsiders to provide the means for their livelihood. They have lost confidence in themselves as well as in the outsiders.

Rural development projects are often implemented without adequate planning. In the absence of an integrated approach to tackle multidimensional interrelated problems, sectoral development activities may not deliver expected results. Apart from integration of various sectors, many of these projects also lack proper planning and resource mobilisation. Unlike industries, rural development projects are not implemented on sound management principles taking into consideration the required inputs, technologies, human skills and opportunities for marketing the produce.

## Rural Development: Systemic Essentials

The present approach in rural development programmes suffers not only from the difficulty of upscaling them without bureaucratic or mechanical replication, but also from the lack of any coordination and consistency between the goals of the myriad projects being launched through governmental or donor support. Nor are they able to mobilise any degree of collective support for the poor against the elites, which protect their interests, often by joining and pre-empting the benefits of such projects for themselves. A more comprehensive rural development strategy needs to encompass:

a) Access to land and land reforms
b) Possibilities of rural industrialisation
c) Rural governance
d) Decentralisation and
e) Local Government structures

## Access to Land and Land Reforms

An issue, which is of basic significance to rural development and yet has not become a part of the architecture of rural development programmes is the access to land and the related issue of land reform. Empirical evidence has shown the incidence of poverty is highly correlated with lack of access to land, although it does not necessarily imply a causal relationship. Studies have shown that households that depend on agricultural wage labour account for less than a third of all rural households but make up almost half of those living below the poverty line.[24] Many of these households also own some land, but in holdings that are so small or unproductive that their owners derive a greater share of their livelihoods from their own labour than from their own land. Land plays a strategic role in rural India—aside from its value as a productive factor, land ownership confers collateral in credit markets, security in the event of natural hazards or life contingencies, social status and, in the case of those with large landholdings, considerable political and economic leverage. Those who control land tend to exert a disproportionate influence over other rural institutions, including labour and credit markets, as well as access to education and other social programmes. Rosenzweig (2002) showed that "the distinction between those who own land and those who do not in rural India is both important for studying distributional issues and useful for under-standing the role of democratisation in aiding the poor ... because the large majority of the rural poor are landless and the ownership mobility is quite limited, so that classification by land ownership is related to lifetime welfare".

The principal assets available to the rural poor tend to be land and water. The three areas of agrarian reform which could be considered politically feasible as well as economically sustainable are:

a) Transforming tenancy rights into either ownership rights for the tenant or through right of permanent tenancy.

b) Redistribution of ownership of uncultivated land.

c) Giving title to lands and watercourses owned by the state.

Transfer of tenancy rights into permanent leaseholds has been successfully implemented in West Bengal, with the active participation of local bodies and peasant organisations. The issue is to give direct stake in the land to those who actually cultivate it. Without legal title to ownership or tenancy of land, the cultivators have negligible incentive to invest in the land nor are they able to use land as collateral to access the credit market.

A study based on empirical evidence of the Indian experience from 1955 to 1988 concludes: "... there is robust evidence of a link

24. Agarwal (1996).

between poverty reduction and two kinds of land reform—tenancy reform and abolition of intermediaries. Another important finding is that land reform can benefit the landless by raising agricultural wages. Although the effects on poverty would probably have been greater if large-scale redistribution of land had been achieved, the results are nonetheless interesting as they suggest that partial reforms, which mainly affect production relations in agriculture can also play a significant role in reducing rural poverty".[25] Considerations of both equity and efficiency would therefore suggest that some form of agrarian reform remains part of an unfinished agenda of economic reforms and as a prerequisite for rural development.

## Possibilities of Rural Industrialisation

The virtuous cycle between agriculture and non-agricultural enterprises plays a strategic role in providing employment opportunities in rural areas.[26] The countries that made substantial progress in poverty reduction created off-farm opportunities. There has been a spurt in the growth of non-farm enterprises in the Chinese countryside after liberalisation around the late 1970s where off-farm employment grew at a rapid rate of 12 per cent per annum, currently employing 31 per cent of the rural labour force.[27] As such, rural enterprises can become both an engine of growth as well as major contributors to the reduction of rural poverty. In most South Asian countries the potential for labour absorption is high in agro-based industries, small and medium industries and the rural services sector. Most of these activities are highly labour-intensive and provide employment opportunities for semi- and unskilled rural labour and the semi-skilled urban labour force.

The rural non-farm economy plays a significant role in providing employment and income for the poor in rural areas in rural India. Its importance is rising as neither agricultural production nor urban industry can absorb the increased labour force. Non-farm sources of income for the rural poor are important for two reasons:

a) The direct agricultural income of the poor is not enough to sustain their livelihood, either because of landlessness or because of insufficient owned or tenanted land.

25. Besley & Burgess (1998).
26. Mellon (1978).
27. Stern (2001).

b) Wage employment in agriculture is highly seasonal and requires supplementation of income and as employment during lean periods.

As most rural non-farm activities require little capital and generate more employment per unit of capital, they provide a good source of raising employment and income opportunities for the poor. The non-farm economy accounts for 40 to 60 per cent of total national employment, and the rural non-farm economy accounts for 20 to 50 per cent of total rural employment.[28] Non-farm income shares are typically 5 to 10 per cent larger than non-farm employment shares in rural areas. The importance of non-farm employment and earnings rises as the land available to the household for cultivation diminishes.[29]

The non-farm sector also has considerable scope to complement farming because of the strong linkages between the two sectors and because the non-farm sector forges linkages between rural and urban areas. Service activities dominate the non-farm economy in rural areas in South Asia. The non-farm sector is also an important source of income for women, small farmers, landless workers and the poor living in rural towns. Manufacturing, services and trade activities are the most important sources of employment for both male and female workers in rural areas, though women are relatively more concentrated in these activities than men.

The rural non-farm sector is particularly important to the rural poor. Households with less than 0.5 ha earn between 30 and 90 per cent of their income from non-farm sources. There is a strong negative relationship between non-farm shares and farm-size. Low-investment manufacturing and services (including weaving, pottery, gathering, food preparation and processing, domestic and personal services and unskilled non-farm wage labour) typically account for the greater share of income for the rural poor than the wealthy.[30] Non-farm income is also important to the poor as a means to help stabilise household income in drought years.

China provides an excellent example of how a rural development strategy focusing on the non-farm sector can bring about a significant

28. ADB (2000).
29. IFAD (2002).
30. Haggblade (1998).

change in the structure of the national economy[31]. This is in addition to boosting the rural economy, increasing farmers' incomes and contributing to poverty reduction. The effects of developing rural enterprises reveal the importance of expanding non-agricultural sectors in the rural areas to generate employment for increasing surplus labour. Rural industrialisation, which plays a vital role in shaping China's economic growth and economic structure, is regarded as one of the major successes of the country's reforming economy. They now employ nearly 30 per cent of rural labour, and comprise a major source of new rural employment. China's experience demonstrates the importance of institutional reform, price and market reform, rural industrialisation and other policies that diversify the agriculture sector and rural economy, as ways to promote farmers' income growth. The shift from the collective to the household responsibility systems also enhanced the price-responsiveness of farm households.

The slow growth of rural industrialisation in India is owing to the lack of public policies to promote the non-farm sector, both direct and indirect, such as macroeconomic and trade policies. Among the support policies directed at non-farm sector enterprises, financial assistance and credit facilities to the non-farm sector and technical services of various kinds are the most important. These policies help reduce the discrimination and disincentives suffered by small-scale rural enterprises through lack of access to credit, technology and markets. Given the urban bias in policies, these enterprises also suffer from underdevelopment of social, human and physical infrastructure in the rural areas. The provision of human capital is important to give the poor the capacity to enter the rural non-farm sector. This does not necessarily include formal education, as there is scope for teaching basic literacy, numeracy and book-keeping in a non-formal, hands-on manner.

Financial assistance to medium, small-scale, and micro-level enterprises is usually channelled through government-owned commercial banks or specialised financial institutions, or by requiring private commercial banks to allocate a certain percentage of their loans to these enterprises. In the past, small enterprises often received loans at subsidised interest rates, resulting in credit rationing. The rate of repayment was very low, resulting in losses for financial institutions burdened with a large proportion of non-performing

31. Lin & Yang Yao (2001).

loans. The rural areas are also generally excluded by institutions of financial support to small and medium industries, as they are focused mainly on urban areas.

Another source of stimulus to the growth of the rural non-farm sector is through local institutions, which can help facilitate the development of physical, social, and human infrastructure at the local level. Decentralisation tends to shift the focus of expenditure toward small-scale infrastructure projects, encouraging the growth of small-scale private sector projects. It is also likely that there will be greater equity in the distribution of public expenditures within localities because there is greater transparency and accountability in a local setting, although the Indian experience in this regard is mixed. On the other hand in China and Taiwan Province of China, where land reforms have eliminated the political influence of large landowners, local bodies have played an important role in the development of infrastructure and industrialisation.

## Rural Governance

More than five decades of rural development efforts by the state and civil society, have transformed the nature of governance in the rural areas in India. The Panchayati Raj Institutions in the rural areas are in a state of flux and a new governance paradigm for rural areas is yet to emerge. The growing economic differentiation of rural society, rapid diversification of activity and its commercialisation has loosened traditional social structures. The process will intensify and lead to a significant re-alignment of the power structure in substantial parts of rural India favouring the disadvantaged groups. Such realignments will not of course occur in all cases spontaneously and in a manner, which gives an effective voice to the poor and promotes their interests. The process unleashed and the potential for change created by them must therefore focus on creating conditions which will facilitate a favourable outcome. In this context three aspects deserve special attention.

First, the state will have to continue to play a supportive role in rural development. A great deal of knowledge and expertise is needed to assess local resources and their potential, different ways of exploiting the potential, the costs involved and raising resources. This knowledge, much of it technical in nature, is often not available locally. Strong support from outside government is necessary to make it accessible to the communities and their leaders. Along with this support, the role of government agencies also needs to change. Instead of planning, deciding and implementing schemes on their own, as they now do, the agencies will have to play a less intrusive role by facilitating coordination between the related schemes of different communities and providing a broader perspective.

Second, the creation of democratic institutions of local self-government and assured representation for disadvantaged groups is a necessary condition to ensure the vulnerable group's interests are safeguarded. The determination of priorities, in the context of limited resources, inevitably involves a process of bargaining between different groups. In order for this to work in favour of the marginalised, various groups have to articulate their needs and actively persuade the relevant forums to take necessary action to meet their needs. None of these occur easily or automatically. Conscious measures to encourage and strengthen institutions of civil society at the local level are essential. Moreover the elected local institutions cannot merely generate demands for a larger devolution of resources from the state and central government should be required to mobilise their own resources to meet a significant part of the costs of their programmes.

Third, civil society has a key role in obtaining and disseminating information on the working of functionaries, including local self-government, making people aware of their entitlements and obligations and enabling them to vent their grievances and seek redress. Besides interceding with the concerned authorities to secure benefits for the eligible and minimise leakages, they have a role in motivating and organizing local communities to take active interest in the working of specific programmes and persuading bureaucracy to work with the community for improving the effectiveness of programmes.

All this implies a basic change in the relations between the state and local governments, the role of the bureaucracy and the attitudes of local governments. There are no standard blueprints for accomplishing the change. A great deal of experimentation and learning from experience is inevitable.

## Decentralisation and Local Government Structures

*Panchayats* are being formed in all states and powers are being delegated to them. These institutions have little or no control over rural development programmes. Instituting parallel structures and active involvement of the civil society have resulted in serious problems of duality or duplication of responsibilities and efforts. For enabling local PRI to genuinely articulate and implement the aspirations of the poor, it is essential that functioning of these institutions remain insulated from bureaucratic interference and elite manipulation and capture. Within India there is a wide variation in the degree of success of local governments among different states. To some extent the success has been correlated with the level of literacy and political consciousness of the electorate and the activism of civil society in the state. To ensure successful decentralisation, two issues deserve top priority:

a) Support for developing an effective framework for and management of the decentralisation process; and

b) Capacity-building of local Governments to meet the demands of their new roles.

*Panchayati Raj* aims to empower the local bodies at the grass-root level to promote micro-level planning, initiate need based development programmes and ensure transparency. The *gram panchayats* are expected to develop their plans through a participatory approach and discuss such plans in the *gram sabha,* watch dog of local democracy. This concept is ideal for the upliftment of the rural areas and to ensure transparency in all public works. The realisation of this concept is totally dependent on a change in the attitude of the local people, who are the members of the *gram sabha*. Since members of *gram sabha* are members of the SHGs and other members of civil society, their existence will have multiple benefits. The formation of self-help groups of women and active participation of the local families in the process of planning and project implementation will also help in developing harmony and build unity among the members of the community, irrespective of their caste and economic diversities. This is an ideal method to empower the women and disadvantaged sections of the society.

## Rural Business Hub: An Alternative Plan for Rural Prosperity

Markets have played a strong role in development. An alternative to the existing rural development initiatives could be integrating rural markets for the poor. As it is evident that non-existent linkages between farm produce and production and processing centres is non-existent, the paradigm shift in the development strategy could be in targeting from the individual beneficiaries to strengthening agri-markets. Since rural market is one of areas transferred to the PRIs, the responsibility of market development rests on the *panchayats*. The local bodies must become an enabler and stakeholder to establish such linkages through partnerships.

It is a paradox that all development strategies deliberately choose to ignore linking the word 'urban' to rural plans and proposals. But without linking rural with urban, it is development in isolation. Perhaps, inequitable growth patterns between the rural and urban economy is the result of last five decades of isolated development. Indian economy comprises both, rural and urban, thus establishing links between rural and urban centres is essential for economic prosperity. Farm produce needs to be linked with the urban markets. It should not be misconstrued that such links were not existing in the past. Such links exist but its effectiveness is marred due to wide ranging market distortions. Another feature of our rural economy is the changing population size, which has resulted in many rural areas emerging as semi-urban centres.

In the last decade, many semi-urban townships at district and *taluka* level have come up both in terms of population and market size. Therefore, an alternative approach will be to establish links between surrounding villages with semi-urban centres, usually at *taluka* and distict levels.

The Census-2001 reports that total number of villages in India are 6,67,843, out of which only 2 per cent villages have a population of more than 5000 people or more than 1000 households. There are 14 per cent villages in India with a population of less than 200 people or 40 households. The relevance of such villages as part of rural development strategy is completely non-viable, especially connecting these villages with grid electricity or constructing a school or establishing a dispensary, *etc*. Perhaps such villages continue to exist because poor infrastructure facilities all around provide no incentive to the inhabitants to opt for better life outside their farming land. With the absence of proper means of road connectivity or

## Table 10.6

*Population-wise Classification of Villages (2001)*

| *States/UTs* | *Population* | | | | | |
|---|---|---|---|---|---|---|
| | *1-200* | *201-500* | *501-1000* | *1001-2000* | *2001-5000* | *5001-* |
| Andhra Pradesh | 3083 | 3397 | 466 | 6470 | 6911 | 2286 |
| Arunachal Pradesh | 2766 | 676 | 266 | 126 | 26 | 3 |
| Assam | 4765 | 6000 | 6231 | 5430 | 2494 | 204 |
| Bihar | 3258 | 5666 | 8487 | 10105 | 8573 | 2943 |
| Chhattisgarh | 2258 | 5500 | 6455 | 4182 | 1263 | 86 |
| Goa | 32 | 60 | 56 | 77 | 96 | 26 |
| Gujarat | 784 | 2301 | 4261 | 5612 | 4151 | 957 |
| Haryana | 273 | 582 | 1203 | 2092 | 2013 | 601 |
| Himachal Pradesh | 8950 | 5618 | 2085 | 659 | 174 | 9 |
| Jharkhand | 6701 | 9213 | 7433 | 4164 | 1641 | 202 |
| Jammu & Kashmir | 684 | 1494 | 1662 | 1546 | 887 | 144 |
| Karnataka | 3333 | 5557 | 7364 | 6373 | 4020 | 834 |
| Kerala | 2 | 4 | 0 | 10 | 69 | 1279 |
| Madhya Pradesh | 7196 | 14329 | 16254 | 10409 | 3548 | 381 |
| Maharashtra | 2966 | 7371 | 12067 | 11554 | 5858 | 1279 |
| Manipur | 754 | 730 | 323 | 202 | 156 | 34 |
| Meghalaya | 2762 | 2084 | 687 | 185 | 60 | 4 |
| Mizoram | 144 | 257 | 197 | 76 | 31 | 2 |
| Nagaland | 104 | 323 | 373 | 252 | 171 | 55 |
| Orissa | 12710 | 14025 | 11410 | 6799 | 2401 | 184 |
| Punjab | 1087 | 2125 | 3381 | 3400 | 1986 | 299 |
| Rajasthan | 5372 | 9155 | 11048 | 8764 | 4653 | 761 |
| Sikkim | 42 | 82 | 157 | 120 | 40 | 9 |
| Tamil Nadu | 486 | 1346 | 2797 | 4484 | 4865 | 1422 |
| Tripura | 12 | 55 | 99 | 188 | 370 | 134 |
| Uttar Pradesh | 9132 | 16912 | 25580 | 27197 | 16559 | 2562 |
| Uttaranchal | 7797 | 4902 | 1878 | 752 | 350 | 82 |
| West Bengal | 4296 | 7560 | 8925 | 8479 | 6814 | 1881 |
| Andaman & Nicobar Islands | 273 | 89 | 62 | 52 | 23 | 2 |
| Chandigarh | 3 | 1 | 2 | 2 | 7 | 8 |
| Daman & Diu | 0 | 2 | 5 | 4 | 5 | 7 |
| Dadra & Nagar Haveli | 1 | 7 | 12 | 15 | 28 | 7 |
| Delhi | 6 | 9 | 29 | 60 | 50 | |
| Lakshwadweep | 1 | 1 | 0 | 0 | 3 | 3 |
| Pondicherry | 0 | 0 | 7 | 18 | 45 | 22 |
| **Total** | **92033** | **127433** | **219466** | **129858** | **80341** | **18712** |

communication and security, the farmer continues to live on his land, thus the village exist. If the incentives are high in terms of better infrastructural facilities, especially in terms of road connectivity, electricity and communication system, and established links with semi-urban markets, almost 33 per cent of existing villages will vanish[32]. Therefore, the objective of rural development converges on rest of 67 per cent villages. In terms of population size, about 10 per cent of villages are presently existing in semi-urban form. Thus, the entire market development strategy revolves around the connecting 57 per cent villages to 10 semi-urban centres. This will require formation of village clusters for creation of rural business hub.

Each village is a production centre in terms of farm produce or horticulture and its residents are consumers. The concept of rural business hub rests on the essentials of rural development, namely, access to land and land reforms, possibilities of rural industrialisation, rural governance, decentralisation and local government structures. If the essentials of rural development are appropriately established, this will pave way for establishing a strong panchayat empowerment network using ICTs, the foundation for local democracy and link for creating a rural business hub through public-private partnership.

## Establishing a Panchayat Empowerment Network (PEN)

'Information' is a major resource, which could empower the rural population. Although deprivation in all its forms is quite evident in rural India, but asymmetry of access to information is major shortcoming. At the *gram panchayat* level, lack of access to information results in wide variety of distortions and deprivation, for instance, lack of information distorts rural markets, absence of information allows rent-seeking, *etc.* Had there been equal access to information, many of the problems of poverty and deprivation at a village level would have disappeared. Therefore, the major challenge for the PRIs is to bridge the informational requirements between the district level system and the village level system and integrate it such that the objectives of socio-economic development and upliftment, and creation of awareness amongst the target groups in rural communities is effectively met. A vacuum in information and mass communication within the rural community and between the rural community and

32. Population of less than 500 people or 100 households.

*gram panchayats* exists. Thus, the foremost challenge is to bridge this info-communication gap.

Aiyar (2004) suggested a time-bound action plan for establishing *Panchayati Raj* in India, both in letter and spirit. Besides the legislative and financial devolution, his action plan categorically focuses on five fundamental issues for strengthening PRIs, namely Planning, Implementation, *Gram Sabhas*, Empowerment and Capacity Building, and connecting rural population to markets. Building on the action plan, the ICT as a tool must be utilised to integrate the action plan with the essentials of rural development.

*Planning*

"Planning is required to be undertaken at each level, including village panchayat." Effective planning requires fair idea of the resources that will be available to them and clear idea of the resources they can raise and retain on their own. The consolidation of information at all levels requires appropriate information and accessibility to *panchayats*. Government agencies generate information on programmes, welfare schemes, evaluation reports, etc., useful for the rural community. Valuable data and information is being generated in R&D projects in Universities and civil society. A number of field level activities in progress adds to information content available on PRIs. All such information is of critical importance for planning and by the rural community. But more than that the information on *gram panchayat* is required by the governmental and non-governmental agencies for planning and decision making process.

*Implementation*

"Effective implementation requires participation of all *panchayat* members at all levels.... with the consent of all concerned.... for the implementation of works. A key element of effective implementation must be restructuring of the line departments into no more than secretariat office...". Progress in this regard has been most ineffective. The PRIs often work as implementation agencies of government programmes than as "institutions of local self-government". Nexus established between the official agencies and *Sarpanch* has fostered widespread corruption, leading to almost dysfunctional transparency and accountability in the PRIs decision making process. Access to information on the respective projects is vital for monitoring and evaluation. Such information will facilitate in the creating transparency and accountability of all the implementing stakeholders.

*Gram Sabha*

"For meaningful empowerment of *Gram Sabha*, the *Gram Sabha* must be entitled for all the information required for transparent and good governance, as well as given duties, which would make the elected *panchayat* answerable to the *gram sabha*". Making the *Gram Sabha* into an effective instrument of local self-government to fulfill the aspirations of the people is one of the major requirements. Accessibility to information will add to the importance of *gram sabha* meetings. It is also required to strengthen the institution of *gram sabha* to built in transparency and accountability in the decision making process of the PRIs. This initiative will facilitate in conducting social audit and fixing responsibility on the *panchayat* functionaries. It will also assist in defining the role of *gram sabhas* in the decision making process for major socio-economic development.

*Empowerment*

The Bangladesh Grameen Mobile Phone experiment is one of the successful case studies of ICT that has positively influenced the income generation capabilities and empowerment of marginalised sections of the society. Information is vital resource for empowerment. Lack of informational power leads to exploitative practices and rent seeking. Often the elites enjoy their power in the rural society due to their monopoly on the information. ICTs offer double benefit, namely expansion of income generating activities and connecting villages and its people to markets and authorities. Besides, ICTs have other spin-off benefits, like creating awareness of legal and human rights, as shown by the experiments in Asia, Latin America and Africa. Putting a village *panchayat* on the global network paves way for creating the foundation for an information society in the long run.

*Capacity Building & Training*

".......The electronic medium constitutes the single most-cost effective method of reaching large numbers of those concerned........" Although the connecting all *panchayat* bodies with Internet was one of the recommendations of the Prime Minister's Task Force on Information Technology, however it remained a pipedream for the last government. As an alternative to traditional connectivity, the peer group influence cannot be overlooked and ignored. It is proposed that each year the portal will attempt to identify 10 best practices by the *gram panchayats* for replication by other *gram panchayats*. The electronic medium will complement the other medium to create awareness on various successful examples. Also competitive pressure between peers will motivate the *gram panchayats* to perform better due to political compulsions. Such an initiative provides a platform for exchange of ideas and dialogues between individual *panchayats*, official agencies and civil society. Creating the 'PEN' portal will be a primary requirement of building the *panchayat* network in India.

Thus, to make PRIs more effective, there is an urgent need to improve communication not only between rural masses and *panchayat* members but also between the other *panchayats*. Focus of the 'PEN' is to create a network of *panchayats* for drawing strength from mutual association and making them an effective instrument of democracy and development.

**Box 10.5**

*Need for Farmer to Farmer Cooperation*

- Direct involvement of farmers for better communication
- Greater degree of success if congruency of objectives
- Conformity in perceptions about management issues
- Better commmunity cohesion for achievement of common objectives
- Overall improvement in productivity and environmental protection
- Better interface with markets and support institutions
- Adequate physical infrastructure

Some of the direct beneficiaries of the database:

1) Government functionaries at the national, state and district level
2) Planners, researchers and policy makers
3) Civil society
4) *Panchayat* Members
5) *Gram Sabha*
6) Markets
7) Rural society, especially the weaker sections of the society.

A single point data resource on *panchayats* in India will assist in the creation of basic infrastructure for building markets at the *gram panchayat* level and allowing horizontal and vertical linkages between them and distant markets, usually the district mandis.

## Establishing 'Apna Bazaar'

The growing number of small farms and declining average size of operational holdings indicate the weakness in their access to critical production resources. Rural producers operate at a lower equilibrium. Several studies indicate that small farmers encounter entirely different set of problems in both input and output markets. The input markets include, land, labour, credit, information and technology and purchased inputs. They also face the consumption market in addition to the output market. To bring them to a high level of equilibrium, it is essential to build linkages between the farmers and markets. Already public-private partnership in education, real estate, tourism, etc. has exhibited the resilience of private sector in rural development. Thus, it is all the more important to experiment with the concept of public-private partnership for creating rural business hubs.

### Box 10.6

*Need for Farmer Cooperation for Sustainable Farming*

- Introducing new technologies if needed
- Marketing- better bargaining power
- Avoid middlemen
- Provide extension service
- Infrastructure development
- Producers welfare
- Decision making and self-governance

Public-private Partnership (PPP) is recognised as a crucial aspect in attaining sustainable human as well as local development. It is primarily initiated to mobilise private sector, producers, investors, businessmen and other partners together with local communities to form institution for the enhancement of local governance, rural employment, poverty alleviation and enterprise development. Liberalisation acts as a catalyst to mobilise the underutilised resources at the district level for the economic upliftment and to create employment opportunities. Another important assumption behind PPP is that private sector has resources, skills and expertise but poor access to organised supply of raw materials and poor access to auxiliary services of the public sectors. The PPP initiates establishment of mechanism for partnership. (See 'Cognitive Space: Farmer')

**Box 10.7**

*Objective of PPP*

- To initiate and support mechanism to create mutual trust between the private and the public sector for the promotion of co-ordination in planning and implementation of the district development programme;
- To initiate and support mobilisation of the private sector, producers, investors, businessmen and other partners together with communities to form institution for the enhancement of local governance, rural employment and enterprise development;
- To ensure the sustainable development of the rural community.

The rationale behind using a PPP is that many communities produce quality products but there is neither proper marketing channels nor any direct linkages with the existing marketing networks. This results in low economies of scale and poor performance of a business enterprise. On the other hand the public sector fails to fully exploit the available resources thus resulting in stunted economic development. In fact, lack of coordination between the private sector and government agencies have resulted in serious imbalances in the rural markets. Good quality of product is available but fails to reach the right market.

PPP has also benefited some of the rural districts in Maharashtra. Eight districts, namely Dhanusa, Dolakha, Sankhuwasabha, Siraha, Sindhuli, Tehrathum, Sunsari and Udayapur, have initiated PPP for rural development, tapping business opportunity and employment creation. In few districts, the programme has already gone into action while some are in preparatory phase. In Dhanusa, the Public Private Management Committee (PPMC) has selected dairy plant for the partnership project implementation. In Tehrathum also the PPMC has selected Milk Chilling Plant for partnership project implementation. In Sindhuli the study has been completed for the cold storage plant. The feasibility study of dairy plant in Siraha also has been presented to the PPMC of the district for further action. These projects have shown promise and village development committees under the *panchayats* supervising the successful implementation of these programmes.

Likewise, *Apna Bazaar* is the establishment of market place at a semi-urban centre at the *Taluka* Level. A consortium of *gram panchayats* under the *Taluka panchayat* invites proposals from private investors to develop an 'Apna Bazaar' on PPP terms. The consortium provides an appropriate land (approx. 1 acre) to the private enterprise on lease. The private enterprise develops the place by constructing sheds, adequate storage facilities, canteen, sanitation facilities, etc. The *gram panchayat* consortium takes the responsibility of providing road connectivity and other area development works to suit the requirements of the *Bazaar* through the rural development funds. The private agency constructs the shops with the *Bazaar*'s premises and leases it out to the local entrepreneurs. The *Bazaar* will seek membership from the local farmers to sell their produce at the designated place within the *bazaar*. Since the private enterprise will also equip the *Bazaar* with modern communication facilities, the *bazaar* could emerge as an informational resource for the local population.

The private agency displays the prevailing prices of the agricultural commodities in other markets. On this basis, the farmers will fix their prices on a day to day basis. The revenues generated are shared between the consortium and the private enterprise. The concept of *Apna Bazaar* benefits the entrepreneur with direct access to farmers for building linkages between the producers and processing plants in urban areas. They are also benefited in terms of recovery of maintenance costs through receipt of rent and leasing fee. Local producers get direct linkage with the local consumers. Besides, they have a platform to get connected with the production/processing units in urban areas. Local population has access to a developed market, where the premium level is low on agricultural produce. The *panchayats* are benefited in terms of revenues, which could be spent on construction of schools and dispensary at designated places within the *taluka*.

*Apna Bazaar* will be the first step towards the creation of rural business hub. Once the *Bazaar* is operational, local entrepreneurship will follow soon. *Apna Bazaar* will provide a platform to establish forward and backward linkages between rural entrepreneurs and manufacturers and processors. Thus, all the stakeholders in the rural society will have the *Bazaar* as an enabler and facilitator to achieve their respective objectives.

Figure 10.3

*Cognitive Space: Farmer*

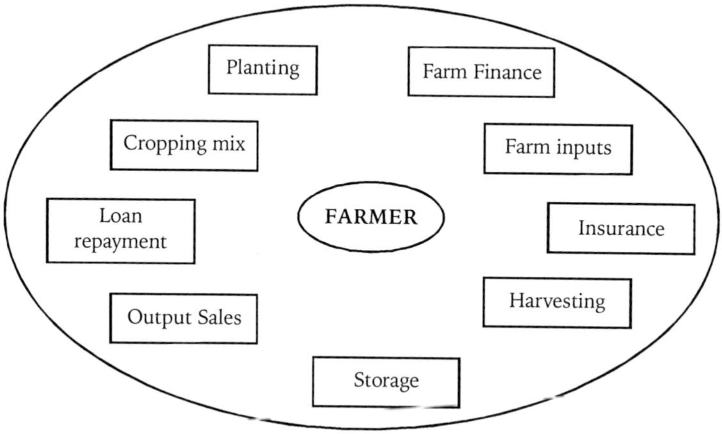


Figure 10.4

*Opportunity for a Rural Business Hub*

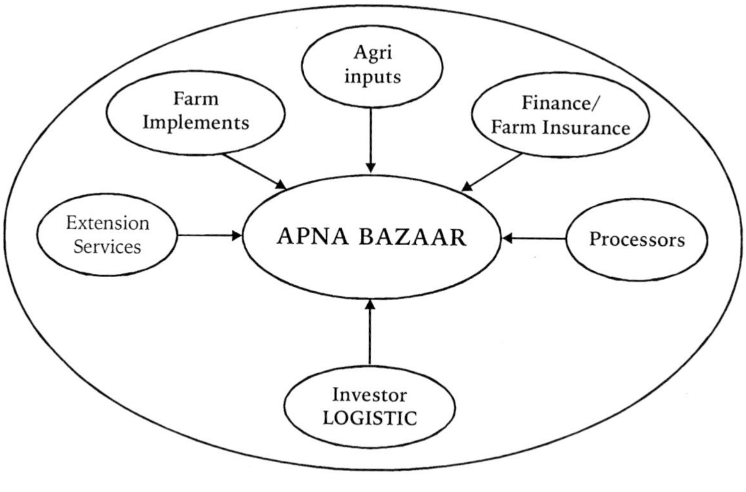

**Figure 10.5**

*The Potential Rural Market Hub*

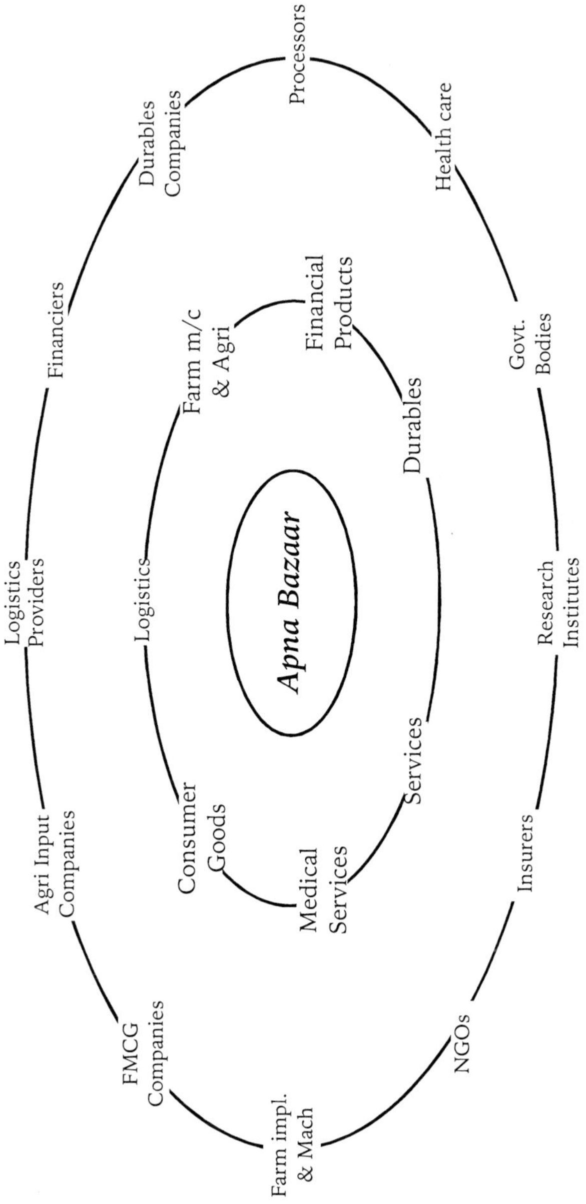

## Some Case Studies: Rural Development through Markets

*"Apni Mandi"* – Such *mandis* are set up in the major towns of Punjab including Chandigarh where farmers can sell directly to consumers, thereby creating direct marketing facilities where the farmer income is considerably enhanced. The *Panchayat Samiti* provides infrastructural and transportation facilities to the farmers. No user charges are levied on the participants. Farmers are provided with 20 crates at 50 percent subsidy. At the farm level extension services are provided to the farmers and benefits provided in terms of better quality inputs, loans, subsidies on inputs etc. However, the *Apna Mandi* and *Kisan* Market experience in Punjab and Haryana has not become self-sustained in the long run and still runs on the State exchequer and is viewed as a Development Activity of the State Agriculture Marketing Board.

*"Uzhavar Sandai"* – Over 100 such markets have been established in semi-urban centres in Tamil Nadu. Sales at such markets exceed 150 crore per year. Farmers benefit greatly for little extra effort. Over 250,000 tonnes sold per annum. Mega farmer markets are being planned for instance in Ottanchatram in Dindigul where auctions will take place. A huge cold store & electronic weighing facilities are to be provided in the new market. If a farmer wants to sell his products in the *Uzhavar Sandai*, first he ought to register his name and get an identity card with his photo affixed. To become a member, a government official inspects the farmer's land and quality of his produce. Only farmers are allowed to sell their farm produce. The farmers are provided carry bags, tamper-proof weighing scales by the government. Shops are allotted to the farmers on first-come-first-serve basis and each farmer gets a different shop daily. They bring their produce and sell directly to the consumers. The retail prices are arrived at based on the wholesale and retail prices in the open market centres in the region by a committee consisting of farmer representatives and officials of the 16 Agriculture Marketing Committees (AMC) which manages the markets. These prices are mentioned on a notice board and people are urged not to pay more than the rate mentioned on the board. The markets in Hosur, Coimbatore, Tirupur and Tiruchi are doing exceedingly well. In some markets the consumer density is more than 5,000. The agriculture department is giving training to the farmers in modern agricultural

practices and is encouraging them to expand cultivation. This is a part of development activity of the Directorate of Marketing as there is no marketing board to supervise the functioning of the market.

*"Agriculture Market"* – In Kerala, agriculture marketing is not regulated. The Kerala Horticulture Development Programme of the European Union has demonstrated a unique concept of grower owned fruit processing facilities. Kerala has the unique advantage of successfully implementing the Self Help Group model through the EU funded Kerala Horticulture Development Program in the Fruit and Vegetable Sector. This project has efficiently organised and integrated the activities of over 35000 fruit and vegetable farmers in the State.

This scheme offers strategic advantages to the State as follows:

- Well defined clusters of vegetable production in major districts
- Empowered farmer community
- Well-established R&D linkages and motivated extension support.
- Well developed market information systems
- Cluster level market infrastructure

The market development programme should integrate with the locally available *haat/mandi*. Thus, the proposed *bazaar* will have an established membership at the start. The *panchayat* must identify the availability of resources such as quality of the land, quantity of water, weather conditions and select suitable crops, which are most productive. The project must also ensure timely supply of inputs and finance. Besides the project must also identify a suitable markets where price recovery for the produce will be maximum. In this process, it is also necessary to develop the capacity of the target groups through establishment of local organisations. Availability of labour and their level of education to adopt necessary skills are also an important consideration. However in most of the villages, idle labour is available in plenty but skills required for implementing agro-based projects is less sophisticated. Hence the labour availability is not a critical factor, but motivating them to take active part in the programme is the key to success.

## Conclusion

We need to develop a strong infrastructure at various levels. Apart from mobilising people, infrastructure is also necessary to organise input supply, finance, post-production processing and marketing of the produce. Inadequate marketing network is another major bottleneck in agriculture. Adequate information channels must be put in place to make swift forecast of the demand for various commodities and exploit the opportunities. There is good scope for setting up market outlets to reach the customers without involving too many middlemen. Such support systems are an integral aspect of sustainable rural development.

Marketing services are presently provided by the state agencies, like Agricultural Marketing Boards, Milk Cooperatives and Federations, which are inefficient and politically oriented. Many of these cooperatives are not competent and are outdated. Very often they end up in losses because of mis-management and ignorance. In this process, the innocent farmers suffer heavily. Private sector can play a significant role in strengthening such market oriented village level organisations and building rural entrepreneurship network.

An ideal linkage of various stakeholders at various levels of agricultural development is an efficient and effective way for a sustainable rural development plan. The role of voluntary sector becomes all the more critical in establishing such linkages between the stakeholders. Self-Help Group (SHG) of 10-20 farmers can be an effective non-formal organisation to provide necessary services and facilities to the community. These groups can share their concerns and plans on various development activities to be undertaken jointly and individually. Successful initiatives from the voluntary sector have shown better scope for rural development outside government agencies, especially in the organisation of procurement of agricultural inputs, credit, technical services and marketing of the produce. Voluntary sector working at the block level has played a significant role in capacity building of the SHGs and Farmers' Organisations and facilitates a close link between the SHGs and *Gram Panchayats*. The present practice of extension services by *gram sevaks* has for long been found ineffective and inefficient. Thus, the technology transfer in backward areas is extremely slow. Even the earlier effort to disburse bank loans to farmers either directly or through the cooperative societies have not been successful due to lack of motivation and inadequate pressure from their peer groups. These drawbacks can be minimised through pushing and strengthening the voluntary sector in rural India.

# 11

# Addressing Food Security Concerns in India: An Analysis of Various Policy Options

DEBASHIS CHAKRABORTY

## Right to Food

The right to food for the citizens is considered to be a basic human right in any welfare state or society. Article 25 of the *Universal Declaration of Human Rights* (1948) states, "Everyone has the right to a standard of living adequate for health and well-being of himself and his family, including food." *The Rome Declaration on World Food Security* during World Food Summit (1996) set the standard as, "Food Security is achieved when all people, at all times, have physical and economic access to sufficient, safe and nutritious food to meet their dietary needs and food preferences for an active life." Hurting this right of others is also condemned as per Article 14 of the International Humanitarian Law. "Starvation of civilians as a method of combat is prohibited. It is therefore prohibited to attack, destroy, remove or render useless, for that purpose, objects indispensable to the survival of the civilian population, such as foodstuffs, agricultural areas for the production of foodstuffs, crops, livestock, drinking water installations and supplies of irrigation works."

It becomes a moral obligation for governments in developing and least developed countries, in scenarios of food shortage, to provide minimum dietary supplements to their citizens, especially to the poorer and most vulnerable sections. India, being a democratic and socialist republic, has enshrined the right to life among the Fundamental Rights in the Constitution.[1] In the post-Independence period, the country faced a problem of persistent poverty and food insecurity in various regions, and more stress was laid on poverty

1. Article 21 protects the right to life of citizens.

alleviation strategies, which in turn was supposed to have a positive impact on food security. However, the food crisis in the mid-sixties demanded a much wider government intervention to solve the problem, and a Public Distribution System (henceforth PDS) was established. Although the system initially depended on food imports, India subsequently achieved self-sufficiency in foodgrains. The poverty ratio in the country has declined drastically in recent years. However, the working of the Targeted Public Distribution System (TPDS) introduced in 1997 has often come under fire, and there is a growing concern that the food security scenario is actually worsening in the country. Academicians, various government committees and others have explored several policy options for improving food security. While a number of studies are of the view that a universal approach, *i.e.*, universal PDS is the way out, introduction of a more focused framework, *e.g.*, a food stamp programme (henceforth FSP), has also been proposed from various quarters. Recently, the Finance Minister, Mr. P. Chidambaram has proposed, in his budget speech for the year 2004-05, initiation of an FSP in several states on a pilot basis.

This analysis intends to focus on various aspects of introducing a FSP, and other suitable policy alternatives in India to ensure food security for the poorest segment of the population. The paper is organised along the following lines. First the PDS system is discussed in brief, and the systemic problems are outlined. Second, the recent scenario on food security is analysed. Third, the views of recent official documents like the Tenth Plan approach papers, and the *Report of the Committee on Long Term Grain Policy* are discussed in brief, and recent Government proposals are summarised. Fourth, a cross-country experience of FSPs and their effectiveness for addressing the concern on food security is provided. Finally, based on the findings, a number of policy observations and recommendations are drawn.

## The PDS System

The PDS system was introduced in India with the goal of addressing food security concerns during scarcity, maintaining price stability, keeping a check on dishonest practices in private trade and raising the welfare of the poor community.[2] The working of PDS can

---

2. For a detailed analysis of PDS in India, see Swaminathan (2000). This paper draws from Swaminathan (2000) for discussing the PDS provisions.

be divided into four distinct Phases. Phase-I ranges from 1943 to 1960. During the war period, rationing in several towns and cities was initiated to discipline supply of foodgrains, and was abolished in 1947. During the 1950s it was reintroduced and was extended to certain food-deficient rural regions as well, and procurement was still dependent on imports. Phase-II spans 1960 to 1978. Facing the food crisis in the mid-sixties, the Government set up two bodies, namely, Agriculture Prices Commission (later Commission on Agricultural Cost and Prices, or CACP) and Food Corporation of India (FCI) in 1965 for managing procurement operations. The coverage of PDS during this period was expanded in a major way, although the reliance on imports was still there. During Phase-III (1978-1991), a comfortable buffer stock was built up through the procurement operations of FCI, and the volume of PDS operations also increased. The Phase-IV was initiated in 1991 and continued up to 1997. However, various systemic problems were noted during this Phase.

The major achievement of the PDS system has been coverage of a substantial population of the country under its network, although there were significant cross-state variations in the volume of off-take.[3] However, the PDS has been subjected to various systemic problems. The first and foremost problem was inefficiencies in functioning of the FCI machinery, resulting in a huge increase in operational cost. The continuous increase in the support price for procuring crops played a major role in this regard.[4] In addition, the urban bias of the PDS has often been subject to criticism on various occasions.[5] Moreover, leakage through widespread corruption, illegal sales, creation of false ration cards, accession of ration facilities by relatively well-off households *etc.* made the situation even worse. In short, although PDS

3. While the share of both Andhra Pradesh and Kerala in all-India off-take stood at 11.5 per cent, for Madhya Pradesh and Rajasthan this was 3.4 and 2.6 per cent respectively in 1998. The volume was very low for the North-Eastern states, *e.g.* – Arunachal Pradesh (0.5 per cent) and Manipur (0.4 per cent).

4. The *Committee on Long Term Grain Policy* recommended that, ".. the MSP should truly be a national level floor price, rather than remaining confined to established surplus regions. The existing MSP system was developed with reference to a closed economy, and must obviously adapt to the context of liberalised trade." However, the Government has for the last couple of years always set the MSP at a higher level than the one recommended by the CACP. Parikh *et al.* (2003) have shown that the MSP, set at a higher than market price, has worsened the welfare of 80 per cent of the rural population and all persons in urban areas.

5. See Dev and Suryanarayana (1991).

was accessed by a huge section of the population, it failed to reach the below poverty line (BPL) households in many instances.[6] Given this background, the government decided to minimise economic losses incurred in running PDS, while reaching the deserving section of the population at the same time. Since 1991, various government policy changes resulted in an increase in the price of commodities obtained through fair price shops, and subsequently, the price differential between the PDS price and the private market price has narrowed down and eventually disappeared.[7] Quite naturally, the volume of off-take of rice and wheat through the PDS network, the two major food-grains, also declined up to 2000-01 (Table 11.1).

In 1992, the government introduced a new scheme called Revamped Public Distribution System (RPDS), whose objective was to cover poorer households with more varieties and quantities of foodstuff at a cheaper price. Government of Maharashtra introduced a special action plan for 115 *tehsils* for this purpose, of which 68 were in the tribal belt.[8] A survey by Swaminathan in 1995-96 revealed that despite limited success, foodgrain entitlements among the targets remained lower and full coverage of households was never achieved.

In June 1997, the government tried to reorganise the system by introducing special cards to BPL families and selling foodgrains under the Targeted Public Distribution System (TPDS) to them at specially subsidised rates. Under the TPDS scheme, each poor family was entitled to 10 kg of foodgrains per month at specially subsidised prices. This was expected to benefit about 60 million poor families identified as 'targets'.[9] Later the Government increased the allocation

6. The Tenth Plan document notes, "The PDS in its original form was widely criticised for its failure to serve the below poverty line (BPL) population, its urban bias, negligible coverage in the states with the highest concentration of the rural poor and lack of transparent and accountable arrangements for delivery."

7. Swaminathan (2000), p. 83.

8. The scheme included establishment of mobile fair-price shops in target areas, apart from introducing special prices and quantities for target households. The additional commodities supplied to the targets through the new scheme included *tur dal*, salt, tea and soap. Swaminathan (2000), p. 91.

9. Specifying the targets, the Tenth Plan document notes, "The emphasis is on including only the really poor and vulnerable sections of the society such as landless agricultural labourers, marginal farmers, artisans/craftsmen (potters, tappers, weavers, blacksmiths, carpenters etc.) in the rural areas and slum dwellers and daily wagers in the informal sector (porters, rickshaw pullers and hand cart pullers, fruit and flower sellers on the pavements etc.) in the urban areas." However, Swaminathan (2000) has noted that the TPDS even excluded households, which have been defined as 'poor' under the IRDP scheme, and therefore, adequate care should be taken in the identification process.

to BPL families from 10 kg to 20 kg per month at 50 per cent of economic cost from 1 April 2000. Although the allocation for above poverty line (APL) families was kept unchanged at the June 1997 level, the Central Issue Prices (CIP) were fixed at 100 per cent of economic cost from that date in order to direct the entire consumer subsidy towards the BPL population. However, it is clearly seen from Table 11.1 that the off-take declined sharply from 1998-99 to 2000-01 for wheat, and in 2000-01 for rice. The off-take has increased during the last three years, thanks to the *Antyodaya* scheme. However, as seen from the third and the sixth column of Table 11.1, there is ample scope for expanding the volume of off-take under the TPDS scheme.

**Table 11.1**

*Foodgrains Allocation and Off-take under the Public Distribution System*

*(Million Tonnes)*

| *Year* | *Wheat* | | | *Rice* | | |
|---|---|---|---|---|---|---|
| | *Allocation* | *Off-take* | *Off-take as % of Allocation* | *Allocation* | *Off-take* | *Off-take as % of Allocation* |
| 1992-93 | 9.25 | 7.47 | 80.76 | 11.48 | 9.55 | 83.19 |
| 1993-94 | 9.56 | 5.91 | 61.82 | 12.41 | 8.87 | 71.47 |
| 1994-95 | 10.80 | 4.83 | 44.72 | 13.32 | 8.03 | 60.29 |
| 1995-96 | 11.31 | 5.29 | 46.77 | 14.62 | 9.46 | 64.71 |
| 1996-97 | 10.72 | 8.52 | 79.48 | 15.10 | 11.14 | 73.77 |
| 1997-98 | 10.11 | 7.08 | 70.03 | 12.83 | 9.90 | 77.16 |
| 1998-99 | 10.11 | 7.95 | 78.64 | 12.94 | 10.74 | 83.00 |
| 1999-00 | 10.37 | 5.76 | 55.54 | 13.89 | 11.31 | 81.43 |
| 2000-01* | 11.57 | 4.07 | 35.18 | 16.26 | 7.97 | 49.02 |
| 2001-02* | 13.14 | 5.68 | 43.23 | 17.23 | 8.16 | 47.36 |
| 2002-03* | 38.66 | 9.78 | 25.29 | 36.02 | 10.35 | 28.73 |
| 2003-04* | 37.11 | 10.71 | 28.86 | 34.46 | 12.08 | 35.05 |

*Source: Economic Survey (2003-04)*

* Including *Antyodaya*

This leaves the country in a major dilemma in the aftermath of TPDS introduction (or stated alternatively, reduction in the coverage of PDS); while the food-stock is increasing due to regular public procurement of foodgrains; the proportional off-take has gone down. A number of populous states like Andhra Pradesh, Karnataka, Tamil

Nadu and West Bengal have witnessed decline in their off-take level. The government cannot abandon procurement operations, owing to its responsibility in avoiding shortages in crisis periods. However, during the late nineties, the actual level of procured foodstock crossed the prescribed level by a hefty margin. In Table 11.2, we report the scenario in the months of July and October for wheat and April and July for rice respectively, the two months when procurement requirement is the maximum for these crops. It is seen that from the year 1997 and 1998 onwards, for rice and wheat respectively, the procured foodstocks are well above the minimum requirement level. The huge foodstocks created by more-than-adequate procurement, coupled with reduced off-take, leaves the government with two problems. First, the cost of storage of this huge volume of foodgrains in FCI warehouses is increasing, which is constraining FCI from allocating more funds towards productive operations.[10] Second, the procurement operations, in absence of distribution, is deteriorating the quality of foodgrains stored in FCI warehouses for more than the reasonable period, while a significant proportion of the population is starving.[11]

Taking note of various concerns, Swaminathan (2000) and the *Committee on Long Term Grain Policy* (2002) have recommended re-introduction of the universal PDS system. However, it seems unlikely that the Government would revert back to the universal PDS system once more for disposal of the procured foodstock. Recently, the Tenth Plan document has strongly advocated in favour of targeted programmes to address the concern of food security as it recommends, ".. identify vulnerable groups/families, undernourished individuals and provide them with well-targeted subsidised food items through TPDS." For supplementing the dietary requirements of the identified vulnerable sections, the document suggested provision of locally procured coarse grains, pulses and iodized salt, apart from

10. The Committee on Long Term Grain Policy (2002) commented, "These stocks are deteriorating because of shortage of storage space, but to hold these the Centre is spending more than what it expends on Agriculture, Rural Development and on Irrigation and Flood Control taken together."

11. Taking note of the fact, the Committee recommended, "All stocks of three years age and more and all grain bought under relaxed specification, including lustre loss, should be taken out of Central pool food-stocks and not be offered to the PDS and other welfare schemes. The grain identified above should be sold immediately, in a phased manner, at commercial terms. The lustre loss wheat acquired in 2001 should be liquidated by March 31, 2003. All grain unfit for human consumption should be disposed of as animal and poultry feed at formula rates, which if necessary may be reviewed downwards."

supply of rice and wheat. The recent *Economic Survey* (2003-04) has also advocated in favour of decentralisation of the procurement system, where states would undertake the operation locally. FCI would concentrate only on maintaining the reserve for food security at the national level or on behalf of selected state governments on the basis of their requests. Decentralised procurement has already been introduced in a limited sense in Bihar, Madhya Pradesh, Rajasthan and Uttar Pradesh. However, because of limited financial resources and inadequate infrastructure, most of the states are not too enthusiastic about this scheme.

**Table 11.2**

*Central Foodgrain Stock and Minimum Buffer Stock Norms*

*(Million Tonnes)*

| *Beginning of the Month* | *Wheat* | | *Beginning of the Month* | *Rice* | |
|---|---|---|---|---|---|
| | *Minimum Norm* | *Actual Stock* | | *Minimum Norm* | *Actual Stock* |
| July – 1992 | 13.1 | 6.5 | April - 1992 | 10.8 | 8.9 |
| October – 1992 | 10.6 | 4.3 | July - 1992 | 9.2 | 7.4 |
| July – 1993 | 13.1 | 14.9 | April – 1993 | 10.8 | 9.9 |
| October – 1993 | 10.6 | 13.7 | July – 1993 | 9.2 | 9.3 |
| July – 1994 | 13.1 | 17.5 | April – 1994 | 10.8 | 13.5 |
| October – 1994 | 10.6 | 15.6 | July – 1994 | 9.2 | 13.2 |
| July – 1995 | 13.1 | 19.2 | April – 1995 | 10.8 | 18.1 |
| October – 1995 | 10.6 | 16.9 | July – 1995 | 9.2 | 16.4 |
| July – 1996 | 13.1 | 14.1 | April – 1996 | 10.8 | 13.1 |
| October – 1996 | 10.6 | 10.5 | July – 1996 | 9.2 | 12.9 |
| July – 1997 | 13.1 | 11.4 | April – 1997 | 10.8 | 13.2 |
| October – 1997 | 10.6 | 8.3 | July – 1997 | 9.2 | 11.0 |
| July – 1998 | 13.1 | 16.5 | April – 1998 | 10.8 | 13.0 |
| October – 1998 | 10.6 | 15.2 | July – 1998 | 9.2 | 12.0 |
| July 1999 | 14 3 | 22.5 | April – 1999 | 11.8 | 12.2 |
| October – 1999 | 11.6 | 20.3 | July – 1999 | 10.0 | 10.6 |
| July – 2000 | 14.3 | 27.8 | April – 2000 | 11.8 | 15.7 |
| October – 2000 | 11.6 | 26.9 | July – 2000 | 10.0 | 14.5 |
| July – 2001 | 14.3 | 38.9 | April – 2001 | 11.8 | 23.2 |
| October – 2001 | 11.6 | 36.8 | July – 2001 | 10.0 | 22.8 |
| July – 2002 | 14.3 | 41.1 | April – 2002 | 11.8 | 24.9 |
| October – 2002 | 11.6 | 35.6 | July – 2002 | 10.0 | 21.9 |
| July – 2003 (P) | 14.3 | 242 | April – 2003 (P) | 11.8 | 17.2 |
| October – 2003 (P) | 11.6 | 18.4 | July – 2003 (P) | 10.0 | 11.0 |

*Source*: Compiled from *Economic Survey* (various years)

P: Provisional

## Food Security: Improving or Worsening?

Before going into the current state of food security in India, a quick look into the working of poverty alleviation programmes would not be inappropriate. The poverty level has declined from 39.4 per cent in 1987-88 to 37.1 per cent in 1993-94, and went further down to 26.8 per cent in 1999-2000. The result has been interpreted as a huge success of the poverty alleviation programme. However, there is a theoretical debate on the validity of the methodology used for calculating poverty in the 55$^{th}$ round, and the criticism takes out a certain amount of luster from the portrayed success.[12] Even in that case, there is no denying that the poverty ratio has declined from the 1993-94 level and therefore, the government decision to streamline foodgrain distribution through the TPDS is somewhat justified. In Table 11.3, the cross-state poverty rates over various NSS rounds are reported. It is seen that in the post-TPDS period, there has been a proportional increase in the off-take of the relatively poorer states, signifying a more efficient targeting mechanism in force.

Despite achieving self-sufficiency in foodgrains, the average net production of cereals has not increased over the nineties, while public stock has increased considerably in the last couple of years. In other words, the government procurement boiled down to withdrawal of available foodgrains from the market. As seen from Table 11.4, net availability of cereals has actually declined 1997 onwards, *i.e.*, since the initiation of the 9$^{th}$ Plan and the TPDS regime.[13] The more recent figures on net availability obtained from the *Economic Surveys* also support this contention. A Plan-wise comparison will help to understand the scenario better. Chakraborty (2004) has shown that the average level of net production of cereals increased from 422.7 grams in the 7$^{th}$ plan to 449.96 grams in the 8$^{th}$ plan period, *i.e.*, increased by 6.44 per cent. The production also increased during the 9$^{th}$ plan period, but experienced a much lower growth rate of 0.55 per cent. However, the availability of cereals, which reached a peak during the 8$^{th}$ plan (443.50 grams per person per day), has declined during the 9$^{th}$ plan (431.25 grams per person per day).[14]

---

12. For a detailed criticism of the methodology, see Sen (2000) and Deaton and Dreze (2002).
13. A similar declining trend is noticed for pulses as well.
14. The Human Development Report (2003) noted that the proportion of undernourished people in India, which stood at 25 per cent in 1990-92 came down only by 1 per cent in 1998-2000.

## Table 11.3

*Percentage of Population Below Poverty Line and Off-take*

*(Percentage)*

| *States* | *Poverty Rate* | | | *Share of State in All-India Off-take of Foodgrain* | |
|---|---|---|---|---|---|
| | *1983* | *1993-94* | *1999-00* | *1995* | *1998* |
| Andhra Pradesh | 28.91 | 22.19 | 15.77 | 17.10 | 11.50 |
| Assam | 40.47 | 40.86 | 36.09 | 5.40 | 4.20 |
| Bihar | 62.22 | 54.96 | 42.60 | 1.50 | 5.00 |
| Gujarat | 32.79 | 24.21 | 14.07 | 4.40 | 3.50 |
| Haryana | 21.37 | 25.05 | 8.74 | 0.40 | 0.60 |
| Himachal Pradesh | 16.40 | 28.44 | 7.63 | 1.10 | 1.30 |
| Jammu & Kashmir | 24.24 | 25.17 | 3.48 | 2.60 | 2.30 |
| Karnataka | 38.24 | 33.16 | 20.04 | 7.90 | 6.50 |
| Kerala | 40.42 | 25.43 | 12.72 | 11.60 | 11.50 |
| Madhya Pradesh | 49.78 | 42.52 | 37.43 | 2.30 | 3.40 |
| Maharashtra | 43.44 | 36.86 | 25.02 | 6.50 | 9.30 |
| Orissa | 65.29 | 48.56 | 47.15 | 3.70 | 5.40 |
| Punjab | 16.18 | 11.77 | 6.16 | 0.02 | 0.10 |
| Rajasthan | 34.46 | 27.41 | 15.28 | 3.50 | 2.60 |
| Tamil Nadu | 51.66 | 35.03 | 21.12 | 12.10 | 8.20 |
| Uttar Pradesh | 47.07 | 40.85 | 31.15 | 3.10 | 7.70 |
| West Bengal | 54.85 | 35.66 | 27.02 | 9.20 | 6.80 |
| **All India** | **44.48** | **35.97** | **26.10** | **100.00** | **100.00** |

*Source*: *NHDR* (2001) and Swaminathan (2000).

## Table 11.4

*Cereal Availability in the Nineties*

*(Grams per person per day)*

| *Year* | *Net Production* | *Net Imports* | *Net Change in Public Stocks* | *Net Availability (1+2-3)* |
|---|---|---|---|---|
| 1985-89 | 422.7 | 2.0 | –5.3 | 430.1 |
| 1990 | 456.9 | 0.3 | –5.0 | 452.1 |
| 1991 | 447.9 | –1.4 | 0.4 | 446.1 |
| 1992 | 446.8 | 1.3 | 4.2 | 443.8 |
| 1993 | 446.4 | 2.5 | 16.6 | 432.3 |
| 1994 | 456.3 | 0.2 | 16.6 | 439.9 |
| 1995 | 448.6 | –5.9 | –2.3 | 445.1 |
| 1996 | 451.7 | –6.9 | –11.7 | 456.4 |
| 1997 | 445.5 | –6.7 | –4.2 | 443.0 |
| 1998 | 455.3 | –4.7 | 11.0 | 439.6 |
| 1999 | 456.3 | –5.4 | 25.3 | 425.6 |
| 2000 | 452.7 | –5.2 | 30.7 | 416.8 |

*Source*: Deaton and Dreze (2002).

Apart from the general decline in cereal availability, the decline in the qualitative feature of consumption is another area of concern. Meenakshi and Vishwanathan (2003), on the basis of the 55$^{th}$ round of NSS data, have noted that while income poverty has gone down, calorie deprivation in rural India has increased. The decline in calorie intake in rural India, even if compared with a much older time frame—1983, looks horrible, which amounts to approximately 70 calories per capita over the period 1983 to 1999-2000. More alarmingly, this is a general phenomenon in almost all major states, and true even for a Green Revolution state like Punjab. In addition, the percentage of persons consuming below 2400 calories per day has increased considerably in most of the states. This is illustrated with the help of Table 11.5. Swaminathan (2000) has also pointed out that, on average, 44 per cent of the households are deficient in calorie intake and malnutrition among women and children are especially higher.

## Table 11.5

*Some Summary Statistics on Calorie Intake and Poverty*

| *States* | *Average Calorie Intake Per Capita Per Day (Kcal)* | | *Head Count Ratios Consuming Below 2400 Calories Per Day (Per cent)* | |
|---|---|---|---|---|
| | *1983* | *1999-2000* | *1983* | *1999-2000* |
| Andhra Pradesh | 2204 | 2021 | 68.5 | 80.7 |
| Bihar | 2189 | 2121 | 67.6 | 74.9 |
| Gujarat | 2113 | 1986 | 72.6 | 80.5 |
| Haryana | 2554 | 2455 | 54.1 | 55.1 |
| Himachal Pradesh | 2636 | 2454 | 44.5 | 56.5 |
| Jammu & Kashmir | 2569 | 2631 | 44.5 | 39.7 |
| Karnataka | 2260 | 2028 | 64.0 | 78.9 |
| Kerala | 1884 | 1982 | 81.5 | 81.2 |
| Madhya Pradesh | 2323 | 2062 | 62.5 | 78.4 |
| Maharashtra | 2144 | 2012 | 73.1 | 83.3 |
| Orissa | 2103 | 2119 | 70.9 | 74.6 |
| Punjab | 2677 | 2381 | 46.2 | 62.8 |
| Rajasthan | 2433 | 2425 | 54.2 | 56.7 |
| Tamil Nadu | 1861 | 1826 | 80.6 | 86.5 |
| Uttar Pradesh | 2399 | 2327 | 58.4 | 64.5 |
| West Bengal | 2027 | 2095 | 76.0 | 75.6 |

Meenakshi and Vishwanathan (2003)

Analysing the level of calorie deficiency across households with 1993-94 data, Bhandari and Dubey (2001) concluded that almost half of the rural population and a quarter of the urban population is calorie deficient. They further found that the impact of PDS on the incidence of calorie deficiency and poverty does not appear to be significant. Based on these findings, they have rightly recommended recalculation of the poverty line on the basis of calorie requirements of the population, with a different age profile from that in the seventies. The point is well taken, as Government of India defines the poverty line for urban and rural areas to be Rs. 296 and Rs. 276 per month respectively, defining those earning below Rs. 10 per day as being below the poverty line. As per Government notifications, this amount is just sufficient for buying food equivalent to 2200 calories per day to prevent death.

In short, the recent scenario leaves us with yet another apparent dilemma, where the decline in the poverty ratio has been associated with decline in net availability of cereals and the consequent fall in calorie intake. One possible reason for this is the increase in food prices, causing the poorer households to shift towards less nutritious diets. However, it becomes clear from the construction of the poverty line that, people slightly above the line are equally affected like those below the line in case of any increase in prices. The scenario might actually worsen in relatively drought-prone regions and certain other states in case of any decrease in productivity, as the *Committee on Long Term Grain Policy* has cautioned:

> "A salient feature of India's cereals situation is that most States are deficit. Only five States produced surpluses of rice and wheat over consumption in 1999-2000. The remaining States were deficit by more than a third of consumption. We expect deficits to enlarge in Southern and Western regions of India during the next two decades. If surpluses decline in Punjab-Haryana, it will be essential to realise the potential for production surpluses in Central and Eastern India where presently prices are below full costs of production."

In this light, there is a need to review the various recent government policy decisions to tackle the problem.

## The Tenth Plan Document

The Tenth Plan (2002-07) documents have shown a staggering picture in ongoing subsidisation trends. While the food deprivation of the people below poverty line is continuously worsening, the level of Government subsidies granted for running the system, as seen from Table 11.6, is actually rising. The volume of subsidy on food accounts, which amounted to Rs. 2450 crore during 1990-91, increased by almost 10 times to reach Rs. 21200 crore during 2002-03.[15] Unfortunately this increased expenditure has mostly been spent to run the machinery, *i.e.* to finance the growing administrative and other costs, while the main target group, the poorer sections, have not benefited at all. The per capita food subsidy expenditure by the government is around Rs. 17 per head per month. The document explains, "This, however, does not mean that consumers got Rs. 17 per head per month, for the cost of distributing this subsidy has to be deducted from the subsidy expenditure."[16]

**Table 11.6**

*Food Subsidy of the Central Government*

| *Year* | *Amount (Rs. Crore)* | *% of Total Government Expenditure* |
|---|---|---|
| 1990-91 | 2450 | 2.33 |
| 1991-92 | 2850 | 2.56 |
| 1992-93 | 2785 | 2.27 |
| 1993-94 | 5537 | 3.90 |
| 1994-95 | 4509 | 2.80 |
| 1995-96 | 4960 | 2.78 |
| 1996-97 | 5166 | 2.46 |
| 1997-98 | 7500 | 3.23 |
| 1998-99 | 8700 | 3.11 |
| 1999-00 | 9200 | 3.03 |
| 2000-01 | 12125 | 3.61 |
| 2001-02 | 17612 | 4.83 |
| 2002-03 | 21200 | 5.17 |

*Source*: Tenth Plan Documents.

15. The volume of subsidy reached Rs. 25160 crore in 2003-04 and has further increased to Rs. 27746 crore (budget estimate) during 2004-05.
16. "The high carrying cost of stocks in excess of the buffer norms pushes up the food subsidy bill and actually amounts to subsidy to the cereals producers/surplus farmers. The Expenditure Reforms Commission (ERC) has recommended that the cost of holding stocks in excess of the requirement for food security and for PDS could be reflected in the budget as producers' subsidy rather than consumer subsidy." Planning Commission, Government of India.

In order to check further mismanagement of funds, and to improve food security, the Tenth Plan Document has explored a number of options. First, it has urged the government to lay stress on the working of the TPDS programme in place of the universal PDS, "With a network of more than 4.62 lakh fair price shops (FPS) distributing commodities worth more than Rs. 30,000 crore annually to about 160 million families, the PDS in India is perhaps the largest distribution network of its kind in the world. This huge network can play a more meaningful role only if it ensures the availability of food to the poor households."[17] Second, the Tenth Plan Document has strongly advocated introduction of a FSP, where each eligible household would be given documents specifying the number of household members, their age and entitlements. The number of stamps given to a household per month would depend on their family size, the age distribution and the consequent dietary requirement. The target households would collect stamps every month from the prescribed distribution centre, and use them at the retail outlets to buy food-grains (rice and wheat), while the State Government is supposed to reimburse the retailers. The detailed version of the Planning Commission's proposals on streamlining TPDS and introduction of a FSP is presented in Annexes 1 and 2 respectively.

## The Committee on Long Term Grain Policy

*The Committee on Long Term Grain Policy* (2002) has also addressed the problem of food security and came out with a radically different policy recommendation, as compared to Planning Commission. Although the report acknowledged the extent of inefficiency and economic loss in FCI functioning, it strongly expressed the opinion that universal PDS is the only solution to address the food security concerns of India:

> "We have in the course of our discussions heard suggestions that the high food-stocks require cessation of open-ended procurement and also that this may be an opportunity to dismantle what many believe to be an expensive and outdated food security system. We have considered these views very seriously, and are forced to reject these. End of open-ended procurement at this stage would deal a severe, possibly a crippling, blow to farmers which may be followed by a blow to

17. P. 367.

consumers in about two years time. Despite the many sources of inefficiency which we have identified, particularly in the functioning of the FCI and the PDS, we are convinced that it is reform and not annulment of the existing system that should be on the agenda."

In order to strengthen the PDS mechanism and the procurement system, the Committee recommended various policies, including modifications in APL and BPL prices, changes in determination of Minimum Support Prices *etc.* Legal and procedural modifications were recommended so as to remove compulsory levy orders on rice mills under *the Essential Commodities Act*; and elimination of barriers on private trade was also advocated. The detailed proposals of the Committee are presented in Annex 3. The Committee also warned the Government against adoption of a FSP without consideration, given the adverse experience in a number of countries, although they acknowledged the potential welfare-enhancing capacity of this.

## Recent Initiatives

The United Progressive Alliance Government that assumed office after the 2004 general elections, given the deterioration of food security in the country over the last couple of years, has been quite serious about identifying an efficient mechanism to address the concern. The constituent parties of the government have adopted a basic set of social and economic development objectives during the last week of May 2004, generally known as the National Common Minimum Programme (NCMP). In Box 11.1 shown below, the food security related concerns as discussed in NCMP are presented:

### Box 11.1

*National Common Minimum Programme on Food Security Issues*

- The UPA will work out, in the next three months, a comprehensive medium-term strategy for food and nutrition security. The objective will be to move towards universal food security over time, if found feasible.
- The UPA Government will strengthen the Public Distribution System (PDS), particularly in the poorest and backward blocks of the country, and also involve women's and ex-servicemen's cooperatives in its management. Special schemes to reach food-grains to the most

*Contd...*

...*Contd*...

destitute and infirm will be launched. Grain banks in chronically food-scarce areas will be established. *Antyodaya* cards for all households at risk of hunger will be introduced.

- The UPA Government will bring about major improvements in the functioning of the Food Corporation of India (FCI) to control inefficiencies that increase the food subsidy burden.

The concern has further been reflected in the budget session of Parliament, as the Government has proposed a number of reform measures for the rural sector, where calorie deprivation is notably on the rise. The Finance Minister, Mr. P. Chidambaram, has included the following proposal in his budget speech (for the year 2004-05):

"In the Tenth Plan document, the Planning Commission had suggested that a system of distributing food stamps should be tested on a pilot basis. Every eligible family will be entitled to collect its monthly quota of food stamps from a designated distribution centre, and such stamps could then be used to buy foodgrains from any food shop. I propose to introduce a pilot scheme for distributing food stamps, instead of distributing food through fair price shops, in two or three contiguous districts in a selected State. I sincerely hope that one of the States will come forward to associate with the Central Government in this experiment."

Against this background, in the following section, we review the working of the FSP in various countries, in order to analyse their potential impact in India.

## Effectiveness of Food Stamp Programme: A Cross Country Experience

Before going into the working of FSP, various modes of government food transfer mechanism are presented in Table 11.7 to understand the differences between their working. All of the following measures could be implemented in a country when a shift from universal PDS is undertaken.

The FSP has a major advantage over the PDS type mechanism in terms of operational efficiency, at least potentially. In PDS, the government needs to procure the foodstuffs at a slightly higher than market price, and distribute that to the poorer sections at a cheaper

## Table 11.7

*Definition of Various Food Support Programme*

| *No* | *Name of Programme* | *Definition* |
|---|---|---|
| 1 | Food stamps | Food stamps are pieces of secure paper issued for the purchase of a fairly wide range of specified foods. Consumers are usually free to use food stamps to buy any quantity of foods they wish at market prices. |
| 2 | Food coupons | Food coupons are pieces of paper which consumers may use to buy limited quantities of a limited number of foods at discount prices. One advantage of food stamps over food coupons is that they offer greater freedom to consumers in their choice of food items. |
| 3 | Food vouchers | Food vouchers are similar to coupons, but provide more freedom within a limited range of goods for purchase. Although they usually specify the types of foods which may be purchased, they place no limits on quantities. |
| 4 | Food cash | Food cash transfers are transfers in local currency for the purchase of specified or non-specified foods. Because of the risk involved in traveling with cash, food cash transfer programmes usually give beneficiaries checks, bank deposits, or wire transfers. |
| 5 | In-kind food transfers | In-kind food transfers refer to the direct distribution of foods to beneficiaries. |

*Source*: Quoted from Castañeda (2000).

rate. Clearly, the government operation involves a two-tier mechanism, involving a procuring agency, which later transfers the commodities to selected retailers. Apart from administrative costs, this involves a huge transportation cost, since the crops have to be carried from the markets to warehouses, and finally to the retail outfits. This also involves the transfer of foodgrains from the surplus states to all of the deficit states. On the other hand, another government agency has to function for identifying the targets, *i.e.*, the poor and vulnerable sections. The huge manpower required for maintaining this network, and the consequent expenditure on wages and salaries add to the cost of the project. Leakages through various sources, wrong exclusion of the poorer sections (Type 1 error), wrong inclusion of relatively well-off sections (Type 2 error) and corruption are the other problems that the system broadly faces. However, under the FSP, the government is supposed to restrict its procurement operations only up to the level required for fulfilling the statutory requirement. Food Stamps would be distributed to the poorer households on the basis of the selection criteria. The identified needy households would go to the retail outfits in their locality, hand over the food stamps, and take the foodgrains equivalent. The state governments are supposed to reimburse the dealers at a later date. Here, the government has to only focus on identification of the poor (although on a regular basis), and it saves a huge amount of public money in terms of fixed and variable costs, which could be utilised for other programmes focusing on upliftment of poorer sections. Besides, the limited government operation in the foodgrain markets leads to minimum distortions in these. However, Grosh (1993) focuses on the potential problems mentioned. "Food stamps are easy to target to the poor, are fairly difficult to administer, depending on programme design, but depending on programme design, may encourage the use of schools and primary health care. But there is controversy about whether they encourage dependency and diminish the work ethic."[18]

In the following, the experiences of nine countries, namely – Colombia, Honduras, Jamaica, Mexico, Sri Lanka, Tunisia, the United States, Venezuela and Zambia, where FSP is operational (or, was introduced in the past), have been presented. Barring the exception of the United States, all other countries are developing countries, drawn from Africa, Asia and Latin America. Although Romania did not have a FSP, the input subsidisation scheme introduced there had a significant impact on the rural poor, and so it has also been briefly discussed. The experiences of the countries have been summarised in Annex 6. This section draws on the studies of Castañeda (2000) and Swaminathan (2000) for basic information.

*Colombia*

The FSP was initiated in Columbia through a World Bank-supported Integrated Nutrition Improvement Project in 1975. The target groups included women and children, for whom, the extent of malnutrition was very high. The coupon system allowed these two groups to obtain specified processed foods with high nutritional content (including precooked corn, flour, vegetal mixes, pasta, vegetal proteins, and soya flour) through the retail network. Apart from the food coupons, the project consisted of investments in primary health care infrastructure and equipment, basic sanitation, and nutrition

18. Grosh (1993), p. 2.

education and information. Between 1975 and 1981, the project was able to distribute 64.8 million coupons to about 420,000 beneficiaries. However, the impact of the project after the initial years could never fulfill the objective, due to adoption of over-ambitious goals. The coverage of the project was expanded too rapidly, without corresponding increases in budget allocations, thereby significantly eroding the welfare-enhancing capacity of the project. A survey among the beneficiaries revealed that the project increased food supply for nearly 60 per cent of the interviewed. Assessing the nutritional impact, Castañeda (2000) notes, " .. The impact appears to have been limited due to the small size of the transfer, the fact that processed foods approved by the programme were too expensive, and food quality problems."[19] Owing to its less-than-satisfactory performance, the scheme was not very popular, and therefore, it was easier for a new regime to terminate it in 1981.

*Honduras*

Honduras implemented two food stamp programmes in 1990, against the backdrop of the structural adjustment programme. The first one, named *Bono Escolar* (BE), involved introduction of a food stamp system for poor primary schoolchildren, distributed in all primary schools in selected areas of the country. The second one, named *Bono Materno Infantil*, (BMI), was given to children below five years of age and to pregnant and nursing mothers, distributed at health centres in selected poor regions. Castañeda (2000) notes, "By 1991, the BE programme was benefiting more than 125,000 schoolchildren while the BMI programme was serving more than 56,000 small children and pregnant and nursing mothers." Although the transfer allowed the target households to purchase any food they wanted, apart from school supplies and medicines with the allocated stamps, studies revealed that more than 80 per cent of them were spent on food items only. Both programmes received financial support from the World Food Programme, USAID, Regional Unit for Technical Assistance in Agriculture (RUTA II) and the World Bank.[20] An autonomous agency was in charge for implementing the programme.

19. World Bank (1998), quoted from Castañeda (2000).

20. WFP to reduce drop-out rates in the schools are still operational and increasing in volume. www.asfsa.org/meetingsandevents/archive/anc2003/handouts/honduras.ppt

An USAID study (1995) showed that although food stamps were more effective than food handouts in increasing school attendance and advancement; food handouts were more effective than stamps in increasing utilisation of preventive health care.[21] The overall impact of the programme has been moderately satisfactory. However, there were various problems in functioning of the programme, like in the process of registration of beneficiaries, printing and distributing, redeeming and disposing of food stamps, fiscal mismanagement *etc*. In addition, the health centres were inefficient in responding to the increased demand of the beneficiaries. The lack of monitoring and evaluation mechanism was also a blow for the efficiency of the programme. Further, the targeting has been inaccurate; for instance, the permanent entitlement programme extended to families with malnourished children, living in a poor community, acted as a disincentive on their self-reliant behaviour. In addition, there were serious problems of compliance with participation requirements (especially with respect to health care visits by pregnant mothers and children, and vaccinations). Responding to these problems, the government tried to improve the mechanism by distributing stamps through NGOs instead of teachers and health care workers, who were often reluctant in undertaking the additional work. In 1998, the country was about to launch, with support from the Inter-American Development Bank (IDB), a programme to improve the supply side of the programme (health centres, posts and schools).[22]

*Jamaica*

Jamaica initiated a national FSP in 1984, when due to the structural adjustment programme, there was a general reduction in food price subsidy. The target group included the most vulnerable sections of the community, pregnant and lactating mothers (during pregnancy and six months after birth) and children less than six years of age, elderly poor and disabled, and individuals and families with incomes below an established threshold level.[23] The first two target groups were identified and registered at health clinics and centres and were required to have regular health checkups before receiving food stamps. The foods considered under the FSP included rice, cornmeal, skimmed

21. Rogers *et al.* (1995).

22. McGuire (1998).

23. In 1996, the threshold level was about 40 per cent of the minimum wage.

milk and wheat flour, all of which provide high calories per dollar of food purchased. The programme received assistance from United States (PL480), the World Food Programme (WFP), Canada and other countries. In-kind food assistance is usually sold on the open market, and the proceeds are used to partially finance the scheme. By 1997, over 270,000 people were under the purview of the scheme. Swaminathan (2000) has noted that the stamp was issued on a bi-monthly basis, and the value of the stamp was different for different categories of individuals. On the whole, the programme was successful in increasing consumption of certain foods and, consequently, the intake of calories and proteins by the target groups, to a certain extent.

The programme, upon review, has revealed a number of weak spots. The value of stamp subsidies declined from 7.2 per cent in 1991 to 2.8 per cent in 1996, when increasing inflation caused rapid erosion in stamp values by over 40 per cent during this period. The absence of the much-needed adjustment for inflation caused a severe nutritional deficiency for mothers and children under six, although this for the elderly poor and the disabled was comparatively less severe during the same period. The overall impact on nutrition remained weak, as only 6.8 per cent of mal-nourished children participated in the programme, and on the whole the number of undernourished children increased. The information management system was also very weak. While a large segment of the poorest section with mal-nourished children could not participate owing to lack of information and lengthy bureaucratic channels, the process of excluding the once-registered (but not eligible any more) beneficiaries was always very slow. Type 1 error, *i.e.*, wrong exclusion, was particularly high, as Swaminathan (2000) notes. "Of all households with pregnant or lactating women, 63 per cent were excluded, in the poorest quintile of households with elderly persons, 45 per cent were excluded from food stamps."[24] The problem with distributing and cashing of food stamps was also severe. Ezemenari and Subbarao however, came out with a different finding (1999):

> "The broad finding of the paper is that in the absence of FSP, the poverty gap in Jamaica would have been much higher. In particular, households with the elderly benefited most. Households with young children benefited relatively more (compared to households without

24. Swaminathan (2000), p. 74.

young children), in terms of the contribution of the FSP to a reduction in the poverty headcount and gap for these groups. Also, the programme appears to have had a greater impact on the poverty headcount and gap of extremely poor households compared to those households that moved into and out of poverty... Nevertheless, the programme contributed more toward a reduction in poverty than in smoothing consumption."[25]

Government initiatives to modification and expansion of the system were on their way, as Castañeda (2000) notes, "Recent studies have recommended active involvement by programme administration officials in locating and registering even those mal-nourished children who are more than six years of age." The programme is still operational and in 2003 targeted a total of 199,685 persons, including all target groups under its wings.[26]

*Mexico*

A number of direct food support programmes were initiated in Mexico in the early 1980s, in the aftermath of reforms, when food subsidies were reduced. *Tortibono* food coupon programme, which started in the late 1980s, identified targets on the basis of information on housing quality, availability of basic services and family income *etc.* The target families had to visit authorised food shops to purchase prescribed foodgrains. In 1997, the scheme covered 1.9 million families spread over all the states. Although the cost of this programme was as high as US $135 million in 1997, its effect on volume of food consumption by the poor, or on their nutritional intake, is not very clearly known.

An integrated food support and health and nutrition programme was initiated on a pilot basis in urban localities of Campeche State in 1995–96, covering 32,000 families. By allowing more variety of foods under purchase list and linking food assistance to health and nutrition interventions for pregnant and lactating mothers and small children, the scheme was more efficient than the *Tortibono* programme. The scheme provided a monthly credit of around US$17 per family, regardless of its size. The cards were recredited only when women and children were able to prove their regular health checks every month, which was a major reason for the scheme's success.

25. Ezemenari and Subbarao (1999), p. 30.

26. http://www.jis.gov.jm/labour/index.asp

Another programme named *Progresa* was introduced in mid-1997 for poverty eradication through integrated family interventions in education, health and food programmes. The selection of targets was done through a two-stage operation. In the first stage, the poorest localities were selected on the basis of census information on socio-economic characteristics, and in the second stage, the poorest families in these localities were selected on the basis of family information on economic and other criteria. Castañeda (2000) notes that the scheme extended monetary assistance to families for the purchase of food and school supplies for young children at levels between the third grade of primary school and the third grade of secondary school, where dropout rate is maximum. School upgrading and teacher training are also part of the programme. A health care package to poor families included mother-child pre-natal and well-baby care, food supplements for pregnant mothers and mal-nourished children or children at risk of mal-nourishment, and nutrition and hygiene education, apart from improving primary health care infrastructure in the rural belt. The scheme has been very successful in augmenting the caloric and micronutrient needs of target households. As food subsidy, *Progresa* transferred a certain amount of money through a check or wire to target families, who regularly complied with the health check-up norm. Various awareness-building measures to ensure compliance were also in force. By the end of 1998, the scheme covered 1.9 million of the poorest families spread all across Mexico.[27]

However, Swaminathan (2000) pointed that the targeted programme was less than adequate for ensuring food security to Mexican people and ultimately lowered the number of people getting subsidised food, causing income poverty (as the real wage level has not increased). The substantial increase in the food price level was associated with a consequent decline in the level of consumption, along with a shift towards less nutritious diet.

*Sri Lanka*

Sri Lanka initiated a well-designed FSP in late 1979. The programme selected the target groups on the basis of family income,

27. One major reason for success of this scheme is efficient targeting, "Because it is assumed that women are more concerned about their families' food needs, all money income assistance—both scholarships and cash food assistance—is given directly to the mother every two months. So far, the programme appears to be successful in meeting its stated objectives." Castañeda (2000), p. 19.

and the threshold level was adjusted a number of times on the face of growing inflation. Although the purchase list was limited to certain food items, namely - rice, paddy, flour, bread, sugar, and milk products; in practice, stamps were used to purchase many other food items as well. The programme, in spite of a wide coverage ratio, faced various problems. First, because of inflation, within two years of initiating the programme, the real value of the food stamps was reduced by almost fifty per cent. Second, the government was never able to properly target the operation of the programme, and therefore, excessive registration crippled the system. Apart from the actual needy and vulnerable section, a formidable section of the population above poverty line also registered as eligible persons for the scheme. Castañeda (2000) has blamed the government inefficiency by pointing out:

> " .. as stated in its policy objectives which would mean only 3.5 million beneficiaries, as opposed to the 8 million people who were actually participating in the programme by 1989 (about 50 per cent of the population)... Despite the huge number of beneficiaries, many poor families were excluded while many well-off families were included. In the 1980–82 consumption survey, nearly 30 per cent of the poorest quintile did not participate in the programme, while 20 per cent of the richest quintile and 45 per cent of the second richest were benefiting from the programme. Once initial classifications were made, beneficiary rolls were closed for years. One direct impact of this overreaching was that the value of food stamps provided to each beneficiary was capable of satisfying only 7–10 days of food needs. The programme was ultimately phased out in the early 1990s."

Consequently, the impact of the FSP on the nutritional aspect had been quite modest. Surveys carried out among the targeted families have shown that food stamps could buy only 20–25 per cent of the required food items for a family with four members, which clearly suggests that the nutritional threshold level for children and the mothers were not met. Sahn (1987) reported an increase in the proportion of children suffering from acute mal-nutrition. Anand and Harris (1990) had found that per capita calorie intake for the lowest three deciles of populations had gone down in the post-food stamp period. However, the programme has been quite successful in reducing the fiscal expenditure of the government on this account, from 5 per cent of GDP and 15 per cent of government expenditures in 1978–79 to 1.3 per cent of GDP and 3 per cent of government expenditures in 1984 respectively, and this went down further in later years. Analysing the FSP, Datt and Gunewardena (1997) however found that direct transfer benefits from the programme were progressive, and had a larger impact on poverty than what would have been implied by uniform allocations of the same budget. "The programme seems well-targeted within the rural sector; food stamp receipts are more progressive than uniform transfers approximately up to the higher poverty line. The graph for the urban sector also suggests an element of progressivity ..... Direct transfers from the food stamps programme reduce poverty by more than would be possible under uniform transfers of the same gross budget for all poverty lines up to our higher poverty line."[28]

*Tunisia*

During the seventies and the eighties, Tunisia extended a general price subsidy to major food products like, wheat, cooking oil, sugar, milk, meat *etc*. However, as a part of a structural adjustment programme, the food subsidies were reduced through a combination of self-targeting and introduction of quality differentiation.[29] The targeting was initiated in 1991, but did not produce the desired effect. While the expenditure on food subsidies declined, various studies pointed out that between 1990 and 1993 there was a 14 and 16 per cent fall in total calorie and protein intake respectively, and the decline was much higher among the lowest income quintile as compared to the highest income quintile. Swaminathan (2000) notes that there was a 13.7 per cent loss in calorie intake among the poorest quintile.

*United States*

During the 1930s, US started providing food stamps to the population and this continued up to 1943. However, the formal coupon-based food subsidy system was initiated with the Food Stamp Act of 1964 so as to enable low-income families and individuals to meet their basic nutritional needs. The programme empowers the target individuals to purchase a nutritionally adequate low-cost diet. According to Castañeda (2000), during 1996, the progamme covered 27 million beneficiaries per month, including 14 million children, the

28. Datt and Gunewardena (1997), p. 29.
29. Swaminathan (2000), p. 75.

total cost being over US$24 billion. In addition, states and municipalities were also contributing over $3 billion for this programme. The participation under this programme increased from 1990 to 1994, but decreased later, up to 2000. It has been increasing from 2001 onwards, as noted by USDA (2003), "In an average month in fiscal year 2002, the FSP provided benefits to approximately 19.0 million people living in 8.2 million households across the United States. The total cost of the programme over fiscal year 2002 was $20.7 billion, $18.3 billion of which were for food stamp benefits... Compared with fiscal year 2001, the number of FSP participants increased by 10 per cent and FSP benefit costs increased by 17 per cent." Many studies argued that the improved economy in the second half of the 1990s was responsible for the decline in participation.[30] However, it has been concluded by Wilde *et al.* (2000a) that changing reforms in the FSP also contributed towards this.

The FSP has undergone various changes from time to time. In 1971, national eligibility standards were established in the system through modification of the 1964 law. Castañeda (2000) notes, "In 1995, major changes were introduced under the Personal Responsibility Act (PRA), under which states and local governments can experiment with alternative forms of delivering food subsidies to make the programme more efficient and to reduce administrative costs."[31] In addition, major debates followed at times for deciding efficient modes of delivering cheaper food for the vulnerable section, and cashing out (*e.g.*, checks) option. In favour of the cashing out scheme, benefits like wider freedom and responsibility for beneficiaries, lesser social stigma for the recipients, reduction in administrative and distributive costs *etc.* have been mentioned. On the other hand, the critics have always pointed out that the potential for substitution towards non-food consumption would be quite high in that case, with limited success in cost savings.[32] As of now, food stamps are very much operational, and the obtained benefits are

30. Kornfeld (2002) has attempted to estimate various factors behind the decline in food stamp caseloads and argues that the revival of the economy explains at least 20 per cent of this between 1994 and 1999.

31. Castañeda (2000), p. 22.

32. Castañeda (2000) notes that cashing out in four places in three major states (California, Alabama, and Washington) has shown that food consumption would drop by 18 to 28 cents per dollar of cash-out, as a consequence. Therefore, FSP has an advantage over the cashing out scheme, in terms of ensuring food security.

recipient-specific, *i.e.*, cannot be exchanged or sold for cash. The basic criterion for distribution is necessarily economic, only the population below a threshold level is eligible for receiving it.[33] In addition, programmes of providing breakfast and lunch at schools are also very effective in addressing the concern of child food security. However, adults, students and a certain section of immigrants are also allowed to access the scheme. Presently, 51 and 9 per cent of the beneficiaries are children and people aged 60 or older respectively; while working-age men and women represent 12 and 28 per cent in that order. A brief description of the targets, as obtained from the USDA web-site, is provided in the following:

- *Adults:* The able-bodied adults between 16 and 60, with some exceptions, must register for work, accept suitable employment, or take part in an employment and training programme to which they are referred by the food stamp office. Failure to comply with these requirements leads to disqualification from the programme.[34] In addition, able-bodied adults between 18 and 50 who do not have any dependent children can get food stamps only for three months in a 36-month period if they do not work or participate in a workfare or employment and training programme other than job search. However, this requirement is waived in some places.
- *Students:* Although most able-bodied students enrolled in college or other institutions of higher education (at least for half-time), are not eligible for food stamps, certain exceptions are there. Students obtaining public assistance benefits under a Title IV-A programme are eligible for this programme.[35]
- *Persons on Strike:* Households with a person who is on strike because of a labour dispute are not generally eligible unless they were so the day before the strike and continue to be

33. USDA (2003) notes, "To be eligible for the FSP, a household must have a net monthly income at or below 100 per cent of the poverty guideline ($1,471 for a family of four in the contiguous United States in fiscal year 2002)."

34. According to USDA (2003) 28 per cent of the households receiving food stamps have earnings, up from 19 per cent in 1990.

35. The provisions include taking part in a State or Federally financed work study programme; or working for at least 20 hours a week; or taking care of a dependent household member under the age of six; or taking care of a dependent household member over the age of five but under 12 and do not have adequate child care to enable them to attend school and work a minimum of 20 hours *etc.*

eligible at the time of application. Eligible households cannot get more food stamps just because the striking member is getting less income. This prohibition does not apply to persons involved in a labour dispute in which management has locked the workers out of the work site. *The Personal Responsibility and Work Opportunity Reconciliation Act* of 1996 (PRWORA) limits the receipt of food stamps to three months in a three-year period for able-bodied adults without dependents (ABAWDs) who are not working, participating in, and complying with the requirements of a work programme for 20 hours or more each week. However, individuals not entitled for FSP, and those unfit for employment are exempt from this provision.

- *Immigrants:* According to the *Farm Bill* (2002) most of the legal immigrants, who have lived in US for five years; or are recipient of disability-related assistance or benefits, regardless of entry date are eligible for the programme. Even non-citizens, *e.g.*, those admitted for humanitarian reasons and those admitted for permanent residence are also eligible for the programme.[36] Eligible household members can get food stamps even if there are non-eligible members in the household.[37]

The food stamp approval system is a very transparent and decentralised process in the US. Anybody can access the application process over the Internet, or can visit the local Food Stamp Office, where the application forms are available. The amended *Food Stamp Act* (1977) requires local offices to process the received applications within 30 days of submission. However, applications from households with extremely low income are processed more quickly through the expedited food stamp eligibility verification procedures, allowing the applicants to receive food stamp benefits within seven days of submitting the application. Subsequently, the person seeking food stamps is interviewed at the food stamp office. During the interview, the person needs to establish his claims for coverage under the

36. However, the MIRA Report entitled, Unequal Access: A Report on Barriers Children in Low-income Immigrant Families Face in Accessing Food Stamps and Health Insurance notes, "The number of legal immigrants using food stamps fell by 54 per cent between 1994 and 1997, accounting for 14 per cent of the total decline in food stamp usage." Bollinger and Hagstrom (2003) also found that the participation rate of the immigrants is declining rapidly with time.

37. A number of States have their own programmes to provide benefits to immigrants who do not meet the regular Food Stamp Programme eligibility requirements. *Source*: USDA.

scheme by showing the necessary documents, a list of which is obtained from the office.[38] If interview is satisfactory, the application is approved. In case of rejection, the applicant has the right to know the reason for rejection, without incurring any financial burden. In fiscal year 2002, food stamp households were certified for food stamps for an average of almost ten months.

The eligible households are entitled to use food stamps for buying eatables like bread and cereals, fruits and vegetables, meats, fish and poultry, dairy products and seeds and plants which produce food for the household to eat. However, there is also a negative list for purchase items, which include non-nutrients like beer, wine, liquor, cigarettes or tobacco; and non-food items, such as pet foods, soaps, paper products, household supplies, vitamins and medicines, hot foods *etc*. Although the beneficiaries can obtain the foods mainly from retail outlets, in some areas, restaurants can be authorised to accept food stamp benefits from qualified homeless, elderly, or disabled people in exchange for low-cost meals.

Although the FSP involves a moderate transfer of funds to the beneficiaries, it has been very successful in increasing the level of food consumption among beneficiaries. USDA (2003) mentions, "In fiscal year 2002 the maximum monthly benefit for a family of four in the contiguous United States was $452". Castañeda (2000) notes, "A review of some 17 studies of the effect of food stamps on consumption and nutrient intake in the US estimates the marginal propensity to consume food obtained with food stamps to range between 0.20 and 0.45 (Fraker, 1990). By contrast, the marginal propensity to consume food bought with regular income is only about 0.12." Jolliffe *et al.* (2003) have concluded that FSP has been very effective in reducing food insecurity among children. Wilde *et al.* (2000b) concluded that although participation in FSP increases one's intake of meats, added sugars, and total fats, it does not have any considerable impact on consumption of fruits, vegetables, grains, or dairy products. Hanson *et al.* (2002) found that any attempt to reduce the FSP leaves an unfavourable impact on low-income households.

---

38. The list includes proof of identity, birth date, or evidence of financial condition like 'cancelled checks for child support payments' etc. For details see www.foodstamps-step1.usda.gov.

*Venezuela*

The direct income support programme to poor families in the aftermath of food price increases was introduced in the early 1990s, when in order to achieve fiscal discipline general food price subsidies were drastically reduced. Castañeda (2000) notes, "The subsidy, known as the *Beca Alimentaria*, was given to all families with children attending pre-primary and primary school and consisted of three coupons; one for two kilograms of powdered milk, one for four kilograms of precooked wheat flour and four kilos of rice, and one money coupon for an amount of Bs. 500 per child, up to a maximum of three children."[39] However in 1996, a streamlining of the ongoing system was attempted through unification of all these three coupons into a single cash transfer, named the *Subsidio Unico Familiar*. Under the new scheme, subsidies were given in the form of vouchers by teachers at schools to the children, which could be encashed by parents at participating banks.

The programme aimed to provide basic needs to the poor and vulnerable through income support, apart from promotion of school attendance by pre-primary and primary school children. The identified targets were families with schoolchildren living in poor neighbourhoods in cities, rural areas, frontier regions, and also included indigenous populations. Castañeda (2000) notes, "In 1997, more than 2.8 million children were participating in the programme, representing about 90 per cent of all children enrolled in school, at an annual fiscal cost of Bs. 172,299 million (about US$350 million)." The major advantage of the programme was that since the teachers used to provide the list of the beneficiaries, *i.e.* students, to the government, the cost for maintaining separate machinery for the purpose of identification and distribution was spared. However, the major drawbacks of the system as identified by Castañeda (2000) include high operational cost owing to near-universal nature of the programme, substantially high commission rates charged by participating banks, high administrative costs owing to various other accounts *etc*. However, the programme remained extremely popular in Venezuela, owing to its wide reach and effectiveness in improving the condition of the beneficiaries.

39. Castañeda (2000), p. 25.

*Zambia*

In Zambia the food coupon system was introduced in January 1989, which was given to all urban households. However, rural households were excluded from its coverage. The volume of coupons available to households varied with their family size, and they were permitted to purchase two varieties of maize available either from government retail shops or from registered private shops. From July 1989 onwards, the operation turned more focused, as distribution of coupons began on the basis of incomes of the households. Only households below a cut-off annual income and households with income from the informal sector were permitted to access food coupons. However, Swaminathan (2000) notes that for the informal sector households, the number of dependents was fixed at six. The overall impact of the programme was a reduction in the subsidy expenditure on food items, and worsening of food security of resource-poor rural households, particularly those located in low-income districts. Besides, type 1 error was very high, *i.e.*, many poor and deserving households were excluded from this scheme.[40]

*Romania*

Although Romania did not incorporate a FSP, in 1997 it introduced an input voucher (stamp) programme for farmers to compensate for the decline in agricultural subsidies and modernisation of farm inputs. The financial aid to farmers through this scheme totaled US $200 million and 10.2 million vouchers were issued nationwide. Under this scheme, local governments prepared beneficiary lists and sent them to the voucher-preparing central agency. The farmers utilised over 90 per cent of vouchers on eligible inputs, since there was a very short span of time between distribution and planting, and also between receipt and redemption of the vouchers.[41] However, the working of the scheme suffered to some extent from the lack of adequate monitoring and supervision.

## Feasibility of Food Stamps in India: A Review of Issues

The broad findings from the cross-country experiences reveal that apart from the United States experience, the FSPs in other developing

---

40. Swaminathan (2000), p. 71.

41. Lazaroiu *et al.*, 1998, quoted from Castañeda (2000).

countries have often suffered from problems relating to inefficient initial targeting, weak administration, reluctance in carrying out time-to-time review of the beneficiary list, and inefficiencies in delivery mechanisms *etc*. One major reason for the US success might, apart from the transparency in the system, be the advantage in isolating the target group from rest of the population, and proper self-declaration (owing to the stigma attached with receipt of food stamps). On the other hand, in most of the developing countries, wrong exclusion (type 1 error) and wrong inclusion (type 2 error) has been quite high, and ultimately led to severe leakage, *i.e.*, drainage of government resources, and decline in nutritional level of the actual needy (and vulnerable) sections. However, the problem could be minimised through a rigorous identification exercise like the two-stage screening procedure followed in the *Progresa* scheme in Mexico, which, although effective, adds heavily to administrative costs. Another major problem is regular review of the system, so that people moving over (falling below) the threshold limit are regularly removed from (added to) the list of beneficiaries. This requires an extensive periodic review and the duration of food stamps/coupons acts as a major problem in this regard. While several countries issued annual stamps, the others had gone for shorter periods (*e.g.*, issued on a bi-monthly basis). It is very difficult to undertake an exhaustive analysis of the socio-economic condition of households for renewal at such a short notice, especially if the target households are spread all over the country. In addition, the calorie intake of households had often been adversely affected in times of high inflation in most of the countries, as the value of the stamps could not be altered in the short run. In a country where price volatility is a general feature, PDS is much better than food stamps, as the vulnerable section is assured of a fixed quantity of foodgrains in the former, irrespective of their prices. However, citing various channels of leakages in PDS, Pursell and Gulati (1993) strongly supported introduction of food stamp in India. "... The present methods of distributing subsidised food through the PDS need to be drastically changed and eventually even replaced altogether by a food stamp system."[42] Finally, it has been observed that the volume of food subsidy has usually declined after introducing FSP in all instances.

42. Pursell and Gulati (1993), p. 33.

In short, the experiences of various developing countries suggest that the introduction of the FSP itself might not be a solution to persistence of hunger and nutrient deprivation in the country. Without regular government monitoring, FSP is susceptible to every problem faced by the PDS. On the other hand, given the example of Sri Lanka or Mexico, the probability is quite high that the coverage of the proposed scheme might even cause a decline in the number of people currently accessing the TPDS facility. The Government, therefore, has to decide whether it wants to stick to TPDS or introduce the FSP instead, since a combination of both is not workable, as the Tenth Plan has rightly mentioned. "A system of food distribution running parallel with the current PDS could result in lack of accountability on the part of both. In the long run, therefore, there should be only one system." However, a couple of important points need to be borne in mind. First, all the developing countries discussed here have incorporated the FSP as a part of a structural adjustment programme, and therefore, a cost-saving bias was always there. India is exploring the option voluntarily at a time when the fiscal scenario is reasonably strong, and therefore, no shortfall in state expenditure is expected. Second, the countries experienced a double-digit inflation shortly after initiation of the FSP, which substantially deteriorated the value of the stamps. Although inflation has increased to over 7 per cent recently, for the past ten years it has been well within the permissible limit. Third, most of the countries relied on imported food for the success of the programme, while India has a comfortable surplus of foodgrains. Therefore, the problems faced by FSP in other developing countries might not be a major concern in India. Another important lesson learnt from the cross-country experiences is that the target population, once identified, should not be expanded before a justifiable period, or in the absence of a proper reason. Most of the programmes surveyed collapsed/functioned improperly because of their increased reach as a part of populist policies, without any commensurate increment in budgetary allocations. This should only be revoked in case of drought or similar scenarios. However, it is worth mentioning that even after targeting, the number of people eligible for FSP would be quite large in India.

A major problem of introducing food stamps is identification of the needy sections. In line with *Progresa* in Mexico, a two-tier identification procedure is required in India. The Census and NSS network is quite strong in the country, and data available from them should take care of the first stage, the identification of backward regions. For identification of the second stage, the local bodies should be involved; *e.g.* — *panchayat*s in the rural belt and urban local bodies in the cities and towns. Calorie deprivation in the rural belt is quite high, and the extensive network of *panchayat*s could play a key role in the identification process. In addition, inputs from the academia for selection of a proper identification method are of utmost importance. For instance, Debroy and Bhandari (2003) have identified 69 most backward districts in India, on the basis of six indicators, namely – income poverty, hunger, infant mortality rate, immunisation, literacy rate and enrollment ratios. Identification at the bloc level within these districts would be instrumental in narrowing down the list of beneficiaries. For identifying the needy section in the cities and towns, the NGOs working in these areas, based on their prior performance, could also be involved.[43] However, it is very difficult to comment on the fiscal implications of introduction of a FSP, and detailed work on this issue is an area of future research.[44]

So far, variants of the food stamp/food coupon programme have been explored in India only in a couple of states, and there is mixed opinion regarding their effectiveness. While in case of coupon introduction in Andhra Pradesh, an increase in welfare as well as a decline in leakage has been reported, possibilities of counterfeiting and manipulation have not been completely ruled out.[45] On the other hand, Swaminathan (2004) notes that the food coupon introduced in Tamil Nadu in July 2002 had suffered from a number of administrative and other related problems, and was withdrawn because of huge public dissatisfaction.

---

43. Quoting a number of instances, Nayak, Saxena and Farrington (2002) note that NGOs generally perform much better in programme implementation.

44. The cross-country experience shows that fiscal expenditure on food subsidy programmes usually go down in the aftermath of FSP introduction, mainly because of the focused approach followed by the new scheme.

45. 10$^{th}$ Five-Year Plan Documents, Government of India. However, Swaminathan (2004) points out that, "Women's activists found that poor families faced enormous problems in acquiring and preserving these flimsy paper coupons without damage or loss. Following strong people's protests against the food coupons, the scheme was withdrawn before the general elections of 2004."

## Alternate Options

While the government should consider all the pros and cons before introducing a full-fledged FSP in the country, in the interim period, maximum stress should be laid on the following policy measures. All of these policies are quite robust measures for addressing the food security concerns for the most vulnerable sections, namely, the children, womenfolk and the elderly people under the poverty line. Besides, the first, second and the fifth option could well co-exist with either TPDS or a food stamps programme in select areas, where there is an urgent need to augment the calorie requirement of the needy sections. The third one, *i.e.*, vouchers, is a second-best option, and although it might lead to mismanagement of funds, might be considered for appropriate regions. However, the fourth one, the mid-day-meal scheme, should be implemented in all states at the earliest.

### *Increasing the Reach of Various Welfare Programmes*

There is enormous scope to increase the off-take of surplus food-grains under various welfare schemes, although these, including *Annapurna*, Food for Work programme *etc.* are increasing over the years, as seen from Table 11.8. The government should expand the reach of the ongoing programmes, instead of going in for newer ones. In particular, NGOs should be involved for this purpose, with strict performance-based incentives. Furthermore, there should be increasing stress on programmes like *Sampoorna Grameen Rozgar Yojana*, and Food for Work programme. The Food for Work programme was initiated in 2000-01 in eight drought-affected states, namely – Chhattisgarh, Gujarat, Himachal Pradesh, Madhya Pradesh, Orissa, Rajasthan, Maharastra and Uttaranchal. The programme aims at augmenting food security through wage employment, and foodgrains are supplied to states free of cost. However, the working of the scheme could never match its expected potential, as the Tenth Plan document notes, ".. lifting of foodgrains for the scheme from Food Corporation of India (FCI) godowns has been slow. Against an

45. Tenth Five-Year Plan Documents, Government of India. However, Swaminathan (2004) points out that, "Women's activists found that poor families faced enormous problems in acquiring and preserving these flimsy paper coupons without damage or loss. Following strong people's protests against the food coupons, the scheme was withdrawn before the general elections of 2004."

allocation of 35.31 lakh tonnes of foodgrains, only 21.26 lakh tonnes were lifted by the target states up to January 2002." Although the situation has marginally improved since then, a significant proportion of the population is yet to be covered under this programme.[46]

### Table 11.8

*Off-take of Foodgrains (Rice+Wheat) under Welfare Schemes*

*(Lakh Tonnes)*

| *No.* | *Welfare Schemes* | *2000-01* | *2001-02* | *2002-03@* |
|---|---|---|---|---|
| 1 | Annapurna | 0.25 | 0.93 | 0.87 |
| 2 | Earthquake | 10.72 | 0.12 | 0.00 |
| 3 | World Food Programme | 0.05 | 1.50 | 0.32 |
| 4 | Sampoorna Grameen Rozgal Yojana | 0.33 | 18.83 | 54.76 |
| 5 | Indigent People | 0.00 | 0.17 | 0.08 |
| 6 | Nutrition Programmes | 0.18 | 1.35 | 1.22 |
| 7 | Hostel SC/ST/OBC | 0.00 | 0.83 | 1.02 |
| 8 | Food For Work | 5.44 | 28.36 | 1.18 |
| 9 | Mid-Day-Meal | 14.93 | 20.76 | 15.11 |
| **Total** | | **31.91** | **71.85** | **74.58** |

*Source: Economic Survey (2002-03)*
@: Upto December

*Linking Food for Work with Infrastructure Building*

Apart from increasing the reach of the programmes, there should be an explicit focus on employing the manpower for productive purposes. For instance, the study undertaken by Debroy and Bhandari (2003) has identified 69 most backward districts in India, which suffer heavily from their geographical positions. The study reveals that for most of these 69 districts, their connectivity with the rest of the economy is extremely weak owing to their poor infrastructure levels. A major proportion of these districts are marked by absence of national highways, poor presence of state highways and railways. As an obvious outcome, food and health insecurity stems from the absence of adequate means of livelihood in those regions. Therefore, the Food for Work programmes in those districts and other equally impoverished

46. Even though the people covered by the scheme are sometimes unhappy with the working. For instance, Right to Food (http://www.righttofood.com/) notes the wide presence of corruption in the working of Food for Work Schemes, which deserves immediate action.

regions should focus on extension of physical infrastructure. While on the one hand, this would provide employment and food security for the needy sections in the short run; it would also be instrumental for poverty alleviation in future by breaking the isolation of the districts on the other. It seems that the Government is also thinking along these lines, as seen from the excerpt from the budget speech of Finance Minister Mr. P. Chidambaram in Box 11.2.

### Box 11.2

*Budget Provisions on Food for Work Programme*

Investment and growth will create new job opportunities for our young men and women. Nevertheless, currently there is a need to ensure that unemployment does not take a heavy toll on the poor people. Work has begun on the National Employment Guarantee Act. The object is to guarantee 100 days of employment in a year to one able-bodied person in every poor household. The Bill will take into account the experience gained in Maharashtra. Government will also take care to avoid the pitfalls pointed out by responsible critics. My colleague, the Minister of Labour, expects that he would be able to introduce the Bill in Parliament shortly. Pending the enactment of the new law, **I propose to launch a new Food for Work programme in 150 districts classified as most backward and identified as areas in immediate need of such a programme.** Allocations under different schemes will be pulled together to support the Food for Work programme. There are substantial funds totalling over Rs. 6000 crore under SGRY, SGSY, SJSRY, REGP and PMRY. Depending on the demand for such work, more funds will be allocated in the current year. I expect to increase the allocations substantially over the next four years. **Special care will be taken in laying down the guidelines for the programme so that the money and labour expended result in durable and visible assets benefiting the whole community.**

*Source: Budget Speech of the Finance Minister (2004-05)*

## Food Vouchers

The problem of misallocation and breakdown in the delivery mechanism is a long-standing issue in India. Saxena (2000) heavily criticised the current approach to poverty alleviation and emphasised that it is not just spending more money on poverty eradication that matters in the current context, but spending it meaningfully:

> "Government of India ministries spend roughly Rs. 35,000 crore annually on programmes that are meant to achieve poverty alleviation. These funds, if directly transferred to the poor, could buy for every poor household 3 kg of foodgrain every day from the market at the rate of Rs. 7.5 per kg and thus could wipe off poverty from this country. If poverty still continues, the obvious conclusion is that availability of funds can at best be a necessary but not sufficient condition to tackle poverty and backwardness. The determining factor is the capability of the government machinery to formulate viable schemes and the delivery system to optimally utilise funds. Unfortunately the record of the government is poor on both counts.".

Arguing along the same lines, only in the poverty-stricken areas, where the scope for Food for Work programme is limited, food vouchers should be made available to rural households. Given the profile of the villagers, food cash will not be a good option. The *panchayats* or even NGOs at the lower level could be involved for identification of the needy households. However, the working of the vouchers should be subject to regular monitoring and the beneficiary list should be accordingly revised on a regular basis. The scheme could also be considered for implementation in selected poorer sections of the cities as well, with proper identification of the beneficiaries. However, the probability of efficient functioning of this scheme is highest in poverty-stricken village areas, where it could be launched almost universally.

## Mid-day Meal Schemes

During the drought in 2001, the food insecurity of the vulnerable sections in general and the drought-prone regions in particular increased, and to tackle the problem, the possibility of providing mid-day meals to the school-going children was explored. The idea was to provide cooked food in the primary school premises, which was expected to ensure food security and reduction in child under-nourishment on one hand and reduce the high dropout rate in the schools on the other. However, given the face of delays in proper consideration of this proposal in a number of states, the People's Union for Civil Liberties (Rajasthan) filed a writ petition in the Supreme Court in April 2001, demanding the immediate utilisation of the country's food-stocks for drought relief and prevention of hunger. The writ petition also urged not to restrict the scope of this exercise only to drought situations. The guiding motive of the petition was the general need to uphold "right to food" of the people, following from right to life (Article 21). The Supreme Court responded positively to the writ petition, and asked the government to act immediately. A brief account of the Supreme Court orders on MDMS and several other policies is provided in Annex 4.

It is clearly seen from the Supreme Court verdict that it laid ultimate importance on provision of food to the BPL households and called for involvement of *panchayats* in this exercise. They also welcomed constructive participation of the NGOs to supplement the role of the Governments. Dr. N.C. Saxena and Mr. S.R. Sankaran were appointed as commissioners of the Court to redress complaints. Apart from the operations of the MDMS; the court also asked the government to strengthen the working of other programmes like SGRY, AAY, NOAPS, ICDS, NBMS, NFBS *etc.* with positive welfare implications on the vulnerable sections of the society. The cross-state current status of the implementation of MDMS scheme is provided in Annex 5. It is quite unfortunate to note that even after two years of the verdict, where the court clearly asked the states to provide cooked mid-day meals to every child in the primary schools, a number of populous states like Assam, Bihar, Uttar Pradesh and West Bengal are yet to enforce it.[47] Similarly, relatively backward states like Himachal and Jharkhand are also among the defaulters, thereby causing significant welfare loss for their poorer households with school-going children. Several North-Eastern States like Manipur, Mizoram and Nagaland are yet to provide necessary information to the authorities. The centre should immediately look into the working of the MDMS schemes in these states, and ask for a definitive time-bound schedule for implementation of the same.

## Grain Bank Schemes

Another efficient and very effective way to respond to the food security concerns in the rural belt would be to introduce local participatory approach with minimum government presence. From

47. For successfully enforcing food security, at least for the undernourished pockets, incorporation of a National Employment Guarantee Act would be useful. Mander, Dreze and Vivek (2003) have shown that the estimated cost of such a scheme, in line with Maharashtra's 'Employment Guarantee Scheme', would not be a major burden on the state exchequer. A bill incorporating employment guarantee is likely to be introduced in the winter session of Parliament.

1996-97 onwards, the Government has initiated a Village Grain Banks scheme in remote and backward tribal areas to prevent malnutrition and starvation. Under this scheme, Ministry of Tribal Affairs provides a one-time grant for purchase of grains, at the rate of one quintal per family. The funds are canalised through TRIFED, and managed by an elected village committee. The members can borrow grains from the bank during times of scarcity. The scheme is currently under operation in Madhya Pradesh and its working and expansion plans are provided in the following Box.

**Box 11.3**

*Working of Grain Banks Scheme in Madhya Pradesh*

3.4.64 A grain bank scheme is also being run under the aegis of the Department of Rural Development in the Jhabua district of Madhya Pradesh. The scheme was launched in 1995 on a pilot basis in 18 villages. The performance of the scheme in the last two years encouraged DRDA to adopt the strategy in all villages under the Integrated Watershed Development Programme. Presently, there are 184 grain banks functioning in watershed areas and these are managed by the community itself. In the last season, 12,363 families took loans from the grain bank.

3.4.65 The Madhya Pradesh government has proposed the evolution of community-based support systems to substitute/supplement PDS operations in areas where PDS does not exist. Self-help groups of BPL families will be formed and charged a membership fee of Rs. 50. These groups will be eligible to receive supplies of foodgrains and other infrastructure-based assistance from the government. They will organise activities, under the grain bank scheme, to develop degraded lands on the periphery of forests with significant *Adivasi* populations through food for work programmes. The grain banks will be managed by committees of women beneficiaries to be called *anaj samitis*. The government will give a one-time supply of 100 kg of wheat or rice to each grain bank. The grain will be stored by the traditional method in earthen *kothas* constructed with local material and free family labour.

*Source*: Tenth Plan Documents

The *Tenth Plan Document* has advocated building of grain banks in remote and isolated areas beyond the reach of PDS, and in regions where there is inadequate employment generation. Linking the grain bank scheme with Food for Work programme has also been recommended, so that the generation of income ensures repayment of borrowed grain by the beneficiaries. The M.S. Swaminathan Research Foundation, Chennai has proposed the following structure to be followed for a successful community foodgrains scheme.

## Box 11.4

*Community Food Bank*

Main features of the proposed food banks are:

one bank for every village of cluster of villages with population ranging from 2000 to 5000;

supervised by a society or council chosen by gram sabha;

managed by a stakeholder council, with different operations assigned to different self-help groups;

to be implemented with honestly, political neutrality, fairness, absence of discrimination based on religion, caste, class, gender, and political belief.

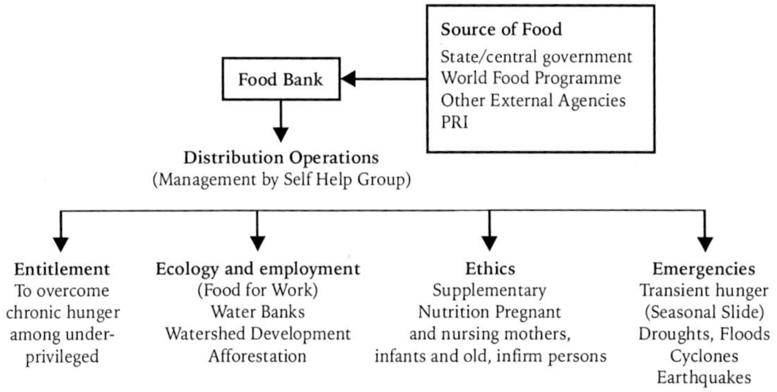


*Source*: Tenth Plan Documents

Apart from providing money to the village grain banks for purchasing food, the government could also directly give them foodgrains from the procured stock. The scheme should immediately be introduced in parts of the country where TPDS is not operational, to have an efficient utilisation of the stored foodgrains, apart from increasing food security of the recipients. In addition, the *Tenth Plan document* has strongly advocated that self-help groups rather than government machinery should run the scheme, in order to avoid shirking. "The moment beneficiaries realise that grain under the scheme is being supplied by the government, there will be a tendency not to repay. However, the government may provide the initial supply of grain and the storage capacity may be created under the food for work programmes." M.S. Swaminathan Foundation has also supported the notion. An ideal solution would be to entrust the local *panchayats* for management of this bank. However, a valid concern is that while the scheme may work well during times of surplus, during drought periods it is likely to show a 'run-on-the-bank' phenomenon. In those circumstances, the government has to come forward and bridge the gap, at the risk of hurting the efficiency in the long run.

## Conclusion

While all of these schemes might be considered for improving food security of the needy sections, before selecting the best one, the actual stress in the long run policies should be on helping people to come out of the poverty trap. That should be the primary goal of all poverty alleviation programmes in the future. To ensure that, suitable policy measures need to be undertaken for raising rural non-farm employment significantly, as well as breaking the isolation of the rural belt with the rest of the economy. The involvement of prime lending agencies like NABARD and SIDBI under various schemes would be a major precondition for the success of any rural poverty alleviation programme. Similar policies need to be formulated for the urban areas as well.[48]

---

48. For instance, in the urban areas, the individuals need to go through a number of bureaucratic channels, which act as a disincentive for entrepreneurship, even at the lowest end. The policies hurt the poorer section much more than the richer one. The internship research papers of Centre for Civil Society establishes the point through studies conducted in Delhi. Needless to add, such unnecessarily protective policies have to be repealed at the earliest.

## Annex 1

*Tenth Plan Document on Targeted Public Distribution System*

3.4.19 The number of BPL families increased with effect from 1st December 2000 because the base was shifted from the population projections of 1995 to the population projections of the Registrar General of India as on 1st March 2000. The change has resulted in increasing the number of BPL families to 65.2 million as against 59.6 million estimated when the TPDS was introduced. The allocation of foodgrains for the BPL category thus increased to 147 lakh tonnes per annum.

3.4.20 In order to reduce the excess foodgrains stocks with the FCI, the Government initiated the following measures under the TPDS from 12th July 2001:

1. The BPL allocation of foodgrains was increased from 20 kg to 25 kg per family per month with effect from July 2001. At Rs. 4.15 per kg for wheat and Rs. 5.65 per kg for rice, the CIP for BPL families is 48 per cent of the economic cost.
2. The Government decided to allocate foodgrains to APL families at the discounted rate of 70 per cent of the economic cost. The CIP of wheat was reduced from Rs. 830 per quintal to Rs. 610 per quintal and the CIP of rice reduced from Rs. 1,130 per quintal to Rs. 830 per quintal.

3.4.21 In addition, 25 kg of foodgrain was to be provided to the poorest of the poor families under the Antyodaya Anna Yojana at a highly subsidised rate of Rs. 2 per kg for wheat and Rs. 3 per kg for rice. The Public Distribution System (Control) Order 2001 was also promulgated which seeks to plug the loopholes in the PDS and make it more efficient and effective.

3.4.22 On 23rd March 2002, the Government reduced the issue price for APL rice and wheat by Rs. 100 per quintal for a period of three months. The scale of issue for APL, BPL and *Antyodaya* households was also increased to 35 kg per month.

3.4.23 Cumulatively, the off-take under TPDS between April 2002 and June 2002 has been 23.54 lakh tonnes for rice and 16.09 lakh tonnes for wheat against 18.46 lakh tonnes and 9.87 lakh tones respecitvely for the corresponding period in 2001. Thus, there is a clear indication that off-take under TPDS has improved at the national level. However, the situation is not uniform across states and there are certain states where conditions need to be improved. For instance, between April 2001 and March 2002, total off-take of rice in Bihar was only 13.8 per cent of total allocation and in the case of wheat this was only 27.9 per cent.

## Restructuring of PDS

3.4.24 The following points need to be taken into consideration in order to make the implementation of TPDS more effective:

a) Items other than rice and wheat need to be excluded from the purview of TPDS. The main objective of providing food subsidy to the poor is to ensure food security. Since rice and wheat are the basic necessities for the poor, food subsidies must be restricted to these two commodities.

b) Sugar should be kept outside the purview of PDS. It should be decontrolled and the system of levy on sugar discontinued.

c) It is argued that encouraging production of coarse cereals in dry land areas can check environment damage like degradation of soil to some extent. However, there is difficulty in supplying coarse cereals through PDS and bringing them under the cover of food subsidy. The average shelf life of coarse grains is limited, making them unsuitable for long-term storage and distribution under PDS. The inclusion of coarse cereals under PDS cannot be taken up as a national level programme since there is no standard variety of coarse grain. However, initiatives on the part of state governments catering to the needs of specific localities are possible.

d) Kerosene oil is also supplied through PDS and is intended for the poor. However, there is large-scale diversion of this commodity and subsidised kerosene is used for adulteration with diesel. The subsidy on kerosene is thus cornered by the non-poor. A study of four states carried out by Indira Gandhi Institute for Development Research (IGIDR), Mumbai shows that there is huge leakage of kerosene meant for PDS. It is irrational, therefore, to continue to subsidise kerosene at such high rates and continue its distribution through the PDS. The subsidy on kerosene should be phased out by raising its supply price under PDS while eliminating all domestic central (e.g. Cenvat) and state (e.g. sales tax) taxes on it so as to encourage private supply through petroleum retail outlets and small dealers rather than FPS. Alternately, if kerosene is to be retained under PDS, the extent of subsidy given should be reduced so that there is less incentive for diversion.

e) All further attempts to include more and more commodities under the coverage of food subsidy should be resisted.

f) The FPS should be permitted to sell all commodities (other than rice and wheat) at full market prices in order to ensure their economic viability.

g) The coverage of TPDS and food subsidy should be restricted to the BPL population. For the APL population, which has the purchasing power to buy food, the Government needs to only ensure the availability of foodgrains at a stable price in the market. Stability in foodgrain prices should be ensured through the maintenance of buffer stock and open market operations of the FCI. Any attempt to revert to the old concept of a universal PDS will be a retrograde step and needs to be resisted. However, in the current situation, where the FCI has huge surplus stocks of foodgrains, it may be necessary to continue supply of cereals under PDS to the APL population at below economic cost as a temporary measure.

h) With the liberalisation of external sector, the operation of the buffer stock can be supplemented by timely exports and imports and this will effectively mean that a smaller buffer stock will be required.

i) Ration cards should not be used by the administration as an identification card for various purposes. That role should be assigned to multi-purpose identity cards.

j) There are several Plan schemes involving distribution of food-grains, which are in the nature of welfare or income transfer schemes. Such schemes could be merged and some sort of convergence achieved.

## Annex 2

*Tenth Plan Document on Food Stamp Programme*

3.4.25 The PDS needs to be restructured and there is a need to explore the possibility of introducing innovative ideas such as smart cards, food credit/debit cards, food stamps and decentralised procurement, to eliminate hunger and make food available to the poor wherever they may be in cost-effective manner.

3.4.26 Under the system of food stamps, the State Governments could issue a subsidy entitlement card (SEC) instead of issuing ration cards. The SEC should show, among other things, the number of members in a poor family and their age and indicate their entitlement level for food stamps.

3.4.27 There could, in principle, be different levels of entitlement based on age. All adult members from a poor family, for example, could be entitled to 'a' number of food stamps per month while the entitlement for a child could be 'b' number of food stamps. There could also be a higher subsidy entitlement for old and infirm people. The SEC will indicate the total number of food stamps a family is entitled to every month.

3.4.28 Each family would collect its monthly quota of food stamps from prescribed distribution centres on showing their SEC. They could then use these food stamps at any food supply shop to buy foodgrains (rice and wheat) at a price (Rs x) below the market price. The retailer will then be reimbursed by the State Government.

3.4.29 There is less scope for corruption under a system of food stamps. Under the existing system, FPS owners declare on paper that they have sold a certain quantity of food to the poor at subsidised prices when, in fact, they have made huge profits by selling the food at market prices. There is less possibility of such diversion of food supplies under the system of food stamps. The retailer can claim food subsidy only if he acquires food stamps by selling food to the poor at subsidised prices. Under this system, it could be made mandatory for retail traders to display the selling price of foodgrains prominently in their shops.

3.4.30 Two potential problems with the system of food stamps need to be kept in mind while designing the system. There is a distinct possibility of food stamps being counterfeited.

Secondly, reimbursement of subsidy to the participating retailers can run into logistical problems. These problems are, however, minuscule compared to the problem of physically procuring, storing, transporting and delivering foodgrains to FPS across the country by the FCI and the state food corporations/agencies.

3.4.31 The food stamp system can be introduced in phases. Initially food stamps can be allowed to be redeemed only at the FPS currently used by the consumer. This will allow food stamps to be printed with the identification number of the FPS so that the totals can be matched and cross-checked later, thus reducing the scope for counterfeiting. This could be followed by the consumer designating any participating retailer and having the identification number of that shop printed on the food stamp. Normally consumers purchase their daily food provisions from the most convenient shop or, in very rare cases, two shops. As the problem of reimbursing money is a fraction of the problem of delivering food, it should not be too difficult to set up a re-imbursement system, perhaps by sub-contracting the task to a financial service provider. To reduce malpractices, there is an opinion that the food stamps should be issued to female members of the family who can be designated as heads of households for the purpose. The system should be introduced cautiously on an experimental basis in areas where a proper market infrastructure exists. The conventional FPS system may have to be continued in remote and inaccessible areas. A food coupon system for distribution of rice and kerosene through PDS was introduced in Andhra Pradesh in 1998-99. Particulars regarding the scheme are in Box 11.5.

## Box 11.5

### *Box 3.4.1: The Andhra Pradesh Experiment*

A food coupon system for distribution of rice and kerosene through the public distribution system (PDS) was introduced in Andhra Pradesh during 1998-1999 in order to improve the delivery system for these two commodities. Under the scheme, mere possession of the card was not enough to draw PDS rice, wheat or kerosene. The cardholder, whose photo was affixed on the card has to be physically present when obtaining the coupons. Coupons are issued once a year and coupon holders are entitled to draw rice and kerosene on a monthly basis. To

*Contd...*

*...Contd...*

help the coupon holder draw rice and kerosene in easy installments in a month, coupons are denominated in smaller quantities like four kg, eight kg etc. The coupon holder/beneficiary is aware of his entitlement. The State Government feels that this system has largely eliminated the scope of cheating by dealers by giving beneficiaries less than their entitlement. The coupon guarantees the stakeholder his right to draw a specific quantity every month. Rice or kerosene is not released unless the coupon is produced. This facilitates proper accounting of the actual quantity distributed in the month as it is calculated on the basis of the quantity covered by coupons produced by the beneficiaries. Quantity distributed *vis-à-vis* the coupons produced could be verified every month by the officials of the Civil Supplies/Revenue Department. Introduction of the coupon system has also reduced the number of bogus cards or those with ineligible families by approximately eight lakh. This system has resulted in saving about 20,000 tonnes of rice and 7,100 kilo litres of kerosene every month. In financial terms, the exchequer has saved Rs. 9 crore per month on rice and Rs. 5.67 crore per month on kerosene as subsidy. The coupon system could be made more effective if the list of beneficiaries is computerised on the basis of FPS so that duplicate names, if any, could be identified and eliminated. This step would also reduce the cost of PDS substantially. However, steps should be taken to prevent counterfeiting of coupons by unscrupulous persons. Regular and staggered distribution of coupons could also prevent mischief and manipulation.

Source: *Tenth Plan Document*, 'The Social Net', Volume II, Chapter 3, p. 371

# Annex 3

*Committee on Long Term Grain Policy's Recommendations*

## Recommendations on the Need to Revive PDS

The Targeted Public Distribution System (TPDS), adopted in 1997, introduced the objective of income redistribution by providing food cheaper to the poor than to the non-poor....

By excluding a large number of families, the TPDS undermined the viability of Fair Price shops and increased scope for distortion and leakage. It penalised States with relatively low incidence of income poverty but relatively high incidence of calorie deficiency. At the same time, it did not reach the poor in States where the PDS was weak prior to its introduction. We feel that it is essential to go back to an universal PDS, which involves one Central Issue Price for each item that is sought to be procured and distributed...

The redistribution objective would be better met if this additional subsidy component is transferred as cash assistance from Centre to States depending upon levels of poverty and linked to actual food distribution, but allowing States to develop their own food schemes for poverty alleviation while retaining centralised MSP and issue prices...

We are convinced that no long run policy can be effective unless present imbalances, specifically, the large excess holding of public stocks, are corrected. For the adjustment of stocks, we have outlined a two year Plan of Action which includes immediate steps to lower procurement inflows on the one hand, and to raise outflows, on the other hand, by several means including a large Food for Work programme, a revitalised universal PDS and other grain-based welfare schemes.

## Recommendations on Focusing Food For Welfare: The Unemployed, the Destitute and Children

India's existing food security system has succeeded relatively well in preventing gross failures of food supply in almost every region, but it has not done enough for the poor and the vulnerable. Certain schemes such as Food for Work and the Antyodaya Anna Yojana have been expanded recently as part of the effort to reduce stocks. In the longer run it should be possible, with resources currently being spent on holding stocks, to eliminate hunger, make a significant dent on the current appalling levels of malnutrition among India's children, and augment the future quality of our human resources.

Social security programmes with some food component in India broadly fall into three groups: employment programmes for the able-bodied, welfare programmes or social assistance for specific vulnerable groups (including infants, pregnant and lactating women, disabled and old age persons) and programmes for basic education and nutrition of children. Once the current high stocks are reduced, we recommend that the resultant savings should be used for:

> Employment schemes, for which there is a strong felt need and which can be used to develop rural infrastructure. We have recommended a major food-based employment programme for the short run. This fiscal commitment should continue after stocks have returned to normal. This should be in the form of a food-linked employment guarantee component in the SGRY which is purely self-targeted, *i.e.* not linked to prior identification as poor. While direct food provision may be necessary in situations involving local food shortage such as in the case of droughts or floods, we see this scheme as also being relevant to cope with extreme seasonal unemployment. Linkage with food in such cases could be through the existing PDS system (by issuing coupons, or other food entitlement as part of wages).

Expanding the existing Antyodaya scheme of food support to become a food security system for the entire destitute population. In particular, we recommend:

> To include other destitute persons, covering those without regular income or economic support, in particular: old people, widows and other single women without regular support; disabled persons and terminally ill persons in BPL families; homeless and other households in extreme poverty. Identification should be by Panchayati Raj Institutions.
>
> Where identification has already taken place and where the PDS works reasonably well, *Antyodaya* persons/families can continue to be supplied grain through the PDS. However, in areas where there are problems with current *Antyodaya* off-take, grain may be made available to *Panchayat*s or other alternative channels to distribute to the identified persons.

Central support to States to the extent of 50 per cent for moving to a cooked Mid-day Meal scheme for all school-going children. In moving from provision of dry rations to cooked meals, the scope for production and distribution of processed foods may be explored.

Supporting and strengthening programmes for infants, children, pregnant and lactating women such as in the Integrated Child Development Services (ICDS).

### Recommendations on Introduction of Food Stamps

In the long run, as markets get better integrated, the PDS function need not remain restricted to designated fair-price shops, and a food coupon system valid even outside PDS outlets may become possible. Food coupons may allow wider choice to consumers in terms of commodities and outlets. In the Committee's view, this is a course, which should be followed with considerable caution in view of the experience of other countries, and the possibility of counterfeiting. However, the most important reason food stamps have not been successful elsewhere has been the erosion in the value of the coupons where it was fixed in nominal terms. If the coupon system is to succeed the PDS suggested above, we recommend that the value of the coupon should be indexed to food inflation. The coupon system should not lead to a dilution of the Central government's commitment to food security.

# Annex 4

*Supreme Court Verdicts on Right to Food*

The broad verdicts passed at various dates in the Supreme Court hearings on the right to food (*PUCL vs Union of India and others*) Case are presented in the following.

## Order of May 2, 2003

- SGRY scheme to be doubled for an interim period of three months (May - July)
- Famine codes will be binding in the months of May, June and July. However, if better measures are incorporated in other schemes, these may be implemented instead.
- Government of India to clarify its response to the Abhijit Sen Committee Report by August 8, 2003.
- Government of India has to evolve a system of ensuring that all poor families are identified as BPL.
- Licences of ration shop dealers to be cancelled if they (i) do not open on time, (ii) overcharge, (iii) retain ration cards, (iv) make false entries in BPL cards, or (v) engage in black marketing.
- BPL households are to be permitted to buy grain in instalments.
- The following groups to be given *Antyodaya* cards:
    1. Aged, infirm, disabled, destitute men and women, pregnant and lactating destitute women;
    2. Widows and other single women with no regular support;
    3. Old persons (aged 60 or above) with no regular support and no assured means of subsistence;
    4. Households with a disabled adult and no assured means of subsistence;
    5. Households where due to old age, lack of physical or mental fitness, social customs, need to care for a disabled, or other reasons, no adult member is available to engage in gainful employment outside the house; and
    6. Primitive tribes.

- States that have not implemented the order on mid-day meal scheme to immediately start providing mid-day meals in at least 25 per cent of the districts (with priority to poorest districts).

## Order of October 29, 2002

- The hearing on 29th October, 02 resulted in the clarification of some points pertaining to the previous orders. The Supreme Court reaffirmed the previous orders and issued some of the following broad points as the order.
- Chief Secretaries will be held responsible if starvation deaths are established in their states.
- Each state will appoint one officer as an assistant to the commissioner.
- One last chance is given to the states to take up the publicity of the orders and translate them.

## Order of May 8, 2002

- The gram *panchayats* shall frame employment generation proposals in accordance with the SGRY guidelines... These proposals shall be approved and sanctioned by the Gram *Panchayats* and the work started expeditiously.
- The respondents shall focus the SGRY programme towards agricultural wage earners, non-agricultural unskilled wage earners, marginal farmers and in particular, SC and ST persons whose wage income constitutes a reasonable proportion of their household income and to give priority to them in employment, and within this section shall give priority to women.
- GoI shall release money entitlements under the different employment generation schemes to each State on schedule, provided that utilisation certificates have been provided by the states certifying that the funds have been used for the specified purpose.
- *Gram sabhas* are entitled to conduct Social Audits into all Food/ Employment schemes.
- Gram Sabhas are entitled to monitor the implementation of the various schemes and have access to relevant information.

- In view of the grievance that the identification of BPL families is not being done properly the central... and the state governments are directed to clarify the issue and work out a policy for...
- The respondents shall ensure that rations shops remain open throughout the months during fixed hours the details of which will be displayed on the notice board.

Dr. N.C. Saxena and Mr. S.R. Sankaran are appointed as commissioners of the Court to redress complaints that have not been resolved by the Collectors and the Chief Secretary. They can take the help of NGOs and individuals to help them monitor the implementation of the court's orders.

## Order of November 28, 2001

*TPDS*

- It is the case of the Union of India that there has been full compliance with regard to the allotment of foodgrain in relation to the TPDS. However, if any of the States gives a specific instance of non-compliance, the Union of India will do the needful within the framework of the Scheme.
- The States are directed to complete the identification of BPL families, issuing of cards and commencement of distribution of 25 kgs. grain per family per month.
- The Delhi Govt. will ensure that TPDS application forms are freely available and are given and received free of charge and there is an effective mechanism in place to ensure speedy and effective redressal of grievances.

*Antyodaya Anna Yojana*

- It is the case of the Union of India that there has been full compliance with regard to the allotment of foodgrain in relation to Antyodaya Anna Yojana. However, if any of the States gives a specific instance of non-compliance, the Union of India will do the needful within the framework of the Scheme.
- We direct the States and the Union Territories to complete identification of beneficiaries, issuing of cards and distribution of grain under this Scheme latest by 1st January, 2002.

- It appears that some *Antyodaya* beneficiaries may be unable to lift grain because of penury. In such cases, the Centre, the States and the Union Territories are requested to consider giving the quota free after satisfying itself in this behalf.

*MDMS*

- It is the case of the Union of India that there has been full compliance with regard to the Mid Day Meal Scheme (MDMS). However, if any of the States gives a specific instance of non-compliance, the Union of India will do the needful within the framework of the Scheme.
- We direct the State Governments/Union Territories to implement the Mid-Day Meal Scheme by providing every child in every Government and Government assisted Primary Schools with a prepared mid day meal with a minimum content of 300 calories and 8-12 grams of protein each day of school for a minimum of 200 days. Those Governments providing dry rations instead of cooked meals must within three months [February 28, 2002] start providing cooked meals in all Govt. and Govt. aided Primary Schools in all half the Districts of the State (in order of poverty) and must within a further period of three months [May 28, 2002] extend the provision of cooked meals to the remaining parts of the State.
- We direct the Union of India and the FCI to ensure provision of fair average quality grain for the Scheme on time.
- The States/Union Territories and the FCI are directed to do joint inspection of foodgrains. If the foodgrain is found, on joint inspection, not to be of fair average quality, it will be replaced by the FCI prior to lifting.

*NOAPS*

- It is the case of the Union of India that there has been full compliance with regard to the National Old Age Pension Scheme. However, if any of the States gives a specific instance of non-compliance, the Union of India will do the needful within the framework of the Scheme.
- The States are directed to identify the beneficiaries and to start making payments latest by 1st January, 2002.

- We direct the State Govts./Union Territories to make payments promptly by the 7th of each month.

*Annapurna*

- The States/Union Territories are directed to identify the beneficiaries and distribute the grain latest by 1st January, 2002.

*ICDS*

- We direct the State Govts./Union Territories to implement the Integrated Child Development Scheme (ICDS) in full and to ensure that every ICDS disbursing centre in the country shall provide as under - Each child up to six years of age to get 300 calories and eight to ten grams of protein; Each adolescent girl to get 500 calories and 20-25 grams of protein; Each pregnant woman and each nursing mother to get 500 calories and 20-25 grams of protein; Each malnourished child to get 600 calories and 16-20 grams of protein.
- Have a disbursement centre in every settlement.

*NMBS*

- We direct the State Govts./Union Territories to implement the National Maternity Benefit Scheme (NMBS) by paying all BPL pregnant women Rs. 500/- through the *Sarpanch* 8-12 weeks prior to delivery for each of the first two births.

*NFBS*

- We direct the State Govts./Union Territories to implement the National Family Benefit Scheme and pay a BPL family Rs. 10,000/- within four weeks through a local *Sarpanch*, whenever the primary bread winner of the family dies.

*Other*

- We direct that a copy of this order be translated in regional languages and in English by the respective States/Union Territories and prominently displayed in all *Gram Panchayats*, Govt. School Buildings and Fair Price Shops.

- In order to ensure transparency in selection of beneficiaries and their access to these Schemes, the *Gram Panchayats* will also display a list of all beneficiaries under the various Schemes.

## Order of September 17, 2001

- States & Union Territories who, according to the learned Attorney General, had not identified the below poverty line families under the Antyodaya Anna Yojana, to identify, we are not satisfied that any such exercise in the right earnestness has been undertaken.
- The Food for Work Programme in the scarcity areas should also be implemented by the various States to the extent possible.

## Order of July 23, 2001

- In our opinion, what is of utmost importance is to see that food is provided to the aged, infirm, disabled, destitute women, destitute men who are in danger of starvation, pregnant and lactating women and destitute children, especially in cases where they or members of their family do not have sufficient funds to provide food for them.
- By way of an interim order, we direct the States to see that all the PDS shops, if closed, are re-opened and start functioning within one week from today and regular supplies made.

---

*Source: www.righttofood.com*

## Annex 5

*Status of Mid-day Meals in Different Parts of India on 12 July 2004*

| *No.* | *State/Union Territory* | *Status of Implementation* | *Extent of Coverage* |
|---|---|---|---|
| 1 | Andaman and Nicobar Islands | Full implementation. | 100 per cent |
| 2 | Andhra Pradesh | Full coverage, details awaited. Recent reports suggest that mid-day meals are being extended to school holidays. | 100 per cent |
| 3 | Arunachal Pradesh | Partial implementation. | Only 34 per cent of the eligible schools and 41 per cent of eligible children are being covered. |
| 4 | Assam | No implementation. "The state government hopes to introduce cooked mid-day meals for a limited number of days in the FY 2004-05" | No money was disbursed by the state government in the FY 2003-04 and 2002-03 on account of conversion costs, however construction of kitchen sheds within SGRY funds has been initiated. The scheme was tried on a pilot basis in one block with funds sanctioned under SSA, but only for limited days. Further in two districts the cooked meal programme was started by asking for "Public Participation and help from *Panchayat*i Raj Institutions" with no corresponding allocation by the state government. |
| 5 | Bihar | No implementation | Only proposal for initiating process has been outlined. Coverage is to be limited to cover 2578 schools in 30 blocks across 10 identified districts, and that too not all the eligible schools in |

*Contd...*

*...Contd...*

| No. | State/Union Territory | Status of Implementation | Extent of Coverage |
|---|---|---|---|
| | | | these selected blocks. Funds worth 13.5 crore are supposed to be transferred to the districts for this purpose. |
| 6 | Chandigarh | Cooked meals are not being provided; only ready-to-eat food is supplied to all schools. | |
| 7 | Chhattisgarh | Full coverage, according to official data. However, field reports suggest that implementation is erratic, with no quality safeguards. Financial allocations are abysmally low (Re. 0.50 per child per day), though recent reports suggest that they are being raised to Re. 1 per child per day. | 100 per cent. |
| 8 | Dadra and Nagar Haveli | Full implementation. | 100 per cent. |
| 9 | Daman and Diu | Full implementation. | 100 per cent. |
| 10 | Delhi | Partial implementation. Quality of MDMs is very poor. Frequent reports of food poisoning. | 77 per cent of eligible schools are being covered. |
| 11 | Goa | Partial implementation. | six out of 11 *Talukas* have been covered and children are provided only ready to eat food. |
| 12 | Gujarat | Cooked mid-day meals have been provided in government primary schools for the last ten years or so. In addition, mid-day meals are linked with regular mass deworming of school children, and a micronutrient supplementation programme (involving vitamin A, iron and iodine). | 100 per cent. |
| 13 | Haryana | Partial implementation. | Only 1382 schools across 17 blocks are being covered. |

*Contd...*

*...Contd...*

| No. | *State/Union Territory* | *Status of Implementation* | *Extent of Coverage* |
|---|---|---|---|
| 14 | Himachal Pradesh | Partial implementation. | Nine (tribal) blocks across three districts are being covered. According to the Director, primary Education, HP "the decision to extend this programme to other non-tribal areas of the state is likely to be taken by the Government of HP on the availability of funds for the state". |
| 15 | Jammu and Kashmir | Information not forthcoming. | |
| 16 | Jharkhand | Partial implementation. | 200 schools per seven districts to be covered. Moreover even in the areas that are deemed covered (*e.g.* Nini centre in Lohardaga district), cooked meals could be served only for seven days. (Visit of Dr Saxena to the State in March 2004) |
| 17 | Karnataka | Full coverage since July 2003. Field survey conducted in three districts of north Karnataka in early 2003 suggests implementation is reasonably good. However, extension to south Karnataka in July 2003 led to serious problems of caste discrimination. | 95 per cent of eligible schools are covered while all government-aided primary schools remain to be covered. |
| 18 | Kerala | Mid-day meals have been supplied in primary schools for many years. However, some reports suggest that they are restricted to children from poor families. | 100 per cent. |
| 19 | Lakshadweep | Full implementation. | 100 per cent. |
| 20 | Madhya Pradesh | Mid-day meals have been supplied in primary schools for many years. However, some reports suggest that they are restricted to children from poor families. | 100 per cent. |

*Contd...*

...*Contd...*

| *No.* | *State/Union Territory* | *Status of Implementation* | *Extent of Coverage* |
|---|---|---|---|
| 21 | Maharashtra | Partial coverage. Quality of MDMs is very poor. Frequent reports of food poisoning. | 80 per cent of eligible schools are covered. State visit (to Purandhar and Pargaon *Taluks* of Pune district) by the Commissioner Mr. Sankaran had revealed several instances where parents had been asked to contribute (Rs. 5-15 per student) towards the conversion costs. It is hoped that after the Court order dated 20 April 2004, the state government will ensure that this does not happen. |
| 22 | Manipur | No information provided to the Commissioners despite several letters sent to the state. | |
| 23 | Meghalaya | Partial implementation. | 88 per cent of eligible children are covered under the cooked mid-day meal scheme. |
| 24 | Mizoram | No information provided to the Commissioners despite several letters sent to the state. | |
| 25 | Nagaland | No information provided to the Commissioners despite several letters sent to the state. | |
| 26 | Orissa | Partial implementation. Cooked mid-day meals were already provided in tribal areas before the interim order of 28th November 2001. | 35 per cent of the enrolled students are being covered under the scheme and 47 per cent of eligible schools are covered. |
| 27 | Pondicherry | Full implementation. | 100 per cent. |
| 28 | Punjab | Full implementation. | 100 per cent. |
| 29 | Rajasthan | Full coverage since mid-2002, but on a shoestring budget (Re. 0.50 per child day). | 100 per cent. |
| 30 | Sikkim | Full implementation. | 100 per cent. |

*Contd...*

...*Contd...*

| No. | *State/Union Territory* | *Status of Implementation* | *Extent of Coverage* |
|---|---|---|---|
| 31 | Tamil Nadu | Full coverage since 1982 – twenty years ahead of the Supreme Court order of November 28, 2001. | 100 per cent. |
| 32 | Tripura | Full implementation. | 100 per cent. |
| 33 | Uttar Pradesh | No implementation. | Only a proposal for initiating the process has been outlined. It had been decided in April 2003 to initiate the scheme in six districts. However even a year later no start has been made. |
| 34 | Uttaranchal | Full implementation. | 100 per cent. |
| 35 | West Bengal | Partial implementation. Just before the Supreme Court order of April 20, 2004, the Government of West Bengal had issued instructions to the effect that mid-day meals should be universalised by March 2005. The latest Supreme Court deadline is September 1, 2004. | 2 per cent. |

*Source*: http://www.righttofoodindia.org/mdm/mdm_states.html

# Annex 6

*Characteristics and Impacts of Food Stamp Programmes in Selected Countries — Jamaica, Sri Lanka, Honduras, Mexico, the United States and Romania*

| *Country* | *Jamaica* | *Sri Lanka* | *Honduras* | *Mexico* | *United States* | *Romania* |
|---|---|---|---|---|---|---|
| Objective | • Buffer impact of structural adjustment policies on vulnerable groups.<br>• Combat hunger and malnutrition of poorest groups. | Compensate for reductions and/or elimination of general price subsidies and ration coupons. | Alleviate impact of structural adjustment on the poor. (Two food stamp programmes. One for poor school children, the other for children 0–5 and pregnant, women and nursing mothers.) | Campeche Pilot: Provide cash assistance to families to replace in-kind subsidies for tortillas, milk, etc. Progresa: Provide integrated cash, health and education assistance to families to reduce extreme poverty and malnutrition. | • Help low-income families and individuals meet basic nutrition needs by ensuring they have means to sustain a low cost diet. | • Provide direct assistance to assistance to farmers as a compensation for reduction of indirect subsidies.<br>• Promote private input market. |
| Implemented | 1984 | End of 1979 | 1990 | Campeche: 1995–96<br>Progresa: 1997 | 1964 | Fall planting season of 1997. |
| Number of Beneficiaries Per cent Population | 277,100 (1997)<br>7.5 per cent (1997) | 7.2 million (1979)<br>50 per cent of population<br>8.0 million (1989)<br>50 per cent of population | • 125,700 school children (1992).<br>• 56,200 children 0–5, pregnant/nursing women (1992). | Campeche: 32,000 families (1997).<br>Progresa: 1.9 million families (end 1998). | 27 million (1995).<br>10.4 per cent of population | 4.4 million farmers.<br>100 per cent of farmers |
| Target Group | • Pregnant and nursing women<br>• Children 0–5<br>• Elderly poor | Households with monthly income below a threshold level (the poorest | • Poor primary school children in selected areas.<br>• All children 0–5 and | Campeche Pilot: Poor families located in three urban areas. Progresa: Extremely | Households have to meet both asset and income tests. | All farmers. Basis for payment was number of hectares of land, |

*Contd...*

*...Contd...*

| *Country* | *Jamaica* | *Sri Lanka* | *Honduras* | *Mexico* | *United States* | *Romania* |
|---|---|---|---|---|---|---|
| | • Incapacitated poor<br>• Selected poor families | 20 per cent of population). | pregnant/nursing women in selected areas. | poor families in mainly rural localities. All family members of selected families are beneficiaries (children, parents). | | from 0.5 hectares up to a maximum of six hectares. |
| General Targeting Criteria (Selection by programme or self-selection) | Self-selection. People apply and register for the programme athealth centres and clinics and parish programme offices. | Self-selection. People apply for registration and are required to show income eligibility. | • Schools are selected by Ministry of Education; teachers choose children.<br>• Self-selection. Mothers who regularly visit health posts and centres with their children. | Campeche Pilot: Selected families were from the rolls of those receiving tortilla (Tortibono) and milk subsidies.<br>Progresa: Families are selected in a two-stage process. First poor rural localities are selected on basis of housing and public services. Second, families are selected within those localities. | Self-selection. People apply for the programme on the basis of asset and income tests. | All farmers are registered by municipal authorities based on cadastral records. |
| Income and/or Other Eligibility Criteria (Threshold levels) | Family income less than the equivalent of 40 per cent of minimum wage (in 1996). | Family income less than SR$300 (US$ 20) per month for a family of five (in 1979).<br>Target: poorest 20 | • Eligible children determined by teacher assessment of family income, size and civil status of parents.<br>• Villages selected based | Campeche Pilot: Families with less than two minimum wages.<br>Progresa: Families are ranked according to poverty index combining | Asset test: Assets less than $2,000, or $3,000 if at least one member is age 60 or older.<br>Income test: | No income or asset test is required. |

*Contd...*

*...Contd...*

| *Country* | *Jamaica* | *Sri Lanka* | *Honduras* | *Mexico* | *United States* | *Romania* |
|---|---|---|---|---|---|---|
| | | per cent of population. | on aggregate poverty index. | a series of socioeconomic variables in a Logit function. | Gross monthly income below 130 per cent, and net monthly income below 100 per cent, of Poverty Guidelines. | |
| Eligible Foods | Rice, cornmeal, skimmed milk flour. There are also kerosene stamps. | Rice, paddy, flour, bread, sugar, milk products, pulses and kerosene (separate stamps that can be changed for food). | Any food, medicines, school supplies. | Campeche Pilot: Rice, beans, cooking oil, eggs, milk, pasta, meat, sugar, fruits. Progresa: Any food. | Any food. Originally, before 1964, stamps were restricted to surplus foods. | Farmers can purchase fertilisers, seeds, pesticides, mechanical works and fuel oil from any supplier. |
| Value of Stamp per Beneficiary | US$3.5 per person per month (1990). Real value declined by over 40 per cent between 90–96 due to inflation. | Real value declined by over 50 per cent between 79–89 due to inflation. | • For school children:$37 per year (distributed biannually).<br>• For children 0–5 and mothers: $44 (distributed monthly in health posts and centres). Data for 1992. | Campeche Pilot:Value was 125 Mexican pesos per family (about US$17) per month. Progresa: Value varies with family size and age composition of children. Subsidy for average family per month was 235 Mexican pesos (about US$26). | Value of stamps is the difference between expected purchases on food and amount budgeted adequate to meet low-cost diet. Expected purchase is 30 per cent of net income. In 1995 maximum amount for a single person was $115; for a family of 8: $695/month. | Value of stamp or voucher was equivalent to US$18 per hectare up to a maximum of 6 per planting season. |

*Contd...*

*...Contd...*

| *Country* | *Jamaica* | *Sri Lanka* | *Honduras* | *Mexico* | *United States* | *Romania* |
|---|---|---|---|---|---|---|
| Importance of Stamps in Consumption expenditure of Food | Value of stamp subsidies was 7.2 per cent of cost of low-income basket in 1991, and 2.8 per cent in 1996. | Value of stamp subsidies for the poorest 20 per cent was 32 per cent of food purchase purchases in 78/79 and 20 per cent in 81/82. | Stamp subsidies increased disposable income of bottom 30 per cent by 26 per cent in urban areas and 13 per cent in rural areas. | Campeche Pilot: Subsidy was about 25 per cent of minimum wage. Progresa: Subsidy amount is about 34 per cent of money income obtained by families in extreme poverty. | Stamps amount to 25–50 per cent of a family composed of a mother and two children, depending on the state's other transfers. | Aggregate value of stamps was about 30 per cent of total expenditures on inputs by farmers in the fall of 1997. |
| Time Profile | No end date has been set. | No end date has been set. | No end date has been set. | Campeche Pilot: Lasted only for 1996. Progresa. No end date for the programme has been set. | No end date has been set. | The program was repeated in spring 1998. |
| IMPACTS<br>Fiscal Costs | Fiscal cost has dropped greatly as a result of drop in value of stamps. Cost as per cent of government expenditure: 1.6 per cent. General subsidy: 3 per cent (1988). | Fiscal cost as share of GDP dropped from 5 per cent in 78–79 before programme to 1.3 per cent in 1984. Fiscal cost as share of govt. exp. dropped from 15 per cent in 1970 to 3 per cent in 1984. | • School children cost: $ 4.6 million (1991).<br>• Young children and mothers cost: $1.4 million (1991) (Pilot). | Campeche Pilot: No final figures were available for this report Progresa: Budget for 1998 was 5 billion Mexican pesos (about US$ 560 million). | $24 billion (1995) plus $3.2 billion in administrative cost. | In 1997, the cost was equivalent to US$200 million |
| Administrative Costs | 4 per cent (Grosh, 1993) | 2 per cent (Cornia & Stewart, 1993) | • 16 per cent in school children programme.<br>• 23 per cent in children | Campeche Pilot: Not available for this report. Progresa: Not available | 13.5 per cent (shared among federal, state | 3 per cent due to very low costs of |

*Contd...*

*...Contd...*

| *Country* | *Jamaica* | *Sri Lanka* | *Honduras* | *Mexico* | *United States* | *Romania* |
|---|---|---|---|---|---|---|
| | | | 0–5 and mothers programme. | for this report. | and local governments). | printing, distribution, redemption and beneficiary identification. |
| Income Distribution | • Transfer to poorest quintile: 31 per cent (1988).<br>• Transfer to richest quintile: 8 per cent (1988).<br>• Elderly poor in programme: 37 per cent. | Target poorest 20 per cent got 40 per cent of FSP (1981/82). | Both programmes appear to be well targeted to the poorest 30 per cent of the population. | Campeche Pilot: Over 90 per cent of beneficiaries had total family expenditures of less than 1.5 times the minimum wage.<br>Progresa: Not known. Evaluation planned for 1999. | Programme available only to poor persons and families. | Most farmers in Romania own between 1–3 hectares and are among the poorest of the population. |
| Food Consumption | Increased food consumption, especially of elderly poor. | Increased food consumption of poor and other segments of population. | Benefits amount to 17–20 per cent of beneficiary food requirements.<br>Over 80 per cent of beneficiaries used food stamps exclusively to buy food. | Campeche Pilot: No studies were done on this.<br>Progresa: Evaluation is planned for 1999. | Food stamps increase food consumption but less than amount of subsidy. MPC food out of FS is estimated to range from 0.20–0.45. | Vouchers increased input purchases. Over 90 per cent of vouchers were used by farmers to purchase inputs directly. |

*Contd...*

*...Contd...*

| *Country* | *Jamaica* | *Sri Lanka* | *Honduras* | *Mexico* | *United States* | *Romania* |
|---|---|---|---|---|---|---|
| Nutrition Impact | Low impact: • Malnourished children in programme was 6.8 per cent in 1996. • Normal children in programme: 11 per cent in 1996. | Transfer too small to have a significant impact on children. Share of calories from programme in total calories was only 11 per cent for poorest quintile. Leakage was also high. | • No study on this has been made. • Important impacts have been noticed on school attendance, preventive visits to health clinics by mothers and children. | Campeche Pilot: No evaluation was done on this. However, reported visits to health posts by mothers and children less than 5 years of age was universal for people in the programme. Progresa: Evaluation is planned for 1999. | n. k. | n. k. |

n. a.: Not available; n. n.: Not applicable; n. k.: Unknown; AEU: Adult Equivalent Unit.

*Source*: Castañeda (2000)

# Annexure

# Annexure

*Suggested Activity Mapping for Panchayati Raj Institutions*
*(As approved by the Cabinet Sub-Committee)*

## Item No. 1

*Agriculture (Including Horticulture) and Extension*

| *Activity* | *Distribution of Functions* | | |
|---|---|---|---|
| | *Zilla Panchayat* | *Taluk Panchayat* | *Gram Panchayat* |
| Increasing Agricultural Production | 1. Prepare comprehensive crop plan;<br>2. Develop and maintain data base for cropping pattern, land use and inputs use for planning;<br>3. Organise Kisan Melas, Fairs and Exhibitions;<br>4. Protect bio-diversity;<br>5. Promote profitable crop technologies. | 1. Assist ZP in organising Farmers' fairs, Kisan Melas, etc.;<br>2. Organise on-farm verification trials and demonstration of new technologies;<br>3. Report and initiate action plans for different items;<br>4. Coordinate activities of field level extension workers and officials;<br>5. Act as a link between ZP and GPs for transfer of knowledge;<br>6. Help in crop yield estimation through maintaining links with various agencies, GPs and farmers;<br>7. Advise suitable cropping system based on location specific characteristics;<br>8. Arrange awards to progressive farmers. | 1. Estimate crop yield and maintain data base regarding crops and cropping pattern;<br>2. Assist in preparation of crop plan;<br>3. Assist in advising farmers about remunerative crop activities and crop diversification;<br>4. Assist in identifying progressive farmers for adoption and diffusion of new technologies;<br>5. Help in providing custom hiring services for plant protection equipment and farm implements;<br>6. Generate awareness in use of organic fertilisers and vermiculture. |

*Contd...*

*...Contd....*

| *Activity* | *Distribution of Functions* | | |
| --- | --- | --- | --- |
| | *Zilla Panchayat* | *Taluk Panchayat* | *Gram Panchayat* |
| Assessment and Distribution of Inputs | 1. Prepare consolidated plan for input requirement;<br>2. Acquire and arrange distribution of inputs in time;<br>3. Improve adequate storage facilities for inputs;<br>4. Monitor distribution of quality inputs. | 1. Assess inputs needs for GPs inputs and forward consolidated request to TP;<br>2. Ensure timely availability of required inputs to GPs;<br>3. Arrange storage and transport facilities for inputs close monitoring of inputs delivery system. | 1. Assist in assessing needs of various inputs such as seeds, fertilisers, pesticides;<br>2. Assist in timely distribution of adequate inputs to farmers. |
| Credit | 1. Prepare credit plan;<br>2. Ensure timely credit availability and linkage between agriculture development and credit institutions, and monitor credit mobilisation;<br>3. Help in strengthening of cooperative credit institutions. | 1. Assist in preparing credit plan;<br>2. Ensure timely credit from formal institutions;<br>3. Monitor credit delivery system. | 1. Assist in assessing credit needs of various groups of farmers and crops;<br>2. Exercise social control and regulate interest areas and recovery of loans from formal and informal credit institutions;<br>3. Help in formation of Self-help Groups. |
| Extension Support | 1. Maintain linkage with research and training organisations;<br>2. Ensure regular visits of extension staff and help in dissemination of new technologies;<br>3. Ensure regular training of extension officials for updating their knowledge of advancements in technologies. | 1. Prepare plan for visit of extension workers and monitor their work;<br>2. Advice and identify extension officials for training;<br>3. Assist scientists in identifying local problems for designing their research work relevant to local needs;<br>4. Ensure better linkages between farmers and extension staff;<br>5. Operate and run farmer service centres, *Kisan Kendras* and *Raitha Samparka Kendras*. | 1. Monitor the visit of extension workers to the village farms;<br>2. Identify suitable plots for conducting trials and demonstration;<br>3. Select farmers for participating in *Kisan Melas* and training. |

*Contd...*

...Contd....

| Activity | Distribution of Functions | | |
|---|---|---|---|
| | *Zilla Panchayat* | *Taluk Panchayat* | *Gram Panchayat* |
| Soil Testing | 1. Establish soil-testing laboratories;<br>2. Monitor soil testing work. | 1. Monitor Soil testing work;<br>2. Help in identifying locations for soil testing work;<br>3. Help farmers for improvement of soil fertility in consonance with soil testing results. | 1. Assist technical experts in conducting soil tests;<br>2. Help in ensuring feed back from soil testing to farmers. |
| Post-harvest Management | 1. Establish and improve storage facilities;<br>2. Develop marketing infrastructure at suitable locations;<br>3. Monitor regulated marketing;<br>4. Ensure correct weights and measures. | 1. Maintain godowns;<br>2. Organise marketing committees and maintain market yards;<br>3. Regulate market charges and ensure correct weights and measures;<br>4. Provide, manage and run market information systems;<br>5. Ensure prompt payment to the farmers. | 1. Help in organising farmers for group sale in bulk;<br>2. Assist in increasing awareness about better storage facilities for seeds and foodgrains. |
| Risk Management | 1. Assess losses due to natural calamities and formulate relief plan;<br>2. Monitor and supervise relief operations. | 1. Estimate crop losses and report action taken;<br>2. Monitor relief operations;<br>3. Assist in providing benefits from crop insurance schemes;<br>4. Arrange crop insurance schemes and coordinate among insurance agencies;<br>5. Prepare contingency agricultural plan. | 1. Report losses due to natural calamities and relief requirements;<br>2. Supervise relief operations and distribution of material;<br>3. Motivate and help in identifying farmers to take up crop insurance schemes;<br>4. Assist in the implementation of contingency plan. |

# Item No. 2

*Land Improvement, Implementation of Land Reforms, Land Consolidation and Soil Conservation*

| *Activity* | *Distribution of Functions* | | |
|---|---|---|---|
| | *Zilla Panchayat* | *Taluk Panchayat* | *Gram Panchayat* |
| Protection and Maintenance of Village Commons etc. | 1. Guide and coordinate the work of GPs & IPs;<br>2. Provide legal, administrative and financial assistance to GPs & TPs as far as practicable, in the conduct of legal proceedings;<br>3. Decide on disposal of village common property or their conversion to other uses with the concurrence of the GP concerned. | 1. Coordinate the work of GPs where inter-GP collaboration is needed;<br>2. Coordinate with the legally constituted machinery involved in the matter. | 1. Primary responsibility for keeping all common property of local nature in good condition;<br>2. Keep watch over them so that they are not encroached upon or converted to uses not in the interest of the community;<br>3. Identify encroachment as well as conversion of illegal or wrong uses of commons;<br>4. Provide assistance in and collection of evidence towards the conduct of the proceedings by such authority. |
| Soil Conservation | 1. Prepare district plan for soil and water conservation projects;<br>2. Disaggregate this plan into TP level, GP level or even lower level deliverable units;<br>3. Harmonise the plan with other employment generating as well as area development plans;<br>4. Coordination with various agencies of the ZP as well as the district administration who will either participate in or whose work will impinge upon the implementation of the plan. | 1. Coordinate with officials of soil conservation machinery;<br>2. Inter GP coordination for smoothly carrying out soil conservation operations cutting across GP boundaries including creation of water channels. | 1. Assist the professional/official machinery for soil conservation work through helping group action by land owners;<br>2. Direct assistance in implementation e.g., organising owner labour as part of contributions of the cost of operations;<br>3. Post-conservation vigilance to ensure that work done is not undone once again;<br>4. Create public opinion in favour of use of soil only in consonance with its properties, gradients, etc.;<br>5. Distribute subsidies and other assistance according to determined scales and priorities. |

## Item No. 3

### *Minor Irrigation, Watershed Management and Watershed*

| *Activity* | *Distribution of Functions* | | |
|---|---|---|---|
| | *Zilla Panchayat* | *Taluk Panchayat* | *Gram Panchayat* |
| Development of MI system, drainage system, water harvesting structures and water management | 1. Formulate MI projects;<br>2. Technically appraise MI projects (outside TP purview);<br>3. Execute MI Projects outside TP and GP plan;<br>4. Assign projects to TP and GP;<br>5. Development of drainage system in water logged areas;<br>6. Sanctioning projects for percolation tanks, check dams and land leveling;<br>7. Supervise, monitor and review of the progress and quality of works by the subject committee;<br>8. Coordinate between various departments and agencies. | 1. Formulate MI Projects;<br>2. Technically appraise MI projects proposed in TP Plan;<br>3. Execute MI Projects included in TP Plan;<br>4. Execute MI Projects assigned by ZP;<br>5. Construct percolation tanks and check dams (outside GP plan);<br>6. Supervision, monitoring and review of the progress, and quality of works by the Subject Committee;<br>7. Coordinate between various line departments/agencies funding for MI projects. | 1. Assist in formulation of MI projects and ratification by *Gram Sabha;*<br>2. Identify locations for projects;<br>3. Execute Community MI Projects;<br>4. Execute MI Projects assigned by ZP and TP;<br>5. Construct percolation tanks and check dams including projects assigned by the ZP and TP;<br>6. Enforce inter-well distance (well density) as per prescribed norms;<br>7. Identify beneficiaries under various programmes for MI projects through *Gram Sabha;*<br>8. Supervise, Monitor and review progress, quality of work. |
| Water Management | 1. Propagate modern water management delivery methods;<br>2. Propagate use of sprinkler and drip irrigation in drought prone/water scarce area; | 1. Guide and motivate people to adopt modern methods of irrigation, on-farm development and proper maintenance of field channels;<br>2. Select beneficiaries for subsidised sprinklers, drip irrigation equipment and delivery system and supply them, including providing technical guidance to beneficiaries;<br>3. Organise farm demonstration for modern water management techniques. | 1. Identify beneficiaries through *Gram Sabhas* for subsidised sprinkler and drip irrigation system;<br>2. Constitute *Neeru Panchayats* for proper utilisation of water including use for drinking purposes;<br>3. Encourage farmers for on-farm development and development of field channels/ delivery system for proper utilisation of water. |

*Contd...*

*...Contd...*

| *Activity* | *Distribution of Functions* | | |
|---|---|---|---|
| | *Zilla Panchayat* | *Taluk Panchayat* | *Gram Panchayat* |
| Watershed Development | 1. Identify, select and approve watershed projects;<br>2. Promote watershed development approach in all areas for better management of natural resources and environment development;<br>3. Supervise, Monitor and review of the progress and quality of works by the Subject Committee. | 1. Prepare watershed project in inter-GP watersheds;<br>2. Organise people to form work committees;<br>3. Form technical team to assist GP in the implementation of watershed projects;<br>4. Integrate various beneficiary oriented and area development oriented schemes to harmonise with watershed projects;<br>5. Monitoring supervision and reporting progress. Coordinate between various agencies and departments implementing watershed projects such as agriculture, forestry, DPAP and DDP. | 1. Participate in planning and implementation of watershed projects;<br>2. Approve land/water use plan for watershed development through *Gram Sabhas;*<br>3. Assist in constituting user/Beneficiary committees in the watershed for their direct participation in the execution of the project;<br>4. Maintain community asset screated under watershed project;<br>5. Supervise and monitor quality of works;<br>6. Select beneficiaries and provide assistance to them for executing individual works under watershed; |

# Item No. 4

## *Animal Husbandry Dairying and Poultry*

| *Activity* | *Distribution of Functions* | | |
|---|---|---|---|
| | *Zilla Panchayat* | *Taluk Panchayat* | *Gram Panchayat* |
| Development of livestock | 1. Assess the need and formulate projects for the establishment, improvement and maintenance of breeding farms for cattle, sheep, goats and hatcheries. | 1. Distribute quality breeds to beneficiaries under various programmes;<br>2. Propagate improved breed of livestock among farmers. | 1. Assist in identification of beneficiaries under various programmes;<br>2. Motivate people to maintain quality breeds and adopt modern methods of maintaining livestock. |
| Veterinary Services | 1. Establish, improve and maintain veterinary hospitals, Dispensaries, Rural Livestock Units (RLUs) and AI Centres;<br>2. Procure and supply medicines, equipment and other materials to hospitals, dispensaries, RLUs and AI Centres;<br>3. Monitor the functions of veterinary services. | 1. Supervise the functioning of veterinary services in the TP;<br>2. Maintain mobile veterinary unit to provide veterinary care and control diseases and epidemics. | 1. Supervise the functioning of RLU and AI service centres;<br>2. Report outbreak of diseases and epidemics. |
| Feeding and Fodder including support during droughts | 1. Propagate production of nutritive fodder and promote proper feeding of animals;<br>2. Procure and establish fodder banks in drought areas. | 1. Organise cooperatives for fodder production and provide financial assistance;<br>2. Supply improved variety of fodder seeds;<br>3. Propagate modern methods of feeding to improve livestock productivity;<br>4. Supply fodder during droughts. | 1. Help in establishing cooperative fodder farm;<br>2. Allocate community land for fodder production;<br>3. Control grazing and improve grazing and pasture lands;<br>4. Distribute fodder during droughts. |

*Contd...*

*...Contd...*

| *Activity* | *Distribution of Functions* | | |
|---|---|---|---|
| | *Zilla Panchayat* | *Taluk Panchayat* | *Gram Panchayat* |
| Dairy Development | 1. Assist Dairy Development Boards or Cooperatives in the development of infrastructure for milk collection, collection centres, transportation and processing. | 1. Develop and open new milk routes for milk collection;<br>2. Promote milk producers, cooperative societies;<br>3. Ensure timely payment to milk producers;<br>4. This has to be done at GP level;<br>5. Supply quality milch animals. | 1. Assist in organising milk producers cooperative societies;<br>2. Identify beneficiaries for dairy development programme;<br>3. Select beneficiaries under various programmes. |
| Poultry Development | 1. Develop infrastructure for poultry farming;<br>2. Production and supply of quality chicks to poultry farmers;<br>3. Allot or lease Community land for establishing poultry complex. | 1. Train poultry farmers;<br>2. Arrange for the supply of poultry feed. | 1. Identify beneficiaries for poultry farming;<br>2. Select beneficiaries and establish poultry complexes for them under various programmes. |

# Item No. 5

## *Fisheries*

| *Activity* | *Distribution of Functions* | | |
|---|---|---|---|
| | *Zilla Panchayat* | *Taluk Panchayat* | *Gram Panchayat* |
| Developing of Inland Fisheries | 1. Formulate Projects for fisheries development;<br>2. Technically appraise and approve projects for development of inland water bodies for fisheries;<br>3. Establish fish seed production farms;<br>4. Formulate Projects for fisheries development;<br>5. Arrange training of fishermen in modern management techniques for fish production;<br>6. Procure and supply fishing equipment for distribution among selected fishermen's cooperatives and beneficiaries;<br>7. Monitor and supervise plan implementation. | 1. Select beneficiaries for fisheries training;<br>2. Organise fishermen's cooperative;<br>3. Distribute boats, nets and other equipment and give assistance to cooperatives and beneficiaries;<br>4. Monitor, supervise and report progress;<br>5. Lease village ponds to fishermen's Cooperatives and groups. | 1. Develop village pond for fisheries<br>2. Identify beneficiaries for assistance under various programmes and assist them in organising fishermen's cooperatives;<br>3. Assist TPs in the distribution of boats, nets and other equipment;<br>4. Supervise and report progress to TPs;<br>5. Execute fishpond and tank improvement projects. |
| Development of Marine Fisheries | 1. Procure and supply motorised and modern boats and equipment to selected groups of beneficiaries and cooperatives;<br>2. Develop brackish water fisheries;<br>3. Enforce environmental restrictions on marine aquaculture and brackish fish production activities;<br>4. Install weather forecasting and early warning system for marine fishermen. | 1. Select sites for marine aquaculture and brackish water fishing;<br>2. Organise fishermen's cooperatives;<br>3. Distribute boats and equipment to selected beneficiaries and cooperatives;<br>4. Monitor impact of marine aquaculture on environment. | 1. Identify beneficiaries and assist them in organising into fishermen's cooperatives;<br>2. Select Beneficiaries for assistance<br>3. Distribute boats and equipment to beneficiaries and cooperatives;<br>4. Create awareness and adopt safety measures during rough weather;<br>5. Monitor the impact of Marine aquaculture on village environment and initiate impact mitigation measures. |

*Contd...*

*...Contd....*

| *Activity* | *Distribution of Functions* | | |
|---|---|---|---|
| | *Zilla Panchayat* | *Taluk Panchayat* | *Gram Panchayat* |
| Development of Marketing Processing Infrastructure | 1. Encourage private entrepreneurs to establish processing, packaging and storage facilities;<br>2. Assist in establishing other marketing infrastructure. | 1. Organise and train fishermen in processing, packaging and preservation of fish and fish products;<br>2. Develop tie-up arrangements between fishermen and processing units. | |
| Welfare Measures | 1. Promote group insurance schemes for fishermen;<br>2. Sanction relief to affected families during natural calamities. | 1. Implement family and group insurance schemes for fishermen;<br>2. Distribute relief to families affected by calamities. | 1. Encourage fishermen to take up insurance schemes;<br>2. Assess loss, damage and relief requirements of families affected by calamities. |

## Item No. 6

*Social Forestry*

| *Activity* | *Distribution of Functions* | | |
|---|---|---|---|
| | *Zilla Panchayat* | *Taluk Panchayat* | *Gram Panchayat* |
| Social Forestry and Farm Forestry | 1. Promote Social Forestry and Farm Forestry;<br>2. Promote and propagate social and farm forestry for improving ecology and environment;<br>3. Establish forest nurseries for supply of seedlings and saplings for distribution;<br>4. Propagate fuel fodder and timber; producing plants and bio-diversity;<br>5. Organise *vana mahotsava*;<br>6. Lease land to groups and individuals interested in social forestry on sharing basis. | 1. Identify degraded and wastelands and formulate social forestry projects;<br>2. Implement TP social forestry projects and those assigned by ZP;<br>3. Plant trees along roads, rails and public places;<br>4. Produce and supply seedlings and saplings for social and farm forestry projects;<br>5. Propagate fuel fodder and timber producing plants; | 1. Identify degraded and waste lands for social and farm forestry and formulate projects with the support of the Gram Sabha;<br>2. Execute social forestry projects through village people;<br>3. Encourage private farmers for farm forestry and assist them;<br>4. Distribute seedlings and saplings;<br>5. Organise and participate in *vana mahostsava*;<br>6. Ensure adequate production of fuel, fodder and timber for local use; |
| Marketing of Fuel/Fodder and Timber | 1. Establish links for marketing of forest products. | | 1. Collect, distribute and sell fuel, fodder and timber. |

## Item No. 7

*Minor Forest Produce*

| *Activity* | *Distribution of Functions* | | |
|---|---|---|---|
| | *Zilla Panchayat* | *Taluk Panchayat* | *Gram Panchayat* |
| Regeneration of MFP Species | 1. Plan raising MFP plantation in concentrated blocks to facilitate collection and marketing;<br>2. Encourage cultivation of MFP in existing forest, degraded forest lands, barren and uncultivable area, and community wastelands;<br>3. Encourage plantation of MFP such as gum, resin, medicinal plants, aromatic plants, leaves, oil seeds, tans and dyes, grasses, seeds, canes, bamboo, etc. particularly in tribal areas;<br>4. Promoting plantation of MFP species in drought prone, desert areas and under social forestry activity under JGSY, particularly in tribal areas. | 1. Establish MFP nurseries for propagation of MFP species. | 1. Assist in identification of families willing to plant MFP species;<br>2. Distribute MFP seedlings for plantation. |
| Training | 1. Organise training for scientific tapping of gums, resins, and grading of MFPs | 1. Organise training at the TP level. | 1. Select and forward trainees names to the TP. |

*Contd...*

...Comtd...

| *Activity* | *Distribution of Functions* | | |
|---|---|---|---|
| | *Zilla Panchayat* | *Taluk Panchayat* | *Gram Panchayat* |
| MFP Collection | 1. Monitor MFP collection activities in forest ranges;<br>2. Timely payment of collection. | 1. Organise item-wise MFP cooperatives like Tendu leaf. | 1. Organise pruning operation of Tendu trees before the leaf plucking season. |
| Processing, and Marketing Charges | 1. Set up small-scale industrial units for value addition to MFPs;<br>2. Fix support prices for MFP procurement;<br>3. Establish godowns for storage of MFPs;<br>4. Strengthen market intelligence and market extension. | 1. Liaise with forest department for constitution of Joint Forest Management Committee for MFP regeneration collection, processing and marketing;<br>2. Ensure value addition to MFP before it leaves the forest area. | 1. Promote collection, primary processing and value addition to MFP before selling;<br>2. Ensure timely payment and adequate collection charges to MFP collectors. |

## Item No. 8

*Small Scale Industries Including Food Processing Industries*

| *Activity* | *Distribution of Functions* | | |
|---|---|---|---|
| | *Zilla Panchayat* | *Taluk Panchayat* | *Gram Panchayat* |
| Industrial Resource potential survey | 1. Formulate Projects by the DIC in coordination with KVIC/KVIB and other agencies based on Industrial Resource Potential survey. | 1. Assist industrial resource potential survey. | 1. Assist survey and project formulation. |
| Development of Infrastructure | 1. Develop inter-linkages in institutions and organisations;<br>2. Establish small industrial estates at suitable locations and develop other related infrastructure activities;<br>3. Identify location and develop food-processing complexes. | 1. Establish small rural industrial estates and complexes. | 1. Identify suitable locations for rural industries. |
| Entrepreneur Development | | 1. Organise entrepreneurial Development Programmes;<br>2. Select entrepreneurs and encourage private investments;<br>3. Establish Industrial counseling Information and guiding centres;<br>4. Assist entrepreneurs in formulating viable projects, and cooperative industrial projects. | |
| Credit and financial assistance from various Govt. Departments and Agencies | 1. Provide information and guidance about credit facilities and other financial incentives;<br>2. Coordinate credit support activities with financial institutions. | 1. Assist in providing financial and other help to small industries. | |

## Item No. 9

### *Khadi, Village and Cottage Industries*

| *Activity* | *Distribution of Functions* | | |
|---|---|---|---|
| | *Zilla Panchayat* | *Taluk Panchayat* | *Gram Panchayat* |
| Planning, Monitoring and Supervision | 1. Consolidate plans prepared by TPs for Khadi, Village and Cottage industries including artisan activities;<br>2. Monitor and supervise the overall progress in this sector, and ISB sector of SGSY. | 1. Prepare plan for Khadi, Village and Cottage Industries and other artisan activities integrating schemes of other agencies such as KVIC/KVIB/ Handloom/Handicraft Development. | 1. Assist TP in activities and identifying potential formulation of projects. |
| Training Skill development and Transfer of technology to beneficiaries | 1. Establish and identify training Centres for Skill Development;<br>2. Allocate and sanction funds for Training and stipend to the trainees;<br>3. Identify appropriate technologies and arrange for their transfer to workers. | 1. Select beneficiaries for Training and Skill development and nominate them to training Institutes;<br>2. Arrange master crafts-persons<br>3. Pay stipend to beneficiaries and honorarium/training cost to the trainers;<br>4. Transfer and upgradation of technology in different areas of production. | 1. Identify beneficiaries for training through *Gram Sabha.* |
| Infrastructure Development | 1. Arrange supply of raw material, equipment, and other inputs to workers;<br>2. Tie up arrangements for marketing of products through Government and non-government marketing agencies;<br>3. Set up retail show rooms for products;<br>4. Encourage cooperatives for production and marketing of products. | 1. Supply of raw material, equipment and other inputs to beneficiary workers;<br>2. Coordinate programmes of various agencies for infrastructure development such as construction of common workplaces, worksheets and market complexes;<br>3. Organise Cooperatives for production and marketing of products. | 1. Assist in Distribution of raw material equipment, etc.;<br>2. Allow beneficiaries to use locally available raw material;<br>3. Construct common worksheds/ workplaces and market complexes. |

Contd...

*...Contd....*

| *Activity* | *Distribution of Functions* | | |
|---|---|---|---|
| | *Zilla Panchayat* | *Taluk Panchayat* | *Gram Panchayat* |
| Credit and Financial Support | 1. Ensure credit support through credit plan;<br>2. Monitor and supervise credit flow and financial assistance from other agencies to cooperatives and individual units. | 1. Ensure credit support;<br>2. Assist beneficiaries in formulating project plan;<br>3. Arrange for subsidy and financial support under various programmes to the beneficiaries;<br>4. Monitor, supervise and report progress. | 1. Identify beneficiaries for financial support under various programmes;<br>2. Assist loan recovery. |
| Credit and financial assistance from various Government Departments and Agencies | 1. Provide information and guidance about credit facilities and other financial incentives;<br>2. Coordinate credit support activities with financial institutions. | 1. Assist in providing financial and other help to small industries. | |

## Item No. 10

*Rural Housing Including Indira Awas Yojana*

| *Activity* | *Distribution of Functions* | | |
|---|---|---|---|
| | *Zilla Panchayat* | *Taluk Panchayat* | *Gram Panchayat* |
| Approval of TP's plan and sanctioning of fund for rural housing schemes | 1. Determine design and unit cost for guidance to GPs keeping in view technical advice and beneficiary needs. | 1. Assist GPs in execution of housing projects;<br>2. Procure and supply of building materials. | 1. Identify beneficiaries and prepare lists through *Gram Sabha*;<br>2. Acquire land for housing layouts, (other than Ashraya housing layouts);<br>3. Assist in allotment and distribute housing and house sites;<br>4. Constitute beneficiaries committee;<br>5. Execute construction work;<br>6. Provide assistance in the distribution of building material. |
| Supervision and monitoring of rural housing schemes | | | 1. Supervise construction quality, use of material and report progress; |

## Item No. 11

*Drinking Water*

| Activity | Distribution of Functions | | |
|---|---|---|---|
| | *Zilla Panchayat* | *Taluk Panchayat* | *Gram Panchayat* |
| Development of water supply system | 1. Formulate major water supply schemes;<br>2. Technically appraise and approve schemes proposed by TPs and GPs;<br>3. Award contracts for the execution of major schemes outside TP and GP plans;<br>4. Establish water testing laboratories for control of chemical and biogenic impurities. | 1. Formulate projects and seek technical approval from ZP;<br>2. Construct schemes within the prescribed cost limits for TPs. | 1. Identify schemes and locations, estimate cost and formulate projects through the involvement of *Gram Sabha;*<br>2. Construct wells, tanks and village water supply schemes of its own or as assigned by the ZP or TP;<br>3. Periodically chlorinate open wells and treat water;<br>4. Ensure proper distribution of water to all households in its villages;<br>5. Collect water sample for testing. |
| Monitoring rural water supply schemes Maintenance of water supply system | 1. Monitor and supervise the progress, quality of work and target achievement. | 1. Monitor and supervise progress and quality of works. | 1. Monitor scheme implementation and report progress;<br>2. Maintain drinking water schemes, collect water charges and appoint operators wherever necessary. |

## Item No. 12

### *Fuel and Fodder*

| *Activity* | *Distribution of Functions* | | |
|---|---|---|---|
| | *Zilla Panchayat* | *Taluk Panchayat* | *Gram Panchayat* |
| Production of Fuel and Fodder | 1. Build awareness for use of fuel-efficient devices and improved fodder species;<br>2. Consolidate assessments of fodder and fuel demands for the district Plan and coordinate fuel and fodder production activities. | 1. Identify wastelands and degraded lands for taking up fuel and fodder plantation; | 1. Assess fuel and fodder requirements;<br>2. Select species and sites for fuel and fodder plantations;<br>3. Identify beneficiaries for fuel and fodder demonstration plots;<br>4. Undertake plantation activities;<br>5. Maintain and protect fuel wood plantations and fodder plots in community or *Panchayat* lands;<br>6. Decide mechanism and oversee the distribution of fuel and fodder produced from community lots;<br>7. Identify sites for fodder nurseries;<br>8. Coordinate nursery establishment programme;<br>9. Distribute fuel efficient wood stoves and smokeless *chulhas*. |

## Item No. 13

*Roads, Culverts, Bridges, Ferries, Waterways and Other Means of Communication*

| *Activity* | *Distribution of Functions* | | |
|---|---|---|---|
| | *Zilla Panchayat* | *Taluk Panchayat* | *Gram Panchayat* |
| Development of road network and accessibility | 1. Survey, technical feasibility, road alignment, and formulate road development projects;<br>2. Approve, allocate and sanction funds;<br>3. Assist in acquiring land, assess grant of compensation;<br>4. Award contracts for procurement of material and equipment for construction of roads and bridges and make supplies;<br>5. Monitor specifications of roads and bridges and supervise quality of works. | 1. Identify villages as per MNP norms inaccessible by all weather road and formulate projects for construction of link roads connecting more than one TP;<br>2. Survey, technical feasibility, sanction of funds;<br>3. Acquire land, assess and grant compensation;<br>4. Construct roads using local labour without contractors;<br>5. Provide technical assistance for road construction projects proposed by GPs;<br>6. Monitor the specifications of roads and bridges and supervise the quality of works and reporting progress to the DP. | 1. Assist in formulating road construction projects and obtain approval through *Gram Sabha;*<br>2. Seek technical advice, feasibility and approval from TP engineers;<br>3. Allocate, approve and sanction funds;<br>4. Construct village link roads and village lanes through works committees, using village labour without contractors;<br>5. Monitor and supervise quality of works through work committee and report progress to IP. |
| Improvement and Maintenance of the existing roads/culverts and bridges | 1. Conduct traffic volume survey and identify road sections needing improvement in capacity;<br>2. Convert ordinary district roads into blacktopped roads; | 1. Convert TP roads into black topped roads;<br>2. Undertake annual repairs and maintenance of roads, culverts and bridges; | 1. Assess costs of improvement, repair and annual maintenance of village roads;<br>2. Raise funds through government or own sources and donations with the help of *Gram Sabha;* |

*Contd...*

...Contd...

| Activity | Distribution of Functions | | |
|---|---|---|---|
| | *Zilla Panchayat* | *Taluk Panchayat* | *Gram Panchayat* |
| | 3. Carry out annual repair and maintenance of roads, culverts and bridges;<br>4. Approve, allocate and sanction funds for all types of improvement and annual maintenance work and award contracts;<br>5. Monitor and supervise the quality of works. | 3. Approve, allocate and sanction funds for improvement and maintenance of IP roads;<br>4. Monitor and supervise quality of works and report progress. | 3. Execute works through Work Committee. |
| Development of waterways, ferrying, ferry services, etc. | 1. Identify waterways suitable for construction of jetties for ferry services;<br>2. Purchase ferries and contract private operators for ferry services;<br>3. Deepen and dredge waterways, Regulate ferry services. | 1. Inspect ferries and boats and maintain vigilance on services and traffic regulations. | |

## Item No. 14

*Rural Electrification Including Distribution of Electricity*

| Activity | Distribution of Functions | | |
|---|---|---|---|
| | Zilla Panchayat | Taluk Panchayat | Gram Panchayat |
| Expansion of electrification | 1. Assess un-electrified villages, hamlets and colonies and formulate projects for their electrification in coordination with KPTCL. | 1. Assist in obtaining power connection for poor and SC/ST/OBC families under various programmes;<br>2. Monitor and report progress of energisation of irrigation pump-sets. | 1. Find land for installing electric transmission poles/electrification;<br>2. Maintain and operate street lights. |
| Monitoring power supply | 1. Ensure power supply for agriculture during critical periods;<br>2. Exercise vigilance against power theft and illegal connection. | | 1. Report position of power supply during prime crop season;<br>2. Exercise Vigilance and report against power theft and illegal connections;<br>3. Monitor power supply for agriculture and assist in checking power theft and illegal connections. |

## Item No. 15

*Non-conventional Energy*

| *Activity* | *Distribution of Functions* | | |
|---|---|---|---|
| | *Zilla Panchayat* | *Taluk Panchayat* | *Gram Panchayat* |
| Assessment of district's energy requirement | 1. Consolidate TPs plans for energy requirement and supply through non-conventional means. | 1. Formulate projects for use of non-conventional sources of energy in the TP. | 1. Assist TP in identification of potential sources of non-conventional energy devices requirement such as gobar gas, bio-mass, solar energy and wind energy. |
| Promoting non-conventional sources of energy which includes installations of solar panels, wind mills and *gobar* gas plants and extension education | 1. Promote non-conventional energy devices and sources;<br>2. Promote and popularise energy saving devices;<br>3. Coordinate different agencies including NGOs for promotion of alternative sources of energy. | 1. Procure and supply material and equipment for the projects;<br>2. Assist in identifying suitably locations and select individual beneficiaries for installation of community and private sources of energy;<br>3. Train users in the maintenance of non-conventional energy devices;<br>4. Monitor and supervise the operation and functioning of the projects. | 1. Assist in identification of beneficiary for individual biogas plants and other devices;<br>2. Organise beneficiary training;<br>3. Monitor functioning of NCE devices. |

## Item No. 16

*Poverty Alleviation Programmes*

| *Activity* | *Distribution of Functions* | | |
|---|---|---|---|
| | *Zilla Panchayat* | *Taluk Panchayat* | *Gram Panchayat* |
| Planning and implementation of Poverty Alleviation Programmes | 1. Coordinate with other departments and agencies;<br>2. Develop training infrastructure;<br>3. Allocate funds for training and stipend for trainees;<br>4. Procure and supply quality assets, machinery and equipment for beneficiary schemes;<br>5. Develop marketing infrastructure marketing network for SGSY self help group products;<br>6. Prepare plan for poverty alleviation programmes at district level;<br>7. Assist in extending technical assist-tance for planning at GP and TP level;<br>8. Supervise and review implementation of different poverty alleviation programmes;<br>9. Review schemes implemented in Drought Prone Areas;<br>10. The ZP in active cooperation with the TP and District Planning Committee may arrange decentralised Planning; | 1. Assist GPs in providing technical and managerial assistance for implementation of schemes entrusted to TPs;<br>2. Collect and distribute data regarding development and management at the district level;<br>3. Assist in the evaluation of schemes;<br>4. Release of funds to banks for subsidy adjustment, formulation of credit plans through banks;<br>5. Prepare plans at the block level under SGSY for filling up gaps in technology, marketing tie-ups, training, strengthening infrastructure and market facilities;<br>6. Assist GPs in organising self-help groups and implement cluster strategies;<br>7. Review plans prepared by the GPs and accord technical approval and assistance; | 1. Identify beneficiaries under SGSY other individual beneficiary oriented poverty alleviation schemes, JGSY and other employment generation programmes entrusted to GPs after approval of *Gram Sabha;*<br>2. Utilise JGSY for the development of of infrastructure in the GP;<br>3. Assist TP for the distribution of identity cards under Employment Assurance Scheme;<br>4. Put up information boards about all the works taken up under Employment Assurance scheme;<br>5. Assist the TP in preparation of plans for land development schemes coming within TPs purview;<br>6. Select beneficiaries in Drought Prone Areas Programme;<br>7. Identify eligible beneficiaries under *Samagra Awaas Yojana;* |

*Contd...*

...Contd...

| Activity | Distribution of Functions | | |
|---|---|---|---|
| | Zilla Panchayat | Taluk Panchayat | Gram Panchayat |
| | 11. Review and supervise schemes implemented under the grants recommended by the Central Finance Commission for local bodies;<br>12. Review implementation of Rural Sanitation and Water Supply scheme;<br>13. Implement and supervise Employment;<br>14. Review Central Rural Sanitation Programme;<br>15. Plan and review Biogas plants schemes for individuals and community;<br>16. Undertake Planning and review of smokeless *chulhas* scheme and National Project on improved *chulhas*. | 8. Draw action plans, get technical approvals and funds allocated under land development scheme;<br>9. TPs can implement schemes with the help of GPs and integrate other programmes with poverty alleviation schemes;<br>10. Assist in supervision of work under District Decentralised Plan;<br>11. Plan and implement infrastructure development by rural local bodies;<br>12. Plan and implement Integrated Rural Sanitation and Water Supply Scheme;<br>13. Arrange practical demonstration under smokeless *chulhas* scheme. | 8. Ensure proper utilisation of funds of Central Finance Commission by local bodies and ensure that the scheme works permitted within GPs are completed;<br>9. Identify beneficiaries under Rural Sanitation Programme and provision of Drinking Water schemes;<br>10. Arrange live demonstration under smokeless *chulhas* scheme and identification of beneficiaries under National Project on Improved *chulhas* and Sanitation Programme;<br>11. Undertake the national Project on improved *chulhas* and Sanitation. |
| Wage Employment programmes | 1. Prepare ZP level shelf of projects and desegregate it into plans that can be implemented by TP and GP plans;<br>2. Formulate projects outside TP and and GP;<br>3. Assign projects to TPs, GPs, NGOs and various other agencies and departments for execution; | 1. Formulate projects with TP funds;<br>2. Scrutinize and grant technical approval to GP Projects;<br>3. Procure and supply material for projects;<br>4. Technically assist GPs for executing projects;<br>5. Execute projects outside GPs plans; | 1. Assist in identification of labourers in the village requiring wage employment through *Gram Sabha*, list them and provide employment cards to beneficiaries;<br>2. Formulate projects and get approval through *Gram Sabha* and seek technical approval from TP; |

Contd...

*...Contd...*

| *Activity* | *Distribution of Functions* | | |
|---|---|---|---|
| | *Zilla Panchayat* | *Taluk Panchayat* | *Gram Panchayat* |
| | 4. Approve, sanction and release funds to TPs, GPs and other organisations for the execution of ZP projects;<br>5. Release funds to TPs as per prescribed norms;<br>6. Provide funds for maintenance of assets created under JGSY/EAS *etc.*;<br>7. Inspect muster-rolls and check quality of works and wage material ratio as per guidelines;<br>8. Monitor and supervise progress of programmes;<br>9. Submit quarterly returns and utilisation certificates to GoI and State Government for release of next instalments. | 6. Inspect muster-rolls, quality of work, assets created and man-days generated by projects executed by IP and GPs. | 3. Constitute works committee for execution of works and projects;<br>4. Ensure employment to all in the village;<br>5. Distribute projects and works as per norms;<br>6. Monitor and supervise quality of works, assets created and man-days generated. |

# Item No. 17

## *Education Including Primary and Secondary Schools*

| *Activity* | *Distribution of Functions* | | |
|---|---|---|---|
| | *Zilla Panchayat* | *Taluk Panchayat* | *Gram Panchayat* |
| Expansion and development of educational facilities | 1. Assess the requirements of schools, teachers, equipment, etc. in the district and plan for them;<br>2. Supervise and monitor quality of educational services. | 1. Supervise the functioning of primary and upper primary schools;<br>2. Maintain school buildings and related infrastructure;<br>3. Supply and distribute material and equipment to schools. | 1. Ensure full enrollment of school age children;<br>2. Maintain school buildings, and play grounds.<br>3. Exercise vigilance on regular attendance of teachers and students and report to the concerned;<br>4. Campaign for full enrollment and reduction of dropouts;<br>5. Assess the dropout position and initiate appropriate action to reduce it. |
| Establishment and maintenance of hostels, and other welfare measures for target group students | 1. Assess and plan hostel requirements for target group students;<br>2. Maintain hostels;<br>3. Supply school uniforms and books for target group students. | 1. Distribute school uniforms, books and other materials to target group students;<br>2. Assist in the maintenance of hostels. | 1. Assist TPs in the distribution of study material to target group students. |

## Item No. 18

*Technical Training and Vocational Education*

| Activity | Distribution of Functions | | |
|---|---|---|---|
| | *Zilla Panchayat* | *Taluk Panchayat* | *Gram Panchayat* |
| Establishment and maintenance of ITIs | 1. Establish and maintain ITIs;<br>2. Assess and plan for technical training;<br>3. Assess vocational education needs;<br>4. Supervise and monitor functioning of ITIs. | 1. Conduct aptitude tests for selection of students under various trades;<br>2. Recommend for admission and placement in ITIs. | |
| Promotion and identifying suitable courses for vocational according to the needs and potential of different areas in education | 1. Select courses for vocational education and identify education schools and centres for important courses;<br>2. Motivate students for vocational training. | 1. Assist in the promotion of vocational education in schools and centres;<br>2. Select candidates and students for vocational courses. | 1. Assist in identification and recommend eligible candidates for vocational education and training. |

## Item No. 19

*Adult and Non-formal Education*

| *Activity* | *Distribution of Functions* | | |
|---|---|---|---|
| | *Zilla Panchayat* | *Taluk Panchayat* | *Gram Panchayat* |
| Planning and implementation of adult and non-formal education Total Literacy Campaign | 1. Identify suitable locations for establishing adult education centres;<br>2. Select volunteers and supervisors for teaching and maintenance of centres;<br>3. Procure and supply all relevant infrastructure and educational material to centres;<br>4. Supervise and monitor activities of adult education centres;<br>5. Organise total literacy campaign. | 1. Implement Adult and non-formal education programmes and total literacy campaigns;<br>2. Distribute material to the centres. | 1. Help in mobilising people for participation in Adult education and TLC campaigns;<br>2. Supervise and assist in functioning of centres and ensure regularity of learners and volunteers;<br>3. Supervise and monitor functioning of the centres. |

## Item No. 20

### *Libraries*

| *Activity* | *Distribution of Functions* | | |
|---|---|---|---|
| | *Zilla Panchayat* | *Taluk Panchayat* | *Gram Panchayat* |
| Establishment and maintenance of libraries | 1. Plan for establishment of new libraries and maintain and improve existing ones;<br>2. Procure and supply books, reading material and popular literature. | 1. Assist in the maintenance and functioning of libraries. | 1. Establish and maintain libraries;<br>2. Up-keep of library;<br>3. Raise donations and collect books for library;<br>4. Subscribe to vernacular news papers and magazines. |

## Item No. 21

*Cultural Activities*

| *Activity* | *Distribution of Functions* | | |
|---|---|---|---|
| | *Zilla Panchayat* | *Taluk Panchayat* | *Gram Panchayat* |
| Promotion of Cultural activities | 1. Guide, encourage and organise cultural programmes;<br>2. Utilise available popular media for cultural affairs;<br>3. Organise youth festivals, sports events on dates of national and state importance;<br>4. Establish sports complexes, theatres and other infrastructure;<br>5. Identify and mobilise sponsors for cultural and sports events and youth festivals;<br>6. Maintain and supervise the functioning of *Nehru Yuvak Kendras;* | 1. Organise local festivals with the help of GPs;<br>2. Plan and organise sports and cultural meets with the help of local organisations and voluntary efforts; | 1. Organise sports festivals and cultural events in villages using folk media for strengthening of national integration, family planning campaign, literacy, sanitation, etc.;<br>2. To promote sports and organise youth clubs. |

## Item No. 22

*Markets and Fairs*

| *Activity* | *Distribution of Functions* | | |
|---|---|---|---|
| | *Zilla Panchayat* | *Taluk Panchayat* | *Gram Panchayat* |
| Identification of location and development of market yards | 1. Identify locations and develop marketing yards and infrastructure for marketing rural products and formulating projects. | 1. Develop and maintain agricultural market yards;<br>2. Develop and maintain places for fairs/*shandies* and weekly markets. | 1. Maintain village fairs and weekly markets;<br>2. Construct market complex within the GP. |
| Regulating wholesale and retail markets, supervision and monitoring of marketing activities | 1. Assist in regulating wholesale and retail markets;<br>2. Supervise and monitor marketing activities;<br>3. Supervise District service and marketing societies; | 1. Enforce fair trade practices and maintain quality of commodities;<br>2. Assist in the maintenance of statistics on prices and commodity traded;<br>3. Maintain statistics on prices and commodities transacted within the district. | |

# Item No. 23

## *Health and Sanitation, Including Hospitals, Primary Health Centres and Dispensaries*

| *Activity* | *Distribution of Functions* | | |
|---|---|---|---|
| | *Zilla Panchayat* | *Taluk Panchayat* | *Gram Panchayat* |
| Health care | 1. Plan through health committees to provide physical infrastructure;<br>2. Coordinate communicable diseases programme with the State;<br>3. Coordinate construction and maintenance and supervise of PHCs;<br>4. Maintain district ISM (Indian System of Medicine) hospitals;<br>5. Periodically conduct Epidemiological surveys;<br>6. Promote school health programmes;<br>7. Organise health awareness rallies and camps. | 1. Assist in supervision and maintenance of sub-centres and deployment of field staff;<br>2. Supervise mid-day meals schemes for school children;<br>3. Organise health and family welfare camps and conduct demonstration-cum-exhibition programs on, health, family welfare and sanitation;<br>4. Assist in supervision of Indian Systems of Medicine (ISM) dispensaries. | 1. Assist in formation of village health committees comprising *Panchayat* members, representatives of villagers, village health guide (VHG) Trained Birth Assistant (TBA) and Multi-purpose Health Workers;<br>2. Upkeep of village sanitation, cleaning of roads and drainage;<br>3. Mobilise and organise people for health and family planning and immunisation camps;<br>4. Coordinate and supervise construction of sanitary latrines; |
| Sanitation | 1. Plan rural sanitation programmes;<br>2. Promote Information, Education and Communication (IEC) campaigns. | 1. Organise and supervise sanitary marts;<br>2. Formulate plan for assisting in the construction of sanitary latrines;<br>3. Assist in inspection/assessment of quality of public health inputs and services. | 1. Chlorinate village tanks and wells and spraying of DDT;<br>2. Assist in construction of individual sanitary latrines;<br>3. Report of outbreak of epidemics;<br>4. Assist in coordinating emergency medical relief services; |

## Item No. 24

*Family Welfare*

| *Activity* | *Distribution of Functions* | | |
|---|---|---|---|
| | *Zilla Panchayat* | *Taluk Panchayat* | *Gram Panchayat* |
| Maternal and Child Health (MCH) Centres | 1. Plan for Family Welfare programme;<br>2. Establish and maintain MCHs;<br>3. Supply medicines and equipment to MCHs;<br>4. Train mid-wives and para medical functionaries;<br>5. Coordinate with state/international agencies;<br>6. Provide immunisation services;<br>7. Propagate family planning methods, procure supply and distribute contraceptives;<br>8. Organise family planning and immunisation camps;<br>9. Identify and approve NGOs for FW<br>10. Organise IEC/Health and FW promotional campaigns;<br>11. Promote school Health Programmes;<br>12. Plan supervise and monitor ICDS;<br>13. Procure, supply and distribute meals for children, medicines and equipment for ICDS centres;<br>14. Train ANMs and others<br>15. Liaise with State/National level health programmes. | 1. Distribute medicines, equipment and family planning materials to centres;<br>2. Propagate and create awareness about maternal and child care immunisation and family planning schemes;<br>3. Coordinate and assist in monitoring and supervision of family welfare and family planning services;<br>4. Assist in organising family planning and immunisation camps;<br>5. Organise IEC, Health and FW promotional campaigns Distribute materials, medicines and equipment to ICDS Promote school health programme centres. Assist beneficiaries, mothers and children;<br>6. Distribute materials, medicines and equipment to ICDS Promote school health programme centres;<br>7. Assist beneficiaries, mothers and children. | 1. Assist in propagation of maternal child care, family planning and immunisation programmes;<br>2. Assist in identification and recommendation of beneficiaries for maternity aid under NSAP and related schemes;<br>3. Assist in maintenance and supervision of *Anganwadis*;<br>4. Identify beneficiary mothers and children;<br>5. Supervise the activities of ANMs and *Anganwadi* workers;<br>6. Collect vital statistics (*e.g.* births, deaths *etc.*). |

## Item No. 25

*Women and Child Development*

| *Activity* | *Distribution of Functions* | | |
|---|---|---|---|
| | *Zilla Panchayat* | *Taluk Panchayat* | *Gram Panchayat* |
| Socio-economic development of women | 1. Promote equal opportunity to women in all sectors of development—social economic and political;<br>2. Mobilise social support against social evils like dowry, sex determination, gender biases like killing girl child at birth, discrimination in educating girl child, etc.;<br>3. Promote opportunities for women to engage themselves in income generating activities;<br>4. Protect the interests of women workers in the unorganised sector;<br>5. Ensure payment of minimum wages to women agricultural labourers; | 1. Propagate the message of equal opportunity to women in all sectors of development;<br>2. Mobilise social support against social evils that discriminate against women;<br>3. Identify income generating activities for women. | 1. Generate awareness among women about their rights;<br>2. Promote self-help groups of women. |
| Maternity Benefit | 1. Help pregnant women receive maternity benefits under the National Maternity Benefit Scheme. | 1. Generate awareness among women about maternity benefit scheme, proper age of marriage and small family norm. | 1. Identify pregnant women eligible for maternity benefit scheme, and help them in getting benefits. |

*Contd...*

*...Contd...*

| *Activity* | *Distribution of Functions* | | |
|---|---|---|---|
| | *Zilla Panchayat* | *Taluk Panchayat* | *Gram Panchayat* |
| Development of Women Children in Rural Areas (DWCRA) | 1. Supervise, guide and support district level officials concerned with the implementation of DWCRA programme;<br>2. Prepare district annual action plan through consolidation and aggregation of village and block level plans;<br>3. Appraise resources and conduct market surveys to identify demand based income-generating activities;<br>4. Prepare annual action plan for DWCRA in line with the credit plan;<br>5. Ascertain the availability of funds for women and child welfare;<br>6. Identify active NGOs for the implementation of the Programme;<br>7. Ensure coordination in converging services;<br>8. Set up infrastructure facilities in support of the programme. | 1. Prepare annual action plan<br>2. Assist ZP & GP in organising training programmes, workshops and meetings;<br>3. Ensure convergence of services in coordination with other departments at GP level<br>4. Mobilise and organise women through NGOs for implementation of programmes | 1. Assist in development of data base for women and child developmentand programmes;<br>2. Prepare annual action plan;<br>3. Assist ZP and TP in identification of women beneficiaries;<br>4. Assist in identification and selection of demand based income-generating activities;<br>5. Assist in conducting credit camps to provide access to credit for women groups from financial institutions;<br>6. Assist in organising self-help/thrift and credit groups as an entry point to the programme;<br>7. Assist in conducting training programmes in<br>a. awareness building,<br>b. gender sensitisation,<br>c. leadership, and<br>d. skill development (TRYSEM);<br>8. Maintain infrastructure facilities like drinking water, sanitation, *Anganwadi* centers primary schools, common work-sheds and provide accommodation for front line workers; |

*Contd...*

...*Contd*...

| *Activity* | *Distribution of Functions* | | |
|---|---|---|---|
| | *Zilla Panchayat* | *Taluk Panchayat* | *Gram Panchayat* |
| | | | 9. Assist in ensuring convergence of services to women groups; literacy, health, immunisation and family welfare;<br>10. Assist women groups in procuring raw materials. |
| Integrated Child Development | 1. Supervise, guide and support Services (ICDS) for implementation of ICDS projects;<br>2. Monitor functioning of the Scheme in the district;<br>3. Promote people's participation in programmes through involvement of local leadership;<br>4. Coordinate with the District Collector for elimination of child labour. | 1. Supervise project staff of woman and child welfare department;<br>2. Assist officers concerned with the programme in procurement and distribution of nutrition material and other medical supplies;<br>3. Provide infrastructural facilities and other logistic support to facilitate implementation of the programme;<br>4. Identify child labour working in hazardous and other occupations;<br>5. Construct *Anganwadi* Centres in GPs; | 1. Assist ICDS staff in TPs in ducting surveys;<br>2. Assist in selection of beneficiaries;<br>3. Assist in selection of sites for locating *Anganwadi* centers;<br>4. Ensure community participation through organising regular meetings;<br>5. Involve women GP members in supervising the functioning of *Anganwadi* centres particularly while ensuring attendance in the centre, maintenance of cleanliness and hygiene, supplementary nutrition in terms of dietary schedule and timings, proper child care and meeting of educational needs, regular health check up and immunisation;<br>6. Assist in the distribution of nutrition and conduct of regular health check-up. |

## Item No. 26

*Social Welfare, Including Welfare of the Handicapped and Mentally Retarded*

| *Activity* | *Distribution of Functions* | | |
|---|---|---|---|
| | *Zilla Panchayat* | *Taluk Panchayat* | *Gram Panchayat* |
| Welfare of the Disabled | 1. Survey and classify disabled persons according to the nature of disability;<br>2. Make available text books in Braille to visually handicapped children in the schools;<br>3. Facilitate easy access to and mobility with buildings and public places for persons with disability especially for people on wheel chair and persons with visual disabilities;<br>4. Inspect, supervise and monitor voluntary organisations receiving grant-in-aid from the Ministry of Welfare GoI for rehabilitation of persons with disability;<br>5. Identify and promote voluntary organisations receiving grant-in-aid from the Ministry of Welfare, Govt. of India for rehabilitation of leprosy patients;<br>6. Identify voluntary organisations and assist them to set up Special Schools for disabled persons with Grant-in-aid from the Ministry of Welfare<br>7. Coordinate with organisations and government in getting assistance for purchase of aids and appliances for disabled persons. | 1. Identify disabled persons and coordinate with ZPs for their rehabilitation. | 1. Assist in identification of disabled persons and coordinate with Block and *Zilla Panchayats* for their rehabilitation. |

*Contd...*

*...Contd...*

| *Activity* | *Distribution of Functions* | | |
|---|---|---|---|
| | *Zilla Panchayat* | *Taluk Panchayat* | *Gram Panchayat* |
| | 8. Coordinate with Special Employment Exchanges and Vocational Rehabilitation Centres for assisting disabled persons to secure employment;<br>9. Coordinate with District Rehabilitation Centres for providing rehabilitation services to disabled persons;<br>10. Organise Sports Meet and Cultural Programmes for disabled people. | | |
| Street Children | 1. Identify street children suffering from destitution, neglect, abuse and exploitation and help them in getting integrated community based non-Institutional basic services through voluntary organisations who get grant-in-aid from Ministry of Welfare, Government of India. | 1. Identify street children and coordinate with the ZP for their development. | 1. Assist in identification of street children Coordinate with the TP and ZP for rehabilitation and development |
| Adoption of Children | 1. Identify voluntary organisations which deal with the adoption of destitute, abandoned, orphaned and relinquished children by giving the child for growth and development to parents other than the child's biological parents, and help in the adoption of orphaned children. | 1. Identify parents willing to adopt children and coordinate with the District *Panchayat* for their growth and development. | 1. Assist in identification of parents willing to adopt children and coordinate with the TP and ZP for their growth and development |

*Contd...*

*...Contd...*

| *Activity* | *Distribution of Functions* | | |
|---|---|---|---|
| | *Zilla Panchayat* | *Taluk Panchayat* | *Gram Panchayat* |
| Welfare of the Aged | 1. Identify destitute and aged persons and help them in taking shelter in voluntary organisations which receive grant-in-aids from the Ministry of Welfare, State Governments for running Old Age Homes; and for giving old age pension. | 1. Identify the aged and coordinate with the ZP for their maintenance, and giving old age pension. | 1. Assist in identification of the aged and coordinate with the ZP and TP for their maintenance and giving old age pension. |
| Drug use Prevention | 1. Build awareness and educate people about ill-effects of drug abuse and prevent it;<br>2. Assist drug addicts through a well rounded up programme of motivation, counselling, treatment, follow up and social reintegration of cured drug addicts at Counselling Centres for drug addicts run by voluntary organisations for which they get grant-in-aid from the Welfare Ministry;<br>3. Take drug addicts to counselling, de-addiction and after care centres, de-addiction and awareness generating camps for their rehabilitation. | 1. Build awareness and educate people about ill-effects of drug abuse and prevent it.<br>2. Coordinate with the ZP for their rehabilitation.<br>3. Take drug addicts to counseling, de-addiction and after care centres, de-addiction and awareness generating camps for their rehabilitation. | 1. Assist in building awareness and educating people about ill effects of drug abuse and prevent it;<br>2. Coordinate with the ZP and TP for the rehabilitation of drug addicts;<br>3. Take drug addicts to counseling, de-addiction and after-care-centres, de-addiction and awareness generating camps for their rehabilitation. |

# Glossary, Acronyms and Abbreviations

## Glossary

| | |
|---|---|
| *Abhiyan* | Campaign |
| *Adhiniyam* | Act |
| *Adhyaksha* | President |
| *Adhosarovachna Samiti* | Infrastructure Committee |
| *Adivasi* | Tribal |
| *Adim Jati/Adivasi* | Scheduled Tribes |
| *Anganwadi* | A child-care centre, under a centrally sponsored programme – Integrated Child Development Services (ICDS), where supplementary food is provided to pregnant women and infant children. |
| *Anna Kosh* | A kind of store where people are supposed to deposit their extra grain that can be used by other persons on some terms and conditions. |
| *Avamand Bhawan* | Building |
| *Crore* | Ten million |
| *Culvert Nalla* | Small bridge on a canal or drain |
| *Dalit* | Scheduled caste/Scheduled tribe |
| *Dharmshala* | Inn |
| *Gram* | Village |
| *Gram Kosh* | Village account |
| *Gram Nyayalaya Adhiniyam* | Village Court Act |

| | |
|---|---|
| *Gram Panchayat* | The lowest tier of the *Panchayati Raj* Institutions, which is formed on the basis of population and consists of one or more than one revenue village. The population of a *Panchayat* cannot be less than 1,000. |
| *Gram Raksha Samiti* | Village Protection Committee |
| *Gram Sabha* | The assembly of the persons of a revenue village whose names are included in the voters list. |
| *Gram Swaraj* | Village self-rule |
| *Gram Sevak* | Village worker working for the government |
| *Gram Suraksha Adhiniyam* | Village Protection Act |
| *Gram Vikas Samiti* | Village Development Committee |
| *Harijan* | Term used by Gandhiji for Scheduled Castes |
| *Indira Awas Yojana* | Shelter assistance for the families living below the poverty line. |
| *Janpad Panchayat* | Second tier of the *Panchayati Raj* institutions, *i.e.* the council of the elected representatives at the block level. |
| *Janmabhoomi* | Literally, 'Land of one's birth', a State-sponsored, people-centred participatory development programme in AP |
| *Janpad* | Block, an administrative subdivision of the district |
| *Janpad Panchayat (Adhyaksh)* | Block-level government (President) |
| *Jan Swasthya Rakshak* | A village level health worker |
| *Jeevan Dhara* | Scheme where financial assistance for digging wells is provided to families below the poverty line. |
| *Jawahar Rojgar Yojana* | An employment guarantee scheme |
| *Kalyan* | Welfare. |

| | |
|---|---|
| *Kanji* house tax | Kanji house is the place where stray livestock is taken by the local authorities and a fine is imposed on the owner for releasing the livestock. |
| *Karmi* | Employee |
| *Khiranja* | Brick road |
| *Krishi Samiti* | Agriculture Committee |
| *Kosh* | Account |
| *Kotwal/Chaukidar* | The person who works as the guard of the village. |
| *Lakh* | One hundred thousand |
| *Lok Sabha* | The lower house of Parliament |
| *Lok Shakti* | Civil society |
| *Mahila* | Woman |
| *Mahila Mandal* | A small group of women working as a Self-Help Group. |
| *Mandal* | Territorial and administrative unit (with a population of about 50,000 to 70,000) between the village and district levels |
| *Mandal Praja Parishad* | Intermediate level council in the *Panchayati Raj* system, made up of the heads of the *Panchayat*s and representatives of the territorial constituencies (MPTCs) within the *Mandal* |
| *Mandir* | Temple |
| *Mandi* | Market |
| *Mela* | Fair/Fete |
| *Moolbhoot Yojana* | Basic Needs Programme |
| *Munadi* | Public announcement |
| *Nagad Kosh* | Cash Account |
| *Nal Jal Yojana* | Hand-pump water scheme, applicable in villages with population under 2,000. |
| *Nirman* | Construction. |

| | |
|---|---|
| *Panch* | The elected representative of a *Gram Panchayat.* |
| *Panchayat Samiti* | Block level |
| *Panchayat* | A middle-level unit of rural local government existing prior to 1986, made up of the heads of village *Panchayat*s |
| *Panchayati Raj* | System of rural local government with three ascending tiers, *viz.*, *Gram Panchayat, Mandal* or *Panchayat Samiti* and *Zilla Parishad* |
| *Panchayati Raj Adhiniyam* | Local self government Act |
| *Panchayat Karmi* | The person who works as the Secretary of the *Gram Panchayat.* |
| *Panjikaran* | Registration |
| *Patta* | Land on lease |
| *Patwari* | The lowest official of the Revenue Department posted at the village level. |
| *Purdah* | A veil |
| *Rajiv Gandhi Shiksha* Mission | Rajiv Gandhi Education Mission |
| *Rajya Sabha* | The upper chamber of India's Parliament; in Hindi, 'States assembly' in Parliament |
| *Rojgar Yojana* | Employment Scheme |
| *Sabha Manch* | Podium |
| *Samajik Nyaya Samiti* | Social Justice Committee |
| *Samiti* | A committee |
| *Sanshodhan* | Amendment |
| *Sarpanch* | Head of a *Gram Panchayat* |
| *Sarpanchpati* | Husband of the *Sarpanch* |
| *Sarvjanik Sampada Samiti* | Common Resources Committee |
| *Shram Kosh* | Labour Account |
| *Shanti Bhawan* | Peace building |

| | |
|---|---|
| *Shiksha Karmi* | Persons engaged in the teaching at the schools that are being run under the Rajiv Gandhi *Shiksha* (Education) Mission. |
| *Shiksha Samiti* | Education Committee |
| *Swasthya Samiti* | Health Committee |
| *Taluka* | An administrative category denoting a zone smaller than a district. |
| *Tehsildar* | Officer in charge of a *Tehsil* |
| *Tehsil* | An administrative category denoting a revenue zone, much smaller than a district. |
| *Upsarpanch* | Deputy Head of the *Gram Panchayat*, elected among the members of a *Panchayat*. |
| *Vastu Kosh* | Material Account |
| *Zilla Panchayat* | The highest tier of the *Panchayati Raj* institution, formed at the district level. |
| *Zilla Parishad* | Advisory body |

## Acronyms and Abbreviations

| | |
|---|---|
| AP | Andhra Pradesh |
| BC | Backward Castes |
| BDO | Block Development Officer |
| BPL | Below Poverty Line |
| BDO | Block Development Office/Officer |
| CBO | Community Based Organisations |
| CEO | Chief Executive Officer |
| CFC | Central Finance Commission |
| CPO | Chief Planning Officer |
| DC | District Collector |
| DDRC | District Development and Review Committee |

| | |
|---|---|
| DPB | District Planning Boards |
| DPC | District Planning Committee |
| DRDA | District Rural Development Agency |
| DWCRA | Development for Women and Children in Rural Areas |
| EAS | Employment Assurance Scheme |
| EGS | Education Guarantee Scheme |
| FFW | Food for Work |
| FPC | Forest Protection Committee |
| GoI | Government of India |
| GS | *Gram Sabha* |
| GP | *Gram Panchayat* |
| HDI | Human Development Index |
| IAY | *Indira Awas Yojana* |
| IRDP | Integrated Rural Development Programme |
| JP | *Janpad Panchayat* |
| JRY | *Jawahar Rojgar Yojana* |
| JFM | Joint Forest Management |
| MLA | Member of Legislative Assembly |
| MLC | Member of the Legislative Council |
| MORD | Ministry of Rural Development |
| MP | Member of Parliament |
| NABARD | National Bank for Agriculture and Rural Development |
| NGO | Non Governmental Organisation |
| NSAP | National Social Assistance Programme |
| OBC | Other Backward Castes |
| PESA | *Panchayat Extension to Scheduled Areas Act* |
| PMRY | Prime Minister's *Rojgar Yojana* |
| PRI | *Panchayati Raj* institutions |
| PRIA | Participatory Research in Asia |

| | |
|---|---|
| PHC | Primary Health Centre |
| PSC | Public Service Commission |
| SC | Scheduled Caste, as per articles 341 and 342 of the Constitution of India |
| SDM | Sub District Magistrate |
| SDO | Sub Division Officer |
| SEC | State Election Commission |
| SFC | State Finance Commission |
| SHG | Self Help Group |
| ST | Scheduled Tribe, as per Articles 341 and 342 of the Constitution of India |
| TRYSEM | Training for Rural Youth for Self-Employment |
| TOT | Training of Trainers |
| UFC | Union Finance Commission |
| UP | Uttar Pradesh |
| VFC | Village Forest Committee |
| ZP | *Zilla Panchayat* |

# Consolidated Bibliography


ADB (2000). *Asian Development Outlook, 2000*, Asian Development Bank, Oxford University Press, New York.

Agnihotri, V.K., Krishna, S. and A. Mukherjee (1994). "Human Resource Development for Panchayats", in Amitava Mukherjee, ed. *Decentralisation, Panchayats in the Nineties*, Vikas Publications, New Delhi.

Agrawal A. & Gibson C. (1999). "Enchantment and Disenchantment: The Role of Community in Natural Resource Conservation", *World Development*, Vol. 27(6) 1999.

Alagh, Y.K., (1990). "The Newly Industrialising Economies and India", *Asian Development Review*, Vol.7, No.2.

————. (1991). "Sustainable Development, From Concept to Action: Techniques for Planners", UNCED.

————. (1991). *Indian Development Planning and Policy*, WIDER Studies in Development Economics, Helsinki and Delhi, Vikas.

————. (1991). *The Post Socialist Transformation from A Development Point of View*, MIT.

————. (1994). *Planning and Policies for Indian Agricultural Research*, 25th Lal Bahadur Shastri Lecture, reprinted in ICAR, Landmarks in Indian Agriculture.

————. (1994). *The Rocky Road to Reform*, Helsinki, WIDER.

————. (1995). "India's Agricultural Trade with the ESCAP Region", in U.N., ESCAP, *Agricultural Trade in the ESCAP Region*, New York, U.N.

————. (1995). "Development Models: The Next Phase", *Indian Journal of Pure and Applied Mathematics*, Vol.26, No.6 reprinted in B.L.S. Rao, *Statistics and its Applications*, New Delhi, Indian National Science Academy.

————. (1999). "India's Agricultural Trade", *Indian Economic Journal*, First Dantwala Memorial Lecture.

————. (1999). Presidential Address, *Indian Journal of Labour Economics*, Jan. 1999.

————. (2000). "Global Sustainable Future and Developing Countries", in, Fu chen Lo, H. Tokuda and N.S. Cooray (ed.), *The Sustainable Future of the Global System*, Tokyo, OECD-UNU, Ch.19, pp.323-333.

————. (2000). *Sustainable Development: India 2020*, Tokyo, UNU/IAS.

————. (2001). "Development and Governance", in Hans van Ginkel and Ramesh Thakur, UNU Millenium Series, *Embracing the Millenium*, below, pp. 73-84.

————. (2001). Committee of Experts for Legislation to Incorporate Cooperatives as Companies, in *Statement of Objects and Reasons, The Companies Second Amendment Bill, 2001, Bill No. 88 of 2001*, pp. 25-26.

————. (2002). "Agricultural Investment Strategies: Prioritising Land and Water", in FAO, pp. 67-78.

————. (2002). "Emerging Institutions and Organisations: Some Aspects of Sustainable Rural Development", in Lok Sabha Secretariat, *Fifty Years of Indian Parliament*, New Delhi, Lok Sabha Secretariat, pp. 491-504.

————. (2003). "Technology Policies and Investment Strategies", in Braga de Macedo and Tadao Chino, *OECD-ADB Asia Forum*, OECD, Paris, pp. 165-180.

Alexandratos, N., ed., (1995). *World Agriculture Towards 2010, An FAO Study*, Chichister, Wiley.

Alsop, R., Krishna, A. and D. Sjoblom (2000). "Are Gram Panchayats Inclusive? Report of a Study Conducted in Rajasthan and Madhya Pradesh", Background Paper No. 3, *Overview of Rural Decentralisation in India*, Vol (3), World Bank.

Anand, S and C. Harris (1990). "Food and Standard of Living: An Analysis based on Sri Lankan Data", in J. Dreze and A. Sen ed., *The Political Economy of Hunger*, Volume 1, Oxford: Clarendon Press.

Anderson, T. W., (1984). *An Introduction to Multivariate Statistical Analysis*, John Wiley and Sons Inc.

Baland J. and J. Platteau (1996). *Halting Degradation of Natural Resources: Is there a Role for Rural Communities?* Food and Agriculture Organisation, Clarendon Press, Oxford.

Bandopadhyay D. and A. Mukherjee (2004). *New Issues in Panchayati Raj*, Rajiv Gandhi Foundation, Concept Publishimg Co., New Delhi.

Bandopadhyay, D. (2000). "Land Reform in West Bengal", *Economic and Political Weekly*, May 27-2 June.

————. (2003). "Land Reforms and Agriculture: The West Bengal Experience", *Economic and Political Weekly*, March 1-7.

Behar A. and Y. Kumar (2002). "Decentralisation in Madhya Pradesh, India: from Panchayati Raj to Gram Swaraj (1995-2001)", *Working Paper: 170*, Overseas Development Institute, London.

Bhandari, Laveesh and Aarti Khare (2002). "The Geography of Post-1991 Indian Economy", *Global Business Review*, Vol. 3, No. 2, pp. 321-340.

Bhandari, Laveesh and Amaresh Dubey (2001) "Caloric Deficiency, Poverty and the Public Distribution System – A Household Level Analysis for 1993-94", *RGICS Working Paper, No. 24*.

Bhatnagar, Subhash & Schware, Robert, (2000). "Wired Village: The Warana Experiment", in *Information and Communication Technology in Development - Cases from India*, Sage Publications, New Delhi.

Blair, H. (2000). "Participation and Accountability at the Periphery: Democratic Local Governance in Six Countries", *World Development*, Vol. 28(1).

Bohra, O.P. (2000). "Decentralisation and Devolution of Powers and Functions to Panchayats", *Journal of Rural Development*, Vol. 19(2).

Bollinger, Christopher R. and Paul Hagstrom (2003). "Food Stamp Programme Participation of Refugees and Immigrants", June.

Braga C. (1996). "The Impact of Internationalisation of Services on Developing Countries", *Finance and Development*, March.

Braga de Macedo, J., and Tadao Chino, (2003). *Technology and Poverty Reduction in Asia and the Pacific*, Paris, OECD and ADB, Development Centre Seminar Series.

Brahm Prakash, (2003). "Asia's Software Industry", in Braga de Macedo and Chino.

Buch, N. (1997). *A Study of Rashtriya Mahila Kosh (RMK)*, Centre for Women's Development Studies, New Delhi.

Burgess R. and N. Stern (1989). *Social Security in Developing Countries: What, Why, Who and How?* STICERD, London School of Economics and Political Science, London.

Byrd, William and Allen Gelb, (1990). "Why Industrialise? The Incentives for Rural Community Governments," chapter 17 in William Byrd and Qingsong Lin (eds.), *China's Rural Industry: Structure, Development, and Reform*, Oxford University Press.

Byrd, William and Qingsong Lin, (1990)."China's Rural Industry: An Introduction," chapter 1 in William Byrd and Qingsong Lin (eds.), *China's Rural Industry: Structure, Development, and Reform*, Oxford University Press..

Byrd, William, (1990). "Entrepreneurship, Capital, and Ownership," chapter 9 in William Byrd and Qingsong Lin (eds.), *China's Rural Industry: Structure, Development, and Reform*, Oxford University Press.

Castañeda, Tarsicio (2000). "The Design, Implementation and Impact of Food Stamp Programmes in Developing Countries", *Human Development Network*, The World Bank, April.

Centre for Civil Society, "Grassroots Research on Public Policy Issues", *Research Reports by Summer Interns* (Various years).

Chadha, G.K., and Sahu, P.P., (2002). "Post-Reform Setbacks in Rural Employment: Issues that Need Further Scrutiny", *Economic and Political Weekly*, May 25-31.

Chakraborty, Debashis and D. Shyam Babu, (2004). "What Can State Do To Tackle Rural Poverty?" in Bibek Debroy and D. Shyam Babu, ed. *The Dalit Question: Reforms and Social Justice*, pp. 157-212, Globus Books, New Delhi.

Chakraborty, Debashis, (2004). "How is the State Functioning? A comparative analysis of Growth, Governance and Social Issues During $8^{th}$ and $9^{th}$ Plan Period, in Bibek Debroy, ed., *Agenda for Improving Governance*, pp. 49-104, Academic Foundation, New Delhi.

Chakraborty, S.K. (1996). "Ethics in Co-operatives: In Search of a Theory" in R. Rajagopalan (Ed.) *Rediscovering Co-operation* (Vol.1), Anand : IRMA, 1-14.

Chang, Chun and Yijiang Wang, (1994). "The Nature of the Township Enterprise," *Journal of Comparative Economics*, 19: 434-452.

Chowdhury, D. (1987). "Critical Appraisal of Voluntary Effort in Social Welfare and Development Since Independence", *The Indian Journal of Public Administration*, Vol. 33 (1987).

Clark, J. (1991). *Democratising Development: The Role of Voluntary Organisations*, Earthscan, London.

Crook, R.C. and Sverrisson, A.S. (2001). "Decentralisation and Poverty Alleviation in Developing Countries: A Comparative Analysis", *IDS Working Paper 130*, Institute of Development Studies, Brighton.

Crook, R.C. and J. Manor (1998). *Democracy and Decentralisation in South Asia and West Africa*, Cambridge University Press, Cambridge.

Datt, Gaurav and Dileni Gunewardena, (1997). "Some Aspects of Poverty in Sri Lanka: 1985-90", *Working Paper No. 1738*, The World Bank, March.

Datta, S.K. and Singh Gurdev (1998). "Relevance and Sustainability of Co-operatives in the Current Economic Scenario" in Sanjeev Chopra (Ed) *Co-operatives: Policy Issues for the SAARC Region*, DehraDun: Book World, 28-45.

Datta, Samar K. (2004). "Co-operatives in Agriculture", Vol. 24, "State of Indian Farmer: A Millennium Study", Academic Foundation, New Delhi.

Datta, Samar K. and Kapoor Sanjeev (2000). *Revitalisation of Credit Co-operatives Through Business Development Planning*, CMA Monograph No. 183, Centre for Management in Agriculture, Indian Institute of Management, Ahmedabad.

de Souza, P.R. (2000). "Multi-State Study of Panchayati Raj Legislation and Administrative Reform", Background Paper No. 1, *Overview of Rural Decentralisation in India*, Vol. (3), World Bank.

Deaton, Angus and Dreze, Jean, (2002). "Poverty and Inequality in India: A Re-examination", *Economic and Political Weekly*, September 7.

Debroy, Bibek, and Laveesh Bhandari, (2003). ed., *District Level Deprivation in the New Millennium*, Konark Publishers, New Delhi.

Dev, Mahendra and Suryanarayana, M.H., (1991). "Is PDS Urban-Biased and Pro-Rich?, An evaluation", *Economic and Political Weekly*, Vol. 26, No. 41.

Dev, Mahendra S., Piush Antony, V. Gayathri, and R.P. Mamgain, (2001). "Social and Economic Security in India", Institute for Human Development.

Diamond, L. (1993). *Political Culture and Democracy in Developing Countries*, Johns Hopkins Press, Baltimore.

Dreze J., Lanjouw P. and N. Sharma, (1993) "Credit in North Indian Village - an Empirical Investigation", cited in the *Design of Poverty Alleviation Strategy in Rural Areas*, FAO Paper No. 115, FAO, Rome.

Dreze, J. and A. Sen (1996). *India: Economic Development and Social Opportunity*, Oxford University Press, Delhi.

Edirisinghe, N., (1987). "The Food Stamp Scheme in Sri Lanka: Costs, Benefits, and Options for Modification", *Research Report No. 58*, International Food Policy Research Institute, Washington, D.C.

Edwards, M. and D. Hulme (eds.) (1996). *Beyond the Magic Bullet: NGO Performance and Accountability in the Post-cold War World*, Kumarian, W. Hartford.

Ezemenari, Kene and Kalanidhi Subbarao, (1999). "Jamaica's Food Stamp Programme: Impacts on Poverty and Welfare", *Working Paper No. 2207*, The World Bank, October.

FAO, (2002). *Investment in Land and Water*, RAP Publications 2002/09, March.

Farrington, J. and C. Lobo (1997). *Scaling up Participatory Watershed Development in India: Lessons from the Indo-German Watershed Development Programme*, Natural Resources Perspectives, Overseas Development Institute, London.

Farrington, J., Turton, C. and A. J. James, (eds.) (2000). *Participatory Watershed Development: Challenges for the Twenty-First Century*, Oxford University Press, Delhi.

Fraker, T., (1990). "The Effects of Food Stamps on Food Consumption: A Review of the Literature." Mathematica Policy Research, Prepared for United States Department of Agriculture.

Gaiha R., (1991) "Poverty Alleviation Programmes in Rural India: An Assessment", *Development and Change*, Vol.22.

Gaiha R., Kaushik P.D. and V. Kulkarni (2000). "Participation or Empowerment? The Case of Panchayats in India" in M. Unnithan-Kumar and V. Damodaran (eds.), *The State Development and Participation*, Manohar Publications, New Delhi.

Government of India, Ministry of Finance, *Economic Survey* (various issues).

Government of India, *The Companies (Amendment) Act*, (2002). (http://dca.nic.in/companies_amendment_act_2002.pdf)

Greer J., Foster J. and E. Thorbecke (1984). "A Class of Decomposable Poverty Measures", *Econometrica*, Vol.1.

Grosh, M.E., (1993). "Administrative Costs and Incidence of Targeted Programmes in Latin America: Towards Quantifying the Trade-Off", The World Bank.

————. (1993). "Five Criteria for Choosing among Poverty Programmes", *Working Paper No. 1201*, The World Bank, October.

Gupta, V.K. and Gaikwad, V.R. (1986). *Guide to Management of Small Farmers' Co-operatives*, Concept Publishing Company, New Delhi.

Hall P. (1996). "Distance Education and Electronic Networking", *Information Technology For Development*, Vol. 7 (2), October 1996, The Netherlands.

Hanson, Kenneth, Elise Golan, Stephen Vogel, and Jennifer Olmsted, (2002). "Tracing the Impacts of Food Assistance Programmes on Agriculture and Consumers: A Computable General Equilibrium Model", United States Department of Agriculture, April.

Haq M. (1996). *Reflections on Human Development*, Oxford University Press, New Delhi.

Hart, Oliver, and John Moore, (1990). "Property Rights and the Nature of the Firm," *Journal of Political Economy*, 98(6), pp.1119-1158.

IFAD (2001). *Rural Poverty Report 2001: The Challenge of Ending Rural Poverty*, Oxford University Press, Oxford.

ISS (2000). *Status of Panchayati Raj in the States & Union Territories of India, 2000*, Institute of Social Sciences, Concept Publishing Co., New Delhi.

Jain, S.P. (1996). *Action Plan for Training of Panchayati Raj Functionaries*, National Institute for Rural Development, Hyderabad.

Jha, S. (2000). "Fiscal Decentralisation in India: Strengths, Limitations and Prospects for Panchayati Raj Institutions", Background Paper No. 2, *Overview of Rural Decentralisation in India*, Vol. (3), World Bank.

Jin, Hehui, and Yingyi Qian, (1997). "Ownership and Institutions: Evidence from Rural China," mimeo, Stanford University.

Johnson C. (2003). "Decentralisation in India: Poverty, Politics and Panchayati Raj", *Working Paper No. 199*, Overseas Development Institute, London.

————. (2001). "Institutions, Incentives and Identity in Common Property Regimes: Community Formation and Fisheries Conservation in Southern Thailand," *Development and Change*, Vol. (32): 5 (2001).

Johnson, C. and D. Start (2001). "Rights, Claims and Capture: Understanding the Politics of Pro-Poor Policy," *ODI Working Paper 145*, Overseas Development Institute, London.

Jolliffe, Dean, Laura Tiehen, Craig Gundersen, and Joshua Winicki, (2003). "Food Stamp Benefits and Child Poverty in the 1990s", United States Department of Agriculture, September.

Kaushik P.D. (2000). "Information Technology: Decentralisation and the Rural Poor in India" in S. Gangopadhaya and Wilima Wadhwa (eds.), *Economic Reforms for the Poor*, Konarak Publishers, New Delhi.

Kaushik, S. (1993). *Women and Panchayati Raj*, Haranand Publications, New Delhi.

Kenney G.I. (1995). "The Missing Link- Information", *Information Technology For Development*, Vol. 6 (1), January 1995, The Netherlands.

Kornfeld, Robert, (2002). "Explaining Recent Trends in Food Stamp Programme Caseloads - Final Report", Abt Associates Inc. and Economic Research Service, March.

Krugman, P., and M. Obstfeld, (2000). *International Economics: Theory and Policy*, New York, Addison Wesley.

Kuhn, B. *et al.*, (1996). "The Food Stamp Programme and Welfare Reform.", *Journal of Economic Perspectives*. Vol. 10, No. 2. pp. 189–198.

Kundu, A., N. Sarangi and B.P Dash, (2003). "Rural Non-farm Employment: An Analysis of Rural Urban Interdependencies", *Working Paper 196*, Overseas Development Institute, London.

Lazaroiu, S., L. Luca. and E. Tesliuc, (1998). "Assessing the Impact of the 1997 Voucher Scheme", Unpublished Document, Bucharest.

Lele, U., N. Kumar, Y. Alagh, N. Saxena, and K. Mitra, (2000). *Forestry in India: An Evaluation*, Washington, World Bank.

Li, David D., (1996). "Ambiguous Property Rights in Transition Economies," *Journal of Comparative Economics*.

Lipton M. and J. Van der Gaag (1991). "Poverty: A Research and Policy Framework, in M.Lipton and J. Van der Gaag (eds.) *Including the Poor*, FAO, Rome.

Ma, Rong, *et al.*, (1994). *Zhongguo Xiangzhen Qiye de Fazhan Lishi he Yunxing Jizhi* (*Development History and Operating Mechanisms of China's Township Enterprises*), Peking University Press.

Mander, Harsh, Jean Dreze, and Vivek S., (2003). "Freedom from Hunger and Fear: Priorities for Action", *RGICS Agenda for Improving Governance Series – XV*.

Massachusetts Immigrant and Refugee Advocacy Coalition, "Unequal Access: A Report on Barriers Children in Low-income Immigrant Families Face in Accessing Food Stamps and Health Insurance", *http://www.miracoalition.org/UnequalAccess.pdf*,

Mathew, G. (2001). "Panchayat Elections: Dismal Record," *Economic and Political Weekly*, 20 January 2001.

Mayo, H.B. (1960). *An Introduction to Democratic Theory*, Oxford University Press, Oxford.

McGuire, J., (1998). "Back to Office Report, Honduras Health Reform Project", 19–23 October. World Bank.

McKinnon, Ronald, (1994). "Gradual versus Rapid Liberalisation in Socialist Economies: Financial Policies in China and Russia Compared," No. 10 in the ICEG Sector Studies Series, a publication of the International Centre for Economic Growth.

Meenakshi, J.V., and Brinda Vishwanathan, (2003). "Calorie Deprivation in Rural India, 1983-1999/2000", *Economic and Political Weekly*, January 25.

Meenakshisundaram, S.S. (1999). "Gram Sabha: Lessons from Karnataka", *Kurukshetra*, Vol. 48(1).

Ministry of Finance and Company Affairs, *Budget Speech of Finance Minister*, Government of India (various issues).

Ministry of Finance and Company Affairs, *Economic Survey*, Government of India (various issues).

Molyneux M. (1994). *Panchayati Raj from Legislation to Movement*, Concept Publishing Company, New Delhi.

Mooij, Joss, and S. Mahendra Dev (2002). "Social Sector Priorities: An Analysis of Budgets and Expenditures in India in the 1990s", *IDS Working Paper* 164, September.

Mukherjee, A. (ed.) (1995). *Participatory Rural Appraisal Methods and Applications in Rural Planning*, Vikas Publishing House Pvt. Ltd., New Delhi.

Mukherjee, N. (1993). *Participatory Rural Appraisal: Methodology and Applications*, Concept Publishing, New Delhi.

National Sample Survey Organisation, (2000). *Employment and Unemployment in India: 1999-2000 – Key Results*, Ministry of Statistics and Programme Implementation, Government of India.

————. (2001). *Differences in Level of Consumption among Socio-Economic Groups 1999-2000*, Ministry of Statistics and Programme Implementation, Government of India.

————. (2003). *Report on Village Facilities, NSS 58$^{th}$ Round (July – December 2002)*, December.

Naughton, Barry, (1994). "Chinese Institutional Innovation and Privatisation from Below," *American Economic Review*, Vol.84, No. 2, pp. 266-270, May.

Nayak, Radhika, N.C. Saxena, and John Farrington (2002). "Reaching the Poor: The Influence of Policy and Administrative Processes on the Implementation of Government Poverty Schemes in India", *Working Paper No. 175*, Overseas Development Institute, London.

Nee, Victor, (1992). "Organisational Dynamics of Market Transition: Hybrid Forms, Property Rights and Mixed Economy in China," *Administrative Science Quarterly*, 37.

NIRD (2001). eds. Choudhury, R.C. and Jain, S.P., *Emerging Patterns of Decentralised Rural Institutions* (Vol. I & II). Hyderabad, India, NIRD.

Norton S. (1992). "Transaction Cost, Telecommunications, and the Microeconomics of Macroeconomic Growth", *Economic Development and Cultural Change*, Vol. 41.

Oi, Jean, (1992). "Fiscal Reform and the Economic Foundations of Local State Corporatism in China," *World Politics*, Vol.45, No.1, October.

————. (1994). *Rural China Take off: Incentives for Reform*, mimeo, Harvard University.

Oommen, M.A. (1999). "Panchayat Finance and Issues Relating to Inter-governmental Transfers", in S.N. Jha and P.C. Mathur (eds.), *Decentralisation and Local Politics: Readings in Indian Government and Politics*, Sage Publications, London.

Parikh, Kirit S., A. Ganesh-Kumar, and Gangadhar Darbha, (2003). "Growth and Welfare Consequences of Rise in MSP", *Economic and Political Weekly*, March 1-7, 2003, pp. 891-895.

Patil, Y.S. (1999). "Case Study of Parshwnath Co-operative Bank Kolhapur on Computerisation", *Co-operative Perspective*, January-March.

Planning Commission, (2002). *National Human Development Report 2001*, Government of India.

Planning Commission, *Tenth Plan Documents (2002-07)*. Government of India.

Pomeroy, R.S. and Berkes, F. (1997). "Two to Tango: the Role of Government in Fisheries Co-management", *Marine Policy*, Vol. 21(5).

PRIA (2002). *Newsletter*, Apr- Jun 2002, Vol. 2, PRIA NEWS.

Pursell, Garry and Ashok Gulati, (1993). "Liberalising Indian Agriculture: An Agenda for Reform", *Working Paper 1172*, The World Bank, September.

Qian, Yingyi, and Barry R. Weingast, (1996)."China's Transition to Markets: Market-Preserving Federalism, Chinese Style," *Journal of Policy Reform*, 1: 149-185.

Qian, Yingyi, and Chenggang Xu, (1993). "Why China's Economic Reforms Differ: The M-Form Hierarchy and Entry/Expansion of the Non-State Sector," *Economics of Transition*, 1(2):135-170, June.

Radhakrishna, R. and K. Subbarao with S. Indrakant and C. Ravi (1997). "India's PDS: A National and International Perspective", *World Bank Discussion Paper No. 380*, The World Bank.

Ravallion M., (1989). "On the Coverage of Public Employment Scheme for Poverty Alleviation", World Bank Publication, Washington D.C. (mimeo).

Renshaw, L. R. (1994). "Strengthening Civil Society: The Role of NGOs", *Development*, Vol. 24(4).

*Report of the Committee on Long Term Grain Policy* (2002). Ministry of Consumer Affairs, Food & Public Distribution, Government of India.

Ritchey-Vance, M. (1996). "Social Capital, Sustainability, and Working Democracy: New Yardsticks for Grassroots Development", *Grassroots Development*, Vol. 20(1).

Rogers, B., *et al.*, (1995). "Food and Income Subsidies and Primary Schooling in Rural Honduras: An Evaluation of the Impact of the Bonos (BMJF) and PL 480 – Title II School Feeding Programmes", USAID ADAI LAC HNS.

Rondinelli D., McCullough J. and R.W. Johnson (1989). "Analysing Decentralisation Policies in Developing Countries: A Political Economy Framework," *Development and Change*, Vol. (20):1, 1989.

Rustam, I. (ed.) (1996). *The Indonesian NGO Agenda: Toward the Year 2000*, CESDA-LP3ES, Jakarta.

Sahn, D.E., (1987). "Changes in the Living Standards of the Poor in Sri Lanka During a Period of Macroeconomic Restructuring", *World Development*, Vol. 15, pp. 809-30.

Saxena, N.C. "Issues in Panchayats", *http://www.panchayats.org/downloads/Panchayats%20NC%20SAX.pdf.*

Saxena, N.C. (2000). "How Have the Poor Done? Mid-Term Review of Ninth Plan," *Economic and Political Weekly*, October 7-13.

Saxena, N.C. and Farrington, J. (2003). 'Trends and Prospects for Poverty Reduction in Rural India: Context and Options', *Working Paper* 198, London: ODI.

Sen A. (1992). "The Political Economy of Targeting", The World Bank Publication, Washington D.C. (mimeo).

Sen, Abhijit (2000). "Estimates of Consumer Expenditure and its Distribution: Statistical Priorities after NSS 55th Round", *Economic and Political Weekly*, December 16.

Sidhu, H.S., (2002). "Crisis in Agrarian Economy in Punjab: Some Urgent Steps", *Economic and Political Weekly*, July 27– August 2.

Singh, N.P. *et al.*, (1996). "Information Technology Implementation in Indian Co-operatives: Issues and Suggestions", International *Journal of Management Systems*, May-August.

Stopford, J. M., (!994). *The Impact of the Global Political Economy on Corporate Strategy*, Pittsburgh, Carnegie Mellon University, Carnegie Bosch Institute.

Swaminathan, Madhura, (2000). *Weakening Welfare: The Public Distribution of Food in India*, Leftword.

Swaminathan, Madhura, (2004). "Targeted Food Stamps", *The Hindu*, Tuesday, August 3.

Taylor, Lance, (1988). *Varieties of Stabilisation Experience*, Oxford, Clarendon Press.

UNDP (2000). "Decentralisation in India: Challenges & Opportunities", *HDRC Discussion Paper No.1*, UNDP, New Delhi.

————. (2001). *Human Development Report 2001*, UNDP Publication, Oxford University Press, New York.

United States Department of Agriculture, (2003). "Characteristics of Food Stamp Households", Nutrition Assistance Programme Report Series, The Office of Analysis, Nutrition and Evaluation, Report No. FSP-03-CHAR02, December.

————. "Food and Nutrition Service", *http://www.fns.usda.gov/fns/*

Van Ginkel. H., and R. Thakur, (2002). *Embracing the Millenium: Perspectives and Challenges for the United Nations and the International Community*, Tokyo, UNU Millenium Series.

Vyasulu, V. (2000). "Decentralisation, Democratisation, Finances, and the Constitution: Reflections Based on Local Reality", Paper prepared for the Panel on Decentralisation of the National Commission to Review the Working of the Constitution, *www.internationalbudget.org/cdrom/papers/decentralisation/Vinod.htm*

Wade, R., (1992). "East Asia's Economic Success", *World Politics*, Vol.44, pp.270-320.

Weitzman, Martin and Chenggang Xu, (1994). "Chinese Township Village Enterprises as Vaguely Defined Cooperatives," *Journal of Comparative Economics*, 18: 121-145.

Whiting, Susan, (1995). *The Micro-Foundations of Institutional Change in Reform China: Property Rights and Revenue Extraction in the Rural Industrial Sector*, Ph.D. dissertation, University of Michigan.

Wilde, Parke *et al.*, (2000a). "The Decline in Food Stamp Programme Participation in the 1990s", United States Department of Agriculture, Economic Research Service, *Food Assistance and Nutrition Research Report No. 7*, June 2000.

————. (2000b) "The Effect on Dietary Quality of Participation in the Food Stamp and WIC Programmes", United States Department of Agriculture, Economic Research Service, *Food Assistance and Nutrition Research Report No. 9*, September.

Wong, Christine, (1992). "Fiscal Reform and Local Industrialisation," *Modern China*, 18(2):197-227, April.

World Bank, (1988). "Project Performance Audit Report: Colombia", *Integrated Nutrition Improvement Project (Loan 1487-Co)*. Operation Evaluation Department.

World Bank (1996). *Harnessing Information for Development*, A Proposal for a World Bank Group Strategy, The World Bank, Washington D.C., 1996.

————. (1998). *World Development Report 1998*, The World Bank Publication, Washington D.C.

————. (2000). *World Development Report 2000/1: Attacking Poverty*, Oxford: Oxford University Press.

Xiangzhen Qiye Tongji Ziliao, (1992). *Statistical Materials of Township Enterprises*, 1992, Beijing, Department of Rural Enterprises, Ministry of Agriculture.

Zhang, Gang and Per Ronnas, (1993). "The Capital Structure of Township Enterprises," mimeo, Stockholm.

Zhonghua Renmin Gongheguo Xiangcun Jiti Suoyouzhi Qiye Tiaoli Tiaowen Shiyi, (1990). *Explanations of the Regulation on Township and Village Collective Enterprises of the People's Republic of China*, edited by the Ministry of Agriculture, Beijing: China Legal Press.

# Index

## N



## O



## P



## Q

## R



## S



## T



## U